T0305039

THE FIFTEENTH CENTURY

VOLUME I

CONCEPTS AND PATTERNS OF SERVICE
IN THE LATER MIDDLE AGES

CONCEPTS AND PATTERNS OF SERVICE IN THE LATER MIDDLE AGES

Edited by
ANNE CURRY and
ELIZABETH MATTHEW

THE BOYDELL PRESS

First published 2000
The Boydell Press, Woodbridge

Transferred to digital printing

ISBN 978-0-85115-814-3

The Boydell Press is an imprint of Boydell & Brewer Ltd
PO Box 9, Woodbridge, Suffolk IP12 3DF, UK
and of Boydell & Brewer Inc.
668 Mt Hope Avenue, Rochester, NY 14620, USA
website: www.boydellandbrewer.com

A catalogue record for this book is available
from the British Library

This publication is printed on acid-free paper

CONTENTS

LIST OF ILLUSTRATIONS

CONTRIBUTORS

Jeremy Catto is Fellow and Tutor of Oriel College, Oxford

Kathleen Daly is Staff Tutor at the Open University, South Region

Virginia Davis is Senior Lecturer in History, Queen Mary and Westfield College, University of London

Chris Given-Wilson is Professor of Late Medieval History at the University of St Andrews

P.J.P. Goldberg is Senior Lecturer in History, University of York

Alexander Grant is Reader in Medieval British History at Lancaster University

Ralph Griffiths is Professor of Medieval History and Pro-Vice-Chancellor in the University of Wales, Swansea

Michael Jones is Professor of Medieval French History at the University of Nottingham

David Morgan is Senior Lecturer in History at University College London

ABBREVIATIONS

Abdn.-Banff Ills.	*Illustrations of the Topography and Antiquities of the Shires of Aberdeen and Banff*, ed. J. Robertson and G. Grub (5 vols, Spalding Club, Aberdeen, 1843–69)
AD	Archives départementales
Annales ESC	*Annales: Economies, Sociétés, Civilisations*
APS	*The Acts of the Parliaments of Scotland 1224–1423*, ed. T. Thomson and C. Innes (12 vols, Edinburgh, 1814–75)
BIHR	*Bulletin of the Institute of Historical Research*
BJRL	*Bulletin of the John Rylands Library*
BL	British Library, London
BNF	Bibliothèque Nationale de France, Paris
Borthwick IHR	Borthwick Institute of Historical Research, York
CCR	*Calendar of Close Rolls*
CFR	*Calendar of Fine Rolls*
CP	G.E. Cokayne, *The Complete Peerage of England, Scotland, Ireland, Great Britain and the United Kingdom*, ed. V. Gibbs et al. (12 vols, London, 1910–59)
CPR	*Calendar of Patent Rolls*
CRISIMA	*Cahiers du centre de recherche interdisciplinaire sur la société et l'imaginaire au moyen age*
DNB	*Dictionary of National Biography*, ed. L. Stephen and S. Lee (63 vols, London, 1885–1900)
EETS	Early English Text Society
EHR	*English Historical Review*
Emden, *BRUC*	A.B. Emden, *A Biographical Register of the University of Cambridge to A.D. 1500* (Cambridge, 1963)
Emden, *BRUO*	A.B. Emden, *A Biographical Register of the University of Oxford to A.D. 1500* (3 vols, Oxford, 1956–9)
Exch. Rolls	*Rotuli Scaccarii Regum Scotorum: The Exchequer Rolls of Scotland*, ed. J. Stuart et al. (23 vols, Edinburgh, 1878–1908)
Hampshire RO	Hampshire Record Office, Winchester
HMC	Historical Manuscripts Commission
Morton Reg.	*Registrum Honoris de Morton*, ed. T. Thomson et al. (2 vols, Bannatyne Club, 1853)
MSHAB	*Mémoires de la société d'histoire et d'archéologie de Bretagne*
NAS	National Archives of Scotland, Edinburgh
NLS	National Library of Scotland, Edinburgh
PPC	*Proceedings and Ordinances of the Privy Council of England*, ed. N.H. Nicolas (7 vols, London, 1834–37)
PRO	Public Record Office, Kew

RMS	*Registrum Magni Sigilli Regum Scotorum A.D. 1306–1424*, ed. J.M. Thomson et al. (11 vols, Edinburgh, 1882–1914)
Rot. Parl.	*Rotuli Parliamentorum* (6 vols, London, 1767–77)
RRS	*Regesta Regum Scottorum 1153–1424*, ed. G.W.S. Barrow et al. (Edinburgh, 1960–)
SHF	Société de l'Histoire de France
SHR	*Scottish Historical Review*
SR	*Statutes of the Realm* (11 vols, London, 1810–28)
TRHS	*Transactions of the Royal Historical Society*
VCH	*Victoria County History*
WHR	*Welsh History Review*

ACKNOWLEDGEMENTS

The publication of this book has been assisted by a grant from the Scouloudi Foundation in association with the Institute of Historical Research; the editors also gratefully acknowledge the financial assistance of the Marc Fitch Fund, the Scottish Historical Review Trust and the Richard III and Yorkist History Trust. Finally, the editors wish to thank the University of Reading for providing financial guarantees pending the outcome of grant applications.

INTRODUCTION

THE nine essays in this volume were originally presented as papers at the Fifteenth-Century Conference held in September 1998 at the University of Reading. Those who regularly attend the normally annual meetings in this series in the U.K. will know that the usual pattern has been to alternate between 'senior' programmes of contributions invited from established scholars, and 'junior' events primarily devoted to work offered by postgraduate students. As 1998 was a 'senior' year, the organizers were able to choose, and request work on, a particular theme. 'Concepts and patterns of service' recommended itself immediately and positively for two reasons. Firstly, it seemed a promisingly inclusive topic, one of either direct, or at least tangential, relevance to most people working on late medieval history, and one which might help to bridge boundaries between a wide variety of areas of interest. Secondly, it was a topic to which particular attention had recently been drawn by the work of Michael Jones and Simon Walker on private indentures for life service,[1] and by Rose-mary Horrox's essay on medieval attitudes to service, which opens with the resonant pronouncement, 'Service has some claim to be considered the domi-nant ethic of the middle ages'.[2]

Much earlier, different, but similarly emphatic, points about the importance of service in the later middle ages were made by K.B. McFarlane. 'Patronage and service were the essence of contemporary society', he stated when, in 1938, he called for a new interpretative order in late medieval English history in the wake of 'the Collapse of the Stubbsian "Framework"' of 'Lancastrian constitutionalism triumphing ... breaking down ... and giving way ... to the autocracy of York and Tudor'.[3] Seven years later, his famous paper on 'Bastard Feudalism', or 'the social order in England in the two centuries following the death of Edward I', declared: 'Its quintessence was payment for service'. Amongst the sources quoted was the apparently autobiographical epitaph of the Derbyshire knight, Sampson Meverell (1388–1462).[4] Its neat résumé of the subject's life in terms of the salient features of the four consecutive periods of service to different patrons into which it had been divided formed the model for a good many of McFarlane's own brief sketches of gentry

---

[1] 'Private Indentures for Life Service in Peace and War 1278–1476', ed. M. Jones and S. Walker, *Camden Miscellany XXXII*, Camden Fifth Series, vol. 3 (1994), pp. 1–190.

[2] R. Horrox, 'Service', *Fifteenth-Century Attitudes: Perceptions of Society in Late Medie-val England*, ed. Horrox (Cambridge, 1994), pp. 61–78, quotation at p. 61. See also her earlier discussion of the incentives to, and demands of, service, and the relationship between service and lordship, in Horrox, *Richard III: A Study of Service* (Cambridge, 1989), pp. 1–26.

[3] K.B. McFarlane, *The Nobility of Later Medieval England: The Ford Lectures for 1953 and Related Studies* (Oxford, 1973), pp. 279–97, quotations at pp. 279, 290.

[4] K.B. McFarlane, 'Bastard Feudalism', *BIHR*, XX (1945), 161–80, reprinted in McFar-lane, *England in the Fifteenth Century* (London, 1981), pp. 23–43, quotations at p. 24, epitaph at pp. 33–4.

careers.[5] In 1953 his Ford Lectures on 'The English Nobility, 1290–1536' identified service as one of 'five certain . . . road[s] to success' for those seeking wealth
and advancement.[6] Here, and in later work, he demonstrated the importance of
this not only to the nobility, but to men of lower rank – the shipowner's grandson and military adventurer, Sir John Fastolf, and his servants, the brothers-in-
arms and heritage hunters on a more modest scale, Nicholas Molyneux and
John Winter, and the energetic and versatile lay clerk, William Worcester.[7] But
McFarlane also stressed 'the impermanence' of service connections, both in the
'loosely-knit and shamelessly competitive society' revealed by the *Paston
Letters*,[8] and amongst leading combatants in the Wars of the Roses. 'Disloyalty
could all too often be seen to pay', particularly under the strains of civil war.[9]

Uncovering some contrasting evidence of permanence and loyalty,[10] later
writers, examining the late medieval nobility and gentry in biographical or
regional contexts, have followed their subjects down all five of McFarlane's
roads to success. He himself – initially at least – was uncertain of the 'precise
order of importance' of these routes.[11] Most late medievalists, however, would
probably now agree with Horrox's view that service was the most effective,[12] or,
to adapt the original imagery, perhaps the most frequently travelled approach to
the crossroads from which the other four – the church, the law, trade (including
industry and finance) and war – diverged. Marriage, which McFarlane named
as a possible sixth road, was also often attained through connections between
families, friends, or patrons and clients which had been initially formed by

---

[5] E.g. those of John Willicotes, John Norbury, Sir Richard Sturry, Sir Lewis Clifford,
Sir William Nevill and Sir Thomas Latimer: K.B. McFarlane, *Lancastrian Kings and
Lollard Knights* (Oxford, 1972), pp. 76–7, 81, 164–5, 167.

[6] McFarlane, *Nobility*, p. 11.

[7] Ibid., pp. 158, 161, 233; see also K.B. McFarlane, 'The Investment of Sir John Fastolf's
Profits of War', *TRHS*, fifth series 7 (1957), 91–116; McFarlane, 'A Business Partner-
ship in War and Administration 1421–1445', *EHR*, LXXVIII (1963), 290–308; McFarlane, 'William Worcester: A Preliminary Survey', *Studies Presented to Sir Hilary
Jenkinson*, ed. J.C. Davies (London, 1957), pp. 196–221; all three articles are reprinted
in McFarlane, *England in the Fifteenth Century*, pp. 151–224.

[8] K.B. McFarlane, 'Parliament and "Bastard Feudalism"', *TRHS*, fourth series 26
(1944), 53–79, reprinted in McFarlane, *England in the Fifteenth Century*, pp. 1–21,
quotations at p. 18.

[9] K.B. McFarlane, 'The Wars of the Roses', *Proceedings of the British Academy*, L
(1964), 87–119, reprinted in McFarlane, *England in the Fifteenth Century*, pp. 231–61,
quotation at p. 259.

[10] See particularly M.C. Carpenter, 'The Beauchamp Affinity: A Study of Bastard
Feudalism at Work', *EHR*, XCV (1980), 514–32, esp. p. 518; G.L. Harriss, 'Introduction' in McFarlane, *England in the Fifteenth Century*, pp. xi–xii; S. Walker, *The Lancastrian Affinity 1361–1399* (Oxford, 1990), pp. 94–116; C. Carpenter, *Locality and
Polity: A Study of Warwickshire Landed Society, 1401–1499* (Cambridge, 1992),
pp. 621–3; M. Hicks, *Bastard Feudalism* (London and New York, 1995), pp. 100–1.

[11] Quotation from McFarlane, *Nobility*, p. 11. Ten years later, however, he gave service
more emphasis: 'The truth is that the aristocracy was in the main one of service, that
it was entered by service, and that acceptable service was the cause of promotion
within it' (ibid., p. 233).

[12] Horrox, 'Service', p. 67.

service.[13] But if we pursue McFarlane's metaphor much further, we find ourselves at a veritable spaghetti junction. While service offered access to the other
roads, they, in their turn, offered new opportunities for service. As Horrox
points out, in a society ordered by hierarchy and deference, 'all forms of medieval activity rested on service'.[14] Service may therefore be studied in a much
wider social context than that of those most obviously affected by bastard feudalism, namely the landed élite and their retainers.

Since McFarlane, however, it has undoubtedly been patronage, rather than
service, that has received the greater share of attention. Significantly, no less
than three early volumes of papers from the Fifteenth-Century Conference series
took patronage as a main theme;[15] until now, service has figured only as the
subject of individual contributions.[16] The surviving sources are frequently much
more informative about the top-down, rather than the bottom-up, view of what
has been described as the 'symbiotic relationship' between man and master.[17]
Moreover, definitions of patronage have widened. Many use the term in a sense
that embraces both sides of the relationship: it is thus seen as including service,
not as something distinct from it.[18] Others, while finding it useful to employ
separate terms, would argue that the two sides of the relationship are so closely
linked that they are essentially one subject, not two.[19] But while separation may
seem difficult or unnecessary, attention has been drawn to the fruitfulness of
the 'shift in focus' that particular attention to service entails.[20] Those impatient

---

[13] Studies of the military community of Lancastrian Normandy have provided particularly sharp examples of this: see C.T. Allmand, *Lancastrian Normandy, 1415–1450*
(Oxford, 1983), chs 3–4; A.E. Marshall, 'The Role of English War Captains in England
and Normandy, 1436–1461' (unpublished M.A. dissertation, University of Wales,
Swansea, 1975). For examples in England, see Walker, *Lancastrian Affinity*, pp. 89–
90, 114–15; Carpenter, *Locality and Polity*, pp. 100–5.

[14] Horrox, 'Service', pp. 61–63, quotation at p. 63.

[15] *Patronage, Pedigree and Power in Later Medieval England*, ed. C. Ross (Gloucester
and Totowa, N.J.,1979); *Patronage, the Crown and the Provinces*, ed. R.A. Griffiths
(Gloucester and Atlantic Highlands, 1981); *Church, Politics and Patronage in England
and France in the Fifteenth Century*, ed. R.B. Dobson (Gloucester and New York,
1984).

[16] Most notably at the conference at Keele in 1985: see *People, Politics and Community
in the Later Middle Ages*, ed. J. Rosenthal and C. Richmond (Gloucester and New
York, 1987), pp. x–xii.

[17] Horrox, 'Service', p. 66. The same phrase is used in the context of relations between
the nobility and gentry in Carpenter, *Locality and Polity*, p. 636.

[18] See E. Powell, 'After "After McFarlane": The Poverty of Patronage and the Case for
Constitutional History', *Trade, Devotion and Governance: Papers in Later Medieval
History*, ed. D.J. Clayton, R.G. Davies and P. McNiven (Stroud and Dover, New
Hampshire, 1994), pp. 1–16, esp. pp. 5–6.

[19] 'When we have duly acknowledged that all over Europe, England and Scotland, in
any century of pre-industrial society, men sought lords to protect them and lords
sought men to serve them, then lordship and service, within any society and from one
society to another, become a subject of "infinite variety", with the same endless and
elusive fascination as Shakespeare saw in Cleopatra': J. Wormald, *Lords and Men in
Scotland: Bonds of Manrent, 1442–1603* (Edinburgh, 1985), p. 13.

[20] See the review of Horrox, *Richard III*, by R.A. Griffiths in *EHR*, CVII (1992),
pp. 710–11.

with the preoccupation with patronage have called, fruitfully too, for a return to constitutional history.[21] But in this context it has also been suggested that much might still be gained from 'closer scrutiny [of] the use of patronage terminology'.[22] Further scrutiny of both service and its particular terminology is surely equally worthwhile.

One man with something to say about the importance, and limits, of service – from what might be called a bottom-up perspective within the upper levels of mid-fifteenth-century English society – was John Paston II. Early in June 1469, having taken all possible steps to strengthen his garrison at Caister against the attack (which he clearly hoped could still be averted) of the duke of Norfolk, he wrote, of the latter, to his brother, John III: 'I wolde do my lorde plesure and seruyse and so I wolde ye dyde if I wyst to be sure of hys god lordeschyp in tyme to kome'.[23] In the event, Caister was besieged on 21 August and surrendered to the duke just over a month later. In January 1476, on the duke's death, after all efforts to recover it in the interim had proved unavailing, Sir John saw and seized his opportunity to regain possession. He wrote again to John III:

wher that som towardys my lady off Norffolk noyse that I dyd onkyndely to sende so hastely to Caster as I dyd, ther is no dyscrete person that so thynkyth; fore iff my lorde hade ben as kynde to me as he myght have ben, and acordyng to suche hert and seruyce as my grauntffadre, my fadre, yowre-selff and I have owght and doon to my lordys off Norffolk that ded ben, and yitt iff I hadde weddyd hys dowghtre, yitt most I have doon as I dydde. And moore-ovyre, iff I had hadde any demyng off my lordys dethe iiij howrys ore he dyed, I most nedys, but iff I wolde be knowyn a foolle, have entryd it the howre byffore hys dyscesse.[24]

These statements were prompted by particular circumstances, but all three surviving collections of gentry correspondence – those of the Oxfordshire Stonors and the Yorkshire Plumptons as well as the Norfolk Pastons – offer eloquent testimony to how frequently the word 'service' occurred in everyday fifteenth-century English usage and how extensive its applications were.

At all social levels, 'service' was the word commonly used for the work, whether paid or unpaid, performed by a servant, attendant or official for his or her lord or lady, master or mistress. Margaret Paston's will directed that 'euery persone being my seruuant the day of my decesse have a quarter wages beside that they at her departing have do seruice fore'.[25] In a letter of 1465 to John

---

[21] See Powell, 'After "After McFarlane"'; C. Carpenter, 'Political and Constitutional History: Before and After McFarlane', *The McFarlane Legacy: Studies in Late Medieval Politics and Society*, ed. R.H. Britnell and A.J. Pollard (Stroud and New York, 1995), pp. 175–206; J. Watts, *Henry VI and the Politics of Kingship* (Cambridge, 1996), pp. 1–6.

[22] Powell, 'After "After McFarlane"', p. 6.

[23] *Paston Letters and Papers of the Fifteenth Century*, ed. N. Davis (2 vols, Oxford, 1971–6), Part I, no. 240, p. 401. For the garrisoning of Caister, its ensuing siege by the duke's forces and John II's 'incorrigible' optimism, see C. Richmond, *The Paston Family: Fastolf's Will* (Cambridge, 1996), pp. 30, 192–209.

[24] *Paston Letters*, Part I, no. 296, p. 491; the relevant passage is quoted at greater length in Richmond, *Fastolf's Will*, p. 252.

[25] *Paston Letters*, Part I, no. 230, p. 388.

III, her son, she had welcomed the possibility of her daughter entering the household of the duchess of Norfolk in the following terms: 'asfor your sustrys beyng wyth my lady, if your fadere wull aggrey ther-to I hold me right wele pleasyd, for I wuld be right clad that she shuld do here servyse be-for any othere, if she cowde do that shuld pleas my ladyes good grace'.[26] In 1479 the bishop of Lincoln's agent in Oxfordshire sent Sir William Stonor confirmation of receipt of his 'letter conteynyng that ye wol do my lord service in thoffice of Stewardship at Thame'.[27] In their turn, those for whom such service was performed spoke of having the service of a particular servant or attendant,[28] or of servants being in their service,[29] coming into, or to, it, put out of it or departing from it,[30] or being in service elsewhere.[31]

Variations on the formula, 'I recomaund me to yow with all my service', were employed by servants and officials to convey respectful assurance of their loyalty and willingness to do whatever work might be required of them.[32] By extension, 'any service' or 'some service' was used in the sense of a particular piece of work or the performance of a particular instruction. William Stonor's steward, Henry Makney, promised in a letter of the mid-1470s: 'if ther be any odire servise, that I may do aboute your business, sende me word, and y shalbe redy'.[33] This usage is also found in the letters of the Pastons,[34] but here 'a service' was also frequently used in the sense of an appointment or position of employment. In 1469 John Paston III sought urgent instructions from John II as to whether several family servants should 'sek hem newe seruysys or not', pointing out that 'if ye kowd get ... eny of thes seyd folkys whyche that ye wyll not kepe, eny seruyse in the mene seson it wer more worchep for yow then to put them from yow lyek masterles

---

[26] Ibid., no. 186, p. 308.

[27] *Kingsford's Stonor Letters and Papers 1290–1483*, ed. C. Carpenter (Cambridge, 1996), no. 255, p. 349.

[28] 'We haf and long tyme haf had the seruice of Thomas Denys' (letter from the earl of Oxford to John Paston I, 1453); 'as for hys seruyse, ther shall no man haue it be-for yow and ye wyll' (letter from John III to John II, 1469, discussing Richard Calle): *Paston Letters*, Part II, no. 490, p. 84; Part I, no. 336, p. 549.

[29] 'He myght do no more for vs but lose hys lyfe in your seruyse and myn ...' (John Paston III to John II, 1470): ibid., Part I, no. 339, p. 554.

[30] 'He came into my service now at Michelmasse and ys my ploughman' (John Croocker to Thomas Stonor, 1468): *Kingsford's Stonor Letters*, no. 92, p. 186; 'she hath not a cloth to hir back but which I haue given hir since she came to my service' (William Whitaker to Sir Robert or Master William Plumpton, no date): *The Plumpton Letters and Papers*, ed. J. Kirby, Camden Fifth Series, vol. 8 (1996), p. 103; 'my modyre hatte causyd me to putte Gregory owte of my servyse' (Edmond Paston II, 1472): *Paston Letters*, Part I, no. 394, p. 634.

[31] John Paston III's reference for Richard Stratton, keen to become clerk of the kitchen to Lord Hastings, described him as 'now in seruyse wyth Master Fitzwater' (1476): ibid., no. 370, p. 600.

[32] Quotation from a letter to William Stonor from his receiver, Henry Dogett, *c.* 1474: *Kingsford's Stonor Letters*, no. 143, p. 237. For other examples, see ibid., no. 215, p. 307; no. 272, p. 364; nos 284–5, pp. 374–5; no. 289, p. 380; *Plumpton Letters*, no. 12, p. 35.

[33] *Kingsford's Stonor Letters*, no. 190, p. 287, and for further examples, see ibid., no. 213, p. 306, no. 314, p. 403; *Plumpton Letters*, no. 38, p. 59; no. 77, p. 86.

[34] E.g. *Paston Letters*, Part I, no. 116, p. 200; no. 234, p. 394.

hondys'.[35] In 1471 John III was asked by his younger brother, Edmond II, to help him find 'any profytabyl servyce', adding, 'I woold haue rytgh an hesy seruyse tyl I were owthe of detys'.[36] Isolated examples in the other two collections confirm familiarity with this usage elsewhere.[37]

In an ecclesiastical context, 'a service' was the word used for both a ceremony of worship and the text prescribed for it. A riotous assembly in Norwich, allegedly demanding admission to Whitefriars to hear evensong, was told that 'suche seruice was non vsed to be there, nor with-yn the sayd citee, atte that tyme of the daye'.[38] Margaret Paston wanted the priest 'to seye ouer me at the tyme of my berying all the hole seruice that to the berying belongeth'.[39] But priests did not merely 'sey servys' or officiate at 'dyvyne service and other sacramentes'.[40] At least on the lower rungs of the church ladder, they too might think of 'a seruyse' as an opening for employment or preferment.[41] Moreover, candidates for benefices or chantries within the Stonor sphere of influence were put forward, in Collinsian guise, with warm recommendations of the 'servysse and plesur', 'feith and service' and 'good service' that they had previously performed for, or could be expected to render to, their lay patrons.[42] Professionals practising law and medicine also

[35] Ibid., no. 335, p. 547.

[36] Ibid., no. 394, pp. 634–5. Their mother used the word in the same way, pressing John III to persuade John II 'to take Pampyng to hym, or ell to get hym a serwyce in the Chauncery or in summe othere place were as he myth be proferryd': ibid., no. 209, p. 355.

[37] Protesting in the early 1460s, at the height of a crisis in the long-running Stonor–Fortescue dispute, that the Fortescue servants 'mauneseth me dayly, and put me in suche fere of my lyffe', John Frende, Thomas Stonor's bailiff at Ermington in Devon, vowed that unless his master came to defend him he would 'do the service no lengher, for I may not ne dernot' (*Kingsford's Stonor Letters*, no. 64, pp. 144–5); in the late 1480s, Sir Robert Plumpton received a request from William Catton, canon of Newburgh in Yorkshire, to use his influence 'that my brother, your trew servent, myght haue that service of the clarkship [of Coxwold]', then vacant (*Plumpton Letters*, no. 58, p. 74). For the Stonor–Fortescue feud, see C. Carpenter, 'The Stonor Circle in the Fifteenth Century', *Rulers and Ruled in Late Medieval England*, ed. R.E. Archer and S. Walker (London and Rio Grande, 1995), pp. 175–200, esp. p. 190.

[38] *Paston Letters*, Part I, no. 48, p. 77.

[39] Ibid., no. 230, p. 384.

[40] Quotations respectively from a letter written *c.* 1471 by William Stonor to his father requesting leave for one priest to be temporarily absent to answer a charge against him and for another to be found to officiate in his place meanwhile, and a petition of *c.* 1465 to Thomas Stonor from the parishioners of Didcot, Berkshire, complaining that in the absence of their parson the church services 'wer not kept as thei aght to be': *Kingsford's Stonor Letters*, no. 74, p. 156; no. 118, p. 209.

[41] The schoolmaster chaplain, John Still, was one of the family servants whose possible 'newe seruysys' outside Paston employment had been discussed by John III in 1469 (see above, n. 35). In 1471, John III informed his elder brother that he had told Still, who had been employed singing masses for the soul of John Fastolf, that he should 'get hym a seruyse now at thys Crystmas, as so he shall wyth-owt that ye send hym othyr-wyse woord, or ellys that ye or I may get hym som benefyse or fre chapell, or som othyr good seruyse' (*Paston Letters*, Part I, no. 350, p. 570). For Still and his service to the Pastons, see Richmond, *Fastolf's Will*, pp. 65, 67 n. 51.

[42] Quotations from letters of *c.* 1465–70, 1479 and 1482: *Kingsford's Stonor Letters*, no. 75, p. 158; no. 247, p. 341; no. 321, p. 408.

spoke in terms of service of their dealings with those they advised or attended. Edward Plumpton, besides applying his 'mynd and service' to all kinds of business in London at the pay and behest of his patron, Sir Robert Plumpton,[43] gave legal advice on at least one occasion in his capacity as a lawyer of Furnivall's Inn to Sir William Stonor, offering his 'servyce ever at your commaundement'.[44] William Goldwyn, physician to William Stonor's second wife, Agnes, whom he described to the apothecary in a prescription as 'a specyall Mastres of myn', promised, in return for a timely gift of venison, that 'my service schall be the more redyer to yow at all tymys'.[45] And service did not necessarily mean peaceful service only: the word was equally applicable - with or without explicit reference to 'seruice in werre'[46] – to service in arms, whether in royal armies or private quarrels. The 'servis' which various men in the half-hundred of Ewelme were listed, *c.* 1480, as 'abull to do the kyng' was undoubtedly military, as mention in each case of 'harnes', 'bowe', 'staffe' or 'bill' testifies.[47] In 1469 John Paston II was informed by John III that four men (who had been specifically engaged by the former as 'prouyd men and connyng in the werre and in fetys of armys' to bolster the Paston forces against the duke of Norfolk in the siege of Caister Castle) had each been paid 40*s* 'for the sesun that they haue don yow seruys'.[48]

Beyond these applications, 'service' had an even wider currency, used in the contexts of catering and of manorial or tenurial obligations,[49] to express the respect and obedience of children to parents and the devotion of lovers,[50] and

---

[43] *Plumpton Letters*, no. 38, p. 59; no. 80, p. 88; for Edward Plumpton, see also ibid., pp. 330–1.

[44] *Kingsford's Stonor Letters*, no. 329, p. 415. Similarly, Sir William Plumpton's legal advisers had promised him to 'shew you such service ... that shall be pleasing vnto you', and assured him of readiness 'to doe you service and pleasure' in 'any matter ye haue to do in the Law': *Plumpton Letters*, no. 4, p. 26; no. 28, p. 52 (letters of 1461 and *c.* 1477).

[45] *Kingsford's Stonor Letters*, no. 271, p. 364; no. 274, p. 366.

[46] A phrase sometimes used in formal contracts, including Edmond Paston II's indentures for military service under Richard, duke of Gloucester, in Edward IV's French expedition of 1475 (*Paston Letters*, Part I, no. 396, p. 636); see also, 'Private Indentures', ed. Jones and Walker, p. 22.

[47] *Kingsford's Stonor Letters*, no. 258, pp. 352–3.

[48] *Paston Letters*, Part I, no. 238, p. 398; no. 334, p. 546. For the siege, see Richmond, *Fastolf's Will*, pp. 192–209, where it is described as 'a militarily-conducted affair. On both sides.' (p. 199).

[49] E.g. 'a servys of Trenchers' (*Kingsford's Stonor Letters*, no. 96, p. 189); 'the seid issues and profytes of the seid maneres, londes, and tenementes, rentes and seruices' and 'no londes ne tenementes in demeane ne in seruice of our seid souerein lord' (*Paston Letters*, Part I, no. 97, p. 175; Part II, no. 437, p. 20); 'ye clame suyt, seruice of the maner of Colthorpe': *Plumpton Letters*, no. 38, p. 60.

[50] Edmond Paston II offered his 'duté and seruyse' to his mother (*Paston Letters*, Part I, no. 399, p. 640); John III urged his suit to two different women in terms of 'that servyse that I owe yow' and 'syche pore seruyse as I now in my mynd owe yow' (ibid., no. 362, p. 590; no. 373, p. 604), while Agnes Wydeslade wrote 'with alle suche servise as y can or may' to her prospective husband, Sir William Stonor in 1480: *Kingsford's Stonor Letters*, no. 262, p. 356.

as an appropriate term for help or assistance offered by an equal or near equal. In 1478, Edmond Hampden, writing with some impatience and no undue deference to his cousin, Sir William Stonor, promised, with reference to one of the latter's servants, 'to do yow better servyce in on owyr then yt scall ley in hys powyr to do all the dayys off hys lyve'.[51]

It should not surprise us that the notion of service permeated medieval society so thoroughly. Even in the later middle ages, the most commonly expressed and, one must assume, accepted social theory was that of the three orders: those who fought (*bellatores*), those who prayed (*oratores*) and those who worked (*laboratores*). This is a functionally based categorization. What you do is what makes you what you are. Even in other attempts at classification, such as that based on the image of the body, the service or function element was to the fore. So, in John of Salisbury's *Policraticon*, as developed by Jean Juvenal des Ursins in mid-fifteenth-century France, the officers of justice were the 'limbs of the body politic'. In other such interpretations, the nobility were seen as the 'arms', serving the will of the 'head' of state.[52]

There were many different groups embraced within the *bellatores* and the *oratores*, and it was never clear which of the two occupied the topmost position in society. The complex nature of society is also disguised by the lumping together of everyone else under the category of *laboratores* or workers. The first two papers in this volume concentrate on this last group. Yet even here there was variation and complexity, as Goldberg reveals in answer to the fundamental question, 'What was a servant?'. He urges us to understand the terms implying 'servant' or 'service' as 'discursive constructs', in order that we may arrive at a 'more subtle and nuanced picture of what medievals meant when they drew upon the vocabulary of service'. His opening case study reminds us again of semantic issues. A girl revived by the miraculous intervention of St Thomas de Cantelupe is described as *ancilla* (maidservant) of the saint, the word ancilla having a variety of connotations. Goldberg goes on to discuss other terms used to describe servants in the period, before looking more closely at the identity of the servant. Many such servants, especially in towns, were young and female, and service formed a distinct period in their life cycle. The servants Goldberg discusses were essentially free agents who had entered into a contract with the employer, usually on an annual basis. Evidence on pay rates is surprisingly thin, but, as Goldberg reminds us, rewards should not simply be calculated in terms of money alone. Other benefits, not least those resulting from 'living in', must be taken into account. Moreover, some servants lived in the employer's household on broadly equal terms with the employer's own children, and enjoyed their master's or mistress's affection, or at least respect, although by the late fifteenth century it would seem that there was a growing demarcation, at least in spatial terms, between master and servant.

[51] *Kingsford's Stonor Letters*, no. 219, p. 314. For the comparable standing of the Stonor and Hampden families, see Carpenter, 'Stonor Circle', pp. 183–4.

[52] For a general discussion of social categorization, see J. Mann, *Chaucer and Medieval Estates Satire* (London, 1973); for the use of service terminology to describe the functioning of bodily parts, see *Middle English Dictionary, Part S.4*, ed. R.E. Lewis (Ann Arbor, 1987), pp. 478, 490.

A century or more before, however, there was already a clear perception on the part of the masters about the expected function of those who laboured, especially those who worked on the land. Indeed, there was increased emphasis after the Black Death on the latters' duty (as expressed in a sermon of the 1380s) to 'travail bodeliche and with their sore swete geten out of the earth bodelech livelode for hem and other partes',[53] prompted by fears that it was not merely demographic change which was undermining the workforce, but also more insidious changes within the minds and ambitions of the labouring classes. Service at this level was thus a sensitive, perhaps one could even call it a political, issue in this period. Historians have tended to see the matter of labour legislation as a fourteenth-century concern, but Given-Wilson's detailed study reveals how it persisted as a major preoccupation well into the next century. As he notes, 'more than a third of the seventy-seven parliaments held between 1351 and 1430 passed legislation relating to labour, and further bursts of activity followed into the mid-1440s and again in the 1490s'. What was at issue was not simply wage levels – the shortage of population having made labour more expensive – but also conditions of service, such as the length of contract, and the attempt to force men and women to work, especially on the land. As Given-Wilson shows, there was continuing concern over the implementation of the legislation. Its reissue was not 'simply the mantra-like repetition of earlier enactments'. Who was to set the wage rates? Were employers, some of whom were clearly willing and able to pay higher wages, also to be subject to prosecution? For whom or what should the fines collected be used? At base there was a fear of mobility of population, which in turn, as Given-Wilson shows, led to 'the development of ideas about vagrancy and mendiancy', some of which even had a more positive side in considering how best to deal with poverty. But, all in all, the parliaments of the period were moved by perceptions of contemporary crisis, of the lower orders being in need of control and 'moral guardianship'.

The theory of the three orders, and indeed of any functionally based model of society, implies that everyone should do their duty, and that their social standing, being defined by their function, should not change. Society should thus be static. One was born a 'fighter' or a 'worker'. Only 'those who prayed' were not born to that station. The church was one of the few areas offering potential to the lower orders of society, although how low is a moot point. But there can be no doubt that the concept of service was central to the essential functions of the clergy to shrive their parishioners, pray, preach and give nourishment to the poor.[54]

Entering a clerical career, or attempting to do so, is the subject of Virginia Davis's contribution. She shows that although it was relatively easy to proceed to ordination, acquiring a benefice was much more difficult. Patronage was crucial to both stages, as was social standing. Thus, in extreme cases, those with the right connections could achieve a benefice even before full ordination, and were often destined for a glittering career in the church. Clerical service was therefore multi-faceted, with many having to settle for unbeneficed positions.

---

[53] G.R. Owst, *Literature and Pulpit in Medieval England* (Cambridge, 1933), pp. 550–1.

[54] William Langland, *The Vision of Piers Plowman. A Complete Edition of the B-Text*, ed. A.V.C. Schmidt (London, new edn 1987), Prologue, p. 4.

Whilst these might seem to the modern eye to be dead-end jobs in that there was little chance of movement from them, this would be to deny the concept of dedication to duty, in this case a man's ultimate duty to God and the church. Davis concludes that historians may have underestimated the level of commitment as well as the piety and devotion of the late medieval clergy. Some men at least had what in later centuries was considered a 'calling' or vocation.

As Davis shows, some churchmen had the benefit of a university education, but by no means all who enjoyed the latter were priests. Jeremy Catto investigates the distinctive forms of service undertaken by fifteenth-century graduates, comparing the careers of those with degrees in arts from the University of Oxford with those of the products of its higher faculties, and noting some interesting parallels and contrasts with the career patterns of those trained in the higher faculties of universities in mainland Europe. Masters of arts – amongst them Fastolf's (and McFarlane's) William Worcester – made valuable notaries and secretaries, capable not only of drafting letters of business, but also of employing their rhetorical skills in the composition of more elaborate documents designed to argue or prove a patron's case. But the intellectual élite and those able to command the highest rewards were the doctors of law, medicine and theology. The first frequently rose to the episcopate and the service of the crown. Doctors of medicine and theology were more often found in the service of the nobility, the latter as confessors. Theologians were also sought after by bishops keen to secure good preachers for their dioceses. Specialist expertise conferred independence: higher graduates were unlikely to give exclusive service to one particular patron. Rather than an ethic of service, Catto concludes, the higher graduates had a professional ethic which demanded that they exercise their skills on behalf of all those who could pay for them.

David Morgan's concern is not simply the reality and the ethic, but also the rhetoric, of service, in this case that rendered to Henry V by his household retinue, the last royal household retinue to be organized primarily on a military basis. Its members, many of whom had served the king's father, and some his grandfather too, played a vital coordinating role at the heart of Henry's army in France. They also figured in the creation, in the late 1430s and early 1440s, of the monuments, both architectural (the king's chantry chapel at Westminster, and All Souls College, Oxford) and literary (the accounts of his life and deeds in prose and verse), that celebrated his posthumous memory as a great war leader. Morgan argues that by the mid-point of the fifteenth century, when the last remnants of Henry's great French conquest was lost by his conspicuously unmilitary successor, the former king and his servants had come to embody an ethos of a much more glorious public life, which was invoked, at different times, by both sides in the ensuing struggle between York and Lancaster. And, despite the fact that the military functions of the royal household died with Henry V in 1422, it was an ethos which resiliantly survived, through an early modern period devoid of sustained English miltary effort abroad, to modern times.

Another aspect of service to the English crown is illuminated by Ralph Griffiths' investigation of the genesis of the scheme for the reform of royal officialdom set out in Chapter 17 of Sir John Fortescue's *Governance of England*, presented to Edward IV in the mid-1470s. An earlier version of this scheme, assumed to have been formulated by Fortescue at the Lancastrian court in exile, constituted one element of a set of recommendations for good government which were addressed to the earl of Warwick as leader of the force that succeeded in briefly reinstating Henry VI on the throne in 1470. It is suggested, however, that this was a scheme devised not necessarily solely or originally by Fortescue, but by a wider group of able and experienced royal servants. The proposal was to make service to the crown exclusive and to reduce the scope for plurality and unnecessary absenteeism by requiring royal servants to serve none but the king and to hold no more than one, or at most two, offices at a time. Griffiths considers the composition and connections of the court in exile from 1463, and changes between the late fourteenth century and the 1460s in patterns of office-holding in different parts of the royal dominions – Ireland, Wales, Normandy, the palatinate of Chester, the duchies of Lancaster and Cornwall and the royal castles along the south coast of England. He argues that the proposed reform was inspired by well-informed appreciation of the contribution that the long-term development of pluralism, absenteeism and increasing control of key offices by the nobility and their retainers had made to the collapse of Lancastrian government in 1460.

Kathleen Daly's contrasting study of royal officials in fifteenth-century France points to some fundamental differences from the English situation. With a strong concept of kingship as an office, the service of the *officiers du roi* was to the institution of monarchy, rather than to the person of the king. Moreover, their functions were becoming specialized enough to encourage the development of what Daly calls 'a professional caste' trained in-house. Some royal officers were, in fact, elected; there was also debate on matters such as whether officers should be appointed for long periods or not. Some considered that this would lead to office-holders becoming complacent or being more likely to abuse their power, but others suggested that longer term occupancy would encourage loyalty and proper behaviour. Offices were in the grant of the king, and repeated political crises in the first third of the century led to changes motivated by partisan factors. Thenceforward, there was greater stability, and Louis XI's attempts in 1461 to make it otherwise proved a failure. By 1482, therefore, notaries and secretaries were able to assert the principle that their offices would not be revoked at the king's death.

France was a different country from England in another significant way. Even in the fifteenth century, it remained highly regionalized both politically and culturally. Brittany, with its higher proportion of nobles than elsewhere in France, was, in Michael Jones' words, 'an all but independent state within the kingdom of France'. As Jones and Kerhervé have previously shown, the duke had his own institutions which functioned like a microcosm of those of the crown. Some of the ducal officials whose residences Jones considers here were personal servants of the duke, members of his ducal household. Others were officers in ducal institutions in the centre or localities. A career in ducal finance was as useful, if not more so, than one in law as 'a path to fortune in late medieval Brittany', as some of Jones' examples of houses and building projects reveal. He emphasizes that some families who might be thought to have prospered simply through office-holding were also those already in possession of large landed endowments. Indeed, for many offices, men of substance were needed, for such men, in Brittany and elsewhere, would be less vulnerable to corruption.

The final contribution to this volume is described by its author, Alexander Grant, as as interim report on a long-term research project on the late medieval Scottish nobility. But it is a substantial revisionist study based on close analysis of what is estimated to be the majority of the now surviving documents produced by Scottish lords between 1314 and 1475 – some 2,061 texts out of a possible 3,000 to 4,000. Grant seeks to overturn previous assumptions about the practicalities of Scottish bastard feudalism and points a number of interesting contrasts with its English counterpart. In late medieval Scotland, twelfth-century practices, such as subinfeudation, and surrender and regrant, survived; the only contract armies were the hostile forces of the English crown. Grant challenges the view that land transactions and tenurial ties had no reality or function in terms of lord–man relations. He also investigates the antecedents of the later fifteenth- and sixteenth-century bonds of manrent and maintenance, the practical, although diplomatically different, equivalent of English indentures of retainer. These antecedents show that pledges of service were frequently matched, not simply, as suggested hitherto, by promises of good lordship from the lord, but by more tangible rewards, annuities or grants of land. He concludes that in late medieval Scotland the concepts of service and land tenure did commonly go hand in hand, at least on a short-term basis, although service relationships cemented by tenurial ties did not normally outlast the lifetimes of the parties to the contract.

There can be no doubt that, had time allowed, the conference could profitably have included papers on many other aspects of service than those considered here. Military service was represented, but the paper given on this topic was offered merely as pre-prandial entertainment and has been published elsewhere.[55] The urban scene might also have repaid further investigation, so too further discussion of the gender perspective. But despite such omissions, there is no doubt that the papers which were given all stimulated lively and extensive debate.

Anyone organizing a conference and editing its proceedings for publication soon discovers that success, as well as their own sanity, depends to a great extent on the invaluable assistance of others. Our thanks go first and foremost to all the contributors; also to Richard Britnell, Tony Pollard, Michael Hicks, Christine Carpenter, Michael K. Jones, Rosemary Horrox and Caroline Barron for ably chairing the various sessions; to St George's Hall for providing participants with accommodation and refreshment; to the Royal Historical Society for a grant enabling us to reduce charges for postgraduate students; to Jennie Matthew who assembled information envelopes for participants, Ben Fulford who assisted with reception duties, and Brian Kemp who led a walking tour of Reading; to Elizabeth Berry who typed a number of letters and, much more importantly, undertook the daunting task of entering on disk the editorial amendments necessary to standardize the presentation of the papers for printing; and to

---

[55] A. Curry, 'Isolated or Integrated? The English Soldier in Lancastrian Normandy, 1417–50', *Courts and Regions in Medieval Europe*, ed. S.R. Jones et al. (York, 2000), pp. 191–210.

Richard Barber and Stephen Taylor for their vital help in arranging publication. Finally we would like to thank the Maidenhead Civic Society for providing the Conference with an exhibition on Ockwells, a mid-fifteenth-century manor house built by John Norreys near Bray, Berkshire, and Ann Darracott for acting as tour guide for the Conference's outing to it, which she arranged by the kind permission of the present owner, Brian Stein. One of the outstanding features of the house is its armorial glass, commissioned by Norreys apparently in celebration of the marriage of Henry VI and Margaret of Anjou in 1445. It was fitting to be reminded that Norreys, no mean pluralist in royal service, as his long list of appointments including the chamberlainship of the exchequer (1446–50) and the office of treasurer of the chamber and keeper of the jewels of Queen Margaret (1445–52) testifies,[56] chose to mark the separate lights with the motto, 'Feythfully serve'.

Anne Curry
Elizabeth Matthew

---

[56] The editors are most grateful to Dr Linda Clark for allowing them to draw on information from her draft biography of John Norreys (John Norris I, d. 1466) prepared for publication in forthcoming volumes of *History of Parliament: The Commons 1422–1504.* Copyright of this material rests with the Trustees of the History of Parliament.

I

WHAT WAS A SERVANT?

P.J.P. Goldberg

IN 1307 during the process of canonization of Thomas de Cantelupe, bishop of Hereford, a young woman known locally as Joan, 'the maidservant (*ancilla*) of St Thomas', testified to the saint's miraculous powers.[1] As a little girl some fifteen to twenty years previously she had fallen and been drowned in a deep fishpond, but the saint had restored her to life in response to the prayers of her parents and other villagers. Since that time she had regularly made pilgrimage with her parents to his shrine in Hereford cathedral and now, a young woman in her early twenties, she expressed herself ambivalent about marrying because of her attachment to the saint. So far as we can tell, Joan probably still lived with her parents who were moderately well-to-do peasant agriculturalists. She was thus not conventionally in service. But her identity as 'the maidservant of St Thomas' cannot go unremarked. Clearly she performed no domestic or other work functions for the long-dead bishop. In what sense, therefore, was she his maidservant? The term used, *ancilla*, has of course biblical resonances. This, according to the Vulgate, was the term used by Mary in response to the angel Gabriel at the annunciation: *Ecce, ancilla Dei* ('Behold, the handmaid of the Lord').[2] The friars who conducted the questioning of deponents and recorded the canonization proceedings could not but have been aware of this when rendering the vernacular of the peasant deponents into the Latin of record, but such resonances would also have been implicit in whatever vernacular term the deponents themselves used.

There are two clues as to why Joan was so described. Firstly she was young – indeed only a child when her fellow villagers must first have given her this title – and unmarried. Secondly she had an obligation to the saint as a consequence of the great mercy he had shown in interceding for the restoration of her life and, we may presume, his continuing spiritual protection. It was an obligation to which Joan was herself sensitive. Her ambivalence about marriage in particular, whether Joan was using her special status in relation to the saint as a reason to deter suitors or even parental pressure to marry, or was driven by contemporary paradigms of female devotion to preserve her virginity, follows from this sense of obligation. The term *ancilla* thus encompasses

---

[1] I am indebted to Sarah Williams who read and commented on a draft of this paper, and to Cordelia Beattie whose own research into single women has influenced my thinking in a number of areas.

[2] Luke 1: 38.

1

implications of youth, of sexual purity, and of spiritual obligation in the context of divine or saintly protection. Like juxtaposition of meanings is not, however, implicit in the use of the same term in, for example, poll tax listings. Here the meanings are purely secular. Meaning must consequently be read in the context of the source. It is, as literary scholars would say, constructed by the discourse. Thus we have no single meaning for the term *ancilla*, but rather a multiplicity of meanings that may shade into one another and may indeed influence one another.

The point of this lengthy discussion of an otherwise obscure early fourteenth-century Herefordshire peasant woman is not to tease as much information as possible from an unyielding source, but to draw attention to some of the bewildering variety of contexts in which terms implying servant or service are found in medieval records. By understanding these terms as discursive constructs we may achieve a more subtle and nuanced picture of what medievals meant when they drew upon the vocabulary of service than if we insisted on finding fixed meanings and definitions. Indeed, it speaks volumes about the medieval understanding of servant that the term is used variously in respect of the relationship of individuals to God, of children to their parents, of employees to their employers, and of lovers to their beloved. What these relationships have in common is a sense of mutual obligation, which may well be contractual and based on consent. They are also unequal relationships since one party is invariably more powerful than the other.[3] Lastly, they are relationships that may have some emotional depth to them even where they are purely contractual in origin.

It is my intention to explore all these relationships. My focus is specifically on the relationship between employer and employee, particularly where the employee is single and in some respects a dependent of a master or mistress below the rank of aristocracy.[4] Nevertheless, the multiplicity of uses of the vocabulary of servanthood must have informed medievals' understanding of the terminology in any specific context. So long as those who employed servants could at the same moment imagine themselves, following the language of contemporary devotional literature or indeed the prayers contained in that most ubiquitous of late medieval devotional aids, the primer or book of hours, as God's servants, then the term cannot have been thought of solely to imply dependence, subordination, or menial office. For medievals 'servant' does not generally appear to have been a pejorative or demeaning term. It implied as much a relationship – between servant and master, mistress, or Divinity – as a status. This relationship was, moreover, dynamic. The servant of God hoped at the end of time to be saved, the lover who was servant to his lady hoped in time to win her heart and possess her body, and the young boy or girl starting service

---

[3] In the case of lovers, the power relationship is of course a fiction.

[4] It was initially envisaged that the programme for the conference would include a paper on servants of the aristocracy, hence my focus on servants employed by persons of non-aristocratic rank. The former is clearly a subject that deserves further attention, since it is evident that only some of the observations made in this chapter are transferrable to an aristocratic context.

hoped in time to grow up, to marry, to become a householder, and even to maintain servants in their own right.[5]

There is a bewildering vocabulary denoting servants to be discovered from late medieval records. The terms most frequently found in wills or in the poll tax returns of the late fourteenth century vary according to the language of the text. In Latin *serviens*, *famulus* or *famula*, and *ancilla* are most usually found. The three former seem to be rendered simply as servant, or perhaps servant and woman servant in English, but *ancilla* is invariably represented as maiden or maid. The English 'ancille' exists purely as a literary form as found, for example, in the work of Lydgate.[6] All are terms used to describe persons resident within their employer's household. Elsewhere we encounter usages that at first sight appear to designate age, thus boy, or its Latin equivalent *garcio*, knave, and woman, but there may be social distinctions implicit here also.[7] We also find nurse (Latin *nutrix*) in the sense of wet-nurse who was likewise resident within the household.[8] It is apparent that different kinds of source use different terminology and hence that the vocabulary used in any given context is dictated by the discourse. Peace session records, for example, invariably use the term 'servant'. This is part of a legal discourse that is concerned with contract rather than status. This is true also of the Statute of Labourers and its various revisions. Only occasionally are alternative terms found in this source and only as qualifications of the generic 'servant'.

Famulus can also have a very specific historical meaning, that is a member of the permanent labour-force employed to work the lord's demesne and hence part of the lord's *familia*. Such workers – carters, ploughmen, shepherds, parkers, dairymaids etc. – were contracted by the year sometimes in return for their tenements, sometimes for payment in both cash and kind. *Famuli* constituted but a handful of workers on any manor and, as demesnes were increasingly leased out during the fifteenth century, their numbers diminished.[9] There is some

---

[5] These remarks must be understood within the specific cultural context of north-western Europe. Service had rather different meanings within other cultural regions. See R.M. Smith, 'Geographic Diversity in the Resort to Marriage in Late Medieval Europe: Work, Reputation, and Unmarried Females in the Household Formation Systems of Northern and Southern Europe', *Woman is a Worthy Wight: Women in English Society c. 1200–1500* (reprinted as *Women in Medieval English Society*), ed. P.J.P. Goldberg (Stroud, 1992), pp. 16–59.

[6] 'Do trewe service, as ancille ... Unto her lord': *The Minor Poems of John Lydgate*, ed. H.N. MacCracken, EETS, original series 192, extra series 107 (2 vols, 1911–34), no. 37. The *Speculum Sacerdotale* uses the term 'ancylle', but immediately glosses this as a damsel that was a servant: *Speculum Sacerdotale*, ed. E.H. Weatherly, EETS, original series 200 (1936), p. 160.

[7] In an aristocratic context the Latin *garcio* can equate to the English 'knave'. I am grateful to Sarah Williams for this observation.

[8] Wet-nurses as household employees are found, for example, in a Yorkshire gentry household noticed in matrimonial litigation in 1365–6: *Women in England c. 1275–1525: Documentary Sources*, ed. P.J.P. Goldberg (Manchester, 1995), pp. 64, 72–3, 78.

[9] M.M. Postan, *The Famulus: The Estate Labourer in the XIIth and XIIIth Centuries*, Economic History Review Supplement, 2 (Cambridge, 1954); D. Farmer, 'The Famuli in the Later Middle Ages', *Progress and Problems in Medieval England*, ed. R. Britnell and J. Hatcher (Cambridge, 1996), pp. 207–36.

indication, however, that they formed part of a larger group of persons contracted by the year, who occupy a sort of middle ground between the 'life-cycle' servant and the hired labourer, who was often a householder or member of a household other that of their employer. The unusually informative Howdenshire (Yorks., E.R.) poll tax returns for 1379 designate taxpayers variously as wife, servant, labourer, husbandman, artificer etc. such that every taxpayer carries some sort of designation by way of justifying the level of tax assessed. Numbers of persons are here designated 'servant' although they appear not to be physically resident within the households of others. Most are unmarried and, within this pastoral economy, women outnumbered men in the ratio 3:2.[10] That the Howdenshire returns also regularly describe children resident in their natal households as servants suggests that notions of dependence are at the heart of this usage; the Howdenshire servants who lived on their own were still seen in some way as dependent on their employers – part of their meinie or mainpasts – whereas labourers were understood to have no ties to their employers beyond the work for which they were duly paid.

The term apprentice seems very rarely to be found outside craft guild ordinances, related borough records, and wills. Where the term is found outside this context it frequently refers in fact to apprentices at law. Once again there is reason for this in as much as other kinds of source, such as poll tax returns or legal records, are more concerned to identify the relationship of the employee, implicit in the term 'servant', to a master or mistress who may thus be held to have some responsibility for them.[11] Craft guild ordinances, however, needed to distinguish apprentices since their training was of particular concern to the guild.[12] Such ordinances regularly required that apprentices be contracted for a period of seven years and attempted to limit the numbers of apprentices an employer might have at any one time. This presumably was to restrict unfair competition from cheap labour, but also to protect apprentices by keeping to a manageable few the number any employer trained and similarly the numbers of persons who, having completed apprenticeships, might be competing for workshops. In other contexts, however, craft ordinances employ the generic term 'servant'.

For the best illustration of the way in which terms may be understood discursively we need to return to *ancilla*. There is some evidence to suggest that this often described the personal servant of the mistress of the household, i.e. a term akin to the much later 'lady's maid'. The *Promptorium Parvulorum*, a mid-fifteenth-century vocabulary, renders maiden servant as *ancilla* in Latin and glosses this as 'Maydyn, or seruaunt folowynge a woman of worschyppe'.[13]

---

[10] P.J.P. Goldberg, 'Migration, Youth, and Gender in Later Medieval England', *Youth in the Middle Ages*, ed. P.J.P. Goldberg and F.J. Riddy (York, forthcoming).

[11] A few apprentices are noted unusually in the Oxford poll tax returns for 1381: *Oxford City Documents 1268–1665,* ed. J.E. Thorold Rogers, Oxford Historical Society, 18 (1891), pp. 24–5, 28.

[12] In theory the apprentice had privileged access to craft mastership and enfranchisement, though in practice this was true of an increasingly small proportion of apprentices through the course of the later fifteenth century. See, for example, the case of York weavers' apprentices: H. Swanson, *Medieval Artisans* (Oxford, 1989), pp. 33–4.

[13] *The Promptorium Parvulorum*, ed. A.I. Mayhew, EETS, extra series 102 (1908), p. 320.

Such a context may explain the use of *ancilla* in the records of the sessions of the peace for Lincolnshire to describe one Alice who was allegedly forcibly abducted from her employer, Sir William de Belesby of Beelsby, by one John Derwent in 1386, but it may not explain the use of the same term in like sources in respect of two alleged assaults in the decade following the Black Death. In 1350 Richard de Spaldynge was said to have broken into William de Byle's house in Lincoln and 'so lay with [—] de Roderham *ancilla* of the said William and did 40s worth of other damage to the same William'. Interestingly this case is not presented as rape, and it is the employer who is said to have suffered damage. A few years later in Bedfordshire another *ancilla* was allegedly dragged from her employer's close by two men who then threatened to beat up another man who came to her assistance. Similarly the female servant allegedly prostituted by her employers in Southampton in 1482 was described as *ancilla*. In all these instances *ancilla* may have been chosen to accentuate the wrong or damage done by the defendants because of the qualities of youth, innocence, and vulnerability implicit in the term.[14]

Ancilla is also found as another synonym for a female servant. Thus the clerk recording the return for the suburban parish of St Thomas in the Oxford poll tax returns for 1381 uses only *ancilla* in respect of women servants; elsewhere in the same returns the term 'servant' is used invariably for both sexes. John Trevisa, translating the *De Proprietatibus Rerum* of Bartholomew Anglicus into English, under the heading *de ancilla* talks generally of the 'seruaunt womman', again suggesting that for him the term had no more specific meaning, although he does write that she 'is ordeined to serue þe wifes rule'. How significant this last distinction is depends on whether his discussion under the head *de seruo* refers specifically to male servants or to servants generally.[15] If, as is likely, the latter, then it is possible to suggest that the term *ancilla* may stand as a general term for a female servant, but may in other contexts indicate the personal servant of the mistress of the house. This would be one way of explaining the particular use of the term *ancilla* as against *famula*, the generic Latin term for a female household servant, to be found in some York wills. In 1428, for example, Agnes Palmar made a substantial bequest to her *famula*, Joan Howsom, but a much more modest bequest to her *ancilla*, Agnes Burnelay, whereas John Walker (d. 1431) left identical token bequests to his *famula*, also Joan Howsom, and his *ancilla*, Marjory. In another instance, however, youth is perhaps the clue to the usage. John Scott, who appears to have been unmarried (perhaps a widower) when he died in 1429, left his *famule*, Agnes Skypton and

---

[14] *Some Sessions of the Peace in Lincolnshire 1381–1396*, vol. II, ed. E.G. Kimball, Lincoln Record Society, 56 (1962), p. 35, no. 88; *Sessions of the Peace in the City of Lincoln 1351–1354 and the Borough of Stamford 1351*, ed. E.G. Kimball, Lincoln Record Society, 65 (1971), p. 5, no. 15; *Sessions of the Peace for Bedfordshire 1355–1359 and 1363–1364*, ed. E.G. Kimball, HMC, Joint Publication, 16 (also Bedfordshire Historical Record Society, 18) (1969), p. 43, no. 29; *The Assize of Bread Book 1477–1517*, ed. R.C. Anderson, Southampton Record Society, 23 (1923), p. 16.

[15] *On the Properties of Things ... A Critical Text; John Trevisa's Translation of Batholomaeus Anglicus De Proprietatibus Rerum*, ed. M.C. Seymour, 2 vols (Oxford 1975), vol. I, pp. 305, 311–12 (book vi, chs 11, 15).

Alice Bayledon, 40s each, but he left only 13s 4d to his *ancilla*, 'little' Joan. Both the epithet 'little' and the absence of a second name are signifiers of youth, but the absence of a widow is telling evidence that Joan was not a lady's maid.[16]

We have here then a range of usages and overlapping meanings associated with the word *ancilla*. These tend to be discursively constructed. Thus Joan was the *ancilla* of St Thomas because, following the language of the Vulgate, this was the term appropriate to a religious discourse. The same process determined the choice of the English 'ancylle' by the author of the *Speculum Sacerdotale* to describe the woman servant who provoked Peter's denial of Christ.[17] Similarly *ancilla* is used in records of the sessions of the peace in order to accentuate the innocence and vulnerability of the female servant, and hence the culpability of the male defendant and the wrong done to the employer under whose protection the female servant lived. *Ancilla* is here used because it is the employer that has been wronged. Where the wrong is presented as having been done to the servant herself, as in the case of a twelve-year-old Lincolnshire *serviens* allegedly raped at knife point in 1379, neither considerations of youth nor of innocence prompted the clerk to depart from the normal conventions of his legal discourse.[18]

Finally, *ancilla* has connotations variously of youth, personal service to the mistress of the household, and service to a lady of rank. Perhaps sexual purity, implicit also in the vernacular 'maid' or 'maiden', is again the common factor. In the context of a culture that placed so much emphasis on the reputation of women, and particularly women of rank, the virtue of the women they employed might be held to be a reflection of their own virtue. Indeed a lady of rank would regularly be seen to be accompanied by her maids as both a projection of her own chastity and as a sort of ambulant *cordon sanitaire*. Whereas the purity of a young girl might be presumed, that of an older servant had constantly to be guarded. This again was partly a matter of social rank. As Phillips has argued, only young women from well-to-do backgrounds were actually socialized to preserve their virginity until marriage, so the older *ancilla* in service to a lady of rank was herself likely to be both sexually inexperienced and of good family.[19]

There are thus a variety of terms found in written sources used to describe servants, the meanings of which must be recovered within the context of the source in which they occur. It is no easier a matter to reconstruct a vernacular vocabulary of servanthood. Servant (ME 'servaunt') appears to have been the generic term, though apprentices, using the normal Middle English form of 'prentice', were probably regularly so called. 'Maid' or 'maiden' was probably the usual term for the Latin *ancilla*, but older female servants may have been described simply as women. The Lincolnshire sessions of the peace for the early 1380s describe two female servants as 'garthwoman' and another as an 'inwom-man'. Likewise the will of Mary or Marion Kent (d. 1500), which although

---

[16] Borthwick IHR, Prob. Reg. 2, ff. 543v (Palmar), 554v (Scott), 658v (Walker).

[17] *Speculum Sacerdotale*, p. 160.

[18] *Sessions of the Peace in Lincolnshire 1381–1396*, pp. 152–3, no. 412. It may be that the girl's age alone made further accentuation of her youth and innocence redundant.

[19] K.M. Phillips, 'The Medieval Maiden: Young Womanhood in Late Medieval England' (unpublished D.Phil. thesis, University of York, 1997), esp. p. 80 et seq.

written in Latin may reflect English usage, makes bequest to every *mulier* or *famula*.[20] The terms 'groom' and 'wench' are also found, but may not have had much currency outside literature. The same is perhaps true of the term 'knave', which seems broadly similar in usage to 'boy'. This last appears to have been in common currency to describe a young male servant. It is found particularly in connection with kitchen employees, but boys are also noted running errands or carrying letters. Only by the later fifteenth century does 'boy' seem to become also a term of contempt or abuse.[21]

So far our discussion has been concerned with terminology. We need now to consider something of the identity of the servant and so move towards an understanding of the terms and conditions by which servants were employed. The economic logic of hiring youngsters as servants, primarily for the cost of their food and clothing, at a time of labour shortage and wage inflation has been described elsewhere.[22] We need note here merely that towns seem to have had a particular capacity to absorb servants into the workshops of artisans and into the grander houses of merchants or their widows, even to the extent that in the early fifteenth-century town most adolescents were probably in service with others rather than living with their natal families. The demand was indeed such that numbers of urban servants were migrants from the rural hinterland and no doubt initially in need of socializing into the mores of urban society.

The demand for servants in the countryside was much less, though in regions where pastoralism or stock raising was practised, servants, by nature of their residence within their employers' households, were available to care for livestock at times when day labourers would be at home with their own families. It should be noted finally that servanthood provided a mechanism for the support of children precisely at the point when they were likely to lose one or both parents. Certainly numbers of London citizens' orphans of both sexes were placed in apprenticeships to give them a surrogate family as well as a training for adulthood, and it is likely that larger numbers of adolescents were more informally sheltered from the trauma of family breakup due to parental mortality by already being in service at the time or by seeking positions as servants as a consequence.[23]

The logic of this institution can only be understood within the context of a distinctive regional culture that permitted, or even encouraged, young people, including girls, to live and work away from their natal homes prior to marriage. But it should not be assumed that the economic pressures that created a demand for servants, particularly in the households of urban artisans and merchants, did not also cause social tensions. There was perhaps a particular anxiety about the welfare and reputation of young women going out to service. This is

---

[20] *Sessions of the Peace in Lincolnshire 1381–1396*, pp. 21 (no. 42), 180–1 (nos 505–6); Borthwick IHR, Prob. Reg. 5, f. 320.

[21] E.J. Dobson, 'The Etymology and Meaning of Boy', *Medium Aevum*, 9 (1940), 121–54.

[22] P.J.P. Goldberg, *Women, Work, and Life Cycle in a Medieval Economy: Women in York and Yorkshire c. 1300–1520* (Oxford, 1992), pp. 74–6, 358.

[23] E.g. *Calendar of Plea and Memoranda Rolls of the City of London 1437–1457*, ed. P.E. Jones (Cambridge, 1954), p. 88.

reflected, for example, in the circulation of the didactic poem *How the Goodwife Taught her Daughter*, written presumably by a clerical author about or before the time of the Black Death, but circulating through the fifteenth century. Evidently a text that was pertinent where daughters were not in fact living at home, it may have served variously to instruct young women in service by warning them against male company, excessive drinking, and unsuitable entertainments, and to instruct employers, particularly mistresses of households, how to socialize adolescent female servants.[24] A like didactic purpose may lie behind a group of ballads that tell of young women seduced and then abandoned by men.[25] One of these ballads, dating to the middle of the fifteenth century, describes the seduction of a female farm-servant (to borrow an anachronistic terminology) on her holiday.[26] She of course is left holding the baby.

It is within the context of this shared clerical and, in respect of *How the Goodwife* at least, bourgeois concern for the virtue and morals of young women in service that we can perhaps understand something of the late medieval English cult of St Sitha. Her cult originated in Lucca where the virtuous life of Zita, the poor servant-girl, was used as an exemplar by the civic authorities there in an attempt to instil some discipline into women servants, an underclass made up variously of impoverished orphan girls, poor widows, and even some married women.[27] Her translation to England involved more than a simple Anglicization of her name. Her whole social context was transformed. Iconographic representations of her in glass, in manuscripts, and on funerary monuments show a well-born and archetypically beautiful virgin with flowing golden hair. Her presence on tombs or in books of hours, as, for example, the prestigeous Hastings Hours, suggests moreover an aristocratic dimension to her cult.[28] A bourgeois patronage is evidenced by her depiction as a full-page illumination within the so-called Bolton Hours, a work probably produced for a York mercantile family in the early fifteenth century. Here a woman, who clearly represents the mother previously shown with husband, son, and daughter before the Trinity, kneels before St Sitha. Elsewhere the daughter is shown in veneration before York's martyred archbishop, Richard Scrope. If we read these hours as primarily intended for the female members of the household and possibly even as a gift from mother to daughter, then we can make sense of her significance.[29] St Sitha provided a paradigm of youthful female conduct that

[24] *The Good Wife Taught Her Daughter*, ed. T.F. Mustanoja, Annales Academiae Scientiarum Fennicae, ser. B, 61 pt. 2 (Helsinki, 1948). For a discussion of this text, see F. Riddy, 'Mother Knows Best: Reading Social Change in a Courtesy Text', *Speculum*, 71 (1996), 66–86.

[25] In several instances these men turn out to be clerics and thus unable to marry by reason of their vows.

[26] 'The Serving Maid's Holiday', *Secular Lyrics of the XIVth and XVth Centuries*, ed. R.H. Robbins (Oxford, 1955), pp. 24–6.

[27] M. Goodich, 'Ancilla Dei: The Servant as Saint in the Later Middle Ages', *Women of the Medieval World*, ed. J. Kirshner and S.F. Wemple (Oxford, 1985), pp. 119–36.

[28] S. Sutcliffe, 'The Cult of St Sitha in England: An Introduction', *Nottingham Medieval Studies*, 37 (1993), 83–9.

[29] There are a number of reasons for thinking this. Books of hours or primers are regularly noted from probate evidence in female possession or passed through the female line, numbers of extant manuscripts are known to have been produced for specific

was chaste, pious, and charitable. She also provided a model of service itself that was pertinent to the daughters of merchants and gentlemen.[30] The mother's devotion to her is thus explained by her desire for the protection, for the virtue, and for the good name of a daughter in service.[31]

St Sitha might offer servants spiritual support, but the law of contract offered more pragmatic protection. Contract lay at the heart of the relationship between the late medieval English servant and his or her employer. Trevisa, following Bartholomew Anglicus, described three kinds of servant under the heading *de seruo*, viz. the bond servant or serf, the slave, and a third kind. Of this last he wrote, 'The þridde manere of seruauntes is bounde frelich and by here owne good wille, and serueþ for mede and for hire, and þis [ben] propirlich iclepid *famuli*'.[32] Three important points are contained within this definition: the servant has no prior obligation to the employer and is a free agent at the point of contract; the servant serves in the expectation of remuneration; the servant, in

female patrons, and the Bolton Hours itself has four illuminations depicting lay women – the two just noted, another of the mother figure before St Michael and All Angels, and a smaller depiction of a woman making confession. Only one (the Trinity page) additionally represents lay men. I have read these as representations of members of the family who commissioned the hours and have elsewhere argued that the manuscript was made for Margaret Blackburn, senior, for use with her daughters. See P.H. Cullum and P.J.P. Goldberg, 'How Margaret Blackburn Taught her Daughters: Reading Devotional Instruction in a Book of Hours', *Medieval Women: Texts and Contexts in Late Medieval Britain*, ed. J. Wogan-Browne et al., Medieval Women: Texts and Contexts, 3 (Turnout, 2000), pp. 217–36.

[30] St Sitha may have had a more plebeian cult following, for whom she was *inter alia* a finder of lost objects, but the point here is that the English Sitha occupied a very different social position from her Italian progenitor.

[31] The cult of St Sitha cannot be understood in isolation any more than the single illumination and associated prayer within the Hours can be divorced from the book as a whole. Her cult must be seen as part of broader devotional fashion here associated with the upper echelons of bourgeois and gentry society. The mid-fifteenth-century inventory of the hospital chapel of St Mary Magdalene in York includes images of Saints Anne, Elizabeth, and Our Lady of Pity, cloths painted with the Veronica, the Trinity, and Saints John the Baptist and the Evangelist, in addition to a relic of the hair of St Sitha. Similarly an English later fifteenth-century manuscript (Biblioteca Statale di Lucca, MS 3540) containing a Latin life of St Sitha, accompanied by prayers and a miniature of the saint, is bound together with the *Meditationes Vitae Christi*, a work on the Name of Jesus attributed to Rolle and extracts from the *Revelations* of St Bridget of Sweden. Such a compilation is not random, and it mirrors the devotional interests of the Bolton Hours, with its comparatively typical but still striking eucharistic and Passion devotions, but less typically, devotions to the Name of Jesus and St Bridget. St Sitha may in particular be seen alongside a devotional interest in Saints Anne and Mary Magdalene. The concern here is with female conduct and reputation. It is a concern couched in essentially familial terms, since within the culture of north-western Europe in the later Middle Ages young, unmarried servants were indeed an integral part of the *familia: Testamenta Eboracensia*, vol. II, ed. R. Raine, Surtees Society 30 (1855), p. 151; T. Turville-Petre, 'A Middle English Life of St Zita', *Nottingham Medieval Studies*, 35 (1991), 104. See also Sutcliffe, 'Cult of St Sitha in England'.

[32] *On the Properties of Things*, vol. I, p. 312 (book vi, ch. 15).

this sense, becomes part of the *familia* or household of the employer and in some ways under the jurisdiction of the employer. The two last are corollaries of the first. Whereas the bond servant owes service as a consequence of his legal status and so is not rewarded, but merely punished for omission, the servant who freely contracts works for reward. Likewise whereas the bond servant is from birth subject to the authority of the lord as a consequence of inherited legal status, the dependency of the servant to the employer is of limited duration and, because voluntarily entered into, may be characterized by good will on both parts. The servant as a member of the *familia* enters into a hierarchy bounded as much by considerations of age and gender as by social or legal status.

There is a parallel here with the position of the married woman. She enters freely into matrimony as a consequence of a contract to which she consents. Her position as wife requires her to serve her husband, but her position as a woman ensures that she is subordinate to her husband's authority. Implicit in her contract, however, are obligations on the part of the husband to protect and provide for her, and though he may lawfully chastise her, he may not abuse her. Experience may have fallen short, but the ideal was of a relationship characterized by mutual respect and affection. In describing the good servant, Trevisa writes that it 'is semeliche þat a seruanunt be merye and glad of chere in his seruyse', and elsewhere writes of the good lord that he 'loueþ more to be iloued þan idrade'. This again appears, though it pertains to ideals and thus ideology and not lived lives, to be about a relationship that is both rooted in a clear hierarchy and is also about mutual respect and affection. This is in marked contrast to his words on the bond servant. 'Hit is' he writes, 'a properte of . . . hem þat ben of bonde condicioun to grucche and ben rebel and vnbuxom to here lordis and ladies' and consequently they must be 'iholde lowe wiþ drede'.[33] This legal distinction may explain why chastisement of servants by employers could be a cause for contention. There are numbers of cases where servants claimed that they had been unreasonably beaten by their employers.

Trevisa's differentiation between the bond servant and the servant who freely contracts is an important one. It is a difference of power relationships. The bond servant is always under the authority of the lord. At the point of contract, however, the *famulus* or *famula* actually stands in a position of equality with the prospective employer. If he or she does not like the terms offered or the duties asked, then no contract need follow. Employers were obliged to bargain with persons inferior in terms of age and household status, and perhaps also in terms of gender and social status. Thus though employers may have had a clear sense of their own authority once the contract commenced, servants would always be mindful of the way in which they had bargaining power and the ways in which a contract bestowed obligations on an employer as it did on a servant. This last helps explain the willingness of servants to bring litigation against the employers and former employers where they found that employers had abused their position or disregarded the terms of their contract.[34] Furthermore, because contracts, other than for apprentices, were invariably short, a year being the

---

[33] Ibid., vol. I, pp. 305–6, 314, 317–18 (book vi, chs 11, 17, 18).
[34] This point is considered at greater length below.

norm, servants retained some bargaining power even after the point of contract where employers wished to retain a servant after the initial year. This last may have been particularly true of the labour-hungry years of the later fourteenth and early fifteenth centuries.[35]

Although a contract was thus central to the relationship between servant and employer, it does not follow that contracts were regularly in written form, nor that terms and conditions were specified in detail. Rather, contracts, other than for apprentices, were normally verbal and hence more immediately accessible to the parties concerned.[36] Moreover, much of what was expected between servant and employer was probably understood as customary rather than matters for negotiation and detailed specification. As such we can only surmise some elements of the contractual relationship. Rarely do we know in any detail what servants were required to do, though this undoubtedly varied according to age, gender, social status, the nature and size of the household, and hence the degree of specialization possible, and over time.[37] Nor is it clear how and in what circumstances contracts were made. Children had to be of sufficient age lawfully to enter into a contract in their own right.[38] In respect of younger servants, therefore, parents may usually have played a role. Thomas Parys of York referred in his will to a contract of service agreed between himself and the mother of his *famula* Alice, but William Nunhouse used his will to remind his (presumably somewhat older) servant, Margaret, of the contract made between the two of them.[39] We have a rare glimpse of a servant being contracted from a cause paper of 1374. Joan, the daughter of Peter atte Enges, was contracted at Pentecost by her master in her house in Clementhorpe, a suburb of York. It is implicit that she agreed to the contract, but equally it is stated that her family were present.[40]

This last example alerts us to the existence, indeed the perdurance, of fixed points during the year when most servants were contracted. The major dates in the calendar were, for much of England north of the Trent, and also Lincolnshire, Martinmas (11 November), and for many other parts of the country and especially midland England, Michaelmas (29 September).[41] Thus the Lincolnshire 'inwomman' noted earlier was hired from Martinmas 1383, and Alice,

---

[35] This is apparent, for example, from a breach of promise cause in the York consistory dating to immediately after the Grey Death (*c.* 1361–2): Borthwick IHR, CP.E.241p, pop popd in *Women in England*, pp. 92–3.

[36] The evidence for the form of servants' contracts is very slight and rests in part on silence. For example, William Coke's deposition (see n. 40 below) appears to relate to a verbal contract. More substantial employers probably kept their own records of the terms and conditions by which their servants were employed.

[37] Goldberg, *Women, Work, and Life Cycle*, pp. 186–94.

[38] Putnam suggests this was somewhere between thirteen and sixteen years: B.H. Putnam, *The Enforcement of the Statutes of Labourers in the first decades after the Black Death, 1349–1359*, Columbia Studies in the Social Sciences, 85 (New York, 1908), p. 186.

[39] Borthwick IHR, Prob. Reg. 2, f. 97 (Nunhouse); 3, f. 282v (Parys).

[40] Borthwick IHR, CP.E.155, deposition of William Coke, pop popd in *Women in England*, p. 137.

[41] Putnam, *Enforcement*, Appendix, pp. 170, 172 (Essex), 246–8 (Bedfordshire), 393 (Gloucestershire), 424 (Nottingham), 447 (Hertfordshire), 453 (Sussex), 458 (Devon), 462 (Somerset).

the servant of William Myche of Bilton (Warwicks.), was hired from Michaelmas 1380. The majority of servants for whom a date of entry or leaving service is noted in York matrimonial cause papers did so at Martinmas.[42] Some servants were also hired at a point about six months before these feasts, at Pentecost and, as the evidence for a Coventry hiring fair demonstrates, Easter, respectively. As we have seen, Joan atte Enges was contracted for a year at Pentecost, and in London a Thomas the Personescosyn, observed in a case from 1371, was contracted for a year from Easter. In the early years of the fifteenth century one Alice, later married to Robert Dalton of Poppleton near York, left service at Pentecost having been contracted at Martinmas.[43]

This last example is indicative of a subsidiary pattern of six-month contracts particularly for some female servants. Although only three of the thirty-one servants whose terms of employment are described in the Oxford sessions of the peace in the early 1390s were contracted for less than a year, two were women serving for half a year.[44] Emma, daughter of Adam le Wright of Chorley (Lancs.), presented in 1350 for refusing employment, was offered a contract from the feast of the nativity of St John the Baptist (24 June) until Christmas. A Beverley woman contracted at Michaelmas – atypically for the region, but this was the year of the Black Death – likewise left service some eight months later at the feast of the translation of St Thomas of Canterbury (7 July).[45] That such contracts of less than a year were recognized as acceptable under the labour legislation is implied by a presentment in the Warwickshire sessions of the peace for 1377. It was said of one Alice, formerly the servant of Adam Walk, that she 'will not serve anyone for the year, nor the half year, nor the quarter year'.[46]

There is some evidence, as the last example suggests, for hirings at points between the half years and thus for a pattern of hirings revolving around quarter days. Thus the York cause papers, in 1366 and 1439 respectively, document a male servant contracted from the feast of the nativity of St John the Baptist and another contracted from Christmas.[47] The Lincolnshire sessions of the peace of the mid-1380s likewise record three different servants presented for having allegedly broken the houses of their employers and left service. The 'breaking' is purely a legal fiction, but the moment of departure – Tuesday before the feast

[42] Goldberg, *Women, Work, and Life Cycle*, p. 173.

[43] Borthwick IHR, CP.E.155, F.202; Putnam, *Enforcement*, Appendix, p. 449. A pattern of biannual hirings at Pentecost and Martinmas is documented for parts of Cumberland as early as 1673: A Kussmaul, *Servants in Husbandry in Early Modern England* (Cambridge, 1981), tab. A4.1, p. 151.

[44] *Medieval Archives of the University of Oxford*, ed. H.E. Salter, Oxford Historical Society, 73 (1921), pp. 70, 88. The third was a male servant employed from Christmas to Michaelmas. I have excluded from my sample a 'servant' paid at the rate of 1*d* and a meal every workday, since such an arrangement implies that he did not live in (ibid., pp. 48, 93).

[45] Putnam, *Enforcement*, Appendix, p. 192; Borthwick IHR, CP.E.79.

[46] *Rolls of the Warwickshire and Coventry Sessions of the Peace 1377–97*, ed. E.G. Kimball, Dugdale Society, 16 (1939), p. 9, no. 17; see also Putnam, *Enforcement*, Appendix, p. 425.

[47] Borthwick IHR, CP.E.89, F.182.

of St Stephen, Monday after the feast of the nativity of St John the Baptist, and Monday after the feast of St Martin – strongly suggests that these were servants leaving to take up new contracts at customary times for hirings. This is explicit in another Lincolnshire case of 1365. One William Gryme, contracted for the year from Martinmas, left at the feast of the nativity of St John the Baptist to work for another employer offering better terms.[48]

The evidence suggests a comparative degree of informality in hirings, as the example of Joan atte Enges cited earlier demonstrates, and there is little to show that the sorts of hiring fairs documented by the early modern era were yet generally established. Neither hiring fair nor intermediary seems to have brought Joan and her master together.[49] Rather we must assume the operation of the sort of informal networks based on trade, kinship, or locality that I have described elsewhere.[50] Servants were sometimes related by blood or marriage to their employers, though this is not always apparent from name evidence alone. Thus John, one of three servants named in the will of William Scoreburgh, a York merchant (d. 1432), is additionally described as his cousin. Likewise John de Wald, apprenticed to Thomas de Wald, potter, at the time of a York matrimonial cause of 1372, was named his cousin.[51] Servants were sometimes related

---

[48] *Sessions of the Peace in Lincolnshire 1381–1396*, p. 95, nos 278–80; Putnam, *Enforcement*, Appendix, pp. 443–5. There is every indication that sorts of regional patterns of customary hiring dates documented by Kussmaul, primarily using eighteenth- and nineteenth-century sources, have long, but not necessarily fixed, historical roots: Kussmaul, *Servants in Husbandry*, pp. 50–1, tab.A4.1, pp. 150–63. One of the more obvious changes over time is that moveable feasts based on Easter came to be fixed on specific days. These long-term patterns would repay further analysis, beyond the scope of this paper. We might, for example, expect a distinctive regional pattern for the west and south-west of the country based around the Marian feasts of the Purification and the Annunciation associated with a pastoral economy. Two Herefordshire men, for example, were both contracted from the feast of the Annunciation to Michaelmas according to presentments of 1355, but servants' contracts in late medieval Exeter tended to run from Michaelmas: M. Kowaleski, *Local Markets and Regional Trade in Medieval Exeter* (Cambridge, 1995), p. 169. What is evident is that the sorts of continuity found in the East Riding are not universal. May Day was the main hiring date in Lincolnshire at the time of Waterloo, but Martinmas prevailed at the time of Poitiers. Since hiring dates can be tied to the needs of the agrarian economy, then it seems plausible to argue that the evidence from the Lincolnshire sessions of the peace still reflects the needs of a heavily arable economy, a legacy of pre-plague conditions, whereas by the late eighteeenth century, and prior to drainage and technological change, a more mixed or pastoral-based agrarian economy had established itself.

[49] It may be that London, by the very nature of its size and the scale of demand for servants, left more room for intermediaries to operate. Cordelia Beattie has observed that priests sometimes so acted from the evidence of later fifteenth-century chancery petitions. For example, in a petition of *c.* 1485–6, the priest, James Gere, claimed that Joan Busshe 'beyng contre woman and of olde acquayntaunce with your said suppliaunt required him to set her in to a service and your said oratour according brought her into the service of one Andrewe Burell': PRO, C1/77/44. I am indebted to Ms Beattie for this reference and transcription.

[50] Goldberg, *Women, Work, and Life Cycle*, pp. 177–80.

[51] Borthwick IHR, Prob. Reg. 2, f. 601v; CP.E.111.

to one another and we may surmise that an older sibling helped find a position for a younger. For example, Joan and Eustachia West, servants in 1358 of John de Scalby of Ottringham (Yorks. E.R.), were probably sisters, and John and Robert Burn, the two servants of the York saucemaker, John Fyschlake, recorded in his will of 1428, were probably brothers.[52]

Such informal networks by which employer and servant found one another are not difficult to infer, but the Lincolnshire man presented in 1381 as 'a common forestaller of labourers and servants so that no one in the area can hire or have a servant save at the will and getting of the said Henry' may imply that such networks were not always adequate to meet demand.[53] Hiring fairs, however, are not much observed. A significant exception is the Good Friday fair recorded in the Coventry Leet Book for 1452 'be which people were lette for service'.[54] We may speculate that established fairs came increasingly to function additionally as hiring fairs from about this time. Taking the East Riding of Yorkshire as an example, where Martinmas hirings prevailed in the later medieval era, we can observe a concentration of chartered fairs in the earlier part of November. It is not, however, until Henry Best's farming book of 1642 that we have documented evidence of servant hirings associated with the then Quarter Sessions which coincided with some of these established fairs.[55] Evidence that fairs often functioned as places where servants could be hired may then be lacking before the early modern era, but equally there is little reason why such a development should have left any record.

The observed pattern of yearly contracts (and the slighter evidence for half-yearly or other contracts for less than a full year) can be understood on a number of different levels. Employers had a vested interest in holding employees to long contracts to ensure their labour needs. Long contracts tended, moreover, to be less costly than employing labour by the day or the week, and indeed this was one of the planks underpinning contemporary labour laws. On the other hand, an employer who had taken on a twelve- or thirteen-year old, the earliest age at which children seem normally to have gone into service, to run errands, to mind livestock, or whatever other task was appropriate to an unskilled and physically immature youngster, had no desire to continue to employ the same servant at the same tasks once they had grown into a strapping youth with matching appetite.[56] Rather it made sense to employ a succession of

---

[52] *Yorkshire Sessions of the Peace, 1361–4*, ed. B.H. Putnam, Yorkshire Archaeological Society Record Series, 100 (1939), p. 7, no. 14; Borthwick IHR, Prob. Reg. 2, f. 538. John Burn was evidently the older. He received a bequest of 20s from his employer, whereas Robert was left only 2s.

[53] This particular case appears to be unique: *Sessions of the Peace in Lincolnshire 1381–1396*, p. 150, no. 404.

[54] *The Coventry Leet Book*, ed. M.D. Harris, EETS, original series 134–5, 138, 146 (1907–13), p. 272.

[55] *The Farming and Memorandum Books of Henry Best of Elmswell 1642*, ed. D. Woodward, Records of Social and Economic History, new series, 8 (London, 1984), pp. 140–1. Best noted that sessions were 'always' held at Kilham on 1 November. This coincides with the established fair there.

[56] For the ages of young people in service, see Goldberg, *Women, Work, and Life Cycle*, pp. 168–73.

youngsters.[57] From the servant's perspective, the boy or girl who had spent a year or two running errands would necessarily expect to graduate to some more demanding position. Moving from one employer to another permitted servants to move up a hierarchy of tasks and responsibilities.[58] It also permitted them to negotiate progressively better terms and conditions, and also to build up friendship networks and, in respect of older servants, to engage in courtship. So long as demand for servants remained buoyant, young people retained a vested interest in the opportunity to move from employer to employer over the course of their time in service, though undoubtedly some preferred to remain for longer periods where they enjoyed a particularly good relationship with their employers.[59]

Although point at entry and duration of contract may have been essentially customary, the level of remuneration was more obviously a matter for negotiation. In practice we have only limited evidence for the amounts paid to servants. Some useful evidence survives for Oxford in the period 1390–2 using presentations for 'excessive' wages under the labour legislation, although by the nature of the source uncertainties arise as to their typicality.[60] Calculations of mean wage rates are probably unhelpful here, partly due the paucity of the sample, partly to the uncertainty of the identity of all as live-in servants, but also because wage rates must have reflected differing ages and levels of experience as well as gender. It is unlikely that young servants received any wage at all. Elizabethan justices of the peace were prepared to issue injunctions against payment of money wages to boys below sixteen and girls below eighteen years, but this may well represent a codification of earlier custom.[61] For the male servants in our sample, two principal annual wage bands are apparent, viz. 10*s* (N = 6) and 13*s* 4*d* (N = 8). Three servants received 20*s*, the highest rate recorded.[62] A couple of male servants received 9*s* and the lowest recorded rate of remuneration was 6*s* 8*d*. Of the much smaller sample of women servants we may observe three

---

[57] It should be noted that employers probably remained responsible for their servants' upkeep and welfare for the duration of their contract even if the servant became incapacitated by illness or accident. Very long contracts could, therefore, be a liability. We may see an example of this in the case of Ellen Taliour of Skelton, near York. In the early 1350s she was contracted as a wet-nurse to the daughter of a minor gentry family from the day of the latter's birth, but was unable to suckle the child after the third week owing to fever. Nevertheless she remained in their service for a whole year from her contract date: Borthwick IHR, CP.E.89, pop popd in *Women in England*, pp. 73, 78.

[58] Analogy with modern evidence would suggest that servants would themselves have been sensitive to a hierarchy of age and experience. See S. Caunce, *Among Farm Horses: The Horselads of East Yorkshire* (Stroud, 1991), pp. 74–85.

[59] Goldberg, *Women, Work, and Life Cycle*, pp. 175–6, 182–3.

[60] *Medieval Archives of the University of Oxford*, pp. 1–128.

[61] Injunctions of the JPs for Bedfordshire, 1561, printed in *Tudor Economic Documents*, ed. R.H. Tawney and E. Power (London, 1924), vol. I, p. 336.

[62] Two of these were butchers, of whom one worked for a widow, and the third was a hosteller. All seem more akin to journeymen, albeit on annual contracts, than the generality of live-in servant, but equally they may simply represent young men at the top of the live-in servant hierarchy.

wage bands each represented by two cases, viz. 6s, 8s, and 10s *per annum*. Only one other female servant is noted, and she was paid a mere 3s.

Such slight data are sufficient to show that money wages were probably graduated according to age and experience. They also indicate a clear gender difference in that male servants' wages were markedly higher, although there is nothing here to show whether a female servant earning say 8s *per annum* was on the equivalent band to a male servant earning 10s or 13s 4d. Clearly, if the first, then the degree of gender-specific wage differentiation would have been comparatively small given that money wages constituted but one part of the total remuneration provided by employers. Using some Norwich lay subsidy evidence for comparative purposes, wage levels seem to have moved remarkably little by the early sixteenth century. Waged male servants received various sums between 10s and 2 marks (26s 8d), the modal rate (N = 2) being 1 mark, but this is based on a tiny sample (N = 6). Waged female servants on the other hand received amounts between 4s and 1 mark, but here the modal rate was 8s (N = 20). Several other women were paid 7s (N = 6) and 10s (N = 4) respectively.

Where the early sixteenth-century evidence from the lay subsidy differs from the late fourteenth-century material from the labour legislation is that it is not limited to waged servants. The return appears to record all household members other than under-age children. Considerable numbers of servants are recorded who are described variously as unwaged, 'for exhibicon', or 'for her fyndyng', none of whom earned wages. In addition there are a significant number of (exclusively) male apprentices recorded who likewise were all unwaged. One reading of the evidence would be to suggest that by the early sixteenth century most juvenile male servants worked without wages, and hence, because service presumably provided them with a training, for the prospect of employment as an adult. Women, on the other hand, served primarily for maintenance and, albeit modest, wages, perhaps in part to save against marriage. The nature of our sources means that we cannot know if this represents a change from a century or so previous, but it is tempting to conclude that it does.

The remuneration given by employers to their servants went beyond a simple money payment. Indeed, unlike the labourer, it was not upon money wages that the live-in servant depended. Those who lived with their employer as a member of the *familia* were – considerations of nurture and training aside – most importantly to be fed, clothed, and lodged. The problem is that the evidence of presentments under labour legislation for the later fourteenth century and for taxable income in the earlier sixteenth century focuses attention on money wages to the exclusion of other considerations. Provision of a bed, food, clothing, and footwear is specified in apprenticeship indentures.[63] Something similar may have been true of other servants. The evidence from the Oxford sessions of the peace in 1390–2 provides a few examples. Thomas Chauntour, brewer, gave his servant, John, a tunic with a hood, an apron, and a 'roket' in addition to his 10s, and another brewer, John Cade, gave his servant, Alice, a tunic in addition to her wages of 6s. In other instances clothing is specified, but not

---

[63] E.g. *York Memorandum Book*, vol. I, ed. M. Sellers, Surtees Society, 120 (1912), pp. 54–5.

itemized.[64] Probate evidence suggests that in addition to the items of apparel specified or customary within their contracts of employment, employers may also have supplied cast-off clothing. Certainly it was common for servants to be so remembered in their employers' wills. For example Agnes Langham (d. 1448) of Snailwell (Cambs.) left Margery Seman, her *famula*, her second-best gown, and Agnes de Lokton (d. 1405), a York draper's wife, left items of clothing to her nurse and each of her three other *famule*.[65]

Although the evidence is slight, there is reason to believe that servants of artisans or husbandmen lived in their employers' households on broadly equal terms with the employers' own children.[66] They probably ate together at meal times, sharing their employers' food.[67] In more modest houses consisting of little more than a kitchen, hall, and solar or chamber, moreover, servants must have shared the same sleeping space as their employers. A reading of extant probate inventories for the diocese of York before 1500 shows that these chambers invariably contained numbers of beds and mattresses of various sorts. Beds or bedding are never found within the hall. A hierarchy of beds is discernible: feather beds often appear alongside board-beds and close-beds, though it is not possible to know which of these beds were intended for children of the employer and which for the servants. Indeed, since it was commonplace – the marital bed aside – for two persons of the same sex to share a bed, and space was at a premium, then servants may sometimes have shared with children of the family.[68]

Employers felt affection or at least respect towards their servants as members of their households. There are various of indicators of this. Oxford employers, for example, spoke up for their employees indicted for transgressions against the labour legislation in the early 1390s. Thomas Chauntour, brewer, said of his servant, John, that 'he works and is on duty (*vigilat*) a lot (*multum*)'. William Chyselhamptone, butcher, likewise said of his servant, Robert, that he was his principal servant and worked hard *et multociens in nimis vili labore in arte predicti* ('and frequently in extremely distasteful work in the aforesaid craft').[69]

---

[64] *Medieval Archives of the University of Oxford*, pp. 14, 25, 70.

[65] *Wills and Inventories from the Register of the Commissary Court of Bury St Edmunds and the Archdeaconry of Sudbury*, ed. S. Tymms, Camden Society, original series, 49 (1850), p. 12; Borthwick IHR, Prob. Reg. 3, f. 227v. Men also left clothing to male servants and apprentices, though a purely impressionistic observation is that male servants were bequeathed clothing less commonly than was true of female servants.

[66] Of course, as has already been noted, in some instances servants were themselves kin: Goldberg, *Women, Work, and Life Cycle*, pp. 177–8.

[67] Ibid., p. 183.

[68] Lady Lisle's son, James, complained to his mother in 1538 that he was having to share a bed with two other boys and a servant, but on investigation she was reassured that the two other boys and the servant were all sons of good families and that he had no cause for complaint: *The Lisle Letters: An Abridgement*, ed. M.StC. Byrne (Harmondsworth, 1983), no. 287, p. 324. Bequests of beds and bedding to servants are not uncommonly found, particularly in respect of female servants, and it may well be that servants were sometimes allowed to take with them the bed they had used whilst in service.

[69] *Medieval Archives of the University of Oxford*, pp. 14, 61.

Such statements were intended to justify the wages paid by the employers, but they seem also to indicate an appreciation of the servants' worth. Another indicator is the frequency with which servants, and even former servants, are remembered in wills. Often these bequests are modest and probably dictated by convention, but sometimes they are much more generous. The York potter, John Sythers, for example, left one of his male servants half his tools, his best pair of bellows, his best and his worst melting pan, and a horse with packsaddle. The married clerk, Thomas Dellabay, even named his servant, Juliana, as one of the executors of his will.[70] Employers also took a paternal interest in the love lives of their older employees. In part this was because their own social reputation as householders depended on their ability to regulate the sexual conduct of their charges, but in some instances employers may have had a genuine desire to see that their employees went on to make satisfactory marriages.[71] Certainly the presence of employers as witnesses to marriage contracts is not unusual, and employers likewise made bequests against the marriages of their female servants.[72]

If affection is one indicator of the closeness of the ties that bound servant and employer, then friction and discord are likewise. At the heart of the service relationship was a contract binding on both parties that created obligations for employers as much as for servants. The corollary of this is that servants were prepared to challenge their employers' actions, to leave if dissatisfied, and even to engage in litigation in the courts. There are, for example, a number of cases of London apprentices who brought successful actions in the mayor's court against masters who had failed to honour their contracts. Perhaps the most striking example is the goldsmith's apprentice who complained that his master sent him out of the city to thresh grain. A Lincolnshire servant allegedly broke his contract because his master 'beat him frequently, did not give him sufficient food, and did not pay the salary due him'. Chastisement was perhaps a particularly contentious issue. Joan Potter of Nottingham brought an action for assault against her master who admitted to striking her on the head and body with an 'elenwand' because she answered him back. He claimed this was reasonable; she claimed damages.[73]

*   *   *

Thus far service has been described in essentially static terms, but the institution experienced change over the period under discussion. On one level this was a simple product of economic change. The combination of acute labour shortage, wage inflation, and, from the 1370s, falling grain prices ensured that servant labour was particularly attractive in the years after the Black Death and indeed well into the first few decades of the fifteenth century. Day labour remained

---

[70] Borthwick IHR, Prob. Reg. 1, f. 76v (Dellabay, d. 1394), 3, f. 87 (Sythers, d. 1402).

[71] For a discussion of such issues, see P.J.P. Goldberg, 'Masters and Men in Later Medieval England', *Masculinity in Medieval Europe*, ed. D.M. Hadley (London, 1999), pp. 56–70.

[72] Goldberg, *Women, Work, and Life Cycle*, pp. 182, 236.

[73] Goldberg, 'Masters and Men', p. 61; Putnam, *Enforcement*, Appendix, p. 444; *Records of the Borough of Nottingham, vol. II (1399–1485)*, ed. W.H. Stevenson (Nottingham, 1883), p. 24.

invaluable for a variety of specialized tasks and for essentially seasonal work, but wherever there were year-round general labour requirements, servants were the more attractive proposition. Labour shortage probably became less acute, however, from the second third of the fifteenth century as a consequence of a contracting economy. This is reflected *inter alia* in the increasing marginalization of women within the public economy from a high point in the early years of the century. From around the 1470s, moreover, the early stages of demographic recovery may both have eroded the advantage of servant labour over wage labour and at the same time increased the numbers of young people within the population. It follows that the demand for servants would have fallen from a high point in the early decades of the fifteenth century to a rather lower level by the final decades. There is some evidence to suggest that this was indeed the case.

Demographic determinism is inadequate to explain parallel trends in social and gender relations. The later fifteenth century witnessed a growing social distance between employer and servant that was not simply a product of age difference. This may be reflected spatially. For example, the will of John Baret of Bury St Edmunds (d. 1463) refers to a chamber with a bed in which his niece slept and to the bedding in the associated 'drawth chambyr for hire seruaunth to lyn in'.[74] It is likewise reflected in the presence of more than one chamber containing beds and bedding, and in the occasional designation within probate inventories of chambers as servants' chambers. Margaret Pigot of Ripon (d. 1485), for example, had beds in her parlour and two chambers, but the second chamber containing five board-beds and another bed was designated a servants' chamber.[75] The wealthy and the well-to-do could afford houses with a multiplicity of rooms, but it appears to have been underlying social changes that created demand for different kinds of housing stock with a multiplicity of rooms that permitted the master and mistress of the household their own private space, and relegated servants to separate accommodation.[76] In the most prosperous households employers may have begun to eat separately from their servants. This is certainly what a Venetian observer writing at the very end of the fifteenth century describes.[77] Bequests to servants appear – a purely impressionistic observation – to become more perfunctory. Even apprenticeship was devalued as fewer former apprentices saw any prospect of ever heading workshops in their own right. Evidence from York wills clearly demonstrates that whereas servants of both sexes were employed in a variety of craft workshops in the earlier part of the century, by the later decades a distinctively gendered pattern emerges. Whereas female servants were employed in number in the houses of

---

[74] *Wills and Inventories from Bury St Edmunds*, p. 23.

[75] University of Leeds, Brotherton Library, Ripon Chapter Act Book 432.1, pop popd in *Probate Inventories of the York Diocese 1350–1500*, ed. P.M. Stell and L. Hampson (York, n.d.), pp. 294–6.

[76] This may sometimes be reconstructed from the evidence of extant buildings as at no. 7, The Shambles, in York. See J. Grenville, 'Houses and Households in Late Medieval England', *Medieval Women*, ed. Wogan-Browne et al., pp. 321–6.

[77] *A Relation ... of the Island of England ... about the Year 1500*, ed. C.A. Sneyd, Camden Society, original series, 37 (1847), p. 25.

the mercantile élite, male servants alone tended to be found in association with craft workshops. The implication is two-fold: first that participation in the activities of manufacture and trade was increasingly deemed inappropriate for young women, and second that female service in an urban context emerged as essentially domestic and concerned with projecting the social rank of the employer. Our earlier speculative observation about wages accords with these findings.

If we extend these tentative findings a stage further, we may suggest that service became less socially inclusive during the course of the fifteenth century, perhaps particularly in respect of women. The sort of concern for the moral welfare of bourgeois and aristocratic young women that is reflected in the circulation of *How the Goodwife Taught her Daughter* or the cult of St Sitha makes most sense in the context of daughters from well-to-do families entering service at the same time, though not necessarily alongside, the daughters of poor labourers and petty artisans. As service for women became increasingly 'domestic' and hence seen as menial, the well-to-do may have felt it an increasingly inappropriate experience for their adolescent daughters. There is a hint of this in John Ely's displeasure reported in a London matrimonial cause of 1487 at seeing his fiancée, Agnes Whitingdon, then in service, carrying clothes to the Thames to be washed. Allegedly he said that he would pay for another to do the job and would even support her prior to their marriage should her master dismiss her for disobedience.[78] By much the same period, following Dobson's chronology, 'boy', previously a neutral term for a young male servant, had acquired pejorative overtones.[79] These are but slight indicators of broader social change and more research is called for, but the case for change is as a whole a compelling one. Just as the meaning of 'servant' changes between different kinds of record and even within the same record, and just as the very concept of service embodies change, so the servant at the end of our period can be seen to have lived in a world subtly different from that which their great-grandparents had experienced.

---

[78] S. McSheffrey, *Love and Marriage in Late Medieval London* (Kalamazoo, 1995), pp. 58–9. Whitingdon's social status is uncertain, but Ely allegedly hoped to obtain a dowry of 5 marks from her father for her marriage.

[79] Dobson, 'Etymology and Meaning', p. 133 et seq. This pejorative usage is found especially in pageant texts which are now thought to be later in date than was the case when Dobson wrote.

II

SERVICE, SERFDOM AND ENGLISH LABOUR LEGISLATION, 1350–1500

Chris Given-Wilson

ACCOSTING a crowd of cowed and desperate Essex men at Waltham in June 1381, in the aftermath of the great revolt of that year, King Richard II declared to them: 'Rustics you were, and rustics you are. And in bondage you shall remain, not as of old, but incomparably harsher'.[1] The contention of this paper will be that, despite the emphasis customarily placed upon the decline of serfdom in late fourteenth- and fifteenth-century England, Richard may have come closer to the truth than even he probably realized. The principal sources employed here are the labour laws enacted in parliament (or occasionally elsewhere) during the century and a half after the Black Death; not simply the statutes (although they certainly provide a formidable enough body of evidence) but also the petitions which lay behind them, a surprisingly neglected source. As can be seen from the Appendix, more than a third of the seventy-seven parliaments held between 1351 and 1430 passed legislation relating to labour, and further bursts of activity followed in the mid-1440s and again in the 1490s.[2] Nor, it is worth noting, was such legislation confined to England: it is a feature of every European country whose records during this period have been examined, where in many cases it was considerably harsher.[3]

What lay behind this prolonged period of concern with working practices was, of course, the depopulation and consequent shortage of labour caused by the Black Death and subsequent plagues of the later fourteenth and fifteenth centuries. It was in June 1349, at the very moment when the country was in the grip of the first and most fearsome outbreak of plague, that the first Ordinance of Labourers was issued. The underlying aims of this legislation over the next century and more were threefold: firstly, to restrict wages from rising above whatever levels were deemed at the time to be acceptable; secondly, to restrict labourers' mobility, so as to prevent them scouring the vicinity for higher wages or better conditions; and thirdly, to enforce working contracts on terms favourable to

---

[1] 'Rustici quidem fuistis et estis; et in bondagio permanebitis, ut non hactenus, sed incomparabiliter viliori': *Chronicon Angliae 1328–1388*, ed. E.M. Thompson (Rolls Series, London, 1874), p. 316.

[2] See Appendix, where, apart from those referenced in the text, references are given to the statutes and petitions cited.

[3] M. Mollat, *The Poor in the Middle Ages: An Essay in Social History*, trans. A Goldhammer (London, 1986), pp. 200–95; M. Rubin, *Charity and Community in Medieval Cambridge* (Cambridge, 1986) pp. 32–3.

employers rather than employees, which usually (though not always) meant longer rather than shorter periods of time.[4]

Before looking at these laws in more detail, however, it is worth saying something about the system which – to some degree – they replaced: namely, serfdom. Before the ordinance of 1349, it was their legal ownership of villeins, enforced in both manorial and higher courts, that had enabled landlords to control the mobility of at least some of their tenants, and to compel them to work on their lands. After the Black Death, however, serfdom gradually withered away, until, by the second half of the fifteenth century, it seems to have been virtually obsolete in many parts of England – although it is now generally acknowledged that reports of its death at this time are somewhat exaggerated.[5] Yet if the labour legislation did, in the long term, come to subsume certain aspects of serfdom, this is certainly not what the framers of the first ordinance had in mind. On the contrary, the initial reaction of the government was to strengthen, rather than to try to replace, the ancient institutions for the enforcement of villeinage. Thus the ordinance of 1349 stated that complaints against recusant workers were to be heard 'in the court of the lord of the place where such case shall happen'. There was no mention here of justices of labourers or justices of the peace, no centrally controlled or nationally regulated system of enforcement. In the attempt to compel the able-bodied to work, lords were also 'to be preferred in their bondmen or their land tenants' (i.e. they were to have preference over any other potential employers in compelling their own bondmen and tenants to work on their land), and as for lords who paid excessive wages, they could be sued in county or hundred courts. It was the old local and manorial courts, in other words, which were seen as providing the most effective enforcement agency. Two years later, however, the power to enforce the statute was handed over to the justices of labourers, who were ordered to hold their sessions four times a year in each county. Manorial and local courts were thus by-passed; appeal from the justices was to the central courts, most notably the king's bench. The statute, in other words, was to be enforced through the public authority of centrally appointed justices, rather than through the private authority of the lord in his manor court.

This was potentially quite a significant change as far as lord–villein relationships were concerned, and it led to some rather anomalous legal disputes during the next few years. For example, in one case recorded on the common plea roll for Oxfordshire in 1355, a lord and his villein jointly brought a case against a third party (the prior of the Hospitallers in England) who claimed that he was the villein's legal employer. The object of their plea was to prove that the villein

---

[4] The building trade seems to have been the major exception: here employers tended to prefer short-term contracts, the nature of the work being obviously very different from agricultural labour.

[5] See, for example, M. Bailey 'Rural Society', *Fifteenth-Century Attitudes*, ed. R. Horrox (Cambridge, 1994), pp. 150–168, at 157: 'serfdom was rigorously maintained on the East Anglian estates of the duke of Norfolk throughout the fifteenth and sixteenth centuries'. See also A. Savine, 'Bondmen under the Tudors', *TRHS*, new series XVII (1903), 235–89, and R. Hilton, *The Decline of Serfdom in Medieval England*, Studies in Economic History (London, 1969).

was indeed a villein, since his lord wished to reclaim him, and he wished to return. The prior, on the other hand, attempted to prove – contrary to the wishes of the villein – that he was a free man, in order to keep him. The lord and his villein won.[6] Another case which arose a few years later, and which is related by the chronicler of Meaux abbey, is that of the villeins of the abbey's manor of Dimlington, near Wawne in south Yorkshire. A family of villeins called the Cellarers fled from the manor, and when the abbot tried to reclaim them, they brought a suit against him, alleging that he had acted 'contrary to the form of the statute and ordinance of labourers, artificers and servants, which had been published and ought to be observed in Yorkshire'. Interestingly, the Cellarers did not deny that they were the abbot's villeins, but they claimed that he had transgressed against the statute by forcibly detaining *their* servants, whom they were employing in accordance with the form of the statute. In the end, however, they lost their case, though not before it had been heard by the local justices of labourers, the assize justices, the royal chancery, and even the king's council – all of which took about four years. And, although he won his villeins back, the abbot was strictly enjoined not to punish them for their defiance.[7]

Cases such as these are in line with Putnam's general observation that, in most cases during the 1350s, neither the clause compelling men to work, nor that which stipulated annual contracts as the norm, was allowed to undermine the legal bond between a lord and his villeins. For example, in a number of cases in which villeins pleaded that their lord could not reclaim them because he already had as many workers as he needed, this plea was disallowed without consideration. In one case where five brothers who were villeins sued their lord for loss of earnings, because he had reclaimed them to his manor after they had made contracts with a different employer, their claim was rejected and his right upheld.[8] On the other hand, the number of cases brought under the statute in which villeinage was an issue *at all* was very small, so that Putnam's overall conclusion was that 'as far as the quarter sessions went, the effect of the legislation on free and unfree was identical.... No distinction between the two categories had to be made by the justices'.[9]

Yet the playing-field had certainly not been entirely levelled. Petitions to the parliaments of 1376, 1377, 1385, 1391, 1397 and 1402 were all explicitly directed at preventing villeins – not labourers in general – from evading the obligations of their servile tenure.[10] The most frequent complaint was that villeins were fleeing to towns in order to gain their freedom. The petition of 1391 is of particular interest: it was submitted not by the commons but, specifically and unusually, by 'the knights of the counties' (*les chivalers des countees*), who claimed that townsmen were obstructing their attempts to reclaim their villeins.

---

[6] P. Vinogradoff, *Villainage in England* (Oxford, 1892), pp. 53–5, 412–5.

[7] *Chronica Monasterii de Melsa*, ed. E.A. Bond, 3 vols, Rolls Series (London, 1868), vol. III, pp. 127–42.

[8] B. Putnam, *The Enforcement of the Statutes of Labourers in the first decades after the Black Death, 1349–1359*, Columbia Studies in the Social Sciences, 85 (New York, 1908), pp. 202–5.

[9] Putnam, *Enforcement*, p. 78.

[10] *Rot. Parl.*, vol. II, p. 340; vol. III, pp. 21, 212, 294, 296, 448, 499.

The implication is of a rift between knights and burgesses on this issue.[11] From the early fifteenth century onwards, however, villeinage as a distinct and separate issue disappears almost entirely from both the legislation and the petitions of parliament. In fact the words 'villein' and 'villeinage' do not appear once in the rolls of parliament for the reigns of Henry V and Henry VI – a point which helpfully corroborates the widely held view that it was the decades around the turn of the fourteenth and fifteenth centuries which saw the decisive phase in the decline of unfreedom in England.

Collective resistance doubtless played its part in this process,[12] but at the same time, the fact that landlords and employers had new weapons available with which to bridle their workers probably meant that they were less concerned to brandish the old ones. So what were these new weapons? Were they effective, and if so why did they constantly have to be repeated? Almost a century has now passed since Putnam established that, during the 1350s, strenuous attempts really *were* made to enforce the labour legislation, and that these met with a fair degree of success.[13] Even so, an important distinction needs to be made here between enforcement of terms and enforcement of penalties. The fact that 7,556 people in Essex – perhaps a quarter of the labouring population of the county – were fined for taking excessive wages in 1352, seems to me evidence not that the legislation was effective – quite the contrary – but that, presumably, a large number of labourers reckoned that there was more to be gained from breaking the law and paying the penalty; in other words, the fine was less than the profit.[14]

Yet Putnam's research did not extend beyond the 1350s, and it is strange how little attention has been paid to the legislation on labour enacted by parliament between the 1360s and the 1440s – with the exception of the statute issued from the Cambridge parliament of 1388, which is rightly seen as a substantial extension of the agenda of working-class control. The reasons for this neglect, where stated, are various, but the most common is the argument that these eighty years or so simply witnessed the constant reiteration of the statutes of 1351 and/or 1388. This point is frequently held, by extension, to demonstrate that the statutes must therefore have been ineffective, or else why would they continually require reassertion?

This, however, is to ignore a number of facts. Firstly, it is not true that the labour laws are simply confirmed over and over again: they are in fact constantly debated and modified, and although several of the resulting enactments *begin* with a clause confirming earlier statutes, they then go on to proclaim

---

[11] *Rot. Parl.*, vol. II, p. 296.

[12] C. Dyer, *Standards of Living in the Later Middle Ages: Social Change in England c. 1200–1520* (Cambridge, 1989), pp. 137–8; R. Hilton 'Peasant Movements in England before 1381', and 'Popular Movements in England at the end of the Fourteenth Century', both in Hilton, *Class Conflict and the Crisis of Feudalism* (London, 1985), pp. 122–38, 152–64.

[13] Putnam, *Enforcement*, passim.

[14] PRO, E 137/11/2: 80 per cent of these were men, 20 per cent women. Analysis of the figures is provided by L. Poos, 'The Social Context of Statute of Labourers Enforcement', *Law and History Review*, I (1983), 27–52.

amendments or extensions to the legislation. Secondly, there are a number of occasions when petitions relating to the labour laws were submitted to parliament, and in some cases even received the royal assent, but were not subsequently enrolled among the statutes. This happened, for example, in 1354, 1372, 1373, 1376, 1379, and 1421. Thirdly, in those cases where the statutes were simply confirmed, this was often for a particular reason. Take the legislation of the 1420s, for example: with the king a minor – and a very minor minor at that – the council evidently thought that this was a subject on which it did not have the authority to legislate on a permanent basis, and therefore simply renewed the laws from parliament to parliament – though, as we shall see, not without modifications.[15]

The labour laws of the 1360s to the 1440s did not, therefore, consist simply of the mantra-like repetition of earlier enactments, but instead reveal ongoing tensions and disagreements over the scope and thrust of the legislation. Three of the most common areas of disagreement were as follows:

(i) Who should be responsible for determining wage-rates? Should they be set nationally or locally? And what criteria ought to be used to decide them?

(ii) The question of where responsibility lay for the payment of excessive wages: was it with grasping employees, or with competing employers? On whom, therefore, should punishment fall?

(iii) What should be done with the profits accruing from these penalties? In particular, could they be used as an incentive to local communities to make the statutes more effective?

To take the first of these questions, there is no doubt that control of wage-rates was seen, at least initially, as the backbone of the labour legislation. Before 1349, they had generally been determined by custom, and indeed the ordinance of 1349 reinforced that view, stating that labourers should continue to take what had been 'customary' in 1346 or the five or six years before that. The statute of 1351 took a different view, however. Presumably the problem of deciding what should be regarded as customary involved so much imprecision as to be virtually unenforceable; at any rate, it was now decided to specify a table of wage-rates, applicable on a national scale, for all kinds of workers, from carters, ploughmen and threshers, to masons, carpenters and plasterers. Some of these were piece-rates, some of them daily rates. It is perfectly clear that these rates were not enforced, although, as we have seen, the penalties for exceeding them quite frequently were.[16] Nevertheless, the attempt to impose national wage-limits persisted, with new rates being proposed for the building

---

[15] This was not uncommon in the parliaments of the minority of Henry VI. In 1423, for example, six of the twenty-one statutes were only 'to endure until the next parliament'. In 1427, the statute on labourers' wages was the only one (of six) for which this was specified.

[16] According to Dyer and Penn, 'After a very large number of cases were brought in some areas in the early 1350s, the justices in normal years dealt with only a few hundred offenders in each county for which we have information': C. Dyer and S. Penn, 'Wages and Earnings in Late Medieval England: Evidence from the Enforcement of the Labour Laws', *Economic History Review*, 43 (1990), 356–76, at 359, reprinted in C. Dyer, *Everyday Life in Medieval England* (London, 1994), pp. 167–89, at p. 170.

trade in 1361, for chaplains in 1362,[17] and for a wide range of agricultural workers in 1388.

The attempt to impose national wage-rates was accompanied by a corresponding effort to peg prices on a national scale, although not with anything like the same precision. This, however, proved to be an even more intractable task than setting wages, and when, eighteen months after the statute of 1388, famine struck and grain prices soared, the policy was quickly abandoned. Instead, it was agreed at the parliament of January 1390 that in future the justices of the peace in each county would, twice a year, proclaim the level of wages to be paid within that county during that year, and that they should be guided in their pronouncement by the current prices of grains and other victuals in their areas. To what extent this was done is very difficult to know, but it did not signal the end of the debate. The statute of 1427 renewed the stipulation that justices of the peace, mayors and bailiffs should proclaim wage-rates annually, and in fact the first surviving schedule of locally assessed rural wages dates from 1431 in Norfolk.[18] In 1446, however, another attempt was made to establish a national wage-scale. Interestingly, the rates set now were approximately double those set in 1388, and sometimes more: a 'common servant of husbandry', for example, could receive almost exactly three times what was prescribed in 1388. Fifty years later, in 1495, it was declared that the 1446 statute was ineffective, and a new national scale was established, which this time included regulations as to the hours to be worked: from March to September, labourers were to be at work by 5 a.m. and remain there until between 7 and 8 p.m. An hour and a half was allowed for breakfast, and the same for dinner, during which a short rest was also allowed. During the winter they were to work from dawn to dusk, but not to sleep during the day. This whole statute was, however, abolished two years later.

The second question – who should be punished for breaches of the wage-regulations – was a tricky one. The original ordinance of 1349 had decreed that both givers and takers – in other words, those who paid or offered excessive wages as well as those who demanded or received them – should be punished (the former by fines, the latter with imprisonment), and if the chronicler, Henry Knighton, is to be believed many landlords were subsequently fined.[19] However, the 1351 statute is silent on the question of penalties for givers, and it seems not to have been until 1388 that these were reinstated; the Statute of Cambridge even threatened givers with imprisonment for persistent infringement of the law.[20] The first thirty years of the fifteenth century witnessed frequent changes of policy: in 1402 the commons asked for penalties to be imposed upon both givers and takers, but the resulting statute restricted the fines only to the takers. The act of 1414 restored the penalties for both, but that of 1416 once again

---

[17] *SR*, vol. I, pp. 373–4.

[18] Poos, 'Social Context', p. 30, who also points out that an urban schedule (for Oxford) survives from the 1390s.

[19] *Knighton's Chronicle 1337–1396*, ed. G.H. Martin (Oxford, 1995), pp. 102–4.

[20] However, the 1362 statute on chaplains' wages had specified that anyone who paid over the odds to a chaplain should forfeit that amount to the king (*SR*, vol. I, pp. 373–4).

exempted givers; and the same happened in the following decade, with the statute of 1423 once again imposing the penalties on givers and that of 1427 once again lifting them.

The thinking behind these changes of policy is reasonably clear from the petitions. Competition for labour was intense, and employers probably had little option but to offer higher wages in order to secure it. If the legislation was to retain its effectiveness, therefore, they had to be discouraged. On the other hand, as the commons pointed out in both 1416 and 1427, employers brought before the justices were hardly likely to present their own workers for taking excessive wages if it led to them (the employers) being fined as well. Yet comparison of the petitions with the statutes over this period as a whole suggests that it was generally the commons who were keener for penalties to be imposed on givers as well as takers, while the government preferred to fine the takers only. This may tell us something about the type of employer being referred to: when they asked for givers to be punished, the commons were probably thinking not of themselves – the landholding class – but of the 'kulaks' and other villagers of much the same social status as the labourers whom they employed. Such people probably required labour only on a casual basis, but were prepared to pay over the odds to get it and were in a good position to secure it. Despite what Knighton says about the initial enforcement of the 1349 ordinance, there are very few examples of knights or esquires being had up before the justices for paying excessive wages. The government, on the other hand, may have reasoned that if the legislation was to be effective at all, employers of all kinds should be given every inducement to present offenders, without fear of personal detriment.

Similar concerns are revealed by the debate over the third question – what was to be done with the fines accruing from enforcement of the legislation. This is a subject which both Putnam and Poos have discussed at length in relation to the 1350s, during which the general principle adopted for the most part was that they should be set aside as contributions to the triennial tenths and fifteenths, with – and this is the crucial point – the fines levied on individuals within each village or hundred being set against the contribution at which that village or hundred was assessed for the tax. Here, surely, was a clear incentive for villagers to present their neighbours, for the result would be that their own contribution to the tax would thereby be lightened. Out of the £115,000 raised for the triennial tenth of 1352–4, for example, nearly £8,000 came from fines under the labour laws, although in some areas the proportion was much higher. In Essex in 1352, for example, £675 out of the county's subsidy assessment of £1235 – about 55 per cent, in other words – was met from fines on labourers, which, as Poos points out, gave villagers 'profound financial incentives towards vigorous statute enforcement'.[21] It needs to be remembered too that the 1351 statute had also stated that individuals who sued others for breach of the statute were still entitled to a share of the penalty.

The statute of 1361 abolished monetary fines for breaches of the labour legislation, and replaced them with imprisonment and branding on the forehead with the letter 'F' for Falsity (although there is no surviving evidence that the

---

[21] Poos, 'Social Context', pp. 44, 50, and see Putnam, *Enforcement*, pp. 100–149.

latter was ever enforced). In the following year, however, the fines were reinstated, and this time it was said that they should be put towards the arrears still outstanding from the triennial tenth and fifteenth. Fifteen years later, in Richard II's first parliament, the commons requested that the fines should be used as a contribution to the war effort, but from the early fifteenth century onwards the usual position was that they should be shared between the king and the person who sued. On the whole then, the policy seems to have been one of combining profit to the king with the provision of incentives for townsmen and villagers to present their neighbours.

The debate over issues such as these gives some indication as to why it continued to be thought necessary to update and reissue the labour laws for a century and more after the first ordinance. The successive statutes and petitions also reveal longer-term shifts in attitudes towards labour, not just to 'labourers' in the narrow sense of that word. Indeed the so-called labour legislation might, in fact, just as well be called the 'service legislation', for it was almost invariably described by its drafters as being directed against 'labourers, servants and artificers'. Take, for example, the question of compulsion to work. The basic idea was there from the beginning: the ordinance of June 1349 had declared that all able-bodied persons, male or female, bond or free, under the age of sixty, who did not practise a craft or own their own land, were to be 'bounden to serve him which so shall him require', and that any man or woman who refused to do so should be gaoled. By 1376, however, the commons were demanding that further powers be brought into operation: unemployed servants should now not merely be compelled to serve, but to 'return to the trades at which they worked before', and not only to the same trades, but, in the case of those who had migrated, to the same localities. Another petition to the same parliament requested that no artisan be allowed to take on as an apprentice any labourer or servant who was required by anyone in his home vill to work the land.[22]

These ideas clearly influenced the 1388 Statute of Cambridge. Migrant servants or labourers were now to be forcibly returned to their home vills, where they were to work at whatever occupation they had formerly undertaken; any child who had worked on the land up until the age of twelve must henceforth 'abide at the same labour, without being put to any mystery or handicraft'; and artificers and craftsmen whose products were not in demand at harvest time were to be compelled to 'cut, gather and bring in the corn' until the harvest had been completed. Yet even this apparently failed to secure an adequate labour supply in the fields, for in 1406 the commons complained that landless parents in the 'upland' region had been putting their children into apprenticeship at or below the age of twelve, thereby evading the intent of the legislation. It was now decreed, therefore, that parents should not be permitted to put their children into apprenticeship, or any other work in any city or borough, *at any age*, unless they could prove that they held at least 20*s* of land or rent *per annum*. Rather, children were to be 'put to serve at such labour, be it within city or borough or without, as their said father and mother used, or other labours as

---

[22] *Rot. Parl.*, vol. II, pp. 332, 340–1.

their estate requireth'. Nor can this act have been entirely ineffective, because a petition from the Londoners in 1429 complained that it had infringed the ancient right of the citizens to take on apprentices, and they therefore requested, and were granted, exemption from the terms of the statute.[23] As late as 1495, the citizens of Norwich were making the same complaint, claiming that, as a consequence of the 1406 act, the crafts in their city were 'greatly decaied', and their youth 'be growen to idleness and vices'; they too were allowed exemption.[24] Meanwhile, in 1446, the justices of the peace had been given power to take any servants whom they deemed not to be gainfully employed out of the service of their masters and to compel them to serve others 'in the occupation of husbandry', treating them in every respect just as they treated vagabonds.

What we see here, then, is a steadily growing conviction, not simply that the able-bodied should work, but that the state should have the power to compel people to undertake certain types of work; in other words, control of labour became specifically directive. And it is perhaps not surprising that the best way to achieve this was considered to be by eschewing change. The insistence upon agricultural labourers remaining in their established localities, and continuing to pursue their established occupations, has all the hallmarks of an attempt to eliminate precisely that mobility and flexibility which by now characterized the labour market.

This growing emphasis on immutability of occupation and residence led also to the development of ideas about vagrancy and mendicancy. This was not new, of course: village by-laws of the thirteenth century had included provisions against strangers, as had the Statute of Winchester of 1285;[25] and in 1331 a statute was enacted empowering village constables to have suspicious vagrants committed to prison.[26] After 1349, however, restrictions on vagrancy and begging acquired a new edge, a new language and, to some extent, a new *raison d'être*. The ordinance of 1349 had forbidden the giving of anything 'under colour of pity or alms' to any person capable of labouring, so that they would be forced to work, and in 1361 the power to arrest 'those who go wandering, and will not labour as they were wont in times past' was transferred to the justices of the peace.[27] It was only in the 1370s and 1380s, however, that vagrancy rose to the top of the commons' agenda. A lengthy petition submitted to the parliament of 1376 complained of idle and vicious labourers who had become wandering beggars (*mendinantz beggeres*), 'staffstrikers' and 'fugitive servants whose names are not known' (*servantz corores desconuz*), and it was suggested that they be seized throughout the realm and put in the stocks or in prison until they were prepared to return to their homes and labour in accordance with the statutes. If they attempted to maintain their anonymity, they were to be kept on bread and water until they revealed their own names, the name of the master

---

[23] *SR*, vol. II, p. 248; *Rot. Parl.*, vol. IV, p. 354.
[24] *SR*, vol. II, p. 577.
[25] *English Historical Documents, vol. III, 1189–1327*, ed. H. Rothwell (London, 1975), pp. 461, 842.
[26] *SR*, vol. I, p. 268.
[27] *SR*, vol. I, p. 364.

whom they had previously served, and the counties and hundreds from which they had come.

Another petition in the same parliament complained of the 'sturdy menials' (*fortz ribauds*) who begged and lived a life of idleness in the towns, and further petitions on the same subject were submitted to the parliaments of 1377, 1378 and 1379.[28] Yet none of these petitions resulted in legislation, and when, in 1383, a statute on vagrancy was eventually drawn up, it was in surprisingly mild terms: they were to be compelled to find sureties for their good behaviour – admittedly not a simple matter for the rootless – and to be imprisoned if they failed to do so, but the more unsparing recommendations of the commons over the previous few years were rejected. However, the Statute of Cambridge went considerably further. All those found wandering outside their hundreds or wapentakes were now obliged to carry with them letters testimonial certifying the reasons for their absence, and any who failed to do so, or whose letters were found to be forged, were to be condemned to the stocks or to forty days' imprisonment. These letters were to be sealed with seals naming both the county and the hundred, and kept by *probi homines* of the hundred under the supervision of the justices of the peace. A file of writs returned by sheriffs to the exchequer testifies to the fact that they were indeed made: fifteen seals in Worcestershire, twenty-three in Yorkshire, nineteen in Somerset and Dorset, and so on.[29] Pilgrims, 'approved hermits', university students and those returning from abroad were also to have letters testimonial approving their travels.

The statutes of 1414 and 1446 also tackled the issues of vagrancy and mendicancy, but it was the 1388 statute which had really established the ground rules for dealing with the problem. There were clearly a number of different concerns at work here. The most obvious of these was the desire to compel the able-bodied to work, but others included an apparent desire to stem migration from the countryside to the towns, the need to clamp down on itinerant Lollard preachers, and – for a decade or so after 1401 – an attempt to keep trouble-making Welshmen out of England.[30] Thus, as so often, the language and remedies applied to one marginalized group came to be applied to others,[31] while at the same time the definition of vagabondage gradually expanded. In 1446, for example, it was decided that any man who had no land of his own, but who refused to accept a contract for a full year's work, was to be declared a vagabond, and dealt with accordingly by the justices of the peace. It was simultaneously decreed that if the latter ordered a servant to leave one master and serve another who, in their opinion, needed him more, and if he refused, he too was to be declared

---

[28] *Rot. Parl.*, vol. II, pp. 332, 340–1; vol. III, pp. 17, 45–6, 65.

[29] PRO, C255/15. The surviving writs cover fourteen counties; they were issued on 8 March 1391.

[30] See the statutes of 1382 and 1401 against Lollard preachers, and of 1402 against Welsh minstrels, rhymers and vagabonds (*SR*, vol. II, pp. 25, 125–8, 140).

[31] The word 'Lollard' is a good example, its use being extended to include not just religious activists but also 'idle layabouts' and vagabonds; a petition of 1417 against insurrections claimed that those who rebelled 'are likely to be of Lollard convictions' (*Rot. Parl.*, vol. IV, p. 114).

a vagabond.[32] Thus were elided the three evils of vagrancy, improper employ-ment, and short-term contracts.[33]

These attempts to clamp down on vagrancy and to acquire greater control over the labour market represent the sharp edge of the labour legislation. Indeed, it is far from difficult to view the whole of this legislation as implacable and reactionary, which much of it undoubtedly was. Yet behind the intemperate language and the apparent knee-jerk reaction to working-class assertiveness, there was also a certain amount of constructive thinking going on about the best way to deal with the problem of poverty. Once again it is the 1388 Statute of Cambridge which provides the clearest example of this. Historians of the social legislation of the sixteenth and seventeenth centuries have sometimes referred to the Statute of Cambridge as the 'first English poor law',[34] and there is some justification for this. The crucial point which it made was that it was ultimately the responsibility of each locality to make provision for its own poor. What the 1388 statute actually said was that all beggars who were genuinely unable to work should remain in the towns or vills where they were residing at the time of the proclamation of the statute; or, if those towns and vills were unable or unwilling to support them, they should, within forty days of the proc-lamation of the statute, return to other vills within the hundreds or wapentakes where they were born, 'there to remain continually throughout their lives'.[35] Nothing was said about how they were to be supported, but nevertheless the implications of this line of thought were considerable, and in this sense the statute of 1388 can indeed be seen as the distant forerunner of both the Tudor Poor Laws and the 1662 Act of Parochial Settlement.[36]

Poverty and charity are topics which have received a good deal of attention in the 1980s and 1990s, and much has been written on subjects such as the sharpening distinction between the deserving and the undeserving poor.[37] There

---

[32] See Dyer and Penn, 'Wages and Earnings', p. 179; also Putnam, *Enforcement*, p. 191; as an example, in 1389, John Smyth of South Benfleet (Essex), having been offered work as a shepherd (*bercarius*), demanded higher than the statutory wages, which was refused, 'et sic adhuc vagrans est' (PRO, KB 9/25, m. 13). On vagrancy generally, see also E. Clark, 'Social Welfare and Mutual Aid', *Journal of British Studies*, XXXIII (1994), 381–406, at 399–400.

[33] *SR*, vol. II, p. 337.

[34] E.M. Leonard, *The Early History of English Poor Relief* (Cambridge, 1900), p. 5; Dyer, *Standards of Living*, p. 252.

[35] *SR*, vol. II, p. 58.

[36] It is interesting to note that Roger Bacon had anticipated such a scheme more than a century earlier, declaring in his *Opus maius* that it was the duty of a prince to prohibit idleness; those who 'cannot be disciplined by compulsion' should be expelled from the state, unless they were too old or sick to work, 'for which cases a house should be founded wherein such may live, and a guardian should be deputed for them'. The state should possess a 'common and public fund composed partly from the law of contracts, partly from pecuniary amercements, partly from the estates of confiscations of rebels, and partly from other sources; and this fund should be devoted partly to such as are hindered of their livelihood by sickness or age, partly to doctors of medicine, and partly to common uses': cited in G.G. Coulton, *Social Life in Britain from the Conquest to the Reformation* (Cambridge, 1918), p. 350.

[37] Rubin, *Charity and Community*; Dyer, *Standards of Living*, pp. 234–57.

is no point in going over this ground again, therefore, but a few points are perhaps worth making. Almost immediately after the Black Death, the government began intervening to try to ensure that at least some of the profits from the enforcement of the labour laws were used to alleviate genuine poverty. In 1351, for example, it was decreed that sworn reports should be made to the justices as to the relative impoverishment of each town or hundred in the county, and that any surplus fines should be distributed among them in accordance with their need, in order to alleviate the tax burden.[38] It is noticeable also that after 1388 – once the principle of local responsibility had been enunciated – the commons began to take a closer interest in the way in which the church discharged its responsibilities to the poor.

The problem of appropriated parish churches, for example, was one which regularly attracted their attention. It has been estimated that something like 40 per cent of England's 9,000 or so parish churches had been appropriated by this time,[39] and the commons were clearly convinced that one unfortunate result of this was that the tithes which should have been distributed as alms were simply being appropriated too. In 1391, therefore, it was agreed in parliament that whenever a parish church was appropriated in future, the diocesan should specify the sum which, 'each year and for ever', should be set aside for the poor parishioners.[40] During Henry IV's reign, the commons pursued this subject relentlessly: the parliaments of 1401, 1402, January 1404, and 1406 all witnessed further petitions on the same topic. According to that of 1406, the main reason for non-residence among vicars was precisely *because* they wished to avoid their obligation to distribute a portion of their tithes to the poor.[41] Then in 1414 and 1416 the commons turned their attention to hospitals, claiming that they too were no longer fulfilling their charitable functions, and asking for a comprehensive commission of enquiry to ensure that in future they did so.[42] And in 1425 and 1432 there were further petitions relating to appropriations: that of 1425 claimed that there was an ancient custom that 'a third part of the goods of holy church should be spent within the same parish upon the poor and the needy of the parish', but that sustenance was now denied to them, and sermons no longer preached, so that they 'lack both ghostly food and bodily'.[43] In 1394 there was even a petition from the commons complaining that the lack of small change in the kingdom discouraged would-be benefactors from giving alms, and requesting that more halfpennies and farthings be minted.[44]

This concern for parish almsgiving to be effective would seem to follow logically from the Statute of Cambridge. However, it also followed from the charitable trends of the age, for, as Rubin has pointed out, it is at just this time that 'the parish gains prominence as a chosen administrator of relief';[45] in other

---

[38] Putnam, *Enforcement*, pp. 105–13.
[39] W.K. Jordan, *Philanthropy in England 1480–1660* (London, 1959), pp. 82, 308.
[40] *SR*, vol. II, p. 80.
[41] *Rot. Parl.*, vol. III, pp. 466–8, 542, 594; *SR*, vol. II, p. 80.
[42] *Rot. Parl.*, vol. IV, pp. 19–20, 80–1.
[43] *Rot. Parl.*, vol. IV, pp. 290, 404.
[44] *Rot. Parl.*, vol. III, p. 319.
[45] Rubin, *Charity and Community*, p. 245.

words, a growing number of lay persons was leaving bequests to parish churches to be distributed as alms – which makes it hardly surprising that there was a corresponding increase in their concern that parishes should discharge their functions honestly. If the problem of the deserving poor was one that should be dealt with at the local level, the church must fulfil its charitable obligations at the local level; if it failed to do so, moreover, it was up to the lay authorities to compel it to do so. That was an important departure, and it was, arguably, the first step on the road to the assumption by the lay authorities of responsibility for poor relief, although it would be a century and more before that became reality.

One interesting question concerns the extent to which Lollard thinking influenced the commons' views on poor relief. The timing is certainly suggestive: it was during the quarter century after 1388 that parliament evinced its greatest concern with the problem, and that is also the period during which Lollards exercised the greatest influence over the commons' agenda. The pronouncements made by Lollard authors at this time are also suggestive. The first of the Twelve Conclusions of 1395 described parishes as being 'slain by appropriation to divers churches', and several Lollard texts advocated the giving of tithes directly to the poor rather than to the church, since clerics simply kept them for themselves. Others said that the king and the lords should intervene directly in order to compel the clergy to distribute their tithes to the poor – precisely what the commons were advocating between 1391 and 1406.[46] The 'Disendowment Bill' of 1410 went further than this. From the 'temporalities proudly wasted by worldly clerks', it declared, a 100 almshouses should be founded in towns throughout the realm, each of which would have a 100 marks *per annum* to spend 'by oversight of good and true seculars'. Yet these almshouses were apparently envisaged only as a last resort, for the bill went on to advocate that 'every town throughout the realm should keep all poor men and beggars who cannot work for their sustenance, in accordance with the statute made at Cambridge; and in case the aforesaid people are not able to sustain them, then the aforesaid almshouses might help them'.[47] In other words, each town had an *a priori* responsibility to provide for its own poor, but in cases where there was not sufficient to allow this, the envisaged 100 almshouses would provide a fallback.

The provision of these 100 almshouses was not a new idea in 1410: the seventh of the Lollards' Twelve Conclusions mentioned a very similar scheme, though in less detail.[48] To what extent these Lollard authors differentiated between 'old-style' hospitals and 'new-style' almshouses is by no means clear. The 1410 Disendowment Bill also mentioned 'leper houses called hospitals' (*spytells*), but listed them at the end of the bill amongst the ecclesiastical institutions whose revenues were yet to be computed following their disendowment.[49] The

---

[46] A. Hudson, *The Premature Reformation* (Oxford, 1988), pp. 343–6; *Selections from English Wycliffite Writings*, ed. A. Hudson (Cambridge, 1978), pp. 19, 24, 95.

[47] *English Wycliffite Writings*, pp. 135–7.

[48] Ibid., p. 26.

[49] Ibid., p. 137. This point seems to be misunderstood in N. Orme and M. Webster, *The English Hospital 1070–1570* (New Haven, 1995), pp. 134–5, which suggests that these 'spyttels' and the other institutions bracketed with them were being excluded from disendowment.

implication seems to be that they favoured almshouses but not hospitals. However, the distinction between the two types of institution is not always very clear. Generally speaking, it lay in the more restricted responsibilities of the almshouse for a smaller and more specific number of poor persons chosen from the locality, whereas hospitals had tended to assume a wider responsibility to offer temporary refuge and assistance to any who sought it. This in itself may have made almshouses more attractive to the Lollard way of thinking, but perhaps more to the point was the fact that almshouses were usually secular institutions.[50] The transformation from hospitals to almshouses took a long time, and was not completed until after the Reformation, but it is easy to see why the Lollards were urging such changes more than a century before the Reformation. Poor relief, they believed, should be provided by a mixture of organized local self-help and secular (which ideally meant state) intervention. The petitions of the commons between 1388 and 1414 seem to reflect this thinking.

This interest in poor relief indicates that coercion was not the sole motive behind the social legislation of this period. On the other hand, it was certainly the *leitmotiv*, and it may be useful, in conclusion, in an attempt to provide a slightly broader context for the labour legislation, briefly to mention a few of the other areas in which parliament legislated on matters of social policy at this time.

What we see in the period after the Black Death is an attempt to regulate wages and prices, mobility, vagrancy, and working contracts for the first time on a *national* scale. It was a policy for society: a social policy. As such, it represented a significant extension of what the English government and parliament regarded as their proper concern.[51] This concern was by no means simply a consequence of the Black Death, for national legislation on a widening range of social matters – vagabondage, for example, or the sumptuary laws – certainly pre-dated the first onslaught of plague.[52] On the other hand, there is no doubt that the demographic crisis of the later fourteenth century provided a pressing and unprecedented incentive to try to broaden the scope and deepen the impact of this legislation. This social policy also encompassed a number of other matters which at other times – both before as well as after the fourteenth century – have often been regarded as the concern of the individual. Among the most obvious of these were, firstly, the acts of 1336, 1337, 1363, 1463 and 1483 which specified the types of food and clothing allowed to various types of person – the

---

[50] W.H. Godfrey, *The English Almshouse* (London, 1955), pp. 15, 19, 44–5. See Orme and Webster, *The English Hospital*, pp. 138–46, for the differences between hospitals and almshouses. It is worth noting that a Lollard treatise of 1396 condemned 'alle almes houses of Ingelond' (Rubin, *Charity and Community*, p. 96), but other Lollards evidently thought differently (unless, in this case, 'almes houses' was simply loose terminology for hospitals).

[51] A point made some time ago by David Crouch, *The Image of Aristocracy in Britain 1000–1300* (London, 1992), p. 41; see also Ormrod's comments in *The Black Death in England*, ed. M. Ormrod and P. Lindley (Stamford, 1996), p. 156. An extreme version of this argument is advanced by R.C. Palmer, *English Law in the Age of the Black Death 1348–1381* (Chapel Hill, 1994).

[52] *SR*, vol. I, pp. 268, 278.

so-called sumptuary laws;[53] secondly, the prohibition on playing certain types of games, such as tennis, quoits, dice, skittles and football – legislation banning these games was decreed in 1351, 1388, 1410, and 1478;[54] and thirdly, the proscription of confederacies and conventicles – sometimes in the context of Lollardy, sometimes in order to prevent workers in the building trade from banding together to improve their working conditions, and sometimes for more bizarre reasons. In 1390, for example, persons of low status were banned from owning hunting-dogs, on two grounds: firstly, because it was alleged that, under cover of their sport, 'they make their assemblies, conferences and conspiracies for to rise and disobey their allegiance', and, secondly, because it encouraged them to go hunting on Sundays and feast days, 'when good Christian people be at church'.[55] This latter point is a reminder that an unmistakeable tone of moral guardianship is detectable in some of the legislation of the time – anticipating the sixteenth-century idea of the 'moral reform of the poor'.[56] In 1413, for example, the commons petitioned for those found guilty of the 'great sins' of adultery and lechery to be punished corporally rather than by monetary fines.[57] The statute regulating food consumption in 1336 asserted that as a result of eating meat 'many evils have happened, as well to souls as to bodies'.[58] Numerous further examples might be cited, but especially remarkable in this context is the preamble to the statute of 1449, which banned the holding of fairs and markets on Sundays and feast days because of the 'great earthly covetise' that occasioned them, 'as though they did nothing remember the horrible defiling of their souls in buying and selling, with many deceitful lies and false perjury, with drunkenness and strifes'.[59] Such sentiments are a reminder of the extent to which, by this time, the state had begun to appropriate the kind of language traditionally associated with ecclesiastical decrees.

Yet this assumption by the state of that moral guardianship which had in former times generally been seen as the preserve of the church (or, in certain circumstances, of the lord in his manorial court)[60] is perhaps understandable in a society which perceived itself to be experiencing a crisis of authority. There is no doubt that the English ruling classes *did* perceive themselves to be undergoing such a crisis at this time – or, to be more precise, three crises in one, a *damnosa trinitas*: the military crisis of the Hundred Years War, the crisis of orthodoxy occasioned by Lollardy and the Schism, and the demographic and occupational crisis resulting from the shortage of labour.[61] Emergencies, real or

---

[53] *SR*, vol. I, pp. 278, 280–1, 380–2; vol. II, pp. 399–402, 468–70.

[54] *SR*, vol. II, pp. 56–7, 163, 462; Coulton, *Social Life in Britain*, p. 320. For an interesting contemporary reaction to this legislation, see *Joannis Rousi Antiquarii Warwicensis Historia Regum Angliae*, ed. T. Hearne (Oxford, 1716), p. 136.

[55] *SR*, vol. II, p. 65.

[56] A.L. Beier, *The Problem of the Poor in Tudor and Early Stuart England* (London, 1983), pp. 17–18.

[57] *Rot. Parl.*, vol. IV, p. 9.

[58] *SR*, vol. II, p. 278.

[59] *SR*, vol. II, pp. 351–2.

[60] Through the exaction of fines such as leyrwite and childwite, for example.

[61] I hope to say more about this elsewhere.

imagined, have so often proved the occasion for governments to assume more extensive and more summary powers – indeed there are theories of governmental development based on precisely this premise. The trick, naturally enough, is not to allow such powers to lapse once the crisis has passed.

Having said that, however, it is worth asking, finally, whether the real achievement of the English government in the century or so after the Black Death lay more in the winning of hearts and minds than in the breaking of heads. That is a much more difficult point to prove, but it is surely very doubtful whether legislation of such a sweeping nature *could* be enforced in a society such as late medieval England, unless a sufficient number of 'ordinary people' could be persuaded that it was in their own interests to enforce them. It was in the perceptions of these ordinary people that the critical distinctions needed to be sharpened: between deserving and undeserving, settled and rootless, productive and unproductive. There is certainly some evidence – in literature such as *Piers Plowman*, for example,[62] or in the patterns of communal behaviour analysed by historians such as Poos and McIntosh – that such distinctions were indeed being sharpened at this time.[63] To cite but one example, Professor McIntosh's study of attitudes towards 'anti-social' behaviour in England between 1370 and 1600 indicates that whereas in the late fourteenth century only about 15 per cent of lesser courts reported such cases, a century later this figure had risen to about 40 per cent, and by 1600 to about 60 per cent.[64] If the laws worked, in other words – and that is a big 'if' – it was because enough people, at enough levels of society, believed that it was in their interests to make them work. Yet once they *had* taken root, these distinctions continued to provide ammunition for both the governing and the governed long after the conditions which gave rise to them had changed. It may well be that much of this legislation was not systematically enforced, but then many of the theoretical impositions of serfdom had not been systematically enforced.[65] What is at any rate clear is that the end of serfdom in England was by no means an unmixed blessing for the English working classes. While economic conditions continued to favour them – that is, through the late fourteenth and much of the fifteenth centuries – their increased bargaining power probably enabled them not merely to throw off the shackles of villeinage, but also to blunt the sharp edge of the labour laws. Yet these laws had, inescapably, created a new public authority with powers of a sweeping nature, and when population began to rise from the late fifteenth

[62] See for example D. Aers, *Community, Gender and Individual Identities: English Writing 1360–1430* (London, 1988), pp. 20–72; Derek Pearsall made similar points in a paper on '*Piers Plowman* and the Problem of Labour' delivered to the conference on 'The Problem of Labour in the Fourteenth Century' at the University of York, July 1998.

[63] Poos, 'Social Context', passim; M.K. McIntosh, 'Local Change and Community Control in England, 1465–1500', *Huntingdon Library Quarterly*, XLIX (1986), 219–42, and 'Local Responses to the Poor in Late Medieval and Tudor England', *Continuity and Change*, III (1988), 209–45.

[64] M.K. McIntosh, *Controlling Misbehaviour in England, 1370–1600* (Cambridge, 1998), pp. 10, 45. This was published after this paper was first written. It is based on a study of 267 manorial, small borough and hundred courts.

[65] See especially J. Hatcher, 'English Serfdom and Villeinage: Towards a Reassessment', *Past and Present*, XC (1981), 3–39.

century, and land and jobs became scarce again, and real wages slumped, it would prove much harder to evade them. Well might they then have remembered the words of Richard II, that June day at Waltham.

APPENDIX

Labour Legislation 1349–1500, from *Statutes of the Realm* and
Rotuli Parliamentorum

References to the *Rotuli Parliamentorum* (*Rot. Parl.*) are included only when there is no corresponding entry in the *Statutes of the Realm* (*SR*)

Date	Reference
1349 (June)	*SR*, vol. I. p. 307
1349 (Nov.)	*SR*, vol. I. p. 309
1351	*SR*, vol. I. p. 311
1352	*SR*, vol. I. p. 327
1354	*Rot. Parl.*, vol. II. p. 258
1357	*SR*, vol. I. p. 350
1361	*SR*, vol. I. p. 366
1362	*SR*, vol. I. pp. 374–5
1368	*SR*, vol. I. p. 388
1372	*Rot. Parl.*, vol. II. p. 312
1373	*Rot. Parl.*, vol. II. p. 319
1376	*Rot. Parl.*, vol. II. pp. 332, 340–1
1377	*SR*, vol. II. p. 2; *Rot. Parl.*, vol. III. p. 17
1378	*SR*, vol. II. p. 11
1379	*Rot. Parl.*, vol. III. p. 65
1383	*SR*, vol. II. p. 32
1385	*SR*, vol. II. p. 38
1388 (Statute of Cambridge)	*SR*, vol. II. pp. 56–9
1390 (Jan.)	*SR*, vol. II. p. 63
1390 (Nov.)	*Rot. Parl.*, vol. III. p. 279
1402	*SR*, vol. II. p. 137
1406	*SR*, vol. II. pp. 157–8
1414 (April)	*SR*, vol. II. pp. 176–7
1416 (Oct.)	*SR*, vol. II. p. 196
1421 (May)	*Rot. Parl.*, vol. IV. p. 146
1423	*SR*, vol. II. p. 225
1425	*SR*, vol. II. p. 227; *Rot. Parl.*, vol. IV. pp. 292–3
1427	*SR*, vol. II. pp. 233–5
1429	*SR*, vol. II. pp. 244, 248
1446	*SR*, vol. II. p. 337
1449	*SR*, vol. II. pp. 351–2
1495	*SR*, vol. II. pp. 569, 577, 585
1497	*SR*, vol. II. p. 637

III

PREPARATION FOR SERVICE IN THE LATE MEDIEVAL ENGLISH CHURCH

Virginia Davis

THE subject to be dealt with here – motivation for entering the church and the early career patterns of young ordained clerks – is one which has been tackled by many others over the last half-century.[1] I am treading therefore on well-worn ground, and indeed I am in agreement with many of the views previously expressed. I come to the issues from the perspective of ordination. For the last few years I have been working on compiling a computerized database of episcopal ordination lists which offers some insight into clergy at the moment at which they came before the bishop to be ordained. This paper will consider some of the issues which affected the aspiring cleric who was trying to prepare himself for service within the church, in particular, finding support to become ordained, and finding the patronage to obtain a benefice. My overall aim is to try to explain how and why, in the face of the evidence that suggests that there were more men being ordained than there were suitable benefices to support them, did men continue to seek to enter the secular priesthood?

Initially the paper considers the patronage needed for the absolutely basic step of entering the church – becoming ordained. It was not simply a matter of turning up, having attained an adequate level of education and being prepared to make the appropriate commitment. Every man who wanted to be ordained to major orders had to satisfy the bishop's examining officers that he had an adequate income to support himself so that he would not become a charge on the episcopal household. How were young potential ordinands able to find this financial backing? Subsequently the paper explores, more briefly, the major challenge which faced most newly ordained priests, how to break through the glass ceiling of the late medieval church into the privileged network of benefice holders. The first benefice was the hardest to come by; how could this be achieved?

[1] Margaret Bowker devoted a chapter to 'The Way to a Benefice' in her book, *The Secular Clergy in the Diocese of Lincoln, 1495–1520* (Cambridge, 1968); Peter Heath had a chapter on preferment in his *English Parish Clergy on the Eve of the Reformation* (London, 1969). More recently Robert Swanson examined the issue in a section entitled 'Clerics and Careers' in his *Church and Society in Late Medieval England* (Oxford, 1989), while John Thomson in *The Early Tudor Church and Society, 1485–1529* (London, 1993) devoted a chapter to the lesser clergy which deals with issues such as ordination, patronage and career structure. See also A. McHardy, 'Careers and Disappointments in the Late-Medieval Church: Some English Evidence', *The Ministry: Clerical and Lay*, ed. W.J. Sheils and D. Wood (Studies in Church History 26, Oxford, 1989), pp. 111–30.

This paper will be arguing that it was relatively easy for a man to obtain the financial support allowing him to proceed to ordination, but that there was no guarantee that, once this had been achieved, he would become beneficed. It argues that information about titles found in ordination lists may be used as a useful indicator as to future progress in the church. This is in a very general sense, in that the titles offered at ordination provide the historian with an idea of the level of support a man had at this early stage in his career.

What financial support was required by young men who wanted to become ordained? Although relatively little is known about the details of the examination by episcopal officials that potential ordinands underwent, canon law clearly stated that every man who wanted to be ordained to major orders had to satisfy the bishop's examining officers that he had an adequate income to support himself so that he would not become a charge on the episcopal household. The details of these titles which briefly describe the source of this income were then recorded in the episcopal ordination lists. The process was clearly well understood by contemporaries in the fifteenth century, although some doubt as to how thorough this examination might have been is cast by the account of the process in the late medieval text, *Dives and Pauper*. The wide-ranging examination of simony in this literary text includes a discussion of simoniacal practice relating to titles to orders.

Also in receyuyng of holy ordre is on symonye sontyme only on hys syde that makyth ordrys, as whan som frend of hym that shal ben ordryd zeuyth the buschop some gifte withoutyn witynge of hym that shal ben ordrid. Somtyme it is don only on his syde that schal ben ordyrd, as if he geue ony giftis to ony of the buschopys officerys to spekyn for hym that he mon ben ordryd, of whiche gifte the buschop knowith nout. Somtyme it is don on bothin partyys, as whan the on geuyth and the othir takyth. Somtyme it is don and thou in neyther partye, as ef a frend of hym that schal ben ordryd geue or hote ony gifte to som of the buschopys offycers to helpyn hym in that cause and neyther he ne the buschop knowith of tho giftis. And in these manerys may also be don symonye in geuynge of benefycis of holy chirche.[2]

It seems more likely that such simoniacal behaviour may have been invoked to cover deficiencies of the candidate's education or personal characteristics rather than deficiencies of titles, though in the early sixteenth century Thomas More also indicated that bishops might be hoodwinked with regard to titles:

... they delude the lawe & them selfe also. For they neuer haue graunt of a lyuyng that may serue them in syght for that purpose but they secretly dyscharge it ere they haue it or els they could not gete it. And thus the bysshop is blynded by ye syght of the wrytyng and the prest goth a beggynge despite all his graunt of a good lyuynge ....[3]

If acting honestly, how much was needed to satisfy the bishop's officials that one had an adequate living? The sums of money involved are not huge; the intention was that the ordinand would not become a charge on the bishop's household. Minimum sums cited in ordination lists tend to be in the range of 5

[2] *Dives and Pauper*, ed. P.H. Barnum, EETS, original series 275, 280 (2 vols, 1976, 1980), vol. 2, pp. 173–6, quotation at p. 175.
[3] *The Yale Edition of the Complete Works of St Thomas More, vol. 6, parts I & II: A Dialogue Concerning Heresies*, ed. T.M. Lawler et al. (Yale, 1981), p. 302.

marks to 100*s per annum*.[4] For some men, these sums would have been trifling, but for others less favoured, they may have presented a substantial obstacle to ordination. The sums might represent a major commitment on the part of an individual, especially since they would be open-ended commitments which would, legally at least, have to be paid for the duration of the ordinand's life if he failed to obtain another income.

A wide range of titles offered by potential ordinands appear in the records, some rather more secure than others. They range from established benefices, academic institutions, personal resources described as their own patrimony, to annual pensions guaranteed by laity and titles certified by religious houses.[5] The titles can be divided into a number of categories: parochial and non-parochial benefices; the ordinand's own patrimony; titles offered by religious houses or hospitals; titles offered by other ecclesiastics; titles offered by laymen;[6] titles arising from a connection with an academic college.

Interpretation of the brief title cited in the episcopal register cannot always be taken at face value. This evidence of an ordinand's means of support at his moment of ordination is less useful than might be anticipated in providing historians with evidence as to who or what was supporting aspirant clerics. Administrative changes within the church from the mid-fourteenth century onwards reduce the usefulness of the information available. These mean that the majority of the men (some 80 per cent) who came forward gave as their title the name of the religious house. Increasingly the investigation of titles appears to have been carried out by religious houses. Having checked the titles and good repute of men seeking ordination, the ordinand was then presented for ordination by means of a letter from the religious house. This institution was then recorded by the episcopal registrar as guarantor of the title. Religious houses appear to have been acting rather like clearing houses, checking on the character and financial resources of the ordinand before passing him on to the bishop. The houses chosen by the potential ordinand were most usually those close to their home, and it would clearly be much simpler for such houses, with ties in the localities concerned, to check the details of a person's income or guarantee of support than it would be for a distant episcopal official. For such a service, some fee is likely to have been paid by the candidate, perhaps something in the

---

[4] Five pounds would not be a bad income for an aspiring cleric; it was described by Sir John Fortescue as a 'fair living' for a yeoman. However, it would have been a substantial amount of money for many men to provide for a friend or relative; £10 a year was regarded as the minimum required to support a gentleman in the fifteenth century. Men in the lower gentry classes would hardly have been in a position to provide this sort of patronage. Less than 1,000 knights had incomes in the £40–£400 bracket; it seems unlikely that the 6,200 men described as worth £5 to £40 in the early fifteenth century would have been able to offer such support: see C. Dyer, *Standards of Living in the Middle Ages* (Cambridge, 1989), pp. 31–2.

[5] This categorization of titles has been used in the computerization of the ordination lists to enable analysis of titles. For a fuller account of the categorization, see V. Davis, 'Late Medieval English Clergy Database', *History and Computing*, 2 (1990), 81–6.

[6] There may on occasion be some overlap between this category and that of the ordinand's own patrimony; this category has been used when the episcopal registrar has recorded the details of the candidate's income rather than merely noting 'own patrimony'.

region of the 4*d* which the Canterbury convocation stipulated in 1532 when they reformed the presentation system and replaced it by a system of testimonial letters for ordinands.[7] Thus the monastic titles which flood the episcopal ordination lists in the fifteenth century represent an administrative device rather than a record of actual titles. Hidden behind them is much of the information which we as historians would like to find.

Despite these administrative changes, there is information available about early support for ordinands, and a range of different titles can still be identified. Men are recorded with institutional titles such as those provided by academic secular colleges. Some individuals are recorded already in possession of benefices, and details of the patrimony offered by some individuals, or of lay patronage, also occur on occasion. Fifteenth-century records for some dioceses also contain enough evidence of lay titles to indicate that the practice of lay support continued, although the titles in question are unusual and appear to have fallen through the administrative net. This may be because the men came from distant areas outside the diocese where administrative practices were different and thus did not follow the commoner procedure of taking their title to a religious house. Thus their real means of support is recorded, as in the case of the title provided for a Guernsey ordinand, Stephen de Saint-Denis, in 1474 by Nigel Crigiel and Nicholas James.[8] Information about lay patrons is available for about 12 to 15 per cent of ordainees in the diocese of Hereford around the turn of the fourteenth and fifteenth centuries.[9] In fact titles from men's own patrimony may still have been the norm throughout the century, as is hinted at by the statement of Thomas More in the sixteenth century that a man entering the priesthood needed to have a sufficient yearly living, either of his own patrimony or otherwise. It is likely to have been the resources which made up an individual's patrimony which were being checked by religious houses.

We shall look briefly at the different means of support which were offered by young men to see what conclusions can be drawn from this evidence. The titles offered by religious houses are of little real help to the historian investigating support at ordination, as already indicated. The one point which should perhaps be made is to note the fact that where we know in detail the geographic origins of the ordinand, the house is often very close to his home, suggesting it may be a useful indicator of geographic origins for men for whom this is not known. This is particularly valuable in the case of geographically extensive dioceses such as Lincoln because it allows the narrowing of the area from which a man might have come.

Some of the men were already recorded as being beneficed before they came to be ordained. This was true of about 15 per cent of the men being ordained priests in the first third of the fifteenth century, dropping to 5 per cent by the end of the century. This was a situation which rarely arose unless a man had

---

[7] R.N. Swanson, 'Titles to Orders in Medieval English Episcopal Registers', *Studies in Medieval History Presented to R.H.C. Davis*, ed. H. Mayr-Harting and R.I. Moore (London, 1985), pp. 233–45.

[8] Hampshire RO, Register Waynflete II, f. 72v.

[9] This estimate is based on an analysis of the printed ordination lists for the diocese of Hereford in the fifteenth century.

either family connections or had already made a successful career within other areas before he came to enter the church, coming to be ordained only when he had already been offered a benefice as a reward for past service. Some such men can be identified in the ordination lists because they occur amongst the relatively few who are listed already holding benefices when ordained acolyte;[10] they are not numerous, but are of particular interest because they were potentially high flyers, who had already achieved the support necessary for success in the church, or who were born into circumstances where family connections smoothed their paths. Into such a category must be placed men such as Reginald Wellesley from the diocese of Exeter, who was ordained acolyte in 1409, having been presented to the Cornish benefice of Minster Talkern in June 1408. A papal dispensation allowed him to be ordained despite his illegitimacy; he was later described as of noble lineage and was dispensed to hold further benefices in southern England.[11] John Stafford, later to become archbishop of Canterbury, was the natural son of Humphrey Stafford of Southwick in Wiltshire and a local girl. Even before his ordination in 1409, while still only tonsured, he was collecting benefices, the first in 1404, when he became rector of Hulcott in Buckinghamshire.[12]

Those with benefices at the very early stage of acolyte were not yet firmly committed to the church; it was not until they made the move to be ordained to the sub-diaconate, the first of the major orders, that they were committed to celibacy. The exploitation of the system which might be found amongst beneficed acolytes can be seen at its worst in a letter written in 1413 by Bishop Reade of Chichester concerning a presentee to a benefice in his diocese, Thomas Jayat. Reade complained that Jayat had been instituted as rector of Bury, but had only the first tonsure and had made no move to be promoted to the higher orders as the law required. Neither, Reade complained, had Jayat contributed any money towards the upkeep of his benefice, and additionally his clothing was unsuitably coloured and he was not even wearing a clerical tonsure. Reade refused Jayat a *cum ex eo* licence because he felt the latter was not disposed to study. Bishop Reade's letter concluded, 'I do not see that he intends to aspire to Holy Orders but that he wishes to get gain and to consume the fruits of the church aforesaid.'[13] Such men certainly delayed their ordination until a good opening within the church arose, or as the above letter suggests, rather longer than that. Jayat may never have fulfilled his clerical obligation; he was described

---

[10] The figures for acolytes ordained already who are listed as holding benefices are 6 out of 313 acolytes in the diocese of Winchester between 1447 and 1486; 19 of 635 acolytes for Ely during the episcopate of John Fordham (1388–1425); 36 of 942 acolytes in early fifteenth-century Lincoln during the episcopate of Henry Beaufort (1398–1404). The actual figures may in fact be greater because some episcopal officials may not have recorded the title, since it was not necessary to have a title to be ordained to the minor order of acolyte.

[11] Emden, *BRUO*, vol. III, p. 2010.

[12] *DNB*, vol. LIII, pp. 454–5; Emden, *BRUO*, vol. III, pp. 1750–1.

[13] *The Episcopal Register of Robert Rede*, ed. C. Deedes (2 vols, Sussex Record Society 8, 10), 1908–10, pp. 47–52. For Jayat's later appointment as king's controller, see *CPR, 1416–22*, p. 30.

three years later as late king's controller in the counties of Devon and Cornwall.

Most of the men ordained already with titles from benefices, however, were set on a path of a clerical career, and, when their careers are further examined, are the men who are likely to be found amongst the clerical élite. Examining, for example, the titles offered at ordination by men who were to become archdeacons or cathedral canons, it can be seen that a disproportionate number of them were either beneficed at the moment of ordination or offered academic titles. William Barton, ordained in 1416 when already a prebendary of St Paul's cathedral in London, was subsequently to become a canon of Lincoln.[14] Most men who were later to become bishops were also beneficed at the moment of ordination to higher orders.[15] Richard Courtenay, ordained subdeacon in 1399, by then also a prebendary of St Paul's, was by 1413 bishop of Norwich; Master John Swayne, later to become archbishop of Armagh, was ordained in London in the autumn of 1415 with a title indicating that he was already holding the rectory of Upminster in Essex. Examining the careers of some of the twenty-nine men who were ordained as acolyte, already beneficed, in the diocese of London in the first decade of the fifteenth century illustrates this further. Roger Bolter of the diocese of Exeter, who was ordained in 1401, holding the Devon benefice of Blackawton, was to rise to be widely beneficed, primarily within the diocese of Exeter, finally acting as official and keeper of the spiritualities of the diocese. He was presented to Blackawton in July 1401 before he was even tonsured, which did not occur until the following month, when he also was granted a *cum ex eo* licence to go to Oxford.[16] Also ordained in London during this period was John Stafford, mentioned above as the future archbishop of Canterbury, who was ordained acolyte holding the benefice of St Nicholas in Durham.[17] Early benefices are often a very clear indication of those who had the support of patrons at this early stage, a fact which ultimately was to assist them towards a high-flying ecclesiastical career.

The fifteenth century may be described as a century of education, when the foundation of many new Oxford and Cambridge colleges plus numerous substantial endowed schools provided a new wealth of educational opportunities. Education, as has long been recognized, was one major key to advancement.[18] Those men who had found their way to Oxford, Cambridge or one of the growing number of good schools which were becoming increasingly widespread in the fifteenth century had taken a step which was very likely to lead them to ecclesiastical preferment.[19] The men who were ordained with titles from the

[14] Emden, *BRUO*, vol. I, p. 124.

[15] J.T. Rosenthal, 'The Fifteenth-Century Episcopate: Careers and Bequests', *Sanctity and Secularity: The Church and the World*, ed. D. Baker (Studies in Church History, 10, 1973), pp. 117–28.

[16] London Guildhall, Register Braybrooke, f. 58v; Emden, *BRUO*, vol. I, p. 215.

[17] Emden, *BRUO*, vol. III, p. 1751.

[18] See, for example, M.J. Bennett, 'Education and Advancement', *Fifteenth-Century Attitudes*, ed. R. Horrox (Cambridge, 1994), pp. 79–96.

[19] 'The majority of students ... went to university largely as an investment: education paid off': R.N. Swanson, 'Learning and Livings: University Study and Clerical Careers in Later Medieval England', *History of Universities*, 6 (1987), 83.

Oxbridge colleges, or from other major endowed colleges such as Eton College or Winchester College, were also likely to be destined to enter the clerical élite. Men with titles from collegiate fellowships tended to have careers which left them supported by their colleges, or tended to be presented by their own college, or another one, to benefices. To explore how such men got on the ladder of preferment, it would be necessary to explore how they came to school or university in the first place, a subject about which very little is known and which there is not space to discuss here. Many such men were of middling or wealthy families with the resources to send their sons to university; others must have attracted important patrons early on, as can be seen in the case of Walter Parry, *nativus* of Bishopstoke manor in Hampshire who was granted manumission by Cardinal Beaufort in 1446 on the grounds that he wanted to study for ordination. Parry had already been a scholar at Winchester College for three years at this time; he was to go on to New College, which provided the title for his ordination in 1453–4.[20] He was a fellow there for some fifteen years and in 1464 he was presented by Winchester College to be vicar of Heston in Middlesex, a position he held until his death in June 1477. The interesting question in examining this example of social mobility is the unanswered, and perhaps unanswerable, one of how Parry attracted Beaufort's patronage to start with, from his humble position as a member of an unfree family on an episcopal manor.

Either academic colleges tended to look after their fellows, or the men were well connected and well qualified enough to attract influential patrons. The colleges themselves had come relatively late to the scramble for endowments in the form of parochial benefices, but those which did hold wealthy parishes used them to support graduates, either their own or those of other colleges, in the small world of Oxbridge.[21] Queen's College Oxford presented several graduates in the fifteenth century to the Hampshire parish of Knight's Enham. These included Master John Pereson who rose from being a 'poor boy' at the college in 1447 to provost by 1460. It was after his appointment as provost that Pereson was presented to Knight's Enham.[22] Another graduate so presented was Richard Bernard of New College who had no evident links with Queen's College.[23]

---

[20] *The Register of the Common Seal of the Priory of St. Swithun, Winchester, 1345–1497*, ed. J. Greatrex (Hampshire, 1978), no. 247; Emden, *BRUO*, vol. III, p. 1439; Hampshire RO, Register Waynflete I, f. Gr.

[21] This is reflected in the small percentage of benefices (3 to 4 per cent) held by such colleges in the diocese of Winchester, despite the importance of a number of bishops of Winchester in the foundation and endowment of colleges. Within the same diocese some colleges were patrons on a small scale. Merton College Oxford had the patronage of two vicarages, Farleigh and Maldon; Queen's College possessed the patronage of Knight's Enham; Winchester College, despite its situation in the city of Winchester, held only two livings in the diocese, while its sister foundation in Oxford, New College, appears to have held only one. Finally, Henry VI's two foundations, Eton College and King's College Cambridge, were, relatively speaking, among the best endowed of these institutions as a result of the lands they had acquired from alien priories. Eton College had advowsons for four benefices in the diocese of Winchester; King's College had two.

[22] Emden, *BRUO*, vol. III, pp. 1463–4.

[23] Emden, *BRUO*, vol. I, p. 178; Hampshire RO, Register Waynflete II, f. 89.

However, the limited number of colleges in Oxford and their small size makes such cross patronage between colleges hardly surprising.

Other corporate bodies also sought highly educated men to fill their benefices. This can be seen, for example, in the presentations made by the Grocers' Company to the rectory of All Hallows, Honey Lane, in London. They obtained the right to make the presentation in 1456 from the will of Simon Strete, and the pattern of their presentees shows that they sought highly educated men. Thomas Ebrall, theologian, preached before the king a year after his appointment in 1464; on his death in 1471 he was succeeded by Henry Hoddes who had a doctorate in theology from Cambridge. He was followed by the theologian Edward Lupton, while Lupton's successor in 1479 was John Chapman, a theologian who in 1496 preached before Henry VII.[24]

It is the contribution of lay patrons to the support of men at ordination which is most hidden by the administrative changes of the later fourteenth century. Information about lay patrons is given for about 12 to 15 per cent of ordainees in the diocese of Hereford around the turn of the fourteenth and fifteenth centuries. The numbers were even lower in southern England. Most lay patrons appear as giving only a single title during this period, suggesting that – as was found in a study based on Carlisle records in the fourteenth century – they were probably assisting a particular individual relative, tenant, or offspring of a friend.[25] The links of kinship can be seen in some instances where the patron and the aspirant cleric share the same surname: thus one Philip Bayliff provided a title for Richard Bayliff.[26] Even when surnames are different, kindred is sometimes hinted at, as when John Graseley presented a title described as the whole inheritance of John Hereford.[27] The precise lands which were to supply the income may be named. Thomas Mughale had a title consisting of lands at Willey and Rodd granted to him for life by Richard Cornwayle in 1410;[28] John Staunton had a title based on 6 marks from within the demesne of Leominster granted by John Salesbury, *armiger*.[29] In the diocese of Durham, John Greteham was being supported by Thomas Lambard of Owton.[30] Owton and Greatham lie less than a mile from each other within the same parish.

[24] Emden, *BRUO*, vol. I, p. 623 (Ebrall); Emden, *BRUC*, p. 308 (Hodder); Emden, *BRUO*, vol. II, p. 1178 (Lupton); Emden, *BRUC*, p. 131 (Chapman).

[25] R.K. Rose, 'Priests and Patrons in the Fourteenth Century Diocese of Carlisle', *The Church in Town and Countryside*, ed. D. Baker (Studies in Church History, 16, 1979), p. 214.

[26] *Registrum Johannis Trefnant, Episcopi Herefordensis*, ed. W.W. Capes (Canterbury and York Society, 20, 1916), pp. 211, 213 (acolyte, May 1391; subdeacon, March 1395; priest, September 1395).

[27] Ordained subdeacon, September 1410; deacon, June 1411; priest, April 1412: *Registrum Roberti Mascall, Episcopi Herefordensis*, ed. J.H. Parry (Canterbury and York Society, 21, 1917), pp. 146, 149, 152.

[28] Ibid., pp. 147–8.

[29] Ordained as subdeacon in September 1410 with a title of 7 marks; ordained priest, December 1412: ibid., pp. 146, 155.

[30] *The Register of Thomas Langley, Bishop of Durham, 1406–1437*, ed. R.L. Storey (6 vols, Surtees Society 1956–70), vol. I, p. 53.

Some local families provided several successive or concurrent titles. John Wallewayn of Stoke Edith provided titles for both William Carpunter[31] and David Fitz Lawrence Jevan;[32] Hugh Russell, *armiger*, supported Roger Taylour, Richard Taylour and John Smyth, while another member of the Russell family, John Russell, supported William Panyers.[33] Women too might provide titles from their lands. Isabel Downe, lady of Collington, provided the support necessary for Laurence Carpunter to get ordained.[34] Most of the titles are provided by individuals, but on occasion groups might be involved. Thomas Ree was ordained with a title drawn from Henry Cachepoll, Richard Faller and Richard Palmer.[35] Fourteenth-century records show communities acting to provide a title at ordination for a village boy. For example, in 1315 the community of Andover provided a title for William atte Watere,[36] but I have yet to find such references in later records.

The scale of the commitment required can be seen where the ordination lists provide details of the sums of money which laymen were guaranteeing to the men being ordained. Peter Hunte's title was a rent of 100*s* to be taken from the lands of Llewelyn Cornwalle in Herefordshire;[37] in Northumberland, William Hertlipole's title from Lady Matilda Bowes of Dalton-Le-Dale was 5 marks.[38] Although not vast sums, the amounts might represent nonetheless a substantial commitment on the part of an individual, especially since, as mentioned earlier, they would be open-ended commitments which would, legally at least, have to be paid for the duration of the ordinand's life if he failed to obtain another income.

No ordination records survive for London until after the Black Death, so it is not known if the pattern there resembles that of Carlisle, where it can be seen that individual townspeople were supporting members of their community; there, in fact, just over 20 per cent of all titles provided by laymen were provided by townsmen.[39] Most of these people were inhabitants of Carlisle and surrounding villages. Thus we can see men such as Peter the Butcher providing a title for William, son of John the Carpenter. Few London lay titles are provided in the fifteenth century, although exploration behind titles relating to benefices may

---

[31] Ordained subdeacon, April 1408; deacon, June 1408; priest, September 1408: *Registrum Mascall*, pp. 137, 139, 140.

[32] *Registrum Trefnant*, p. 226.

[33] Hugh Russell provided a title for John Smyth to be ordained deacon in March 1406 and subsequently as priest in March 1407: *Registrum Mascall*, pp. 134, 136. In September 1411, Richard Taylour was ordained deacon with a title of 'a rent of 6 marks from the lands of Hugh Russell': ibid., p. 150.

[34] Acolyte, December 1405; subdeacon, April 1408; deacon, June 1408; priest, September 1408: *Registrum Mascall*, pp. 129, 137, 138, 140.

[35] Henry Cachepoll is additionally recorded as giving a title to David ap Jevan ap David Stuckhull; however, when in 1391 he had the right of presentation to Mokkas rectory, he presented a Thomas Bristowe to it: *Registrum Trefnant*, pp. 197, 199, 188.

[36] *Registrum Henrici Woodlock, Dioceseis Wintoniensis, 1305–1316*, vol. II, ed. A.W. Goodman (Canterbury and York Society, 44, 1941), p. 876.

[37] Ordained subdeacon in May 1412: *Registrum Mascall*, p. 153.

[38] *Register of Thomas Langley*, vol. II, p. 36.

[39] Rose, 'Priests and Patrons in Carlisle', p. 213.

reveal laymen supporting kinsmen, as must be the case with John Bys, who was ordained acolyte in 1407, having already been presented to the London parish church of St Magnus the Martyr by two London citizens, Thomas Kemysar and Edmund Bys, the latter almost certainly a relation.[40] However, fifteenth-century records for the diocese of Winchester contain enough evidence of lay titles to indicate that the practice continues behind the administrative cloud. Twenty-six laymen's titles are cited in detail for the period 1447–86. These particular titles are of interest because they are unusual, a number of them deriving from the Channel Islands. In the late 1470s and 1480s, for example, Peter Manger was ordained with a title of £15-worth of land from William Hamptone, gentleman of Jersey; Thomas Costyll, with a title of land of the same value from John de Larane of Jersey, and Matthew Gallier, again with £15-worth of lands, this time from Philip Payn of Jersey.[41]

The patronage of urban and rural laymen of all classes of society thus played a vital role in allowing aspiring clerics to be ordained and to take the first step towards joining the clerical establishment. The numbers of men being ordained and the range of titles suggest that men wishing to become ordained found it relatively easy to do so legitimately (or illegitimately, using the *Dives and Pauper* simoniacal method). Thomas More certainly considered that it was in fact too easy for men to be ordained as priests. In his *Dialogue Touching Heretics* he argued, 'For ye shold haue prestes fewe ynoughe yf ye lawe were truely obserued that none were made but he yt were without colusyon sure of a lyuynge all redy.'[42]

In considering the pursuit of preferment, it is clear that becoming a parish priest was a considerable achievement, even in a poorish parish, and not everyone either achieved it or indeed expected to do so. The first benefice was the hardest to come by. How could it be achieved? I cannot deal here with the very wide range of pressures which faced patrons with parochial benefices at their disposal when they came to find men to fill their parishes. The point should be stressed, however, that there are relatively few links between the patrons who supplied titles which enabled men to become ordained and those who provided the benefices.

Religious houses held an enormous amount of patronage in terms of presentation to benefices. Within the diocese of Winchester, for example, 40 per cent of parochial advowsons were held by religious houses, within the diocese or elsewhere in England. Peter Heath has stressed that monastic patronage was by no means necessarily a matter of free will, and he indicates the pressure put upon the houses by the king, nobles, prelates and magnates.[43] The men they presented were diverse and were subject to many different pressures. On occasions religious houses might present members of their own or of other

---

[40] London Guildhall, Register Bubwith, f. 34r; *Novum Repertorium Ecclesiasticum Parochiale Londinense* (London, 1898), p. 274.

[41] Hampshire RO, Register Waynflete II, ff. 200r, 186r, 183r.

[42] More, *A Dialogue Concerning Heresies*, p. 302.

[43] Heath, *The English Parish Clergy*, pp. 29, 33–4; R. Donaldson, 'Sponsors, Patrons and Presentations to Benefices in the Gift of the Priors of Durham in the Later Middle Ages', *Archaeologia Aeliana*, 4th series (1928), 169–77.

religious houses of the same order. John Gernesey, an Augustinian canon of St Denys, Southampton, was presented, by the Augustinian priory of Merton, to Effingham in Surrey in 1477, and John Warde, canon of Merton, was presented to Mitcham in 1475; the abbot of the Premonstratensian Titchfield abbey was presented to Empshott by the Augustinian Southwick priory.[44] John Winchester, an Augustinian from Mottisfont priory, was presented by his own house to two benefices in succession, King's Somborne and Laverstoke.[45] Hyde abbey, a Benedictine house, presented the Premonstratensian John Ellingham of St Radegund in Kent to two of the benefices in its possession.[46] Bermondsey abbey, a Cluniac foundation, in 1458 presented Thomas Elkington, a Benedictine from Bardney in Lincolnshire, to a benefice in its gift.[47]

Examination of the titles offered by men who were subsequently presented to benefices by religious houses, and also of the subsequent careers of men who were ordained to the titles of religious houses, show no significant correlation between the titles offered by religious houses to those seeking ordination and the presentation to benefices by the same religious houses. This reinforces Swanson's suggestion that it was an administrative function. It was clearly not amongst the men to whom they had given titles that houses seeking potential candidates for benefices looked. Men such as John Holme of Carlisle, ordained with a title from Mottisfont priory in the early 1450s and later presented to Longstock by the same priory by 1460, are very much the exception.[48] John Gedeney of the diocese of Salisbury was ordained in the early 1450s with a title from the Augustinian house of Christchurch. In 1460 he was presented to the parish of Kings Worthy by Hyde abbey.[49] Walter Dyer from Bath and Wells was ordained with a title from Clothall hospital in Hertfordshire in the mid-1450s; his benefice came from Nunnaminster, which gave him the prebend of Itchen [Abbas] in 1459.[50] Master William Skylling was ordained in the late 1460s with a title from Romsey abbey; he was presented to Lainston in 1476 by John Skylling, presumably a family member.[51]

The situation with regard to lay patrons is more clear-cut, but lay patrons made up a relatively small proportion of the total number of advowson holders. Some major lay patrons, members of the great aristocracy, clearly did use patronage to reward their retainers or servants. The Stafford dukes of Buckingham held four advowsons in Surrey which formed just a small part of their extensive ecclesiastical patronage. Of these four, the most valuable was Bletchingley, which was also the seat of a manor occasionally used by the family. In 1451 the duke presented Hugo Hexstall to it, a candidate chosen from a family

[44] Hampshire RO, Register Waynflete II, f. 43r (John Gernesey); f. 31r (John Warde); f. 63r (the abbot of Titchfield).

[45] Ibid., ff. 71r, 100v, 101v.

[46] To Worting, May 1462, and Micheldever, December 1464: ibid., ff. 119r, 135r.

[47] The benefice was Warlingham in Surrey, ibid., f. 92r.

[48] These rather negative conclusions are based on extensive, but inconclusive, work attempting to link these men within the diocese of Winchester in the fifteenth century.

[49] Hampshire RO, Register Waynflete I, ff. E4, 103v.

[50] Ibid., I, f. Mr-v; f. 96v.

[51] Ibid., I, f. N*v; II, f. 40r.

which was already playing an integral role in ducal administration. His brother William had already represented Bletchingley in parliament in 1447.[52]

Overall, it is not an optimistic picture which emerges, when viewed from the perspective of an aspirant cleric who did not have influential connections or patrons. While it was relatively easy to obtain the initial patronage to become ordained, the hurdle of obtaining a parochial benefice defeated all but relatively few. In fact, making a career outside the church, thus attracting a patron who could then promote one's advancement to a benefice, or attending a major academic college, were perhaps the best ways to the richest benefices, though the problem was that such a route to worldly success in the church also required substantial initial support and patronage.

What emerges from this examination of presentation to benefices is that there are clearly two classes in the late medieval church: those who attain the desirable benefices become beneficed at an early stage in their ecclesiastical career, while those without the requisite connections, talents or patrons tend to remain unbeneficed, or at best obtain a parish at a late stage in their career. I do not think the pattern is one of men spending some time as jobbing clergy in a variety of assistant roles within the parishes, as chantry priests, assistant chaplains and so on, and then moving up to being beneficed. Many of those people who were going to be beneficed obtained their benefices early.[53] More often there was little interchange between the two groups, and those who were chantry chaplains or unbeneficed remained so. Of the 26 curates reported as serving Boston in 1500, 4 were still there a quarter of a century later in 1526, and although 8 eventually received a living, it took them some time. In the archdeaconry of Leicester the names of 42 curates were recorded at the archidiaconal visitations of 1517 of whom only 3 appear to have received benefices, and many of them either stayed in the same curacy or simply moved to another curacy.[54]

The ecclesiastical community attached to one large parish helps to illustrate the fate of some of the unbeneficed. The community is that associated with one Somerset church, that of the parish church of St Mary Magdalen in Taunton. A series of visitation and subsidy records in the fifteenth century, combined

[52] C. Rawcliffe, *The Staffords, Earls of Stafford and Dukes of Buckingham, 1394–1521* (Cambridge, 1978), pp. 83–4. Hexstall's successor in Bletchingley in 1476 was William Drayton, one of three men named Drayton who comprised three of the ten men presented to the Staffords' Surrey benefices during Waynflete's episcopate. No direct link can be established between the Draytons and the ducal household, but it is highly probable that the Draytons came from Staffordshire. While it can be dangerous to argue from topographical/surname evidence at this late date, Drayton is not a place-name found in either Hampshire or Surrey, but there is a place of that name in Staffordshire. Other examples of family use of patronage can be seen in P. Hosker, 'The Stanleys of Lathom and Ecclesiastical Patronage in the North-West of England during the Fifteenth Century', *Northern History*, 18 (1982), 214–27; I. Jack, 'The Ecclesiastical Patronage Exercised by a Baronial Family in the Late Middle Ages' *Journal of Religious History*, 3 (1964–5), 275–95.
[53] Margaret Bowker, examining early sixteenth-century Lincolnshire, suggests that of those who were ordained priest, most took about five years after their ordination to do so: Bowker, *The Secular Clergy in the Diocese of Lincoln*, pp. 72–3.
[54] Ibid., p. 72.

with a full sequence of surviving episcopal registers for the period, allow the fate of the clergy attached to it in various capacities to be better documented than is often the case. Surviving records cover the years, 1444, 1450 and 1461, and there is additionally some more intermittent later material.[55] The 1444 episcopal visitation listed 8 chaplains in addition to the perpetual vicar. The latter, William Cogan, had been instituted into this position in 1428; he held it until 1456 when he was promoted to the parochial benefice of Combe Florey by the prior and convent of Taunton. He resigned this benefice in 1461 and was still in receipt of his pension in 1463. Ralph Hilling, anniversary chaplain in 1444, was still holding this post in 1450 and in 1468, suggesting little promotion had taken place. Richard Pomerey was chaplain of St Andrew in 1444 and still in 1450, but he had disappeared from the record by 1461, as was the case with his fellow chaplain, John Waleys. Another anniversary chaplain, Thomas Harding, was first mentioned in 1450; seven years later he was promoted to the parish of Chilton by the Bridgwater hospital of St John. In 1461 he resigned this benefice and obtained a pension of £4. No reason is given for his resignation, but it was most probably due to advanced age. After at least twelve years as chaplain, William Boys, mentioned as chaplain in 1444, was in 1456 presented by Christine, widow of Walter Portman, to nearby Orchard parish church. John Benet was an anniversary chaplain in 1444; in 1459 there is a licence for him to be excused from services. He is described as being 80 years old and having exercised the chantry for 33 years, having been presented to it in 1426 by Anne, countess of Devon. John Baker, described in 1444 as chaplain in St Mary's chantry, was the following year presented to Locking perpetual vicarage. However, when he came to be instituted, he was discovered to be ignorant of letters and scriptures and was ordered to study to remedy this situation. He died in 1455. John Jede, parochial chaplain in 1444, died still in this position in 1460. Nicholas Thressher was ordained in 1451 to the title of the hospital of St John at Wells; by 1461 he was chaplain of St Mary's. The evidence of this single, well-documented and substantial parish church suggests that the chantry priests or other chaplains attached to it were not on the first step of a high-flying career within the church, but that they seem to have reached a plateau, and the most they could hope for, after long service to this church, might at best be late promotion to a local parish. More likely, they would live out their life in this fairly lowly position as auxiliary clergy within the parish.

I have been arguing that there are very clearly two classes in the church, a beneficed and an unbeneficed. A study of ordination records suggests that it was clear early in a man's career to which class he would belong. Mobility between the underclass and the élite was relatively difficult. Yet there is no doubt that the secular church continued to attract entrants in very substantial

---

[55] This material is to be found in *The Register of John Stafford, Bishop of Bath and Wells, 1425–1443*, ed. T.S. Holmes (2 vols, Somerset Record Society, 31, 32, 1915–16); *The Register of Thomas Bekynton, Bishop of Bath and Wells, 1443–1465*, ed. H.C. Maxwell-Lyte and M.C.B. Dawes (2 vols, Somerset Record Society, 49, 50, 1934–5); *The Registers of Robert Stillington, Bishop of Bath and Wells, 1466–1491, and Richard Fox, Bishop of Bath and Wells, 1492–1494*, ed. H.C. Maxwell-Lyte (Somerset Record Society, 52, 1937).

numbers throughout the fifteenth century with little decline seen before the 1520s. It is hard to believe that men in this period did not recognize that their prospects of becoming beneficed, unless they were well educated or had a powerful patron, were fairly slight. Yet men still came to enter the church with enthusiasm and in numbers, even in the face of alternative careers opening up to literate men in the fifteenth century which were not dependent upon ordination to the priesthood.

So, what conclusions can be drawn from this disparity between the flood of ordainees and the relative lack of opportunities to become beneficed? The historiographical debate since the 1970s about the numbers entering the church has been very much couched in terms of careerism and unemployment. I believe that the church still offered reasonable opportunities, even to those who remained unbeneficed, given the demand for masses, for stipendiary chaplains, for chantry priests. A jobbing priest could make a reasonable, if somewhat insecure, living. However, I am increasingly convinced that there was another reason why men continued to enter the church in the fifteenth century. Perhaps historians of the medieval church have seriously underestimated the level of the commitment of many of these men to service in the church and of their piety and devotion. There is a striking divergence in recent historiography. While writing on the laity and the church increasingly stresses lay piety and devotion displayed by major sections of the population, those of us who have been concerned with the lesser clergy have been concentrating almost entirely on their career opportunities or lack of them. Lay people are devout, clergy are cynical careerists. It is an odd divergence, and I am increasingly unconvinced by it. The lesser clergy may have been inadequately educated or ill-prepared for their positions. Indeed, some almost certainly were, but this does not negate their commitment. Historians need to explore in more detail the idea that many of the floods of men entering the church in the fifteenth century came because they had a calling – a concept of service in, and to, the church which they were keen to fulfil, even if wealth, riches and security were not to follow.

IV

MASTERS, PATRONS AND THE CAREERS OF GRADUATES IN FIFTEENTH-CENTURY ENGLAND

Jeremy Catto

THE historiography of bastard feudalism has ensured that the concept of service, the performance of tasks on behalf of a person of superior status by his or her inferiors, has been prominent in the minds of fifteenth-century historians. The deconstruction of bastard feudalism, which was initiated by McFarlane in his 1945 paper on the subject, has equally made clear that they may have exaggerated its distinctive role in that era. It is now a commonplace that service, whether generalized in the affinity or specialized in the household or the armed retinue, was already characteristic of Anglo-Saxon England, and was still normal to the grandees of the eighteenth century, who could command private regiments and pocket boroughs. If the author of the Old English poem *The Seafarer* could lament the paucity of opportunity for service – 'there come now no kings or Caesars, nor gold-giving lords like those gone' – his successor William Wordsworth was more fortunate in being able to do his duty as collector of stamps for Westmorland and election agent to the earl of Lonsdale. What are perhaps now to be remarked on about fifteenth-century service are some distinctive *forms* of serving political masters and social superiors, and prominent among them must be the contribution of the structured professions: both the English, or customary, and the learned laws; medicine; theology, in this century overwhelmingly the practical art of preaching; many would add the art of the secretary, transformed in this period by the adoption of the *studia humanitatis*; some would also add the profession of the receiver and the accountant, taught in the business schools of Oxford and the capital.[1] In 1400 these professions

---

[1] See *Profession, Vocation and Culture in Later Medieval England*, ed. C.H. Clough (Liverpool, 1982), esp. R.L. Storey, 'Gentlemen-bureaucrats', pp. 90–120, C.T. Allmand, 'The Civil Lawyers', pp. 155–80, and E.W. Ives, 'The Common Lawyers', pp. 181–217; J. Barton, *Roman Law in England*, Ius Romanum Medii Aevi, pars v. 13a (Milan, 1971); Barton, 'The Study of Civil Law before 1380', *History of the University of Oxford*, vol. I, *The Early Oxford Schools*, ed. J.I. Catto (Oxford 1984), pp. 519–30; Barton, 'The Legal Faculties of Late Medieval Oxford', *History of the University of Oxford*, vol. II, *Late Medieval Oxford*, ed. Catto and T.A.R. Evans (Oxford, 1992), pp. 281–313; M. Beilby, 'The Profits of Expertise: the Rise of the Civil Lawyers and Chancery Equity', *Profit, Piety and the Professions*, ed. M.A. Hicks (Gloucester, 1990), pp. 72–90; L.E. Boyle, 'Canon Law before 1380', *The Early Oxford Schools*, ed. Catto, pp. 531–64; C.H. Talbot and E.A. Hammond, *The Medical Practitioners in Medieval England* (London, 1965); Talbot, *Medicine in Medieval England* (London 1967); F.M. Getz, 'The Faculty of Medicine before 1500', *Late Medieval Oxford*, ed. Catto and Evans, pp. 373–405; C. Everitt, 'Eloquence as Profession and Art' (unpublished D.Phil. thesis, Univer-

were not new: law, medicine and theology had been taught as organized subjects in Oxford and Cambridge since the 1230s. But it was not until the late fourteenth century, in Italy, Germany, England and France, that the doctors of the higher faculties emerged as 'the pillars of the church, made of deathless cedarwood and arrayed in the gold of wisdom' as one Viennese theologian, Henry Totting von Oyta put it, or as we might say now, a self-conscious intellectual élite.[2] Aware of the high ideals and corruptibility of their several professions, they carefully guarded their standards of training, began to assert the regulatory role of universities in great matters of church and state, and cooperated in the reunion of western Christendom after the Great Schism. Confident if somewhat troubled in conscience, products of the European *grandes écoles* like Pierre d'Ailly, Matthew of Cracow or John Wyclif were not at the beck and call of any master however exalted; but they did put their independent minds and judgement at the service of particular potentates: Louis, duke of Orléans, for d'Ailly, and Rupert III, count palatine and king of the Romans, in the case of Matthew of Cracow. Wyclif's service to John of Gaunt is more dubious. All three were theologians offering counsel to great men with some public responsibilities; jurists were even more at home in a similar conciliar role. The special nature of the professional service, afforded to English patrons by graduates of Oxford, is my subject here.

In the thirteenth and fourteenth centuries the service of professional men was not so sharply defined as it would later become. Edward I and his nobility needed legal advice and advocacy, but took them indifferently from civil law doctors like Robert Pickering and judges trained in the king's own courts such as Ralph Hengham.[3] It is impossible to make any distinction, at that date, between the Oxford-trained lawyers in the service of their clients and the serjeants-at-law, advocates and judges of the king's bench employed by the same lords. Some of the fourteenth-century chancery clerks of the crown were Oxford civilians while others were not; they all learned the mysteries of their profession, the wax, the ribbon and the formulaic Latin through in-house training, living together in the inns of chancery.[4] It would be equally impossible, in 1300, to distinguish a university-trained physician from a colleague trained only in London practice. Only the theologians had developed a standard university *cursus* and a specialist vocabulary, the mark of a mature professional culture. Theologians, however, were not yet in a position to deploy their skills in the service of lay masters, and were therefore no exception to the rule succinctly stated by Jean Dunbabin: 'university training might be highly desirable for many posts,

---

sity of Oxford, 1985); R.A. Griffiths, 'Public and Private Bureaucracies in England and Wales in the Fifteenth Century', *TRHS*, fifth series 30 (1980), 109–30, reprinted in his *King and Country* (London 1991).

[2] G. Sommerfeldt, 'Zwei politische Sermone des Heinrich von Oyta und des Nikolaus von Dinkesbühl (1388 und 1417)', *Historisches Jahrbuch*, 26 (1905), 320–3, at 321.

[3] For Pykering, see Emden, *BRUO*, vol. III, pp. 1532–3. On Hengham, see *Radulphi de Hengham Summae*, ed. W.H. Dunham (Cambridge, 1932).

[4] T.F. Tout, 'The Household of the Chancery and its Disintegration', *Essays in History Presented to Reginald Lane Poole*, ed. H.W.C. Davis (Oxford 1927, reprinted 1969), pp. 46–85.

but it was not essential for any.'[5] During the fourteenth century, the professions founded on study in one of the higher faculties in universities were transformed, both in terms of the expertise they conferred on those who completed the course, and in respect of the opportunities for employment they found as a result. Doctors of civil and canon law (there is little discernible difference between them) could operate in the far more active courts of the Canterbury province as well as in a defined sector of secular courts; doctors of medicine now found they could build established practices in London and elsewhere; doctors of theology, who were no longer mostly friars, were in demand as preachers and confessors. In 1450, it would be difficult to deny that the possession of a degree did make a difference to a man's career, not only because it conferred a mark of respect, but because there was scope for the exercise of some real expertise.

It is clear that in contemporary eyes the arts course did not confer on its masters the professional status of the higher faculties. A master of arts would not, for instance, find himself recommended for a prebend in the rolls of graduates presented by Oxford and other universities to the Roman curia. The dialectical training of the arts schools was of course applicable in many walks of life: Ralph Strode for instance, Chaucer's 'philosophical Strode', whose logic textbooks were prescribed texts in late fifteenth-century Padua, made his career in the legal world of the City of London, as the common serjeant of the City, between 1373 and 1387. The brilliant development of Oxford logic in the fourteenth century had all but made the logician a specialist with his own professional expertise: William Heytesbury, Richard Billingham, Henry Hopton, Richard Feribrigge, Roger Whelpdale, William Milverley and John Tarteys were all the authors of textbooks used long after their time in Oxford or abroad. Yet it is noticeable that those among them who made a career after Oxford took a degree in theology and then enjoyed a conventional clerical *cursus honorum*; Feribrigge, Milverley and Tarteys are unknown to have done so and fell into obscurity or perhaps an early death. Nothing is known of them beyond their writings.[6] So logic alone provided no service, though combined with other arts it was immensely useful, as Strode, the common serjeant, doubtless found.

Masters of arts can also be found in the higher reaches of the notary's profession. Master John Stevens of the diocese of Exeter took his degree about 1400; he found employment, without legal training, in the court of Canterbury in its heroic age under Archbishop Arundel, initially as clerk to the archbishop's registrar. His close association with high fliers like John Langdon, the well-connected Canterbury monk, and John Kempe, later archbishop, cannot have harmed his prospects, but Stevens also deployed considerable rhetorical skill in drafting letters, some of which survive in his formulary, All Souls MS 182.[7] He was able to transfer to the service of Henry V, for whose territorial claims he drew up collections of evidences. He is the most probable author of that highly

---

[5] J. Dunbabin, 'Careers and Vocations', *The Early Oxford Schools*, ed. Catto, p. 576.

[6] On logic and the careers of logicians, see E.J. Ashworth and P.V. Spade, 'Logic in Late Medieval Oxford', *Late Medieval Oxford*, ed. Catto and Evans, pp. 35–64.

[7] On Stevens, see Emden, *BRUO*, vol. III, p. 1774; M.D. Legge, *Anglo-Norman Letters and Petitions* (Anglo-Norman Text Society, Oxford, 1941), and A.L. Brown, 'The Latin Letters in MS All Souls 182', *EHR*, LXXXVII (1972), pp. 565–73.

accomplished tract, the *Gesta Henrici Quinti*. Stevens was verging on professional expertise in an emerging new career category, that of the secretary. Charles Everitt has traced the beginnings of the secretary's expertise, the composition of documents to influence and persuade, or at least to impress, to the years about 1400; it is marked by the appearance of letter-books in which rhetorical rather than legal or dictaminal forms were preserved, most of which were compiled by clerks in the king's service, especially officials of the privy seal, or in the employ of leading, usually curial, bishops. English secretaries were somewhat behind the officials of the French crown, and well behind their Italian counterparts, in adopting the humanist Latin which became standard form for three centuries of polite communication; when they did, in the 1430s, graduates in the service of Humphrey, duke of Gloucester, led the way.[8]

But the most instructive example of an Oxford graduate acting as secretary to a single master is that of William Worcester, the antiquary. After becoming master of arts about 1439, at the charge of the great captain, Sir John Fastolf, he served his master as man of business, letter-writer and possibly even astrologer; he certainly made a table of fixed stars for Fastolf's use. McFarlane has defined the nature of his services: a great landowner's 'riding-servant', whose 'views on building-costs and estate finance are those of an expert ... he put his knowledge of genealogy, heraldry and the laws governing the descent of land to his master's profit'.[9] These valuable attributes were, of course, only the half of it. Fastolf may have retired from active service, but he tried hard to keep some influence on affairs and especially to vindicate his dubious conduct at the battle of Patay. His secretary's historical collections – and they extended beyond contemporary events to ancient Roman examples and moral precepts, much in the style of Leonardo Bruni – were to a very large extent put together to justify the old captain's deeds of war and to fortify his opinions on the defence of Normandy. Like his business dealings, Worcester's historical work was based on specific and exact knowledge. It was also capable of being used to a purpose: to make a case, in his *Boke of Noblesse*, for Fastolf's political views, which it is clear he genuinely shared. Authentic historical knowledge could, as Worcester put it, 'courage and comfort noble men in armes to be in perpetuite of remembraunce for here noble dedis, as right convenient is soo to bee'.[10] His final service was to indulge his master's literary tastes, which were largely French, translating for him Cicero on friendship and old age. Did Fastolf's investment in an Oxford education for his servant pay off? One is obliged to conclude that it did, like most of that canny speculator's investments. Scholarly exactitude, the capacity to marshal facts in support of a case, broad interest in the world – Worcester must have acquired these qualities in Oxford, or at least honed them there. The value added was substantial.

[8] Everitt, 'Eloquence as Profession and Art'; R. Weiss, *Humanism in England during the Fifteenth Century* (Oxford, 1941, reprinted 1967), pp. 71–83.

[9] K.B. McFarlane, 'William Worcester: a Preliminary Survey' in his *England in the Fifteenth Century* (London, 1981), pp. 206–7, originally published in *Studies Presented to Hilary Jenkinson*, ed. J.C. Davies (London, 1957), pp. 196–221.

[10] William Worcester, *Boke of Noblesse*, ed. J.G. Nichols (Roxburgh Club, London, 1860), p. 1.

The secretary, in his informal fifteenth-century phase, was an officer of the household of his master, as Worcester's case shows. The households of some fourteenth-century noble clerks, such as the Trillek and Charlton brothers, impinged on Oxford directly by occupying large premises, Trillock's Inn and Charlton's Inn. They tended to bring companions with them, who were also educated in the schools. But in the fifteenth century noble parents preferred their sons at Oxford to occupy lodgings in existing halls or colleges, and to partake in the way of life and discipline increasingly elaborated in those establishments as appropriate to scholars. The young Richard Holland, son of Thomas, earl of Kent, lived in Canterbury College in 1394, with Master John Giles, who had just ceased to be a fellow of New College, as his tutor: an arrangement seems therefore to have been made with a scholar already studying at Oxford.[11] A longer connexion was put to use by Lord Tiptoft when Master John Hurley, who was living in University College, was appointed to tutor his son John, later earl of Worcester, in 1441. Hurley had been indebted to the elder Tiptoft for his first benefice, conferred in 1432, and was prepared to serve the younger as late as 1459, when he evidently accompanied the newly created earl on his Jerusalem pilgrimage and studies in Padua. At his death he left his patron a gilt cup and a property in Leicestershire. The latter item, however, implies that Hurley was not a mere lackey of the Tiptoft family. As a bachelor of canon law he had independent standing; though he owed his principal benefice at Hanslope in Buckinghamshire to the Tiptofts, his landed inheritance suggests that he was closer to being their associate, though admittedly not of their exalted standing, and not a household servant.[12] The younger Tiptoft's probably legal studies in Padua may have been facilitated by Hurley's own expertise in the field. These details define the benefit of university study as the elder Tiptoft must have envisaged it in 1441: life under the discipline of a college or academic hall under a tutor of academic standing, but known to the family, and a chance for his son to acquire a love of books and a trained intelligence for a career in public service like his own. If the younger Tiptoft's fine Italian hand eventually got the better of his political career when his somewhat Paduan methods of summary justice (as one contemporary stigmatized them) made him too many enemies at home, it was because he had learned too much.[13] He was a dangerous example of the mental independence and receptivity to new experience conferred by a university education.

Tiptoft's study under Hurley exemplifies the relationship between university masters and great patrons: superficially one of service, in effect it was a contract between patrons with material benefits and influence to confer, and careerists with professional skills as well as more general educational benefits to pass on. There are numerous examples throughout the fifteenth century of scholars

---

[11] Emden, *BRUO*, vol. II, pp. 951–2, 769.

[12] Emden, *BRUO*, vol. II, p. 988; vol. III, pp. 1877–8; on Hanslope, to which Hurley was preferred in February 1450, see *VCH Buckinghamshire*, vol. IV, pp. 350, 361; its manor and advowson were part of the dower of Cicely, dowager duchess of Warwick (d. 28 July 1450), who had married the younger Tiptoft in 1449.

[13] John Warkworth, *Chronicle of the first thirteen years of the Reign of King Edward the Fourth*, ed. J.O. Halliwell (Camden Society, London, 1839), p. 5.

endowed by the nobility, but such scholarships seem to have been acts of charity more than investments in future service. The Mortimer family evidently made a practice in the late fourteenth century of sending men of Usk to Oxford out of the issues of that lordship: at least, they sent the ambitious young Adam Porter, better known as Adam of Usk. Usk, writing in his chronicle or memoirs, recognized his obligation with an encomium on the Mortimers and their ancestors, and indeed served Earl Roger at least briefly in 1397, but his main line of advancement as a notary, doctor of laws and advocate in the court of arches owed nothing to them, and in its turn contributed virtually nothing to their rather patchy fortunes in the half-century after 1375. The one, and for Adam crucially important, exception was another act of charity on the part of Sir Edward Charlton, who had married into the Mortimers: in 1408, when Adam could do nothing for him, he intervened with the crown to obtain a pardon for the errant cleric.[14] The influence of the occasional northern peer, the lords Fitzhugh or the earls of Westmorland, can be detected in the selection of secular scholars for Durham College, a mixed society in which the scholars shared with monks. But it does not seem possible to trace any of their future careers and affiliations.[15] William Worcester, at the age of seventeen, was already the scholar of Sir John Fastolf at Oxford in 1432; he must have entered his master's service when he came down, and served the knight not only until the latter's death in 1459, but until his affairs were settled in 1477: virtually a lifetime. Of all the known Oxford scholars in the service of the great, Worcester came closest to being a household servant, living with Sir John ten years, by his own reckoning, from 1449 to 1459.[16]

These examples do not advance us much further than Jean Dunbabin's definition of graduate service in 1300: desirable but not essential. Was this also the case of the doctors of the higher faculties in their professional capacities? It is perhaps useful to bear in mind the larger European context here. The century 1350–1450 was perhaps the high tide of professional esteem for doctors of the learned laws in the courts, cities and universities of Europe: Baldus of Sassoferrato, John of Legnano, Antonio de Butrio, Zabarella, Panormitanus. They were rich men able to dictate their terms of service to their many clients, and to move from chair to chair, and consultancy to consultancy, at will. The popes of the schism sought their judgement on the rightful pontiff, kings on the rights and wrongs of war.[17] The richest plums of ecclesiastical patronage were available for those of them, by no means all, who were in orders; the college of cardinals was full of lawyers, and eight of the twelve occupants of the pontifical throne, or thrones, between 1352 and 1447 were doctors of laws. Over the Alps, civilians and canonists lacked the openings to market their skills so effectively, and doctors like Gilles Bellemère, Jean le Fèvre or Rodrigo Sanchez de Arévalo took service under various lords, the Avignon popes, the dukes of Anjou or Brittany,

---

[14] *The Chronicle of Adam Usk 1377–1421*, ed. C. Given-Wilson (Oxford, 1997), pp. 38–48, 238–40; Emden, *BRUO*, vol. III, pp. 1502, 1937–8.

[15] E.g. Richard Wright (Emden, *BRUO*, vol. III, p. 2097); Thomas Marley (ibid., vol. II, p. 1224).

[16] Emden, *BRUO*, vol. III, pp. 2086–7; McFarlane, 'William Worcester', pp. 202–6.

[17] W. Ullmann, *Law and Politics in the Middle Ages* (London, 1975), pp. 104–16, 184–9.

the counts palatine or of Württemberg, or Spanish grandees like the Mendoza dukes of Infantado, as well as the kings of France and the emperors. Opportunities for service were not limited to enrolment in the bureaucracies of sovereign powers: when Gutierre Alvarez de Toledo, bishop of Palencia, took possession of the not particularly prominent or developed lordship of Alba de Tormes in 1430, his agent was Dr Pedro Gonzalez, *amenistrador e poseedor e juez* (administrator, proprietor, judge) with all the powers and duties appropriate to colonial rule.[18] Michael Jones has pointed out, similarly, the openings for doctors of laws in the government of Brittany, as has Peter Moraw for the service of the Wittelsbach in the Rhineland.[19]

Oxford and Cambridge were entirely up to date in their fostering of the learned laws, and their alumni, like those of their counterparts across the Channel, were among the busiest, and were certainly the most highly rewarded, of public servants. Robert Hallum, Henry Chichele, Philip Morgan and William Lyndwood combined royal service and ecclesiastical office not only to forge for themselves eminently successful careers culminating in the episcopate, but cooperated to bring into being, under Henry V, a highly articulated and intelligent imperial regime.[20] It is striking, however, how limited, if brilliant, their career opportunities were in comparison to French or Spanish doctors of laws. The golden road to advancement in England lay in the practice of the ecclesiastical courts, especially the Ely consistory court and the various courts of Canterbury, at the turn of the fifteenth century. Advocates in these courts were well placed to take advantage of new openings in the courts of chivalry and admiralty and in the equitable jurisdiction of chancery, and to find employment in the diplomacy of the Lancastrian kings. What they did not find, to all appearances, was the chance to serve the nobility in their councils and administrative bodies. Carole Rawcliffe and others have emphasised the crucial role of baronial councils in the politics and equally the law of the fifteenth century, and the emergence of subcommittees, the 'council learned' on which lawyers on permanent or occasional retainer might sit. Civilians and canonists did not sit with them. For example, the composition of the council of Humphrey Stafford, duke of Buckingham, can be reconstructed in unusual detail from the Stafford papers, and the absence of any university-trained lawyers is striking, in contrast to the service of noblemen of equal standing and wealth in France or Italy.[21] There are exceptions. John of Gaunt employed doctors of laws such as Dr William Assheton, chancellor of the duchy of Lancaster, after 1385, and sent him as a

---

[18] J.M. Monsalvo Antón, *El sistema politico concejil: el ejemplo del señorio medieval de Alba de Tormes* (Salamanca, 1988), p. 157 n. 37.

[19] M.C.E. Jones, 'Education in Brittany' in his *The Creation of Brittany* (London, 1988), pp. 321–6; P. Moraw, 'Beamtentum und Rat König Ruprechts', *Zeitschrift für die Geschichte des Oberrheins*, 116 (1968), 59–126.

[20] J.I. Catto, 'The King's Servants', *Henry V: the Practice of Kingship*, ed. G.L. Harriss (Oxford, 1985), pp. 75–95.

[21] C. Rawcliffe, 'Baronial Councils in the Later Middle Ages', *Patronage, Pedigree and Power in Later Medieval England*, ed. C. Ross (Gloucester, 1979), pp. 87–108, and her *The Staffords, Earls of Stafford and Dukes of Buckingham, 1394–1521* (Cambridge, 1978), pp. 219–25.

representative to his rival, John I of Castile. Assheton was not a full-time Lancastrian servant; he combined his duties with the post of vicar-general of the bishop of Lichfield, which was, admittedly, a temporary appointment.[22] The duchy of Lancaster was the nearest equivalent in England to continental lordships like that of the duke of Burgundy or the duke of Savoy. The other exceptions were in the service of princes of the blood: Dr Thomas Southam, a clerk of Edmund, duke of York, in 1389, among many other employments; Dr William Feriby in the service of Henry, prince of Wales, about 1402, and Dr John Macworth, his chancellor, in 1406; Dr Edward Dauntesey, chancellor of Thomas, duke of Clarence, in 1412; two distinguished New College lawyers, Dr John Fyton who had been at Pisa and Constance and Dr Thomas Bekynton, a future intimate royal adviser, in the service of Humphrey, duke of Gloucester, in the 1420s, and Dr Richard Leyot, chancellor of John, duke of Bedford, from 1419 to about 1426.[23]

It is fairly clear that these doctors of laws were in no way beholden to their princely employers, since they had other business to pursue. They were independent experts who could be called on from time to time when their professional advice and expertise was required. This was probably not very often. The nobility's testamentary affairs, suits in the church courts and especially at the Roman curia might bring in business to doctors of the learned laws, but the comparative lack of jurisdiction of their honours and liberties, and the role of English custom and the common law in cases where they could exercise it, must have limited its scope. The role of baronial councils as arbitrators might in theory have given them an opening on the basis of equitable judgement, like the court of chancery, but in practice the parties seem to have been content with English custom and common lawyers.[24] In stark contrast to the diffuse opportunities for civilians in France, in England they were concentrated in the service of the crown and the church courts, where public business was also transacted. Unlike the great nobility of France, English grandees did not send representatives abroad to further their business, with the partial and semi-public exception of princes such as John of Gaunt, claimant to the Castilian throne, John, duke of Bedford, as regent of France, Humphrey, duke of Gloucester, the most continental of English dukes, in pursuit of his Netherlandish claims, and Richard, duke of York, as lieutenant of Normandy, when he aspired to make a royal marriage for his eldest son. The difference in the career patterns of English and French, or German, civilians or canonists brings into sharp focus the greater dominance of the king's government over his subjects in England, eclipsing any lesser jurisdiction, in comparison with the multiplicity of lordships over the Channel to which landowners might attach themselves and jurists offer their professional services.

So we can see the English canonists and civilians of the fifteenth century fairly clearly as distinct in opportunity, but not in training and culture, from their

---

[22] Emden, *BRUO*, vol. I, pp. 64–5.

[23] Emden, *BRUO*, vol. III, p. 1733 (Southam); vol. II, pp. 678–9 (Feriby); vol. III, pp. 2193–4 (Macworth); vol. I, p. 546 (Dauntesey); vol. II, pp. 737–8 (Fyton); vol. I, pp. 157–9 (Bekynton); vol. III, pp. 2189–90 (Leyot).

[24] E. Powell, 'Arbitration and the Law in England in the Late Middle Ages', *TRHS*, fifth series 33 (1983), 49–67, cf. 59, 64–6.

counterparts across the Channel. They were the epitome of a professional culture, with an established and recognized form of training which was common to all universities, a clear pattern of advancement and a developing professional ethic expressed in the notion of equity, or in contemporary language conscience. They were not, however, the only profession to emerge from the university world. The professional physician with a medical degree also made his debut in English society during the century. In medicine as in law, Oxford had been eclipsed by the much larger and more advanced centres of study in Bologna, Montpellier and Paris. Although several scholars in the thirteenth-century university with a knowledge of academic physic (essentially, the works of Galen together with the Arabic writers and some other Greek authors transmitted through the eleventh-century school of Salerno) asserted the pre-eminence of learned medicine in England, they had to compete with a folk medicine going back to pre-conquest times, and practised by unlicensed but popular medicine-men who operated from compendia of empirical remedies. These writers, such as the encyclopaedist, Bartholomaeus Anglicus, and Roger Bacon, who knew something of most subjects, typically treated medicine as part of a wider body of natural philosophy.[25] They were in no position to assert control over the practice of medicine. In the fourteenth and fifteenth centuries, by contrast, a professional practice of medicine centred on the universities did develop in England, largely on parallel lines to the faculty in Montpellier and elsewhere. After 1420 the physicians made a concerted attempt to establish a nationally organized profession, in which the influence of their patients and patrons was crucial. The theme of service, therefore, is a central factor in the development of English medicine.

The development of a standardized medicine had depended, in Italy and France, on the close relation of academic physicians with influential patrons. The medical faculty at Bologna had established its dominance through the pressure of its large and diffuse body of powerful patients; in Paris by contrast, the same result had been brought about by the presence of the king's court, and in Montpellier the patronage of the papal court at Avignon had ensured the control of practice by the medical university. In the absence of a court or powerful clientèle in the vicinity of Oxford, the best the fourteenth-century medical faculty could do was to establish a system of certification for local practitioners, who were required to have qualified for the degree of bachelor of medicine. But by the 1380s Oxford physicians seem to have become fashionable in London society, led by the young Henry of Derby whose wife Mary had rather poor health. Geoffrey Melton was fetched on several occasions from Oxford, and Dr John Malverne probably set up practice in London, where he served Henry both as earl of Derby and as King Henry IV.[26] Royal recognition of Oxford medicine was confirmed by Henry V's medical arrangements for his Agincourt campaign: a double contract was made, one with the London surgeon, Thomas Morstede, and another with the Oxford physician, Nicholas Colnet.[27] Though

---

[25] Getz, 'Faculty of Medicine', pp. 376–80.

[26] Emden, *BRUO*, vol. II, p. 1257 (Malverne); p. 1211 (Melton); Talbot and Hammond, *Medical Practitioners*, pp. 53–4, 166–7.

[27] Emden, *BRUO*, vol. I, p. 469 (Colnet); Talbot and Hammond, *Medical Practitioners*, pp. 350–2; Getz, 'Faculty of Medicine', pp. 393–4.

it would be fanciful to attribute to them much effect on field medicine in the dysentery-ridden army at Harfleur, Henry V's patronage may have led the Oxford-trained London physicians to attempt a general scheme of certification, together with the London surgeons. The leading spirit in this venture was Dr Gilbert Kymer, who had been senior proctor at Oxford in 1412 and who was medical adviser to Humphrey, duke of Gloucester. In 1423, doubtless with the backing of the duke, now the leading councillor of the minority government, they set up the so-called 'conjoint college of physicians and surgeons' with Kymer as rector, with the power to license physicians who had reached the standard of a bachelor of medicine, even if they had not studied at a university. If the scheme collapsed in the following year through the opposition of the barber-surgeons, it still marked the beginning of an official, state-backed medical art, the core of which was the medical faculties of Oxford and Cambridge.[28] Doctors of medicine, far more directly than doctors of law, were in the service of the nobility and the court, without whom their attempt to set a national medical standard could not have been contemplated. But Kymer, close as he remained to Duke Humphrey, was no household servant or retainer; he was an independent practitioner with many patients. His service to his patron, and probably the patron's own preferences, led him to give medicine as professional and national a base as was possible in that era.

Medicine and law by any definition were professions. Was theology, the remaining higher faculty? Not by the criteria of 1300, when it was generally regarded as the completion of the arts degree, a general art in the Aristotelian sense; the philosophical issues discussed in arts faculties were simply taken up on a more metaphysical level by theologians. But after 1370 theologians had participated in the improving fortunes of the other higher faculties; their value in contemporary eyes can be measured in the numerous new faculties of theology in both older universities, such as Bologna, and new foundations, Prague or Heidelberg for instance; and in England, secular clergy were now taking theology degrees in large numbers. The content of theological education, by 1400, was no longer primarily speculative. Moral and pastoral teaching, based on biblical study, was the core of theological education in the lectures of William Woodford and his opponent, John Wyclif, and in the sermons of Wyclif's disciple, Philip Repingdon.[29] The value of theology degrees was clearly perceived outside universities. So could theologians provide service to lay patrons individually, or was their learning, like the learning of civilians, primarily of use to the body corporate of state or church? The second of these alternatives can be given substance by the palpable demand for preachers by fifteenth-century bishops, acting in their public capacity and in accordance with government policy. Repingdon's systematic appointment of Oxford theologians to preach in his diocese of Lincoln; the extensive preaching tours of members of the chapter of Salisbury like Dr Thomas Cyrcetur; the filling of London pulpits by fiery popular preachers like Dr William Lichfield at All Hallows the Great with his 3,083 sermons, between 1425 and 1448; the universally shocked reaction when Bishop

---

[28] Getz, 'Faculty of medicine', pp. 400–3.
[29] J.I. Catto, 'Wyclif and Wycliffism', *Late Medieval Oxford*, ed. Catto and Evans, pp. 196–8, 226–7, 256–9.

Pecock dared to doubt their efficacy; and the sheer number of surviving fifteenth-century sermon cycles bear witness to the powerful and sustained moral leadership assumed by the Lancastrian religious establishment.[30] On this basis the service of theologians is not unlike that of civil and canon lawyers: primarily public service, over which looms the heavy presence of England's uniquely well-articulated government.

After making due allowance for all this, however, there remains the role of the confessor, the intimate religious adviser who might become an integral part of a great household. Here above all, the casuistry of an Oxford doctor of theology could do service to the tender consciences of the great. In the 1390s the Franciscan Dr William Woodford described the penances of road and bridge repair he had set to a lady whom he confessed; this was evidently Margaret Marshal, duchess of Norfolk, whose 1394 account book does indeed contain such items. Woodford evidently stayed frequently at her residence at Framlingham Castle, where he wrote two of his books, but his main base was the London Franciscan convent.[31] Of its nature, his service must be independently grounded, and his quite separate intellectual life and his lively controversies confirm it. In the following decades the nobility, and increasingly their social inferiors, had ample invitation to examine their consciences and develop an interior spiritual life, and references to their personal confessors multiply. Great patrons tended to confess to doctors of theology; Richard, duke of York, and his duchess, Cicely, went to Dr John Keninghale, the prior provincial of the Carmelites, before the latter's death in 1451.[32] As they were largely in France or Ireland and he was a busy man resident in London or Norwich, his service to them must have been occasional, and can hardly have affected a way of life entirely separate from theirs. The officially sponsored foundations of Sheen Charterhouse and the Brigittine community of priests and nuns at Syon may even have provided an approved pool of learned confessors. The confessor of Margaret, duchess of Clarence, was probably Simon Wynter, a priest of Syon; Cardinal Beaufort's was William Mede, a Carthusian of Sheen.[33] We do not know whether they were doctors of theology, but they clearly had some theological training, and above all experience in the contemplative theology which may have been the medium through which the learning of the schools impinged on the penitent in the confessional. In 1441 Henry Percy, earl of Northumberland, had as chaplain and probably confessor a Carmelite bachelor of theology,

---

[30] S. Forde, 'Writings of a Reformer: A Look at Sermon Studies and Bible Studies through Repyngdon's *Sermones super evangelia dominicalia*' (unpublished Ph.D. thesis, University of Birmingham, 1985), vol. I, pp. 293–9; R.M. Ball, 'Thomas Cyrcetur, a Fifteenth-Century Theologian and Preacher', *Journal of Ecclesiastical History*, 37 (1986), 205–39; Ball, 'The Opponents of Bishop Pecok', ibid., 48 (1997), 234–5; H.L. Spencer, *English Preaching in the Late Middle Ages* (Oxford, 1993).

[31] Woodford, *Defensorium Mendicitatis*, Cambridge University Library, MS Ff.1.21, f. 120r; Woodford, *De Sacramento Altaris*, Bodleian Library, Oxford, MS Bodley 703, f. 148v; College of Arms, MS Arundel 49, f. 38r (accounts of Margaret Marshal).

[32] Emden, *BRUO*, vol. II, pp. 1035–6.

[33] A.I. Doyle, 'Publication by Members of the Religious Orders', *Book Production and Publishing in Britain, 1375–1475*, ed. J. Griffiths and D. Pearsall (Cambridge, 1989), pp. 113, 116–7; G.L. Harriss, *Cardinal Beaufort* (Oxford, 1988), pp. 377–8.

Richard Misyn, who is best known as the translator of Richard Rolle's *De emendatione vitae* and *Incendium amoris*.[34] It was perhaps in the form of Rolle's doctrine that learned confessors could most easily put their expertise to the service of their penitent patrons.

The evidence indicates that the service done by the graduates of the higher faculties to lay patrons was a matter effectively of contract: not, of course, between equals in contemporary eyes, but between parties who made the arrangement each from an independent standpoint. McFarlane emphasized the fragility of bonds dependent on the giving and receiving of fees, which by the mid-century had become so indiscriminate that the lords who paid them could not expect to command the exclusive service of their beneficiaries. The civil lawyers, doctors and confessors to whom they occasionally resorted certainly took fees or alms from several of them simultaneously. This was not merely a matter of calculation, as might be expected from the henchmen and local agents of the dukes of Suffolk or earls of Warwick, but a consequence of the recognized professional standing of doctors, indeed bachelors, of the higher faculties, established by the beginning of the century, and indeed of at least one outcrop of an arts training, the profession of secretary, which would attain something of the same position, though not so eminent, by about 1440. In contrast to the Tuddenhams and the Heydons, the professional ethic of the learned callings demanded that they should exercise their skills on behalf of all comers, provided of course that they could pay the fee. There was another distinctive feature of their position, distinctive too in relation to the French and German counterparts whom otherwise they closely resembled. In England the king's government was overwhelmingly the greatest user of their services, which consequently took on a public character. Even medicine, the most individual of services, was almost subject to a system of public licensing under the guidance of Dr Gilbert Kymer in the early 1420s. The expert element in the king's council was represented by lawyers and theologians in clerk's orders who were likely to be, or to become, bishops. The ethic of public service they seem to have developed in the execution of Henry V's will is implied in the preface to Lyndwood's *Provinciale* and in the foundation charter of All Souls: the gift of hard work and technical expertise in the cause of their master and the state. In their occasional service to Duke Humphrey or other potentates they could offer advice from an independent standpoint. It would be pointless to seek to attach them to the affinity of any individual patron. Even a secretary like William Worcester, who did serve only one master and who gave him invaluable and loyal service, rendered it only in office hours; his leisure time recognized no master but the pleasures of poetry and antiquarian inquiry. If these too were of service to Sir John Fastolf from time to time, that was the free gift of friendship and affection that, if not so obviously, were in reality just as well-represented in the fifteenth century as any obligation of service.

[34] Emden, *BRUO*, vol. II, p. 1286.

V

THE HOUSEHOLD RETINUE OF HENRY V AND THE ETHOS OF ENGLISH PUBLIC LIFE[1]

David Morgan

IN 1465 the judges of England assembled in Exchequer Chamber delivered their verdict upon the issue before us in this conference. They found that it really would not do, for this word 'servant' (they pronounced) does not show the condition, state or mystery of a man, for everyone who is in service – whether lords in the service of the king, knights, esquires, gentlemen, yeomen, grooms, ladies, damsels, other women, priests, friars or others being under a master in service – is properly and can be called 'servant'; and every hired labourer or craftsman or artificer is for the time being a servant. The judges parenthetically agreed that 'labourer', despite its lack of such occupational specificity as 'delver', 'diker', 'tyler', was none the less an acceptable designation under the Statute of Additions for the various callings comprehended by the phrase 'common labourers'; that term did not raise those more disturbing issues raised by 'servant', for (they expostulated) 'labourer' does not stretch so generally as 'servant', for every gentleman being in service could be 'servant' as much as every yeoman, groom, labourer or artificer; a gentleman of whatever estate, were he to go at the plough or were he to have nothing in his purse, still he is a gentleman; if he were in service he might be called 'servant', but he should not be given that addition under the Statute, for any man being in service whether lord, knight, gentleman, yeoman (etc.) might be called 'servant', and therefore the term is too general to be a good addition. Case dismissed.[2]

Did the judges here manage their usual feat of being wrong for all the right reasons? Rosemary Horrox has observed, 'Service has some claim to be considered the dominant ethic of the middle ages'.[3] The word is ubiquitous; whatever its connotations, it rings as a refrain through the gamut of social life, and stretches across any distinction we are conditioned to make between 'private' and 'public' spheres. Precisely because service was so pervasive might be thought the best of reasons why we, if not they, should take it seriously; but if so, we need to take equally seriously the implication of the judges' train of thought

---

[1] An earlier version of this paper was given at the Seminar in Medieval History at All Souls College, Oxford: I am grateful to Rees Davies for his initial incitement, and to the Warden, Dr J.C. Davis, for his subsequent encouragement.

[2] *Les Reports des Cases en Ley en le cinque an du roy Edward le Quart, communement appelle Long Quinto* (London, 1680), pp. 32–4.

[3] R. Horrox, 'Service', *Fifteenth-Century Attitudes: Perceptions of Society in Late Medieval England*, ed. Horrox (Cambridge, 1994), p. 61.

that service is something adventitious rather than constitutive of a person's identity. If such a man as John Norreys of Ockwells (to take an instance not entirely at random) – yeoman and usher of the king's chamber, esquire of the king's body, keeper of the great wardrobe, treasurer of the queen's chamber – not only styles himself 'servant', but chooses to emblazon the windows of his house with the motto 'Feythfully serve', is he presenting us with the reality or just the rhetoric of things?[4] It is a question I shall seek to pursue with reference to the service elicited by a master who focuses much of the rhetoric, indeed – but perhaps also much of the reality – of fifteenth-century public life.

*   *   *

I start with perhaps the single most rhetorical of fifteenth-century English public monuments. Between 1437 and 1450, Henry V's feoffees (and more particularly his uncle and servant, Henry, Cardinal Beaufort) carried through the project, stipulated in the king's will, of the building of his chantry chapel at Westminster – an architecturally assertive construction (Gerald Harriss's word is 'grandiose') in which, aloft over his tomb and the shrine of Edward the Confessor, the king's shield, helmet and saddle were displayed in a setting whose sculptural iconography gave elaborate expression to an enhanced ideology of monarchy both English and French, and within which the propitiation of three daily masses were to be offered, and be seen by those standing below in the nave to be offered, over and above the earlier 20,000 masses whose celebration Henry had required as soon as possible after his death. Brynmor Pugh has darkly commented: 'No one else in medieval England ever thought it necessary to invest so heavily in the purchase of paradise; even Henry VII (who had a great deal on his conscience) calculated that 10,000 requiem masses would suffice'.[5] Simultaneously, Archbishop Chichele – Cardinal Beaufort's fellow as both feoffee and godfather to Henry's son – in 1438 began the building of that other monument expressing a commemorative consciousness of Henry V, though doing so in a manner designed to preserve the memory not solely of Henry himself, but also of that wider company of those who served him: 'that certain perpetual college ... within Oxford and its university, to study and to pray for the king's and archbishop's well-being while they live, and after their deaths for their souls and the souls of the most famous king Henry V, Thomas late duke of Clarence, the dukes, earls, barons, knights, armigerous men and other noblemen and commoners who have ended their lives in the king's and his father's reign in the French wars'.[6]

In the case of written rhetoric, it was in those same years of the building of the chantry monuments at Westminster and Oxford that biographical writing

---

[4] E. Green, 'The Identification of the Eighteen Worthies Commemorated in the Heraldic Glass in the Hall Windows of Ockwells Manor House, in the Parish of Bray, in Berkshire', *Archaeologia*, 56 (1899), 323–36. See also above p. xxiii.

[5] W.H. St.John Hope, 'The Funeral, Monument, and Chantry Chapel of King Henry the Fifth', *Archaeologia*, 65 (1913–14), 129–86; G.L. Harriss, *Cardinal Beaufort: a Study of Lancastrian Ascendancy and Decline* (Oxford, 1988), pp. 324–5.

[6] E.F. Jacob, 'The Warden's Text of the Foundation Statutes of All Souls College, Oxford', *The Antiquaries Journal*, 15 (1935), 420–31; J. Catto, 'The World of Henry Chichele and the Foundation of All Souls', *Unarmed Soldiery: Studies in the Early History of All Souls College* (the Chichele Lectures 1993–94, Oxford, 1996), pp. 1–13.

on Henry V was magnified into what became an exceptional – and exceptionally eulogistic – departure from the English historiographical norm, in which such individual 'lives' and 'deeds' were rare.[7] Stylistically, the efforts of those who commissioned their works were not ideally well rewarded: the 'Life' by Tito Livio, commissioned in 1437 by Humphrey of Gloucester, is not the finest flower of Italian humanist panegyric; and the partly derivative *Vita et gesta* (the pseudo-Elmham text), instigated by Walter, Lord Hungerford, circulating in a revised dedication to the king's former tutor and physician, John Somerset, by 1446, for which another immigrant author has been postulated,[8] adopts a particularly orotund variant of the 'flowery beauty of words'.[9] The pseudo-Elmham text drew on the memories of those with the king on his last French expedition; Tito Livio used material such as the celebratory poem on the siege of Rouen, though such products of Henry's own lifetime as Thomas Elmham's *Liber metricus* and the narrative of 1413–16 (the *Gesta Henrici Quinti*) – both angled more especially towards an ecclesiastical readership, whether at home or abroad – were not so utilized.[10] But at least as significant as moulders of contemporary opinion and attitudes are the vernacular writings, both prose and verse, in which a sense of Henry's purpose and policy were transmitted – fully in keeping with his own chosen practice, recorded by the London Brewers'

---

[7] See A. Gransden, *Historical Writing in England, II, c. 1307 to the Early Sixteenth Century* (London, 1982), pp. 194–219 ('The Biographies of Henry V') who rightly urges that 'it is necessary to discover why for over a century Henry V's reputation evoked so much panegyrical literature', p. 197. In doing so the closely connected matter of the king's own self-publicity requires attention: see J.A. Doig, 'Propaganda and Truth: Henry V's Royal Progress in 1421', *Nottingham Medieval Studies*, 40 (1996), 167–79.

[8] *Tito Livio Foro-Iuliensis Vita Henrici Quinti*, ed. T. Hearne (Oxford, 1716); *Thomas de Elmham Vita et Gesta Henrici Quinti*, ed. T. Hearne (Oxford, 1727). See David Rundle, 'On the Difference between Virtue and Weiss: Humanist Texts in England during the Fifteenth Century', *Courts, Counties and the Capital in the Later Middle Ages*, ed. D.E.S. Dunn (Stroud, 1996), pp. 188–91. I am grateful to Dr Rundle for drawing my attention to the humanistic *comparatio* written 1449–51 by or for John Manyngham, in which Henry is made to compare himself favourably to Alexander, Hannibal and Scipio, and to the interesting interpretation of this text (printed in W. O'Sullivan, 'John Manyngham: an Early Oxford Humanist', *Bodleian Library Record*, 7 (1962), pp. 37–9) in his unpublished thesis, 'Of Republics and Tyrants: Aspects of Quattrocentro Humanist Writings and their Reception in England, *c.* 1400 – *c.* 1460' (unpublished D.Phil. thesis, University of Oxford, 1997), pp. 279–83, 348–54.

[9] E.F. Jacob, 'Verborum florida venustas', in his *Essays in the Conciliar Epoch* (Manchester, 1963), pp. 185–206; the phrase occurs in texts of 1417 and 1426: *The Register of Henry Chichele, Archbishop of Canterbury 1414–1443*, ed. Jacob, Canterbury and York Society, vol. 1 (1943), p. 98; vol. 3 (1945), p. 36.

[10] J.F. Roskell and F. Taylor, 'The Authorship and Purpose of the *Gesta Henrici Quinti*', *BJRL*, 53 (1970–71), 428–64, and ibid., 54 (1971–72), 223–40. The *Gesta* survives in only two manuscripts, although Elmham's *Liber Metricus* (which used it) survives in nine, and was used by John Capgrave for his *Liber de illustribus Henricis*, written 1446–7. The chronicle of John Strecche – altogether eulogistic in its commentary on Henry V – has also been thought akin to Elmham in tone, although in genre it is derivative from the *Brut*: see F. Taylor, 'The Chronicle of John Strecche for the Reign of Henry V (1414–1422)', *BJRL*, 16 (1932), 137–87.

Company: 'whereas our mother-tongue, to wit the English tongue, hath in modern days begun to be honourably enlarged and adorned, for that our most excellent lord, King Henry V, hath in his letters missive and divers affairs touching his own person, more willingly chosen to declare the secrets of his will, and for the better understanding of his people, hath with a diligent mind procured the common idiom to be commended by the exercise of writing'.[11] Those English-language proclamations, and letters missive under the king's signet announcing the progress of his enterprise in France, are among the formative exercises which over the following generation brought into being an English idiom of public life.[12] This shaping of English as a language of politics – so much later than is the case with many other European vernaculars – deserves more of our attention than it has yet received; but we may at least feel sure that when that has happened, Henry V will be seen to have played his not inconsiderable part, not only as a user of the idiom, but also as a focus of the thoughts and feelings which the idiom came to express.

Without break from the propagandist writing of his lifetime, the verse and prose of the following years maintained Henry's significance as a point of reference in current concerns. Its public projection in the continuing flow of Lydgate's verse for a generation after 'the excitation of King Harry' had been responsible for *The Troy Book* and *The Life of Our Lady*, clearly made itself heard as a vocal line at least as long-drawn-out as those requiem masses; and if James Simpson is right in his recent suggestion as to the dating and intention of Lydgate's *The Siege of Thebes*,[13] we may have to contemplate a further dimension of coded (but presumably to contemporaries, understood) commentary woven into the texture of the 'political poetics' of the years in which such backward reference to Henry became a frequent topos. In prose – but prose which, from time to time, breaks off to give us the text of those much-publicized 'ballads' on notable events – the *Brut* chronicle still awaits proper assessment as a vehicle for contemporary attitudes and also as a tool for fashioning those attitudes, not least in these decades when its diffusion in variant recensions achieved what our French confrères would surely see as *démarrage* and also as a prime candidate for the attention of an *Institut de recherche des textes*.[14] Any such assessment seems to me unlikely to support the view that the *Brut*'s 'patriotic and chivalric tone' was muted by the enterprise of the London scriveners who from 1414 generated the further tangle of London narrative vernacular writing. The London reading public seems to have been receptive to the same

[11] *A Book of London English 1384–1425*, ed. R.W. Chambers and M. Daunt (Oxford, 1931), p. 139; for correspondence and proclamations relating to the war in France, see ibid., pp. 64–89.

[12] *An Anthology of Chancery English*, ed. J.H. Fisher, M. Richardson and J.L. Fisher (Knoxville, 1984); M. Richardson, 'Henry V, the English Chancery, and Chancery English', *Speculum*, 55 (1980), 726–50.

[13] J. Simpson, ' "Dysemol daies and fatal houres": Lydgate's Destruction of Thebes and Chaucer's Knight's Tale', *The Long Fifteenth Century: Essays for Douglas Gray*, ed. H. Cooper and S. Mapstone (Oxford, 1997), pp. 15–16.

[14] For a listing and classification of 181 surviving manuscripts of the Middle English versions, see L.M. Matheson, *The Prose 'Brut': the Development of a Middle English Chronicle* (Tempe, Arizona, 1998).

impulses as others, to judge from such reflections of political debate as *The Libelle of Englyshe Polycye* – a tract for the times not lacking in a sense of 'the merveillouse werroure and victorius prince kynge Herry the Vth ... prince of honoure ... no better was prince of strenuite', and of his realm as

A myghty londe, whyche hadde take on honde
to werre in Fraunce and make mortalite.[15]

By the late 1430s, when such thoughts on English policy were being aired, the style of argument – hitherto confined to the less public sphere of the king's council – reached a point of significant change. If in the 1420s the lords of the realm had expressed the view that 'the Kyng that ded ys, in his lyf ne might by his last will nor otherwyse altre, change nor abroge withoute thassent of the thre Estates, nor committe or graunte to any persone, governaunce or rule of this land lenger thanne he lyved',[16] that had not prevented them continuing in all essentials to further the policy he had pursued. With the end of his son's minority, the reappraisal of that policy and its continued viability became conceivable. Yet its occurrence marked not a weakening but a strengthening of the invocation of 'the Kyng that ded ys', as a touchstone of the rights and wrongs of policy; and it was in those years from 1437 to 1443 – the years which saw the heightening of commemorative activity in the visual and literary modes at which I have glanced, and in which the conduct of the war he had launched continued without break – that Henry V came to embody more explicitly an ethos of public life defined as the realization of king-led war-enterprise. The defining moment, and the moment at which a new edge of political argument made itself felt in the idiom of public life, was 'the declaracone of Humfrey, sonne, brother and oncle of kynges ... ayainst thenlargissement and deliveraunce of Charles duc off Orliaunce ... taken and yolden into the handes of the moost victorious and mighte prince, kyng Henry the fift, at the bataille of Agincourt, the day of Saintes Crispin and Crispinian'; a trophy of war whose deliverance Henry had instructed in his last will should not take place 'unto tyme that he had accomplished fully his conquest in his royaume of France'.[17] The publicity accompanying the 'declaracone' of 1440, and the council's response, proved the start of a process of argumentative conflict whose non-resolution would be one (possibly somewhat mealy-mouthed) way of characterizing the years ahead.

*   *   *

Before we move ahead to consider the bearing of those years after the suspension of war-enterprise by the Truce of Tours in 1444, we should perhaps

[15] *The Libelle of Englyshe Polycye: a Poem on the Use of Sea-Power, 1436*, ed. G. Warner (Oxford, 1926), pp. 51–3 and lines 10–13; see F. Taylor, 'Some Manuscripts of the Libelle of Englyshe Polycye', *BJRL*, 24 (1940), 376–418; Carol M. Meale, '*The Libelle of Englyshe Polycye* and mercantile literary culture in late-medieval London', *London and Europe in the Later Middle Ages*, ed. J. Boffey and P. King (Westfield Publications in Medieval Studies vol. 9, London, 1995), pp. 181–227, esp. pp. 210–19 on 'the overlapping worlds of city and government'.

[16] *Rot. Parl.* vol. IV, p. 326.

[17] *Letters and Papers Illustrative of the Wars of the English in France during the Reign of Henry VI*, ed. J. Stevenson, vol. II (Rolls Series, 1864), pp. 440–60; *Paston Letters and Papers of the Fifteenth Century*, ed. N. Davis, vol. II (Oxford, 1976), no. 439, p. 22 (letter of Robert Repps to John Paston I, 1 November 1440).

contemplate a little more explicitly the household retinue of Henry V. It has, in fact, been keeping us company, for it figures both in the creation of the memorials to the king and in the images of his kingship which those memorials convey. When his Westminster chantry was put in place, the king's effigy was flanked by the burial monuments of his treasurer of the chamber, Richard Courtenay, bishop of Norwich (a casualty of the 1415 French expedition), and of Louis Robessart, Lord Bourchier, his household esquire since at least 1403, later knight of his body and chamberlain of the household of Henry's son when in 1430 he died in battle in circumstances which I have earlier suggested may express a sense of political commitment.[18] Of his biographies, the *Gesta Henrici Quinti* is the work of one of the household chaplains who campaigned with the king; the pseudo-Elmham drew on the memories of its instigator, Walter, Lord Hungerford, steward of the household in 1421–22, by whom *The Libelle of Englyshe Polycye* was 'oversene'. The poem on the siege of Rouen rehearses the deeds (among others) of

> Syr Robert Babthorpe in that space
> Countroller unto oure kynge he was,
> Both hegge and dyche he ordayned that,
> And mekyl worshiyppe there he gatte . . .
> The countroller the werke [over]-see,
> A besy knyght in chevallere.[19]

The records of Henry's household are not superabundant; the hazards of record-survival have evidently emphasized the scrappy and incomplete features to which the initial circumstances of the truncated time-span of the reign overall, as well as in the period of office of some of the household accountants, and the pace of their activity, gave rise. Only for the first few months of the reign is there an extant book of particulars of account of the household treasurer, whose *Feoda et robe* section is in effect the 'establishment list' of the constituent ranks of those household servants forming the king's immediate entourage.[20] We do have, however, some surviving accounts for the household of Henry while prince of Wales,[21] and the exceptionally full account of Sir William Phelip as treasurer of the household of the late king, and treasurer of his wars, for the period 1 October 1421 to 8 November 1422 (the day of the king's burial), heard

---

[18] A.P. Stanley, *Historical Memorials of Westminster Abbey* (London, 8th edn, 1896), p. 179. See also J. Catto, 'The King's Servants', *Henry V: the Practice of Kingship*, ed. G. Harriss (Oxford, 1985), pp. 75–95, esp. pp. 87–8 on Courtenay; D.A.L. Morgan, 'From a Death to a View: Louis Robessart, Johan Huizinga and the Political Significance of Chivalry', *Chivalry in the Renaissance*, ed. S. Anglo (Woodbridge, 1990), pp. 93–106.

[19] *John Page's 'Siege of Rouen'*, ed. H. Huscher (Leipzig, 1927), pp. 154, 156, lines 397–400 and 435–6.

[20] PRO, E101/406/21, ff. 27–8.

[21] Ibid., E101/404/16, 23, 24; E101/405/1, 17, 26; E101/406/2. See also W.R.M. Griffiths, 'The Military Career and Affinity of Henry, Prince of Wales, 1400–1408', *Profit, Piety and the Professions in Later Medieval England*, ed. M.A. Hicks (Gloucester, 1990), pp. 51–61, which concludes that Henry's 'household and affinity were essentially military in character'.

at the exchequer in 1435.[22] Between whiles there is a miscellany of documents, such as the roll of *c.* 1417 endorsed *Familia regis infra hospicium suum ultra partes transmar[inas],* listing *les gentz esceantz a bouche de courte.*[23] We should count our blessings – though quite what we can count is not all that could be desired, and some matters will no doubt have to remain at best imprecise (such as the scale of increase in household numbers, or the level of household expenditure). With those caveats, what may be ventured as to the distinguishing features of this entourage? (I hasten to add the further caveat that I do not proffer these very summary and tentative remarks as even a sketch of the household 'in the round', for which an altogether more comprehensive analysis of both the strategies of power and the tactics of service, from the standpoints of both lord and follower, would be the necessary grounding.[24])

The Lancastrian household of 1413 – the immediate *familia* of 10 men of knightly rank, 23 esquires of the chamber, 35 other esquires, 31 yeomen of the chamber, a chapel of 27 clerics, with the usual complement of other ranks – was not overblown. Nor does it appear to have become so in the later years of the reign. Its personnel in those higher ranks was catholic rather than sectarian in derivation, some having served with Henry as his household men before 1413, others having at that time been in the household of his father. At the top of its hierarchy, age received its due: the chamberlain, Lord Fitzhugh, and the steward, Sir Thomas Erpingham, were born in 1358 and 1357 respectively;[25] others too could look back on years of service before 1399, whether to John of Gaunt or to other magnates. What they could look forward to was a persistence of their relationship to their master: Fitzhugh remained chamberlain throughout the reign, and all those holding office as steward, treasurer, comptroller, master of the horse, king's carver, were promoted from within. Their interconnexions, by descent and marriage (as well as the interplay of their mutual concerns as feoffees and executors), already in being in several instances, naturally grew over the years. For their rewards, they could expect to benefit from their master's characteristically *dirigiste* style of giving to each his due, whether at his own or others' expense.[26] As to the pattern of their service, that held few surprises.

[22] PRO, E101/407/7.

[23] Ibid., E101/407/10. The 106 names listed are headed by William Kynwolmersshe, cofferer; the listing includes 15 of the king's household esquires, and 13 (unnamed) 'hensemen de Roy'.

[24] As so well demonstrated by S. Walker, *The Lancastrian Affinity 1361–1399* (Oxford, 1990). We lack such a study for the period after 1399, but the observations in J. Catto, 'King's Servants', pp. 83–9, should be noted.

[25] A.C. Reeves, 'Henry lord Fitzhugh' in his *Lancastrian Englishmen* (Washington D.C., 1981), pp. 65–138; T. John, 'Sir Thomas Erpingham, East Anglian Society, and the Dynastic Revolution of 1399', *Norfolk Archaeology*, 35 (1973), 96–108.

[26] E.g. the missive directed to the abbot of Peterborough in 1419: 'Trusty and welebeloved yn god, we grete yow wel. And we wol and pray yow as we have praide yow by oure other lettres afore this tyme that ye wol have atte reverence of us oure welbeloved servant and clerc of oure chapelle Alayn Kyrketon specialy recommended unto the next benefice that shal voide longyng to youre yifte. And that ye thenke hereupon that hit be doon as we trust to yow, notwystandyng any instance or preyere maade or to be made to yow to ye contrarye, so that we may have cause to can yow thanke therfore. And that ye certifie us by youre lettres of youre wille and entent in

Appointment to the commission of the peace and suchlike chores they could not always escape, but less than a third of the chamber esquires of 1413 put in a stint as MP at any time. As Simon Walker has said about the Lancastrian affinity of the fourteenth century, 'the service ... required from retainers was primarily military; the Lancastrian retinue remained, as it began, a society organized for war', and it was this which produced 'a shared ethic of duty and service'.[27] Thomas Walsingham, in his usual libellous vein of armchair camp-follower, described Henry IV's household knights as 'more like Dionysus than Mars', having passed equally wild and wrong-headed judgment on the knights of Richard II's chamber;[28] neither he nor any other contemporary commentator thought so to describe the household retinue of Henry V.

Organizationally, the household was at the heart of the king's enterprise, its personnel employed on the whole spectrum of its widening scope – from the logistics of transport and the artillery train to the channelling of war finance, the prosecution of diplomacy, the administration of conquered territory. How numerically large the household retinue loomed in the larger complex of the army is difficult to compute; Chris Given-Wilson has suggested perhaps one-fifth or one-sixth by the later fourteenth century.[29] Proportionately, it clearly amounted to far less than the half of his military companies which John of Gaunt had raised from his indentured retinue of household men and bannerets, but the comparison is affected by the different scope of Henry's recruitment. Fully deployed for war though it was, his household was not intended to operate as an exclusive war-band; it functioned as a mechanism of royal initiative and control within the larger assemblage of those other retinues provided by the lordly and other captains contracting with the king, and the exploits of the household retainers are recited in the celebratory texts alongside those of their fellow-fighters. That other fellowship to which Henry devoted much attention as the embodiment of his style and purpose, the Order of the Garter, signalled with its careful selectivity of election the common criteria which appraised and co-opted the household men along with those of noble status.[30] The place of the household men was not to displace the workings of the wider aristocratic network of the king's service, but to facilitate its coherent functioning; and its *modus operandi* is perhaps best conveyed in a record such as the listing of the

---

this matere in al goodely haste. And god have you in his kepyng. Yeven under oure signet in oure hoost afore Roan the furst day of Januar'. The required response followed on 16 February, and Kirketon's presentation to the parish church of Alwalton on 10 May: see Register of Peterborough Abbey, BL, Add. MS 25,288, ff. 106–7.

[27] Walker, *Lancastrian Affinity*, pp. 42, 58.

[28] Thomas Walsingham, *Historia Anglicana*, ed. H.T. Riley, vol. II (Rolls Series, 1864), pp. 156, 259.

[29] C. Given-Wilson, *The Royal Household and the King's Affinity: Service, Politics and Finance in England 1360–1413* (New Haven and London, 1986), pp. 63–6.

[30] Hugh Collins, 'The Order of the Garter, 1348–1461: Chivalry and Politics in Later Medieval England', *Courts, Counties and the Capital*, ed. Dunn, pp. 155–80, esp. p. 170: 'Henry V's distribution of garter insignia appears to represent not merely an abstract recognition of individual feats of arms, but the culmination of a long-term policy to cultivate a body of tried and trusted soldiers who were to be the mainstay of his military ambitions.'

appointments in October 1417 and January 1418 of those who were to take the musters of a clutch of garrisons, of the troops forming the advance, middle and rear guards of the army, and of the retinues of lesser men: those appointed included the household almoner, the clerk of the kitchen, and predominantly the knights and esquires of the household.[31]

Among the features of this corps, which so much of the way displayed a behavioural pattern of solidarity and cohesiveness, was none the less a marked individual variety of life-chances. Some died even earlier than the king, and at no greater age; others lasted longer – including both those products of the 1350s, Fitzhugh, the chamberlain, and Erpingham, the steward. Where the survivors stood in the changed situation after 1422 is not easy to generalize. As an operative group their prospects were singularly limited, for the abnormality of the new king's age deprived them of the possibility of continuance as the personnel of his household, whose formation only began in the years 1428–32 and which remained embryonic until the king's tutelage was brought to an end in 1436–37. Some at least pursued the path of functional continuity by continuing to serve in the French war in the retinues of the duke of Bedford and those other captains with whom they had earlier come into such close contact; and of these, some later found a way back into the king's new entourage. A notable example is Ralph Boteler (from 1441, Lord Sudeley), whose career began in Henry V's retinue and continued with service as captain of Arques and Le Crotoy and chief chamberlain in Bedford's household. He became the king's bannerer, and served until 1440 (when he was elected a knight of the Garter) as a member of the king's council in France and Normandy; but appointment as chief butler in 1435 prepared the way for his succession to the post of king's chamberlain in 1441, and from that in 1447 followed a further ten years as steward of the king's household. Such endurance of a man only slightly younger than Henry V (he lasted on until 1473), and his ability to survive (seemingly unscathed and uncriticized) such upsets as the convulsion of 1450, has surely something to teach us about the life of household service and indeed about fifteenth-century political society more generally. If we add the thought that his later years were marked by friendly dealings with his sister's godson, King Edward IV, we might almost be encouraged to imagine a situation of underlying stability, underpinned by supporting networks which in Ralph Boteler's case had provided him with a start in life thanks to a stepfather, Sir John Dallingridge, who served as Henry IV's knight of the chamber (and whose father was retained as a king's knight by Richard II).[32]

In fact, we should not be so deluded. Let us remind ourselves (as Gerald Harriss has put it, with reference to Henry V's chantry chapel): 'Even as this great monument to past glory was being fashioned, attitudes towards the French conquests were changing. To the generation which had served Henry V, the war had represented an ambition to be fulfilled and latterly a commitment to be

---

[31] *Rotuli Normanniae in Turri Londinensi asservati*, ed. T. Hardy (Record Commission, 1835), pp. 357–9.

[32] With Ralph's daughter-in-law, Eleanor Talbot, Edward IV's friendliness allegedly became particularly marked and ultimately consequential (*Rot. Parl.*, vol. VI, p. 241).

shouldered. Now, increasingly, it was becoming an incubus to be shaken off.'[33] Maurice Keen has formulated persuasively the sense of disjunction between Lancastrian France and Lancastrian England in this shift of interests and attitudes, perhaps arising from premises built into Henry V's chosen strategy;[34] though at least until it became apparent that his successor would not fulfil the assumption built into the conduct of affairs during the years of minority – that he would resume the active policy of his father – we may presume that some at least continued to envisage the household as the king's military retinue (an outlook reaffirmed by the staging of the 1430–32 coronation expedition, organized in the traditional mode with the treasurer of the household acting as treasurer of the war).[35] Still in 1440, Richard of York's term of appointment as lieutenant in France stipulated that those of the king's household servants serving with him should be 'better recomaunded unto oure said souvereine lords good grace because of thaire greete labours and goingis'; and in 1443 an instruction was issued 'to such squiers of the Kyngs household as that beth appointed to goo over now in the Kyngs service of werr', in the army led by John Beaufort which proved the last gasp in the effort to maintain military momentum.[36] But beyond those watershed years of 1437–1443, such activity fades away. If Henry V had lived as long as Edward III he would (*per impossibile*) have witnessed the loss of Normandy and Gascony. As it was, by the time of the crisis of 1449–51, not only Henry, but also his household retinue (with only such residual exceptions as Ralph Boteler), had left the scene.

*   *   *

What they left behind was a sense of difference. Already there in the commemorative forms we noted earlier, in the 1450s the invocation of Henry V and his servants took on tones of a heightening nostalgia as a point of emotional reference in the exposition of an ethic of public life in need of reaffirmation if the present were to be put to rights. In, and immediately after, 1451 William Worcester was at work building such feelings into that *Boke of Noblesse*, which, in celebrating the claims of Henry V and his brothers to stand in the heroic sequence of those earlier 'Worthies' of the noble past, also stressed repeatedly the role of their adjutants – Sir Thomas Rempston, Sir Richard Harrington, Sir John Radclyf, as well as the unignorable Fastolf – and the need to see their exploits as aimed at furthering 'the common profit' and 'the comen wele': 'O ye right noble martirs! whiche that for youre verray righte of the coroune of Fraunce, and for the welfare of the kingis highenesse, and for the worship of his bothe roiaumes of Englond and Fraunce, ye forto susteyne righte and forto wynne worship, have ben often put in gret aventure ....'[37] Its interest lies in the

---

[33] Harriss, *Cardinal Beaufort*, p. 325.

[34] M. Keen, 'The End of the Hundred Years War: Lancastrian France and Lancastrian England', *England and her Neighbours 1066–1453*, ed. M. Jones and M. Vale (London, 1989), pp. 297–311.

[35] D.A.L. Morgan, 'The House of Policy: the Political Role of the Late Plantagenet Household, 1422–1485', *The English Court from the Wars of the Roses to the Civil War*, ed. D. Starkey (London, 1987), p. 36.

[36] *Letters and Papers*, ed. Stevenson, vol. II, p. 589; *PPC*, vol. V, pp. 146–9.

[37] *The Boke of Noblesse*, ed. J.G. Nichols (Roxburghe Club, 1860), p. 48. 'The terme of Res publica, whiche is in Englisshe tong clepid a comyn profit', 'the comen wele', 'the comyn publique', is the repeated refrain to the commemoration of their exploits.

way the developing idiom of English politics, whose expression became so loud and excited in these years of unresolved crisis, brings together the concepts of things *public* and the values of personal relationships of which the household retinue and *familia* was the pre-eminent embodiment.

The same juxtaposition marks the chronicle of John Hardyng, which (in the version surviving as BL Lansdowne MS 204) was presented to Henry VI in 1457. Some of its writing may date back to the 1440s, but it was put into such shape as it has in 1456–57. It is basically a rendering into ungainly verse of a *Brut* chronicle, but with extended additions in which Hardyng drew on his recollections and accumulated feelings stretching back over a lifetime that had begun in 1378. Many of those feelings take the form of endlessly repetitive repining about his failure to gain appropriate reward for his service to Henry V as a spy in Scotland and his collection of alleged 'evidence' in support of English claims to sovereignty there. We know the evidence to have been forged; even had it not been, one wonders at the generosity of the treasurer who accorded him payment of £10 in November 1457 in return for the presentation copy of the chronicle. Presumably we should view it as the tribute Lord Treasurer Shrewsbury (elected to the Garter six months before) felt it proper to pay on the king's behalf for an expression of the ethos which had militated the generation of both the king's and the treasurer's fathers, in the stanzas devoted to the memory of Henry V 'with commendation of his governance', and in the further stanzas billed as: 'how the maker of this commendeth his maystir syr Robert Umfrevile, and by exemple of his gude Reule to enforme the Kynge to kepe the publike profite of his Reme'. Hardyng there commemorated the master he had served from 1403 until Sir Robert's death in 1437 – a king's knight to Henry IV and Henry V, elected to the Garter in 1409, who fought at Agincourt and thereafter in France and Scotland; his nephew Sir Gilbert was Henry V's knight of the chamber from the start of the reign until his death in 1421.

> Treuly he was a Iewell for a Kynge
> In wyse counsayle and knyghtly dede of werre;
> For comon profyte above all other thynge
> He helped, ever was nothyng to him derre
> In werr and pees comon profyte he did preferre,
> For that poynt passed never out of his mynde,
> Which poynt he sayde shulde longe a Kynge of kynde.
> Wharfore to yow, moste sovereyn prynce and lorde,
> It fyttethe wele that poynte to execute,
> The comon wele and very hool concorde.

With curious ineptitude, the rhetoric of that encomium is interlarded with the fond reminiscence of his employer's indulgence towards his servants' blatantly thievish proclivities:

> And whan they stale his gode that he did se,
> He wolde it layne fro his other maynee,
> And noght repreve hym more in any wyse,
> So was he kynde withouten covetyse

– a touch obtuse, perhaps, as a way of adorning a tale designed to point a moral as to the direction of master-servant relationship for 'the publike profite' when aimed at Henry VI.[38]

By the mid-1450s, the issue of the interplay of public weal and personal relationship was being voiced not only in the rhetoric of such unofficial commentary as Hardyng's or Worcester's, but also in the immediate reality of political action, and with Henry V again invoked as a touchstone. The occasion for Hardyng's presentation of his work to the king may have been the reactivation of Anglo–Scottish hostilities in 1456–57, though it was the prospect of inward rather than outward war which then stimulated the reaffirmation of a martial ethos and an anxious concern that the Lancastrian heir become its protagonist.[39] But reference back to his paternal grandfather's style of rule became a tactic of those who came to challenge Prince Edward for Henry's legacy. In the parliament of 1455–56, which met in the aftermath of the first battle of St Albans, proceedings were launched with an exposition of the eight 'heads of business' deemed to form the programme for a reformation of the realm, starting with the need to establish an ordinate and substantial rule for the king's household and provide for its expenses, and proceeding to the defence of the realm and how to relaunch active war policy. By the third session in February 1456 bdiscussion had reached the necessary Act of Resumption. Its preamble sets forth the model they had in mind: the 'worshipful, noble and honorable [household kept] in the days of the most victorious prince of blessed memory', the king's father; it also states the connecting rationale, for resumption had to be made in order to make possible financial assignment for the restoration of such a household, 'to the entent that your Enemyes from whos knowlege the penurie of your said Household and the cause therof, and also the agrugyng therfore of your seid peple had is not hidde, wherof without dowte they take a grete corage and boldenesse ayenst your said lond, mowe falle from the seid corage into rebuke, and have your said lond and people in such drede as here tofore in the daies of you and of your progenitours they have hadde'.[40] On the terms of this resumption (so Benet's chronicle tells

---

[38] C.L. Kingsford, 'The First Version of Hardyng's Chronicle', *EHR*, XXVII (1912), esp. pp. 746–51; also his *English Historical Literature in the Fifteenth Century* (Oxford, 1913), pp. 140–9.

[39] In the 1456 Coventry pageants, Queen Margaret was assured that 'the knyghtly curage of prince Edward all men shal ioy to se': R. Osberg, 'The Jesse Tree in the 1432 London Entry of Henry VI: Messianic Kingship and the Rule of Justice', *Journal of Medieval and Renaissance Studies*, 16 (1986), pp. 217–18. And if Fortescue is to be believed, the prince did indeed develop a marked penchant for martial exercises and even for the perusal of Vegetius – no doubt in the 1458–59 rendering into English verse: Sir John Fortescue, *De Laudibus Legum Angliae*, ed. S.B. Chrimes (Cambridge, 1942), pp. 2, 136; *Knyghthode and Bataile*, ed. R. Dydoski and Z.M. Arend, EETS, original series 201 (1935).

[40] *Rot. Parl.*, vol. V, pp. 279–80, 300. The same invocation of Henry V's household had been used in the 'ordenances and appointmentes' issued by the great council on 13 November 1454: *PPC*, vol. VI, pp. 220–2. Few though they must have been, there were still at least some of Henry's servants whose active presence, on whichever side of the political divide they figured, kept him in mind: one could wish to know more than I have managed to discover about Sir John Beke, who on 20 December 1457 was

us)[41] Richard of York's protectorate fell. He took with him into the ensuing civil war and the subsequent affirmations of Yorkist and later kingship this venerated relic of the Lancastrian past.

*   *   *

Let us not follow him along that path. Indeed, merely to think of doing so is enough to stop one in one's tracks: even a route-map, which might be used for a Pilgrim's Progress out from that City of Destruction which was the England of Henry VI, would be difficult to descry in the Slough of Despond of early modern times through which the obscure (and often deceptive) lines of continuity and discontinuity seem to lose themselves. Many unanswered, and even unasked, questions stand in the way of our understanding the outcome of the story I have tried to tell. Not only in the short term, the nexus of policy and service – in which the household retinue and the ethos of public life had served as web and woof – unravelled and fell apart. Despite momentary impulses towards its reconstitution, in the longer term policy in the form of active war-enterprise was not sustained; despite occasional twitches of activity, it remained either still-born or at best susceptible to an extremely high incidence of infant mortality through Tudor and most of Stuart times. Unsurprisingly, any emergence of soldiering as a 'profession' alongside the development of civilian professional vocations, which in the sixteenth and seventeenth centuries strengthened from their earlier origins, proved exceedingly slow and hesitant.[42]

But the rhetoric, if not the realization, of the militant outlook showed more persistance. In public imagery, the legitimating tradition of the king as war-lord still figured as the decor of the hall of the 'pleasaunt Place of Richemond', rebuilt in 1499–1501.[43] Lines of continuity are certainly to be found if one follows the transmission of those various texts which were vehicles for the personalized commemoration of Henry V: the *Brut* became Caxton's *Chronicles of England*, the biographies and other tracts for the times produced notable further crops in both the early and the late sixteenth century. Hardyng (particularly in the second version of his chronicle, reworked in the 1460s) continued to be read and –

---

appointed knight harbinger of the household and master and governor of the king's henchmen (in acknowledgement of good service to the king and to his father), and who on the particularly striking date of 3 February 1461 received a further grant for good service in foreign parts and about the king's person, and in recompense of his losses in horses and other goods at St Albans and in the field at Northampton and elsewhere: *CPR, 1452–1461*, pp. 397, 646.

[41] 'John Benet's Chronicle for the years 1400 to 1462', ed. G.L. and M.A. Harriss, Camden Society, 4th series, vol. 9, *Camden Miscellany vol. XXIV* (1972), p. 216.

[42] I. Roy, 'The Professions of Arms', *The Professions in Early Modern England*, ed. W. Prest (London, 1987), pp. 181–219.

[43] 'In the wallys and siddys of this halle betwene the wyndowes bethe pictures of the noble kinges of this realme in their harnes and robis of goolde, as Brute, Engest, King William Rufus, King Arthur, King Henry – and many othir of that name – King Richard, King Edward, and of thoes names many noble waryours and kinges of this rial realme with their fachons and swordes in their handes, visagid and appieryng like bold and valiaunt knightes, and so their dedis and actes in the croniclis right evydently bethe showen and declared emonge thes nombre of famous kinges'. To these were added 'the semely picture' of Henry VII: *The Receyt of the Ladie Kateryne*, ed. G. Kipling, EETS, original series 296 (1990), p. 72.

appropriately for a work which projected the knights of the Arthurian Round Table, whose mission was 'comon profyte all way to execute', as integral to the 'British history' – through his influence on Malory continued to encourage a sense of 'the hyghe servyse' aimed at by that Arthurian fellowship which was both militant and public-spirited. Wynkyn de Worde's interpolation in his 1498 edition of Malory stated, '. . . in [the *Morte Darthur*] shal ye fynde the gracious knyghtly and vertuous werre . . . Also me semyth by the oft redyng therof ye shal gretly desyre tacustome yourself in folowynge those gracyous knyghtly dedes . . . faythfully and courageously to serve your soverayne prynce.'[44] Such generalized expression of the interdependence of war-enterprise and the public weal remained interestingly recurrent, underpinned by continued attention to earlier material. Let me just instance the translation into English in 1511–15 (the time of Henry VIII's attempt to resume the policy of outward war, which also saw the production of the first life of Henry V in English, drawing on Tito Livio, Monstrelet and Caxton's version of the *Brut*, as well as on family memories)[45] of Nicholas Upton's treatise of *c.* 1446, *De studio militari*, by John Blount, scion of a lineage of household retainers who served the house of Lancaster, and Fellow of that Lancastrian chantry war-memorial, the College of All Souls.[46]

---

[44] A.S.G. Edwards, 'The Manuscripts and Texts of the Second Version of John Hardyng's *Chronicle*', *England in the Fifteenth Century: Proceedings of the 1986 Harlaxton Symposium*, ed. D. Williams (Woodbridge, 1987), pp. 75–84; E.D. Kennedy, 'Malory and his English Sources', *Aspects of Malory*, ed. T. Takamiya and D. Brewer (Cambridge, 1981), pp. 42–8; F. Riddy, *Sir Thomas Malory* (Leiden, 1987), p. 28.

[45] *The First English Life of King Henry the Fifth*, ed. C.L. Kingsford (Oxford, 1911). The original author mistimed his work, completed after Henry VIII's French expedition came to an early conclusion in 1514; it therefore remained unprinted, but nonetheless via Stow and Holinshed influenced Shakespeare and others in the later sixteenth century. W.T. Waugh has argued persuasively, against Kingsford, that the anonymous author's informant was not Henry V's contemporary, James Butler, 4th earl of Ormond (b. *c.* 1390, d. 1452), but the latter's youngest son Thomas, the 7th earl, who was aged *c.* 90 in 1514: J.H. Wylie and W.T. Waugh, *The Reign of Henry the Fifth*, vol. III (Cambridge, 1929), pp. 445–8. For a discussion of the point, which brings out the persistence until the seventeenth century of these family memories of service to Henry V, see E.A.E. Matthew, 'The Governing of the Lancastrian Lordship of Ireland in the time of James Butler, Fourth Earl of Ormond, *c.* 1420–1452' (unpublished Ph.D. thesis, University of Durham, 1994), pp. 113–15.

[46] Bodleian Library, MS Eng. Misc. D227; *The Essential Portions of Nicholas Upton's 'De Studio Militari'*, ed. F.P. Barnard (Oxford, 1931). The translation was done at the behest of William Blount, Lord Mountjoy, great-grandson of Sir Thomas Blount, who served as treasurer of Normandy and fought at the battle of Verneuil, having in 1418 made the transition from his earlier status of the 'unarmed soldiery' of a king's clerk after the death of his childless elder brother, Sir John, knight of the Garter, king's esquire and knight, killed in personal combat at the siege of Rouen; when Thomas's son, Walter, made the further transition in 1454 from a century and a half's family service to the house of Lancaster to the service of the house of York, the change involved no abandonment of the family's wider outlook and behavioural pattern. A mid-fifteenth-century copy of the Pseudo-Elmham *Vita et Gesta Henrici Quinti* was bequeathed to All Souls by James Goldwell in 1499: A.G. Watson, *A Descriptive Catalogue of the Medieval Manuscripts of All Souls College Oxford* (Oxford, 1993), MS 38.

In noting all this bellicosity, we would do well to heed Cliff Davies's reminder that in trying to understand the ethos of a ruling group, we may distort the picture as a whole, passing too lightly over what that ethos entailed.[47] Perhaps some such thought had occurred to the man who thought so big when engaged in computing his need for requiem masses – whether one sees him (as Ernest Jacob proposed) as 'an adventurer, not a statesman', or instead views his rule (as Jeremy Catto has suggested) as 'one of the most vigorous phases of the English state'.[48] Yet however rebarbative, the ethos of English public life which Henry V came to epitomize, thanks not least to the service he instigated, has to be reckoned with. With reference to that generation which so busily fostered Henry's memory, Maurice Keen has remarked: 'It may be thought that the last thing – bar Henry VI – that England needed in the 1440s and 1450s was a "chivalrous king", but that does not mean that the concept was not an influential one'.[49] It would surely be mere wishful thinking to underrate the continuing force of the attitudes and feelings in question. Can it really be maintained that the age of those successive bids (all of them frustrated or at least in part unrealized) aimed at the 'reformation of the realm' produced a convincing and accepted alternative – whether humanist or religiously-radical – to the ethos of English public life fashioned in the age of the Hundred Years War? At all events, when, at last, with the Glorious Revolution the advent of the modern state came to pass in that new British polity within which England and its governing traditions were subsumed, it did so (as John Brewer and others have been at pains to tell us) in the form of the military-fiscal complex of forces in which the conduct of war set the pace and called the tune.[50] Not quite in all respects, of course, did that dispensation replicate its avatar. Policy and ethos prevailed, in the age of the Second Hundred Years War, in something recognizable as an echo of their forerunners; even the personal image of Henry V[51] and his accompanying 'happy few' ('we band of brothers')[52] could from time to time be brought out on parade as a classic exemplification of the charismatic leadership of the politics of conviction, in Max Weber's typology of the forms of

---

[47] C.S.L. Davies, 'Henry VIII and Henry V: the Wars in France', *The End of the Middle Ages?*, ed. J.L. Watts (Stroud, 1998), pp. 235–62. See also his earlier essay, 'The English People and War in the Early Sixteenth Century', *Britain and the Netherlands, vol. 6: War and Society*, ed. A.C. Duke and C.A. Tamse (The Hague, 1977), pp. 1–18.

[48] E.F. Jacob, *The Fifteenth Century 1399–1485* (Oxford, 1961), p. 202; J. Catto, 'World of Henry Chichele', p. 1, and cf. p. 13.

[49] M.H. Keen (review of John Watts, *Henry VI and the Politics of Kingship*), *Nottingham Medieval Studies*, 41 (1997), pp. 192–7, quotation at p. 196.

[50] J. Brewer, *The Sinews of Power: War, Money and the English State, 1688–1783* (London, 1989).

[51] The publication, in the year of the battle of Blenheim (1704), of Thomas Goodwin's *The History of the Reign of Henry the Fifth* no doubt related as both cause and effect to its refurbishment.

[52] The Shakespearean phrases are pre-echoed in the language of some of the variant texts of the *Brut* and other London chronicles, e.g. BL, Cotton MS Cleopatra C IV on Agincourt: '... all the ryall power of ffrensshemen come ayenst owre kynge and his litill meyne ... And than he sayde to his lordys and to his mayne: "Syres and ffelowes ..."'; *Chronicles of London*, ed. C.L. Kingsford (Oxford, 1905), p. 119. Other versions have 'host' in place of 'mayne'.

authority.[53] In the public idiom, 'the services', then and for long thereafter, meant the armed services; but what had disappeared as a still operative vehicle of service, in a process of change from which a new differentiation of 'public' and 'private' emerged, was the household retinue. Is it more than wishful thinking to hope that we may eventually understand why?

---

[53] Max Weber, 'The Profession and Vocation of Politics', *Weber: Political Writings*, ed. P. Lassman and R. Speirs (Cambridge, 1994), pp. 309–69, esp. pp. 311–13 on the grounding of charismatic *Herrschaft* in the personal devotion of the leader's *Gefolg-schaft* as the root from which grows 'the politics of conviction' – as distinct from that 'politics of responsibility' in which authority is founded on rationally devised rules.

VI

'FFOR THE MYGHT OFF THE LANDE, AFTIR THE MYGHT OFF THE GRETE LORDES THEREOFF, STONDITH MOST IN THE KYNGES OFFICERS': THE ENGLISH CROWN, PROVINCES AND DOMINIONS IN THE FIFTEENTH CENTURY

Ralph Griffiths

CONTRASTS can be instructive and the study of fifteenth-century England offers some that are particularly so. On three occasions between 1399 and 1485 wearers of the crown were challenged by claimants of royal blood invading from France: two were successful after brief campaigns, the other unsuccessful – disastrously so – after months of uncertainty as to which way the struggle would go. There was, of course, more to these invasions than naval plans and military confrontations, and not least the political objectives of the intruders.

Nonetheless, it remains unclear what the intentions of Henry Bolingbroke were in 1399, most likely because he himself remained uncertain until a few weeks before he captured Richard II, or else because he changed his mind late in the day. Whichever of these propositions is true, he can have given little thought to his future rule of England and its associated territories before he displaced King Richard, not least because a short period of only five months was spent plotting in Paris, between John of Gaunt's death and Henry's landing in Yorkshire. What indications there are of his attitudes to his own kingship in the summer and early autumn of 1399 seem ill-formed or confused.[1]

We are gradually becoming aware of the intentions of Henry Tudor in 1485, and of the preparations for his enterprise, not simply on the military front, but also in relation to his training in France for kingship and his early actions as king. With few exceptions, this growing awareness has been by way of inference, since Henry and his companions in exile seem not to have committed to writing any discussions they may have had about rulership, or any conclusions they may have come to. In any case, the time-scale was relatively short and the circumstances in Brittany hardly ideal for such planning: only in the two years since Richard III's usurpation – perhaps only in the twenty months after the collapse of Buckingham's rebellion – could the character of future Tudor rule have been seriously considered. However, the busy intrigues of the exiles suggest

---

[1] J. Sherborne, 'Perjury and the Lancastrian Revolution of 1399', *WHR*, XIV (1988), 217–41, reprinted in idem, *War, Politics and Culture in Fourteenth-Century England*, ed. A.J. Tuck (London, 1994), pp. 131–53; N. Saul, *Richard II* (London and New Haven, 1997), pp. 406–18.

that those twenty months were put to good purpose, and not simply a military purpose.[2]

In 1470, circumstances were strikingly different. Henry VI had been dethroned in 1461 and since June 1465 had been a prisoner in the Tower of London. His wife, Margaret of Anjou, accompanied by their only son, Edward of Lancaster, had striven hard to turn the tables on the Yorkist usurper, but in the summer of 1463 she and her entourage had withdrawn and installed themselves in north-eastern France. There they had lengthy opportunity not only to plot a return to England but also to consider future Lancastrian rule in the context of failed Lancastrian government before 1461.[3] Such discussions could hardly have taken place before the end of 1463, but the next seven years provided ample opportunity, and in a better informed environment than that in which the exiled groups were thrown together, for much shorter periods, before 1399 and 1485. And there survives a well-known, written memorandum which may be the outcome of such discussions, and whose conclusions also appear in Sir John Fortescue's *The Governance of England*, which is even better known.[4] It would strain credibility to suggest that Henry VI had similar thoughts whilst he was immured in the Tower of London from 1465. Rather is Shakespeare's portrayal of a captive king overwhelmed by remorse and fateful resignation a compelling one:

> Let me embrace thee, sour Adversity,
> For wise men say it is the wisest course.[5]

Proposals and memoranda for administrative or governmental reform were not unknown in England, especially at times of crisis; they mostly came from within the regime itself or else from the regime's critics, and they tended to focus on particular issues. For example, in the gathering crisis years of the late 1440s, two such sets of proposals were submitted to the king's council and parliament by two intelligent bishops, William Booth of Coventry and Lichfield, and Marmaduke Lumley, the bishop of Carlisle, 'a masterful treasurer' in Gerald Harriss's judgement.[6] Two other sets of proposals, concerning the

---

[2] R.A. Griffiths and R.S. Thomas, *The Making of the Tudor Dynasty* (Gloucester, 1985), chs 8–9; A.V. Antonovics, 'Henry VII, King of England, "By the Grace of Charles VIII of France" ', *Kings and Nobles in the Later Middle Ages*, ed. R.A. Griffiths and J. Sherborne (Gloucester, 1986), pp. 169–84; R.A. Griffiths, 'Henry Tudor: The Training of a King', *Huntington Library Quarterly*, XLIX (1986), 197–218, reprinted in idem, *King and Country: England and Wales in the Fifteenth Century* (London, 1991), ch. 7, pp. 115–36; C.S.L. Davies, 'Bishop John Morton, the Holy See and the Accession of Henry VII', *EHR*, CII (1987), 2–30.

[3] B.P. Wolffe, *Henry VI* (London, 1981), pp. 335, 343–4; R.A. Griffiths, *The Reign of King Henry VI* (2nd edn, Stroud, 1998), pp. 888–90.

[4] The memorandum and *The Governance of England* are accessible in modern English in Sir John Fortescue, *On the Laws and Governance of England*, ed. S. Lockwood (Cambridge, 1997), pp. 139–43, 83–123.

[5] *King Henry VI, Part III*, act III, scene 1.

[6] R.A. Griffiths, 'The Winchester Session of the 1449 Parliament: a Further Comment', *Huntington Library Quarterly*, XLII (1979), 186–8, reprinted in idem, *King and Country*, pp. 158–61; G.L. Harriss, 'Marmaduke Lumley and the Exchequer Crisis of 1446–9', *Aspects of Late Medieval Government and Society*, ed. J.G. Rowe (Toronto, 1986), p. 153.

government of Ireland and Wales earlier in the 1440s, reached the council from the king's servant-administrators.[7] The memorandum of 1470 was similar; yet it was also different in that it emanated from members of a regime that had lost power and was determined to regain it, and it encompassed uniquely broad recommendations for governmental reform that went to the heart of royal rule by loyal servants. Proposals of these sorts invite a commentary on contemporary and past practices, the appropriateness of the proposed reforms, and on the needs of stable royal government as they were perceived by the proposals' authors.

'Ffor the myght off the lande, aftir the myght off the grete lordes thereof, stondith most in the kynges officers': this offers a convenient text for such a commentary on some aspects of the memorandum for reform of 1470. It is taken from Chapter 17 of *The Governance of England*, a treatise whose final version was completed by the notable common lawyer, Sir John Fortescue, probably in England in the early 1470s. That is the view of most commentators and it seems a reasonable one.[8] It is also reasonable to suppose that the formulation of the *Governance*, if not its actual composition, took place over a lengthy period in Fortescue's eventful life. Chapter 17 is one of twenty chapters that make up the most substantial and sustained discussion of comparative political economy and governmental practice written in later medieval England.[9] Fortescue's treatise has long attracted attention from political and constitutional historians and political theorists. But Chapter 17 has not attracted much comment: it is entitled 'Here folowethe aduertysmentes for the geuyng of the kynges offyces', or, to paraphrase, 'Here are some precepts or instructions for making appointments to the king's offices'. This title may not sound immediately exciting, but the circumstances in which Sir John is thought to have offered his advice are interesting enough, somewhat controversial, and even dramatic, in the middle of the Wars of the Roses. The precepts or instructions reflect contemporary ideas of royal administrative practice and, further, reveal some of the problems of government which had become apparent by the mid-fifteenth century in England and in the king's dominions beyond, problems which helped to plunge England into a series of political crises and dynastic revolutions.

Sir John Fortescue returned to England in April 1471 in the entourage of Margaret of Anjou, the exiled Lancastrian queen, and her son, Edward, prince of Wales, the Lancastrian heir to the throne. Fortescue was present in the Lancastrian camp at the battle of Tewkesbury on 4 May when the army of Margaret

---

[7] E. Matthew, 'The Financing of the Lordship of Ireland under Henry V and Henry VI', *Property and Politics: Essays in Later Medieval English History*, ed. A.J. Pollard (Gloucester, 1984), pp. 97–115, esp. pp. 104, 106; R.A. Griffiths, 'The Provinces and the Dominions in the Age of the Wars of the Roses', *Estrangement, Enterprise and Education in Fifteenth-Century England*, ed. S.D. Michalove and A.C. Reeves (Stroud, 1998), pp. 10–11.

[8] The most recent, detailed discussion of the writing of *The Governance of England* is in *The Politics of Fifteenth-Century England: John Vale's Book*, ed. M.L. Kekewich et al. (Stroud, 1995), pp. 53–66; see also Fortescue, *Laws and Governance*, p. xxxiii and n. 31; A. Gross, *The Dissolution of the Lancastrian Kingship* (Stamford, 1996), pp. 71, 102.

[9] The classic edition is *The Governance of England*, ed. C. Plummer (Oxford, 1885), pp. 150–3 (Chapter 17).

and Edward was defeated by Edward IV. Whilst some leading Lancastrians were killed or executed at Tewkesbury, Sir John, who was not a soldier but a lawyer in his middle seventies, and a former chief justice of king's bench during the Lancastrian era, was soon pardoned and allowed his freedom. Edward IV, whom Fortescue had long and consistently denounced, considered him of some use, presumably because of his fund of political, legal and constitutional experience and his skill at propaganda. At some point during the following four years, he seems to have completed *The Governance of England* and addressed this final version of it to Edward IV: his purpose in writing and presenting it is not absolutely clear.[10]

Immediately prior to 1471, Fortescue, as a loyal Lancastrian servant, had spent more than seven years with Queen Margaret and Prince Edward at their court in exile at Koeur Castle, near St Mihiel in the duchy of Bar, in northeastern France, where they had sought refuge with Margaret's father, René, duke of Anjou. As one of Sir John Fastolf's confidants famously reported in 1456, Margaret was 'a grete and strong labourid woman for she spareth noo peyne to sue hire thinges to an intent and conclusion to hir power'. Despite her grave misfortunes, she had lost none of her determination; as Shakespeare put it, in words from Margaret's own mouth in the late 1460s:

Tell him [King Edward] my mourning weeds are done,
And I am ready to put armour on.[11]

She persisted in planning her return to England to free her husband, Henry VI, from the Tower and restore him to the English throne. Accordingly, when the opportunity came in 1470, in alliance – an extraordinary alliance – with the dissident Yorkist lords, George, duke of Clarence, Edward IV's own brother and male heir, and Richard Neville, earl of Warwick, Edward IV's own 'kingmaker', she took it. It is not unreasonable to suppose that some detailed thought had been given during those years of exile to plans for the return, even that some analysis was made of why Henry VI had lost his throne and what governmental changes or reforms would be needed if he should ever regain it.

Warwick and Clarence returned to England first, in September 1470; Margaret and Prince Edward (and Fortescue with them) would follow later when the essential groundwork had been laid. For Warwick's guidance, a set of 'advertismentes' about governmental practice was compiled for 'the good publique' of

---

[10] For a detailed chronology of Sir John Fortescue's life, see Sir John Fortescue, *De Laudibus Legum Anglie*, ed S.B. Chrimes (Cambridge, 1942), pp. lix–lxvii. The later stages of his career are discussed in Gross, *Dissolution of the Lancastrian Kingship*, chs 3–4.

[11] *The Paston Letters*, ed. J. Gairdner (6 vols, London, 1904), vol. III, p. 75 (9 February 1456); *King Henry VI, Part III*, act III, scene 3. Two distinguished, contemporary, Burgundian writers, Georges Chastellain and Olivier de la Marche, who knew Margaret, stressed her fortitude and courage in adversity: *Oeuvres de Georges Chastellain*, ed. K. de Lettenhove (7 vols, Brussels, 1863–6; reprinted Geneva, 1971), vol. VII, pp. vii–viii, 75–143 ('Temple de Bocace', presented to the queen, *c.* 1464); vol. IV, pp. 277–332 ('Chronique'); *George Chastellain: Le Temple de Bocace*, ed. S. Bliggenstorfer (Berne, 1988), pp. 9–12.

the English realm: a sort of manual of good government. It survives and has seven sections or 'articles'. The 'advertismentes' in article 6 of this document form the introduction and conclusion of the more elaborate Chapter 17 in Fortescue's *The Governance of England*. Only one fifteenth-century copy of the articles intended for Warwick's guidance is known to exist, whereas there are ten known of the *Governance*.[12] More than a decade ago, David Morgan noted that the relationship between these two texts was overdue for further investigation, but not much headway has been made since then.[13] Commentators have regarded Fortescue as the author of the articles, mainly because of their resemblance to parts of the much longer and more discursive *Governance*. But it is not necessary to think of him as their sole or original author, especially when one considers the group which shared Margaret's exile (and Fortescue's too) at Koeur Castle, and the schemes that preoccupied them between 1463 and 1471. Indeed, the concise, practical nature and declared purpose of the articles might be thought to have sprung as readily from the experience of some of the others at Koeur as from that of a former chief justice of king's bench.[14]

The seven articles were probably written in the two months between July 1470, when Margaret of Anjou made her surprising alliance with Warwick and Clarence, and September 1470, when Warwick and Clarence left for England; or, at the latest, when news of Warwick's success in England (and Edward IV's flight into exile) reached Margaret's little court in mid-October.[15] It is not known whether or not Warwick ever received the articles; and although only one copy of them survives, in the collection of materials compiled *c.* 1480 by John Vale, in the circle of the prominent London merchant, Sir Thomas Cook, there is no reason to doubt their authenticity. Cook welcomed the Lancastrian 'readeption' in 1470–1, and John Vale's book contains several pertinent writings relating to Edward IV's misfortunes in 1469–70.[16]

---

[12] The 'advertismentes' are in BL, Add. MS 48031, printed in *Governance of England*, pp. 348–53; *John Vale's Book*, pp. 222–5; and in modern English in Fortescue, *Laws and Governance*, pp. 139–43. For the copies of the *Governance*, see *John Vale's Book*, p. 250.

[13] D.A.L. Morgan, 'The House of Policy: the Political Role of the Late Plantagenet Household, 1422–1485', *The English Court from the Wars of the Roses to the Civil War*, ed. D. Starkey (London, 1987), p. 47 n.65. For some comparative comment, see *John Vale's Book*, pp. 50–1, 55 n. 40, 57–8, 60–1; and Gross, *Dissolution of the Lancastrian Kingship*, pp. 83–5.

[14] Fortescue was chief justice of king's bench from 1442 until 1460. The articles are not attributed to Fortescue in BL, Add. MS 48031, unlike the following item ('Secundum Sir John Fortescu knighte', f. 148v).

[15] For the chronology of these events, see C. Ross, *Edward IV* (2nd edn, London and New Haven, 1997), pp. 146–53. The copy of the articles refers to Warwick as Prince Edward's father-in-law, which would date the articles' composition after the formal betrothal of Edward and Anne Neville in Angers Cathedral on 25 July 1470. The articles were 'sente' by Edward to Warwick, which may suggest that the earl had departed from the Loire Valley en route to England: *John Vale's Book*, p. 222.

[16] Ibid., pp. 92–3. For a probable reference to Cook as 'a worthy, honest, and faithful knight' in Fortescue's *De Laudibus*, which was written at St Mihiel in or soon after 1468, see Fortescue, *De Laudibus*, pp. 49, 169.

It seems unlikely that the content of the articles was formulated in a hurry or that Margaret and her advisers had not thought about the issues addressed by the articles well before Warwick's departure from France. It is noteworthy, too, that the articles were addressed to Warwick by Prince Edward, who was barely seventeen years old, and not by the queen herself. It may have seemed wise to address them in the name of Henry VI's heir, who could not be regarded as in any way responsible for the downfall of the Lancastrian regime or for its shortcomings; and wise also that they should not be issued in the name of Margaret, whose French blood, relations with Louis XI, and the memory of her divisive role in late Lancastrian politics might perpetuate resentments rather than remove them. No mention was made of Warwick's shallow-minded confederate, Clarence, who was still Edward IV's male heir. 'Advertismentes' or precepts issued to Warwick in the name of Prince Edward were an unmistakeable signal that they were intended to inform a Lancastrian restoration in which Clarence could expect a negligible part. In this spirit, the seven articles – or 'suche of theym as may be thoughte expediente for the good publique of the reaume' – were to be implemented by a re-established Henry VI and his council.[17] They amount to an analysis and a detailed plan, albeit composed in uncertain times and at a distance.

Now a word about article 6 of these fascinating 'advertismentes' addressed to Warwick. It concerns the appointment of royal officers, on whom depended 'the mighte of his lande', that is, the king's effective power, his dominion.[18] Specifically, these particular 'advertismentes' stated that the king should not give any office, not even a parkership of a royal forest or park, to anyone who was not already a royal servant or to anyone who was in the service of anyone else or in receipt of a pension, fee or other retainer from a person other than the king. They also said that, if these principles were adopted, royal appointments need not prejudice the king's livelihood or resources. Article 6 further stated that no man should hold more than one office at any one time, unless he was a servant or official of the king's household, and then he could enjoy a parkership or an office that could be filled by a deputy who should be in the service only of his master, who in turn should serve only the king. The king's lay counsellors might receive an additional office for, unlike his spiritual counsellors, they could not be rewarded with benefices. If these 'advertismentes' or precepts were adopted, the king would enjoy 'the mighte of his lande' and do so economically; by implication, this 'mighte' had been weakened in the past because (at least in part) these precepts had not been followed.

These and other instructions are widely assumed to reflect the exiled Lancastrians' determination to abandon certain questionable practices of Henry VI's adult reign, and to learn from his regime's mistakes that had contributed to the king's overthrow in 1460–1. This assumption may not be entirely warranted. The articles generally may equally have been a comment on the government of Edward IV since 1461, and indeed on the government of England and the royal dominions over a much longer period. And, in view of the composition of the threadbare court clustered about Queen Margaret and Prince Edward for seven

---

[17] Quotations are taken from the edition in *John Vale's Book*, p. 222.
[18] Ibid., pp. 224–5.

years, it may reasonably be wondered whether the 'advertismentes' reflect in part the thinking of Lancastrian government in the late 1450s, when these same exiles had a noteworthy part to play. In order to appreciate the significance of all seven of the articles addressed to Warwick, it is important to recognize for what they are the assumptions of polemicists from the fifteenth century (including Fortescue himself in the *Governance*), and of nineteenth- and twentieth-century historians of Lancastrian, Yorkist and early Tudor government: in short, it is important to evaluate the articles in their own context and, as far as is possible, without distortion.

First, the circle from which the articles emerged can be partially reconstructed. At Koeur Castle, Margaret's court – perhaps at least fifty strong – was knowledgeable about England and the king's dominions. Details of those exiles were assembled by Stanley Chrimes, assisted by a friend who spent the summer of 1937 exploring St Mihiel and its libraries.[19] No one has added significantly to our knowledge since then. A list of identifiable companions of Queen Margaret can be compiled from, first, a letter written by Sir John Fortescue himself at St Mihiel on 13 December 1464, and addressed to John Butler, earl of Ormond, who was then in Portugal; second, a note included in the annals formerly attributed to William Worcester; and, third, contemporary ecclesiastical records kept at St Mihiel. Together, these identify at least seventeen individuals by name, apart from a group of esquires, gentlemen, clerks and ladies who are unnamed.[20]

Edmund Beaufort, claimant to the dukedom of Somerset, and his younger brother, John; Henry Holand, duke of Exeter; John Courtenay, eventual claimant to the earldom of Devon; and Thomas Butler, brother of the earl of Ormond, provided a noble and chivalric perspective, though they soon moved for a time to the more lively court of Burgundy.[21] Several others at Koeur Castle could offer advice on the practicalities of royal government and service. Among the leading knights, Sir Edmund Mountford, Sir Edmund Hampden and Sir Robert Whittingham had been long-serving officials in Henry VI's household

---

[19] Fortescue, *De Laudibus*, pp. 142, 144–6. A useful study of the exiles is C.J.M. McGovern, 'Lancastrian Diplomacy and Queen Margaret's Court in Exile, 1461–1471' (unpublished B.A. dissertation, University of Keele, 1973).

[20] *The Works of Sir John Fortescue*, ed. Lord Clermont, vol. I (London, 1869), pp. 22–9; *Letters and Papers Illustrative of the Wars of the English in France during the Reign of Henry the Sixth*, ed. J. Stevenson (2 vols in 3, Rolls Series, 1861–4), vol. II, pt. ii, p. 781 (which says that as many as 200 travelled from Scotland with Margaret); C.E. Dumont, *Histoire de la ville de Saint-Mihiel* (4 vols, Nancy and Paris, 1860–1), vol. I, pp. 174–7.

[21] In some penury, they sought a better life at the Burgundian court before the marriage between Duke Charles and Margaret of York in 1468: *The Memoirs of Philippe de Commynes*, ed. S. Kinser (2 vols, Columbia, S. Carolina, 1969), vol. I, pp. 210–11, 219–20, 222 (mentioning Exeter, Beaufort and others). For Courtenay, see R. Vaughan, *Charles the Bold* (London, 1973), p. 61 and n.1 (where he is confused with Exeter). Beaufort 'and all hys bend [band]' seem to have returned to St Mihiel at the time of the Burgundian marriage: *Paston Letters and Papers of the Fifteenth Century*, ed. N. Davis, vol. I (Oxford, 1971), p. 539 (John Paston III writing from Bruges to his mother on 8 July 1468). See also *CP*, vol. XII, pt. i, pp. 57–8 (Somerset); vol. X, p. 131 (Ormond); vol. V, pp. 212–15 (Exeter); vol. IV, p. 328 (Devon).

and knew all about patronage and service, and about those who sought royal offices for their retainers: they had been seconded to the queen's household, and two of them – Hampden and Whittingham – had been assigned to the prince of Wales's council in the later 1450s.[22] Two prominent esquires, William Grimsby and William Joseph, were no less informed about the inner workings of central government, the former as 'under-treasurer' of England and treasurer of Henry VI's chamber, and Joseph as clerk of the signet office, through whose hands instruments of appointment to royal offices had passed since 1448.[23] In addition, Dr John Morton, the able canon lawyer who later became chancellor of England and archbishop of Canterbury, had been the prince of Wales's chancellor and became the Lancastrian keeper of the privy seal in exile; and Thomas Bird, bishop of St Asaph, may be identified as the queen's confessor during her exile.[24]

The most prominent knights and esquires came from a swathe of midland England, between Warwickshire and Lincolnshire, whilst the prince's officials knew Wales, Cornwall and Chester; Thomas Butler's family had extensive interests in Ireland.[25] Sir John Fortescue was at the heart of this group, designated 'the chancellor of England': as a former chief justice, he had judged the effectiveness of royal officials, central and regional, on many occasions.[26] Together,

---

[22] J.C. Wedgwood, *History of Parliament: Biographies of the Members of the Commons House, 1439–1509* (London, 1936), pp. 602–3 (*sub* Montfort), pp. 313–14 (Hampden), pp. 943–4 (Whittingham). Another exile, Henry Roos, was also one of Queen Margaret's esquires: A.R. Myers, 'The Household of Queen Margaret of Anjou, 1452–3', *BJRL*, XL (1957–8), 407, reprinted in idem, *Crown, Household and Parliament in Fifteenth-Century England* (London, 1985), p. 185.

[23] Wedgwood, *Biographies*, pp. 400–1 (Grimsby); J. Otway-Ruthven, *The King's Secretary and the Signet Office in the XVth Century* (Cambridge, 1939), pp. 138–9, 158, 186 (Joseph); C.A.J. Armstrong, 'Politics and the Battle of St Albans, 1455', *BIHR*, XXXIII (1960), 57–8, reprinted in idem, *England, France and Burgundy in the Fifteenth Century* (London, 1983), pp. 57–8 (Joseph).

[24] Emden, *BRUO*, vol. II, pp. 1318–20 (Morton); vol. I, p. 91 (Bird). The records of the abbey of St Mihiel also note 'Guillaume de la Barre, chanoine de la cathédrale de Lincoln,' as being in Margaret's company. The identification is problematic, but he may be identified with William Jey, who was prebendary of Asgarby (dioc. Lincoln) in 1451 and 1459, and was not replaced until 1466: Dumont, *Ville de Saint-Mihiel*, vol. I, p. 174; J. Le Neve, *Fasti Ecclesiae Anglicanae, 1300–1541*, vol. I, compiled by H.P.F. King (London, 1962), p. 30.

[25] Another exile was Dr Ralph Makerell, a scion of a Derbyshire and Nottinghamshire family: *The History of Parliament: the House of Commons, 1386–1421*, ed J.S. Roskell, L. Clark and C. Rawcliffe (4 vols, Stroud, 1993), vol. III, pp. 663–5; PRO, C1/26/425, and Borthwick IHR, York Registry Wills, III, ff. 576–8 (references kindly supplied by Dr S.J. Payling). William Vaux of Northamptonshire, who was married to one of Queen Margaret's French ladies-in-waiting, was another exile: Wedgwood, *Biographies*, p. 904. Sir Robert Whittingham was married to one of the queen's Angevin ladies: Myers, 'Household of Queen Margaret', p. 405. See also D. Dunn, 'Margaret of Anjou, Queen Consort of Henry VI: a Reassessment of her Role, 1445–53', *Crown, Government and People in the Fifteenth Century*, ed. R. Archer (Stroud, 1995), pp. 112, 122.

[26] For his designation, see J. Calmette and G. Périnelle, *Louis XI et l'Angleterre, 1461–83* (Paris, 1930), pp. 69 n. 5, 305.

these people had extensive practical experience of government in England and the king's dominions under Henry VI, and, if they cared to admit it, a shrewd idea of its faults. Moreover, they were in touch with England, Wales and Ireland, and could gauge reactions to Edward IV's rule: not simply by raids and attempted invasions in the 1460s, but also via the sort of agents who were captured in the Thames estuary in 1468 on their way to London, with whose urban élite they also had links. Those arrested in 1468 included one of Sir Robert Whittingham's servants, a former servant of the duke of Exeter, and John Courtenay's brother, Henry.[27] Furthermore, the queen's father, René of Anjou, was close to the French court, where the intrusion of aristocratic retainers had seriously undermined the French king's authority and government earlier in the century. René and his son, John, duke of Calabria, and their counsellors visited Margaret periodically.[28] More important, the comings and goings between Koeur Castle and Louis XI's court appear to have been frequent, to judge by the memoranda which Fortescue was inflicting on Louis' councillors by 1468: these consisted of proposals, some lengthy and some confidential, for the restoration of Henry VI with French aid, and providing, interestingly, that Warwick should have 'the principal government of the realm'.[29] From this restless circle came the 'advertismentes' intended for Warwick in 1470, preparatory to the restoration of Henry VI.

The concerns of article 6 were, therefore, these: plurality of office-holding by royal servants; divided loyalties of royal officers; the need to dispense royal patronage widely; and thereby to secure a broad spectrum of support for the crown. If these concerns were addressed, the crown's influence in the provinces of the realm and in the dominions would be strengthened. When Fortescue completed *The Governance of England*, Chapter 17, he commended these precepts and illustrated their application in more detail.[30] The officers he had in mind were in every part of the land: specifically, he noted foresters and stewards of royal lordships, receivers and chamberlains, constables of castles and justices of the forests. He did not mention the principal royal agents in the English shires, the sheriffs, escheators and commissioners of various sorts, especially of the peace. To ensure that substantial numbers of these officers were reliable servants in a royal affinity was far from straightforward, but at least sheriffs and escheators were appointed, by law, annually, and commissions were ad hoc by nature, and their activities more intermittent and narrowly circumscribed compared to those of the stewards, receivers, foresters, chamberlains and castle

---

[27] Ross, *Edward IV*, pp. 114, 122–4; *CP*, vol. IV, p. 327 n. (a). For the plottings of 1468, see M.A. Hicks, 'The Case of Sir Thomas Cook, 1468', *EHR*, XCIII (1978), 82–96, reprinted in idem, *Richard III and his Rivals* (London, 1991), pp. 419–33; A.F. Sutton, 'Sir Thomas Cook and his "Troubles": an Investigation', *Guildhall Studies in London History*, III, no. 2 (1978), 85–108; *John Vale's Book*, p. 89 et seq.

[28] Dumont, *Ville de Saint-Mihiel*, vol. 1, pp. 174–5 (1464).

[29] *Works of Fortescue*, vol. I, pp. 34–5; Calmette and Périnelle, *Louis XI*, pp. 303–5. As early as late 1464, Fortescue was in Paris, where he seems to have met Jasper Tudor, earl of Pembroke, Henry VI's half-brother: Fortescue, *De Laudibus*, pp. lxvi, lxxiii, 210.

[30] *Governance of England*, pp. 150–3.

constables mentioned by Fortescue.[31] Moreover, in specifying their offices, Fortescue was pointing his finger at palatinates like Chester, the duchy of Lancaster and Cornwall, and the principality of Wales, as well as at the English shires.[32] A stable royal affinity, serving in offices such as these, with pluralism restrained and loyalty to the crown unmistakeably affirmed, would be mighty indeed. He estimated the number of these offices at 1,000, aside from others at the disposal of the prince of Wales in his dominions. And he denounced the braggers, brokers and suitors who turned appointments into a trade that was the cause of 'mony gret trowbels and debates in dyuerse contraes off Englond' and, one might add, beyond. By the beginning of the 1470s, a group of informed and experienced analysts had concluded that these defects of royal government were at the heart of the Wars of the Roses. There is one other important difference between article 6 and Chapter 17 of the *Governance* – a difference which may have a bearing on the date and circumstances of writing of the two texts. Article 6 barely concealed its opinion that the nobility had been at the root of mismanagement of the royal officialdom, and with the exiled nobles off in search of the fleshpots of Burgundy there was no one at Koeur Castle to gainsay this view. Fortescue, in Chapter 17 of the *Governance*, however, felt it prudent to say, in contrast to article 6, that 'the myght' of the land lay in the king's officers 'aftir', or second to, the nobility.[33]

How sound was their analysis? What does it reveal of the features of royal government and royal service as they had developed by the end of Henry VI's reign? How well founded were these particular reforms, with the objective of strengthening the king's authority? These are daunting questions. Research over the past fifty years into aspects of the duchies of Lancaster and Cornwall, the lordship of Ireland and the duchies of Normandy and Gascony, the principality and Marcher lordships of Wales, and some of the counties of England has provided much groundwork for an assessment though probably not yet quite enough; and of course historians' perspectives and objectives have varied a good deal. But some examples are instructive and highlight relevant issues.

Before the fifteenth century, in the king's lordship of Ireland, there was a dearth of able, loyal servants from Ireland itself and from the king's realm and other territories to carry on his government. 'Regarded by English kings first as a source of profit and then as an embarrassment which could neither be surmounted nor relinquished, the country [of Ireland] was denied the resources which alone could ensure effective and stable government.' So say H.G. Richardson and G.O. Sayles, and it is difficult to disagree fundamentally with

---

[31] For a convenient summary of provisions governing such appointments, see *English Constitutional Documents, 1307–1485*, ed. E.C. Lodge and G.A. Thornton (Cambridge, 1935), part III, chs I-V.

[32] For offices in these domains, see, for example, D.J. Clayton, *The Administration of the County Palatine of Chester, 1442–1485* (Manchester, 1990); R.A. Griffiths, *The Principality of Wales in the Later Middle Ages*, vol. I: *South Wales, 1277–1536* (Cardiff, 1972); R. Somerville, *History of the Duchy of Lancaster*, vol. I (London, 1953).

[33] Instructive comparison of the two texts may be made in *Governance of England*, pp. 150–3, 352; Fortescue, *Laws and Governance*, pp. 118–20, 142–3; and *John Vale's Book*, pp. 224–5, 246–8.

them.[34] The Gaelic resurgence from the fourteenth century underscored how burdensome and unrealistic were the king's responsibilities there. Richard II's bold enterprise in the 1390s demonstrated that:

> For violent fires soon burn out themselves;
> Small showers last long, but sudden storms are short;
> He tires betimes that spurs too fast betimes . . .[35]

Moreover the campaigns and conquests of Edward III and Henry V in France diverted resources and starved the English administration in Ireland of men, money and dependable servants.

Henry V had devised a policy to revive effective rule, but the king's preoccupation with France, his early death, and the lack of central vigorous direction while Henry VI was young, undermined it. The Dublin government continued to function, though it was increasingly dependent on Irish resources including administrative manpower. By 1440 the strains were evident.[36] The earl of Ormond's lieutenancies in the 1420s had required that he hold office in person; but all other appointments in Henry VI's reign allowed lieutenants to appoint deputies should they wish to return to England, where most of them had other interests and offices. In these circumstances, the Anglo-Irish lords encouraged the drift towards self-rule, and a separate Irish identity from which these lords benefited.[37] Margaret's circle at Koeur would have been aware of all that, for one of Ormond's sons, Thomas, accompanied Queen Margaret to St Mihiel in 1463, whilst another, John, was corresponding with her and Sir John Fortescue from Portugal, where he and Roger Tonge, described as a clerk of Henry VI's council, were trying to enlist support for Lancaster.[38] They would also have known that, under Edward IV, the trend continued – indeed, it can be said to have accelerated because Edward's father, as a major Irish landowner, had been one of those self-same Anglo-Irish lords.[39]

---

[34] H.G. Richardson and G.O. Sayles, *The Administration of Ireland, 1172–1377* (Dublin, 1963), p. 68.

[35] Saul, *Richard II*, ch. 12 (esp. p. 290).

[36] Matthew, 'The Financing of the Lordship of Ireland'; Griffiths, *Reign of Henry VI*, pp. 162–7, 411–23.

[37] For lists of the chief governors of Ireland and their deputies, see *Handbook of British Chronology*, ed. E.B. Fryde, D.E. Greenway, S. Porter and I. Roy (3rd edn, London, 1986), pp. 163–4, 166–7.

[38] John became earl of Ormond after his brother's execution in May 1461. Queen Margaret, Prince Edward and Fortescue tried to secure a safe-conduct for him to travel through France to St Mihiel, but it is uncertain whether he was able to do so. For letters, dated 13 December, probably in 1464, from Prince Edward and Fortescue to Earl John, who had written to Queen Margaret from Oporto, see *Works of Fortescue*, vol. I, pp. 23–5; 'Original Documents Preserved in the National Library at Paris', ed. E. Green, *Archaeological Journal*, VII (1850), 170–1, from BNF, Baluze MS 9037, 7, art. 173, 175.

[39] A. Cosgrove, 'Anglo-Ireland and the Yorkist Cause', and D.B. Quinn, 'Aristocratic Autonomy, 1460–94', *A New History of Ireland*, vol. II: *Medieval Ireland, 1169–1534*, ed. A. Cosgrove (Oxford, 1987), pp. 557–68, 591–618.

Henry VI and his council were made aware of the difficulties and their potential consequences by one of the king's talented servants, Giles Thorndon, whose
career illustrates some of the features that the circle at Koeur Castle appreciated. Thorndon, from Newcastle-upon-Tyne, laid the foundations for his career
as a royal servant in the households of Henry V, as prince and king, and of
Queen Katherine. Between 1434 and 1446 he devoted almost all his energies to
the Irish administration as constable of Dublin and Wicklow Castles and treasurer of Ireland. It is true that for part of that time, from 1438 to 1442, he also
served as joint constable of the king's castle of Cardigan in the principality of
Wales; his duties there were discharged by deputy, but he gave undivided loyalty
to the king.[40] In 1442, Thorndon produced a notable analysis of the Irish
governmental problem and, in particular, of the need for impartial servants in
key royal offices if the crown's authority were to be re-asserted and the damag-
ing aristocratic faction struggles ended.[41] Four years later, Thorndon himself
had become a victim of the Irish situation and he returned to the king's household; but when, in 1458, the regime under the direction of Margaret and the
prince of Wales's council sought to retrieve the fading Lancastrian position
there, it turned to Thorndon again and affirmed his grants of the Irish offices.
However, as the allied attempt in December 1459 to install James Butler, earl
of Ormond and of Wiltshire, as Henry VI's lieutenant of Ireland, along with
two new deputies, demonstrated, it was already too late to turn a tide that had
been running in Ireland for a century and more.[42] The authors of article 6 of
the 'advertismentes' of 1470 sought a cohort of Thorndons: it is a nice coinci-
dence that Sir Edmund Hampden, one of Margaret's exiles, knew Giles
Thorndon well and held the reversion of his Irish offices and income.[43] It is not
known where Giles Thorndon went after 1460 – perhaps back to Northumberland where he died in 1477, almost ninety years old.[44] If that is where he went,
so too did Henry VI, Margaret, Prince Edward, Fortescue and the rest;
Thorndon may have felt unable to face the journey to Koeur Castle, but one
wonders if he had interesting visitors or struck up an interesting correspondence
in the years before 1470.

In the five counties of the late medieval principality of Wales, the rebellion
of Owain Glyn Dŵr in the first decade of the fifteenth century had caused Henry
IV to rely on senior officers who were generally knowledgeable of Wales and
the Welsh, and devoted to the house of Lancaster, and in this he was followed

---

[40] Griffiths, *Principality of Wales*, vol. I, pp. 216–18.

[41] *PPC*, vol. V, pp. 321–4.

[42] In May 1458, Thorndon's appointment of John Hayne, esquire, as his deputy in the
Irish offices was formally recorded on the Close Roll: *CCR, 1454–61*, pp. 297–8; Griffiths, *Reign of Henry VI*, p. 854.

[43] The reversionary grant, in anticipation of Thorndon's death, was made to Edmund
Hampden and John Wenlock, esquire, jointly and in survivorship; it understandably
made Thorndon a trifle uneasy: *CPR, 1441–6*, p. 424 (16 May 1446), p. 457 (22 July
1446).

[44] A writ of *diem clausit extremum* was sent to the mayor and escheator of Newcastle-
upon-Tyne on 27 August 1477, consequent upon Thorndon's death: *CFR, 1471–85*,
pp. 136–7.

by Henry V. They were prominent nobles with large interests and experience elsewhere, but at least they used conscientious deputies with Welsh Marcher or English border connections. Once the French war began, however, Henry V had little option but to employ lesser men – esquires – as justiciar of south Wales, and several of the deputy-justiciars, who were trained administrators or lawyers, had no previous connection with Wales.[45] A second change, at roughly the same time, imposed a more permanent limitation on the crown in seeking capable, loyal servants in Wales – and more widely in the king's dominions. In staffing the office of chamberlain of south Wales, the senior financial office, in the fourteenth century, heavy dependence had been placed on clerical administrators, sometimes from the English borderland, and their career patterns occasionally extended from Wales to England, Ireland and the royal household. Things changed by the beginning of the fifteenth century and not simply in response to the Welsh rebellion. It had become an overwhelmingly lay officialdom in Richard II's later years, thereby restricting the available pool of officials and denying them reward in the shape of ecclesiastical benefices. Henry IV and Henry V relied for their chamberlains on esquires and a few clerics, usually drawn from the March or the border English counties.[46]

At first, Henry VI's council did not alter radically this approach to either of these senior offices in south Wales, but as the years passed appointments were made increasingly for political motives unconnected with Wales and especially, after the example of Richard II, to reward members of the king's household who were often occupied elsewhere, not least in France. This trend was accentuated after Henry VI came of age, and especially with the appointment of influential nobles – like the duke of Suffolk, and Richard, duke of York – who were frequently absent and promoted their own retainers to offices. '. . . yf hit were yt the kyng hade .ij. gode shirreffs a bidyng opon thair offys in Caern'schir' and Anglesey . . .', lamented one clerk in 1440![47] The consequences were absentee and pluralist officials, the apportionment of fees to a small and favoured group, inadequate supervision and therefore enfeebled royal control, and a drift towards self-rule by local landowners.

Here is an instructive contrast. The chamberlain of south Wales at the height of the Glyn Dŵr rebellion and for long after was John Merbury, a Herefordshire esquire who was a loyal, hard-working and capable royal servant. He was chamberlain from 1400 until 1421, deputy justiciar of south Wales in 1411–13 and he was promoted to be justiciar himself in 1421, serving until 1423. He had proved himself in John of Gaunt's service and in Prince Hal's, and so valued was he in a crisis that he was specifically retained in 1402 to be in personal attendance on the king, the prince and their lieutenants and justiciars in Wales. For about thirty years, whenever a job had to be done for the king in southern Wales and the March and in Herefordshire, Merbury was the first to whom the government turned; presumably he was so valued there that he was not given

---

[45] Griffiths, *Principality of Wales*, vol. I, pp. 126–37.
[46] Ibid., pp. 168–83.
[47] For both north and south Wales, see R.A. Griffiths, 'Patronage, Politics and the Principality of Wales, 1413–1461', *British Government and Administration*, ed. H. Hearder and H.R. Loyn (Cardiff, 1974), pp. 69–86 (with the quotation on p. 84), reprinted in idem, *King and Country*, p. 176.

responsibilities in France, as others were.[48] Contrast Merbury with John Beauchamp, who was justiciar of south Wales from 1447 to 1461 and was created by letters patent Lord Beauchamp of Powick on the day of his appointment as justiciar in tail male; or with William Herbert, justiciar and chamberlain of south Wales from 1461 until his death in 1469 – and much else besides; he became Lord Herbert in July 1461, and his appointments in south Wales were extended to his male heirs in 1466. These noble officers, perforce, were inclined to rely on members of their own affinities with interests and loyalties elsewhere.[49] Into the interstices of local royal administration thus opened up, ambitious local landowners elbowed their way and capitalized on the aristocratic rivalries that accompanied the dynastic struggle in mid-century. There are, then, some contrasts to be drawn with Ireland, but also some comparisons too: namely, problems of English royal authority that are traceable to the fourteenth century; an over-stretched civil service that could not meet all of the responsibilities imposed upon it; an apparent grip by senior nobles on the higher reaches of administration; and local exploitation of the opportunities in royal service by local landowners.[50]

To these dominions – and we must not forget Calais, Gascony and the Channel Islands, too – was added Normandy in Henry V's reign. Henry V's conquests and settlement added significantly to the crown's administrative responsibilities, especially in the early years when reliance on Frenchmen was not altogether safe. English esquires, knights and proven professional administrators – overwhelmingly laymen by this time – were needed alongside army and garrison commanders from England and Wales. The Lancastrians sensibly drew on officials already employed in Wales, Ireland and elsewhere in the king's dominions and realm. Officials developed career patterns that might extend from Dublin to Caernarfon, from Westminster to Bordeaux and Rouen. To take but one example: William Allington, a Cambridgeshire esquire, had served in Brittany as receiver of Brest in 1397 and in Calais as its treasurer in 1398–9, and also in Henry IV's household, before becoming treasurer of the Irish exchequer in July 1403. Later he was whisked off to Normandy as treasurer- and receiver-general from 1 May 1419; in between times, he was a royal official and frequent commissioner in his home shire of Cambridge.[51] The administrative system and its largely lay personnel

---

[48] Griffiths, *Principality of Wales*, vol. I, pp. 132–4, 137, 181, and references cited there. For his indenture of service with John of Gaunt, concluded at Bordeaux on 2 October 1395 while the duke was in Gascony, see S. Walker, *The Lancastrian Affinity, 1361–1399* (Oxford, 1990), pp. 275, 300–1. As chamberlain of south Wales, in 1415 Merbury undertook to raise several hundred archers for service in France, but there is no sign that he went himself on Henry V's expedition: C.T. Allmand, *Henry V* (London, 1992), p. 208.

[49] Griffiths, *Principality of Wales*, vol. I, pp. 152–6; *CP*, vol. II, pp. 46–7; vol. X, pp. 400–1.

[50] See the comment in R.A. Griffiths, 'Wales and the Marches', *Fifteenth-Century England, 1399–1509*, ed. S.B. Chrimes, C.D. Ross and R.A. Griffiths (Manchester, 1972; 2nd edn, Stroud, 1995), pp. 150–2.

[51] J.S. Roskell, 'William Allington of Horseheath, Speaker in the Parliament of 1429–30', *Proceedings of the Cambridgeshire Antiquarian Society*, LII (1959), 30–42, reprinted in idem, *Parliament and Politics*, vol. III (1983), ch. 15, to be supplemented by *History of Parliament: House of Commons, 1386–1421*, vol. II, pp. 27–9, and with further comment in A. Curry, 'L'administration financière de la normandie anglaise: continuité ou changement', *La France des principautés*, ed. P. Contamine and O. Mattéoni (Paris, 1996), pp. 93–7.

were overstretched, and the temptation to accumulate offices and fees, affording only partial service from time to time, and for nobles and commanders to advance their own retainers, posed problems of effectiveness, control and economy.

By the early 1450s, the crown had lost both Normandy and Gascony, whilst in large parts of Wales and the lordship of Ireland the king's 'myght' had been seriously attenuated. Article 6 of the 'advertismentes' prepared for Warwick did not envisage the recovery of either Normandy or Gascony, and Fortescue's proposals made to Louis XI a little earlier, with their comments on England's future commercial relations with the two duchies, implicitly acknowledged that they would remain in French hands.[52] The article's plans for effective service by loyal, royal officials were concentrated on England and its more proximate dominions. It is possible that these dominions did not include Calais either, to judge by Fortescue's early proposals for the future management of the wool trade under a restored Lancastrian regime. Doubtless Queen Margaret and her advisers were ill-disposed towards the merchants of the staple for their support of the Yorkist lords and Edward IV, and of course Margaret had already promised Calais to Louis XI in 1462 in return for French aid.[53] Hence, Fortescue made proposals about 1468 for the re-establishment of the staple either at Rouen or, a second choice, at Calais, both of which were described as being in France; and the arrangement should be without prejudice to the king, or realm, of France. Furthermore, he sought to encourage Louis' support for the Lancastrians by suggesting that its entire cost could be met through the prolonged lawsuit which the rogue London merchant, Richard Heyron, was currently pursuing in the *parlement* of Paris against the merchants of the staple.[54]

Within the realm of England, the palatinate of Chester and the duchy of Cornwall and the scattered estates of the duchy of Lancaster offered opportunities for the development of an effective royal affinity as the basis for the king's 'myght' in large parts of the kingdom. There too developments since the fourteenth century had made this gradually more difficult to achieve, something which Margaret and her circle at Koeur Castle recognized. The senior officers in all three inheritances prized the power and profit involved: the authority and means of patronage to make more junior appointments, to make grants and leases of property, to judge and to punish – powers that lay at the heart of the king's 'myght'.

In the palatinate of Chester, the justiciar's office was held by a succession of nobles from Richard II's reign onwards; they inevitably came to regard the post as a sinecure whose duties needed to be discharged by deputies, even by deputies

---

[52] Calmette and Périnelle, *Louis XI*, pp. 304–5 (*c.* 1468).

[53] C.M. Barron, 'London and the Crown, 1451–61', *The Crown and Local Communities in England and France in the Fifteenth Century*, ed. J.R.L. Highfield and R. Jeffs (Gloucester, 1981), pp. 88–109; Wolffe, *Henry VI*, p. 334.

[54] Calmette and Périnelle, *Louis XI*, pp. 304–5. It was suggested that Louis should accordingly favour Heyron in his suit. For Heyron's relentless pursuit of his claims during 1460–80, see W.I. Haward, 'The Financial Transactions between the Lancastrian Government and the Merchants of the Staple from 1449 to 1461', *Studies in English Trade in the Fifteenth Century*, ed. E. Power and M.M. Postan (London, 1933), pp. 318–20.

of deputies. Thus, there is no evidence to show that William de la Pole, earl (and later marquess and duke) of Suffolk, the justiciar of Chester, Flint and north Wales for life from 1440, ever visited Cheshire, and he had no other links with the palatinate. If a monopoly of senior office-holding gradually came to be enjoyed by the Lancashire and Cheshire Stanleys in the 1450s and under Edward IV, often with hereditary tenure, they nevertheless were often preoccupied with responsibilities at court and elsewhere in the north-west; in 1455 Sir Thomas Stanley had been created Lord Stanley and in 1457 was elected a knight of the Garter.[55]

The chamberlains of Chester in the fourteenth century, like those in the principality of Wales, had usually been capable clerics, but in the fifteenth century their office became a privileged position offered as a reward or a favour; it increasingly became a sinecure and eventually part of the Stanleys' monopoly of formal authority. John Troutbeck of Cheshire had been an all too effective and busy chamberlain (1439–57), who was more inclined to exceed his duties than to forget them or to allow them to languish in the hands of deputies.[56] But his successor in 1457 was Sir Richard Tunstall, a north countryman who had compelling preoccupations at court and in the king's household, and who probably treated the chamberlainship of Chester as a sinecure. The ample forests and parks of the palatinate, which the chivalric classes and landowners valued highly, went the same way, ultimately into Stanley hands in the fifteenth century.[57]

The duchy of Cornwall, which developed a wholly separate administrative structure in the period following the Black Prince's death in 1376, exhibited similar trends that accentuated its physical distance from London and the Thames Valley. The stewardship of Cornwall was held more and more frequently by political and noble personages, and hence the bitter struggle over the office that occurred between the earl of Devon and Sir William Bonville during 1437–43. This trend became yet more pronounced after 1461, when William, Lord Hastings, and then Anthony Woodville, the queen's brother, became receiver-general of the duchy, despite the formidable number of other important offices which they held at the same time and in different parts of England and beyond.[58]

A study of the duchy of Lancaster may be even more instructive, because it was an aristocratic inheritance incorporated into the crown's domains when some of these developments were already under way, and also because its estates were scattered in most parts of the realm and in south Wales. The office of chief

---

[55] Clayton, *Chester*, pp. 142–61; *CP*, vol. XII, pt. i, pp. 250–1.

[56] Clayton, *Chester*, pp. 161–7. Troutbeck's conscientiousness is all the more notable in view of his minor service at the Westminster exchequer and in Henry VI's household.

[57] Ibid., pp. 161–2. For the importance of forests and parks to the landowning classes, see A.J. Pollard, *North-Eastern England during the Wars of the Roses* (Oxford, 1990), p. 200 et seq.

[58] J. Hatcher, *Rural Economy and Society in the Duchy of Cornwall, 1300–1500* (Cambridge, 1970), pp. 47–8; Griffiths, *Reign of Henry VI*, pp. 574–6. The steward of Cornwall from 1461 was Humphrey, Lord Stafford of Southwick (later created earl of Devon): *CP*, vol. IV, pp. 327–8.

steward of the northern part of the duchy was one of the most powerful. Here Henry IV, like his father, John of Gaunt, relied on experienced esquires and professional administrators, men who quickly adapted to wider royal service, as, for instance, did Sir Robert Waterton. But gradually these officers became absorbed with their other duties at the expense of the chief stewardship, as did John Tyrel at Calais as well as at the centre of government and in Henry VI's household: in April 1431 he was given formal authority to appoint a deputy chief steward, and the need for deputies was acknowledged thereafter. Even so, the appointment of the earl of Suffolk in 1437, and for life, was of a different order, and thereafter the chief stewards were political, aristocratic appointees whose deputies seem to have been drawn from their own retinues rather than from the *cadre* of professional lawyers and administrators in crown service.[59] In 1451 Lord Cromwell became chief steward for life of both the northern and southern parts of the duchy; in 1461 Edward IV conferred these same offices, and much else, on Warwick the Kingmaker for life.[60]

Some of the greatest fiefdoms of the duchy reveal the same features. At Knaresborough and Pickering, Yorkshire gentry and lesser nobles served as steward until, in 1461, Warwick secured the office in both lordships; at Tutbury in 1461 the steward of the new king's household, Henry Ferrers, a Kentishman, secured the receivership, whilst Warwick, as steward of the lordship, added the forest and park of Duffield Chase to his portfolio.[61] In the south, the steward of the duchy's Sussex lands from 1440 was James Fiennes, a household man, albeit with local roots, and he secured many other influential offices soon afterwards; in 1461 the stewardship fell to the Woodville circle.[62]

One last illustration of the relationship between service and commitments in the fifteenth century will suffice: it is drawn from the strategically placed royal castles along the south coast of England. From the 1370s, appointments of constables had generally been of soldiers of proven loyalty and personal service to the king, and in recognition of lengthy service in France, though others had demonstrated such loyalty and capability in a non-military environment at home. They were mostly knights or esquires with local interests, and frequently household servants. There had long been a place for constables who held more than one office, but this became more common in the fifteenth century and especially among household servants from the 1430s. This was combined with a tendency to rely on a very small number of faithful companions of kings at the outset of their reigns – notably in 1461 and 1483 – which caused unpopularity and resentment, especially if they were absentees and had little or no connection with the locality.[63]

[59] Somerville, *Duchy of Lancaster*, vol. I, pp. 367–8, 418–22, 424–5.
[60] Ibid., pp. 421–2, 429.
[61] Ibid., pp. 523–4, 533–4, 540, 556.
[62] Ibid., p. 616. Another branch of the Fiennes family was closely associated with Queen Elizabeth Woodville and governed the duchy's Sussex lands from 1453 to 1483. Richard Fiennes, Lord Dacre, was also appointed master forester of Ashdown Forest (Sussex) for life in 1460: ibid., p. 621. Cf. the shift from local gentry to distant nobility in filling the stewardship of the duchy's East Anglian estates after 1461: ibid., p. 594.
[63] This paragraph is based on the analysis in M.J. Roeder, 'The Role of the Royal Castles in Southern England, 1377–1509' (unpublished Ph.D. thesis, University of Wales, 1985), especially chs VI and VII.

By 1470 Margaret of Anjou's circle at Koeur Castle had identified important shortcomings of a lay civil service with formidable responsibilities that had grown over a century and a half, often in challenging political circumstances. There can be little doubt that limiting the number of important offices held by individual royal servants – receivers, chamberlains, constables and master foresters were mentioned by Fortescue – would have been a major reform and one which might have improved effectiveness of administration. The crucial importance of deputies was acknowledged, but so too was their loyalty to the officer they were replacing – and therefore to the king – rather than to any aristocratic affinity. Limiting royal service to those whose first loyalty was to the king, and not simply as a formality, was not a pipedream. The Thorndons and Merburys of the fifteenth century were proof of its advantages, and Edward IV appreciated the steadfast loyalty of John Say, the Lancastrian chancellor of the duchy of Lancaster who, after twelve years' service, moved into Yorkist employ in 1461 and duly proved his worth. According to Henry Bourgchier, earl of Essex and treasurer of England, the king thought him 'the truest and the feithfullest man that any christen Prince may have, of the whiche I am right glad and joyeux that ye have soo borne you'.[64]

Intermittent attempts were made by Richard II in 1399 and by Henry V to insist that the king's officials and retainers should not be retained by anyone else, and this emerged as a desirable objective in the discussions in 1454 about the extent of the duke of York's power and authority as protector of the realm during Henry VI's incapacity.[65] Each of these occasions was in the nature of either a political or a military emergency – just like 1470, when exclusive allegiance to the king was again recommended. If implemented, such a recommendation could promote a loyal officialdom and also, perhaps, provide a means of controlling noble retaining. Others realised its virtues, too. The sheriff of Wiltshire in 1464–5 noted disapprovingly how shire officials – sheriffs, bailiffs, justices and coroners – were employed not only in Edward IV's service but also in noble retinues and on noble estates in the county.[66]

The value of royal forests and parks to a gentry society was appreciated in 1470, including their usefulness when granted to a royal official. Earlier in the century, parks and forests had been frequently assigned to upwardly mobile, valued servants, providing them with leisure, residences and income. William Ludlow and his son, John, from Wiltshire, members of Henry VI's household, acquired Ludgershall park and its lodge, but in 1461 they lost all. Their Shropshire kinsman, Richard Ludlow (died *c.* 1460), a serjeant of the cellar in King Henry's household, acquired the park and manor house at Henley (Surrey) as a residence. Sir Edmund Hampden, one of the exiles at Koeur Castle, had Beckley and its lodge in Oxfordshire. After 1461, however, all three parks and manor

---

[64] J.S. Roskell, 'Sir John Say of Broxbourne', *East Hertfordshire Archaeological Society*, XIV (1959), 11, reprinted in idem, *Parliament and Politics*, vol. II, p. 163, quoting *Original Letters Illustrative of English History*, ed. H. Ellis, 1st series (3 vols, London, 1825), vol. I, p. 15.

[65] J.M.W. Bean, *From Lord to Patron* (Manchester, 1989), pp. 210–11 (quoting *CPR, 1396–9*, pp. 534–71, and *PPC*, vol. VI, p. 109 [23 July 1454]).

[66] M. Condon, 'A Wiltshire Sheriff's Notebook, 1464–5', *Medieval Legal Records*, ed. R.F. Hunnisett and J.B. Post (London, 1978), pp. 415–16.

houses fell into other, absentee or aristocratic, hands.[67] The reformers of 1470 sought to restore an economical mode of patronage and administration that had supported the royal affinity in the past.

There was hardly opportunity in 1471 for the Lancastrians to implement this programme to recast royal service, in order to restore the king's 'myght', and Edward IV gave no signs of trying to do so during his aristocratic regime. But there is a hint, here and there, that those who planned at Koeur Castle may have been groping towards some of their conclusions during the last few years of Henry VI's reign, when government was focused on Queen Margaret and the prince of Wales, and on the king's domains outside the south-east.[68] Whether or not this was so is less significant than the existence of an analysis of English government and royal administrative service that sought to understand developments that had mostly taken place over generations – cerainly beyond the compass of Henry VI's adult rule – and which had contributed to political collapse by 1460.

[67] Wedgwood, *Biographies*, pp. 560–2; *VCH Wiltshire*, vol. XV (London, 1995), p. 130; *VCH Surrey*, vol. III (London, 1911), p. 342; *VCH Oxfordshire*, vol. V (London, 1957), p. 57. Henley came into the possession of Thomas St Leger, one of Edward IV's esquires of the body and, later, the lover of the king's sister, Anne, duchess of Exeter.

[68] Griffiths, *Reign of Henry VI*, pp. 777–89.

VII

PRIVATE VICE, PUBLIC SERVICE? CIVIL SERVICE AND *CHOSE PUBLIQUE* IN FIFTEENTH-CENTURY FRANCE

Kathleen Daly

BY the fifteenth century, the king of France had a dual identity: as an individual or *persona privata* and as the holder of the royal 'office'.[1] As a *persona publica* he was a servant of the *chose publique*, which, depending on its context, we might translate either as 'state' or as the 'common good', or even 'affairs of state'. By the fifteenth century, the crown of France had particular attributes and duties, which the individual king was obliged to honour, if he was to be worthy of his exalted office and rank. The crown was a 'public affair', rather than a private inheritance,[2] for the king was head and soul of the *chose publique*, and that '*chose publique* concerns the people, the country and the community,' intoned Jean Juvenal des Ursins in 1452.[3] Moralists and political theorists, however, were aware of the divergence between the ideal and the real ruler. The extremes of vice and virtue attendant on kingship, and concern to educate the prince in his duty to God and his people, were well-worn themes in French politico–moral literature. Comparable advice was addressed to the nobility.[4]

---

[1] The background to the development of this theory is discussed by E.H. Kantorowicz, *The King's Two Bodies* (Princeton, 1957). There is now an extensive bibliography on the evolution of political ideas about the special attributes of the crown of France. Useful syntheses include J. Krynen, *L'empire du roi. Idées et croyances politiques en France xiii–xve siècle* (Paris, 1993) and C. Beaune, *Naissance de la nation France* (Paris, 1986).

[2] Noël de Fribois, *Abrégé des chroniques de France, (1459)*, discusses 'Des choses qui appartiennent a la decence et office de la dignité royal...': Vatican Library, MS reg. lat. 829, f. 69r. For the evolution of the idea of the crown as dignity rather than property, in response to the problems posed by Edward III's challenge to the Valois succession, see Krynen, *L'empire du roi*, pp. 127-33.

[3] Quotation from 'Verba mea auribus', *Écrits politiques de Jean Juvénal des Ursins*, ed. P. S. Lewis (SHF, 3 vols, Paris, 1985), vol. II, pp. 203–4, vol. III, p. 175, n. 32. He also uses *bien publique* in the sense of 'public good'. For other examples of des Ursins' use of the term, see 'Tres crestien, tres hault, tres puissant roy' (*c.* 1446), ibid., vol. II, pp. 42, 43, 52; and 'Verba mea auribus' (*c.* 1452), vol. II, pp. 185, 203–4, 206, 217, 218, 220, 240–1, 243. On the etymology and concept of the medieval state, B. Guenée, 'État et nation en France au Moyen Age', *Politique et histoire au moyen-âge* (Paris, 1981), pp. 151–64; idem, *States and Rulers in Later Medieval Europe*, trans. J. Vale (Oxford, 1985), pp. 4–6.

[4] For views on kingship, see J. Krynen, *Idéal de prince et pouvoir royal en France à la fin du moyen age, 1380–1440* (Paris, 1981), passim; P.S. Lewis, 'Jean Juvenal des Ursins and the Common French Literary Attitude towards Tyranny in Fifteenth-Century France',

What then, of those who served the king: 'civil servants', *officiers* or *gens du roi*, who held office(s) in the royal administration, and what of their relationship with the *chose publique*? In the last thirty years, prosopographically based studies of different groups of royal officers has revealed their significance in national and regional politics, society and culture. The upheavals of the civil wars and English rule in the earlier fifteenth century were followed by an important phase in the development of the principles and privileges, such as stability and heritability, associated with particular types of office. Despite their relatively low numbers even by the early sixteenth century,[5] royal officials nevertheless emerge as a significant element in what has been termed a 'judicially based state',[6] where, it has been proposed, the 'leading characteristic of public power from 1450 onwards was perhaps that of the royal office'.[7]

Given their importance to modern historians, how were royal officers viewed by contemporaries, and how did they view themselves? How did they view their own role within royal government? Were attempts made to 'educate' them in public service, as writers attempted to educate princes and the nobility in the tasks of government or warfare? And what can be gleaned from their writings about their own views of the state? The field is potentially vast (as is the number of different royal offices and officers in fifteenth-century France). I shall be exploring these questions with particular reference to the *chancellerie*, but also drawing on information concerning the royal *chambre des comptes* and the *parlements* – established branches of the royal administration, with relatively clearly defined functions, personnel, and a tradition of royal service.

Private vices

Towards the end of his life, Alain Chartier, royal notary and secretary in the service of Charles VII, addressed contemporary suspicion that public service equated with private vice in *De vita curiale*, couched as a response on Chartier's part to a friend seeking office at court, and in the *Dialogus familiaris*, in the form of a conversation between two friends on the merits and demerits of public

---

Medium Aevum, XXIV (1965), 103–121. For literature addressed to the nobility, see the summary and references in P. Contamine, *La noblesse au royaume de France de Philippe le Bel à Louis XII: essai de synthèse* (Paris, 1997), pp. 285–96.

[5] Following Pierre Chaunu, David Potter has estimated that royal officers and their families may have constituted 0.4 per cent of the population by 1515: D. Potter, *A History of France, 1460–1560: the Emergence of a Nation State* (Basingstoke, 1995), p. 142, n. 30. Contamine estimates the nobility at about 1.5 to 1.8 per cent of the population by the early sixteenth century: Contamine, *La noblesse au royaume de France*, pp. 54–6.

[6] E. Le Roy Ladurie, *The Royal French State 1460–1610*, trans. J. Vale (Oxford, 1994), p. 3.

[7] Potter, *Emergence of a Nation State*, p. xii. For the uses and limitations of prosopography and some examples of its use, see *Prosopographie et genèse de l'état moderne*, ed. F. Autrand, Collection de l'Ecole Normale Supérieure de Jeunes Filles, no. 30 (Paris, 1986), especially F. Autrand, 'Y-a-t-il une prosopographie de l'état mediéval?', and A. Demurger, 'L'apport de la prosopographie à l'étude des mécanismes des pouvoirs', pp. 13–18, 289–301.

service (both written *c.* 1427). In the first, the author is expected to use his influence to secure an office at court for his 'brother', who, ironically, believes that there is more merit in public service than in attending to his own affairs. The author disabuses him. On the contrary, courtiers prefer the name and rights of office to its duties. Instead of finding virtue in the exercise of public office (*in publico ministerio exercitium invenire virtutis*), the aspiring officer will have to battle against an army of vices, and may well be defeated by them! In the *Dialogus*, the corruption of those who purport to serve the public good is evidence of a more general need for moral reform, without which the French kingdom cannot hope to expel its enemies, the English. The harshest criticism of public servants is voiced by the 'companion' or *sodal*. High office is bound to attract the vicious, who gain it through luck and temerity, who never intend to rule for the public good, and lead others into error by their example. Chartier rebuts his friend's allegation that those with private vices can nevertheless benefit the public good: only the virtuous are worthy to serve, for true service requires sacrifice, even of one's life. The vicious dishonour the offices which they hold, he argues, citing (after Valerius Maximus) the example of the Roman, Manlius Torquatus, who refused to accept a consulship because of the corruption of others who held that office.[8]

Chartier's criticism of royal officers may have been the extension of a traditional literary topos – criticism of the court – but is also representative of a more general perception.[9] Officers made easy scapegoats for the perceived shortcomings of late medieval royal government. Their abuses and iniquities were a familiar theme in royal ordinances, and a target for reformers. In the same tradition, when the *commun* or Third Estate presented their advice for securing the 'good, utility and profit of the kingdom and the *chose publique*' to Charles VIII and his council during the estates general summoned to Tours in 1484, they complained of the 'malice and covetousness' of certain 'perverse and wicked' officers, and echoed the complaints of earlier reformers in urging that the king relieve his subjects of the 'multitude of officers ... and their wages'.[10]

Some of the severest critics of royal government were, like Chartier, from within the milieu of royal officers themselves. Christine de Pizan, for example,

---

[8] For the preceding three paragraphs, *Les oeuvres latines d'Alain Chartier*, ed. P. Bourgain-Hemeryck (Paris, 1977), pp. 68–71, 276, 278, 282, 288, 290, 322, 350. The editor plausibly dates *De vita curiale* as *c.* 1427, and the *Dialogus familiaris amici et sodalis super deploracione Gallice calamitatis* at the latest as March 1427 (pp. 68, 42).

[9] F. Autrand, 'De l'enfer au purgatoire: la cour à travers quelques textes français du milieu du XIVe à la fin du XVe siècle', *L'État et les aristocraties (France, Angleterre, Ecosse) XIIe–XVIIe siècle*, ed. P. Contamine (Paris, 1989), pp. 51–78. See also J. V. Alter, *Les origines de la satire anti-bourgeoise en France: Moyen-Age – XVIe siècle* (Geneva, 1969), pp. 186–206, who nevertheless argues that satire directed specifically against royal officers, though occurring in the fifteenth century, is above all a phenomenon of the sixteenth century.

[10] A. Coville, *L'ordonnance cabochienne, 26–27 mai 1413* (Paris, 1891); *Journal des états généraux de France tenus à Tours en 1484 ... par Jehan Masselin,* tr. A. Bernier, Collection des documents inédits (Paris, 1835), pp. 676, 681. For background, see J. Russell Major, *Representative Institutions in Renaissance France 1421–1559* (Madison, 1960), pp. 60–116. On the pre-eminence of moral concerns, see Krynen, *Idéal de prince*, pp. 144–8, 152–3; Potter, *Emergence of a Nation State*, pp. 36–7.

had married a royal notary and secretary and was the mother of another. In her *Livre du corps de policie* (*c.* 1405), intended for the dauphin, Louis, duke of Guyenne, she is critical of the lack of a sense of public duty among the great officers of the king and princes: they, who can best afford to pay their taxes, are exempt, leaving the burden to be borne by lesser folk.[11]

Jean Juvenal II des Ursins (1388–1473), was another commentator on royal officers and public service from the milieu of royal government. His father, Jean Juvenal I, had served as royal advocate in the *parlement* of Paris in 1400, and as chancellor of Louis, duke of Guyenne, in 1413. When the Burgundians entered Paris in 1418, the family had fled after the dauphin to Poitiers, 'having lost everything, barefoot and clothed as poor people'. There Jean I became successively president of the *parlement* of Poitiers, then president of the newly established regional *parlement* in Toulouse, while Jean II followed his father into the law, becoming an advocate for the king, and successively bishop of Beauvais (1432–1444), Laon (1444–1449), and finally archbishop of Reims, while his brother, Guillaume, was appointed chancellor of France.[12]

In his treatise, *Verba mea auribus percipe Domine*, addressed to the king and completed in 1452,[13] Jean Juvenal II enumerates the vices associated with royal officers in general, and with specific groups. There are officers who encourage the king to take all the taxes he desires from his subjects, and to increase the number of posts, as a means of enriching themselves, so that even a clerk's clerk gets his cut. In the *parlement*, 'thinking more of greed and advancement than to fulfil their duties', and preferring their own or their friends' business to that of the *chose publique*, officers reduce their hours and are slack in their duty. Judges commit more serious crimes than those they judge; royal commissioners inflate their expenses; notaries and secretaries take their pay, but do not write royal letters themselves.[14] 'God grant', he warns the king, 'that those who serve you may be as attentive to the common good (*bien de la chose publique*) as they are to their own advantage.'[15]

The Third Estate at Tours in 1484 voiced similar, if more specific, concerns, singling out for criticism the excessive dues taken by notaries and secretaries, whose ignorance, furthermore, meant that they needed clerks to do their work, who were greedier than their masters. They should charge only the rates specified in earlier royal ordinances (or failing that, rates to be established by new ordinances), and should be forced to make restitution to those they have overcharged.[16]

The royal officer: appointment and disappointment

A more positive role was, however, also envisaged for 'civil servants'. Christine de Pizan distinguishes 'civil' from 'military' service, alleging that Scipio Nasita,

---

[11] *Le livre du corps de policie*, ed. R.H. Lucas (Geneva, 1967), p. 31.

[12] *Écrits politiques*, ed. Lewis, vol. III, pp. 24–102.

[13] Ibid., vol. II, pp. 179–405; vol. III, pp. 215–16.

[14] See, for example, ibid., vol. II, pp. 270, 324–26, 334. These themes echo his earlier treatise, 'A, a, a nescio loqui' (1445): see below, notes 17, 21.

[15] 'Dieu par sa grace veuille que ceulx qui sont autour de vous ayent l'eul au bien de la chose publique autant, comme on dit, que ilz ont a leur proffit': *Écrits politiques*, vol. II, p. 204; vol. III, p. 175, n. 31.

[16] *Journal des états généraux*, pp. 683–5.

though not a soldier, was so prudent 'in serving the *chose publique* ... that he did as much by his wits (*sens*)' as others had done by arms. Jean Juvenal II, developing his twelfth-century source, John of Salisbury's *Policraticon*, described the officers of justice as 'limbs of the body politic'.[17] Although they echoed the complaints of earlier reformers in urging that the king relieve his subjects of the 'multitude of officers ... and their wages', the estates general in 1484 recognized that royal government, and particularly justice, could not operate without them. The obvious course of action was to select worthy servants in the first place, whether these were royal counsellors, or other officers. The sources indicate a conflict, again, between ideals and political reality.

Noël de Fribois (active from *c.* 1420, died *c.* 1467–8), notary and secretary, then counsellor to Charles VII, voiced typical concerns in his abridged chronicle of France presented to the king in 1459. Candidates for office had to be 'worthy and suitable men',[18] able to carry out their duties and morally beyond reproach: 'those who glow through their purity of conscience and outstanding knowledge'; for 'negotiations and affairs [of state] should be entrusted to experts, for whoever is not expert, what can he know, for experience is the mistress of [all] things'.[19]

In spite of the complaints of the ignorance of royal officers, including notaries and secretaries, some of which were probably justified, the degree of expertise required of royal servants probably facilitated the development in the longer term of a professional '*caste*' dominating some royal offices by the early sixteenth century.[20] Some officials, such as Fribois, were licensed in civil and canon law, possibly before they entered royal service. However, Jean Juvenal II advised his brother, the chancellor, that a degree in canon and civil law would not be enough to guarantee the suitability of a candidate for office, 'for God knows nowadays what sort of graduates [universities] produce!'.[21] Canon and civil law did not train officers directly in procedures, or in the application of royal ordinances and their implications, or in the customs of the particular institution(s) to which an officer belonged. More usually, individual branches of the royal administration developed the expertise of their members as servants of the crown 'in house'.[22]

---

[17] *Livre du corps de policie*, pp. 62–3; *Écrits politiques*, vol. II, p. 186. In 'A, a, a, nescio loqui', Jean Juvenal includes a broad range of officers in the central administration, in the *parlement*, the royal household, *chambre des comptes* and *trésor*, as well as those in the localities, such as *baillis*: ibid., vol. I, p. 513.

[18] 'Aux honneurs doivent estre promeuz tant seulement gens preudommes et ydoines': Fribois, *Abrégé*, f. 70r.

[19] Ibid., f. 70r-v.

[20] P.S. Lewis, *Later Medieval France* (London, 1968), pp. 141–2, 151–2. Even a trusted officer could err, however: 'Ce mauvais ... garçon de Serisay [probably Guillaume de Cerisay, *greffier* in the *parlement*] avoit laissé à mettre mes droiz de la couronne', Louis XI complained to the chancellor in a letter dated 6 August 1482: see *Lettres de Louis XI*, ed. J. Vaesen and E. Charavay, SHF (1905), vol. IX, pp. 273–4.

[21] *Écrits politiques*, vol. I, pp. 517, 548.

[22] S. Lusignan, 'La transmission parascolaire de savoirs juridiques: les arts épistolaires de la chancellerie royale française', *Education, apprentissage, initiation au Moyen Age: Actes du 1er colloque international de Montpellier, nov. 1991 (CRISIMA)*, 1 (1993), pp. 249–62, esp. p. 250.

Training could take place through the equivalent of an apprenticeship. Some officers in the *chancellerie* and *chambre* began their careers as clerks to another notary, secretary or clerk, succeeding in their turn to an office.[23] In the fifteenth century, existing tools for retrieving documents, or on protocol in these institutions, were supplemented by more sophisticated letter-books or manuals.[24] Thus, although a few letter collections from the *chancellerie* existed well before the fifteenth century, Serge Lusignan has suggested that Odart Morchesne, clerk to the chancellor, Martin Gouge de Charpaigne, in 1422, and royal notary and secretary of Charles VII from 1427, was a key figure in the development of a tradition of letter-books, copied throughout the fifteenth and into the sixteenth century, to provide guidance for new officers in the 'kingdom of Bourges', divorced from the royal archives in Paris. Many of the same documents were later reproduced in the guides to the style of the *chancellerie* published in the early sixteenth century.[25] Individual officers gained a reputation for their expertise within an institution: for example, Jean Le Bègue and Pierre Amer each compiled manuals to the archives in the *chambre des comptes* for their own use.[26]

The question of morality was, to judge by contemporaries, viewed equally seriously. It is easy to take a cynical view of such demands, in the light of

[23] For example, Laurent Girard was clerk to Etienne Chevalier in 1448-9: *Les notaires et secrétaires du roi sous les règnes de Louis XI, Charles VIII et Louis XII (1461-1515)*, ed. A. Lapeyre and R. Scheurer, Collection des documents inédits sur l'histoire de France, Bibliothèque Nationale (2 vols, Paris, 1978), vol. I, p. 151; Pierre Amer (d. 1484) was pupil and clerk to Jean Le Bègue.

[24] A. M. de Boislisle, *La chambre des comptes de Paris. Pièces justicatives pour servir à l'histoire des premiers présidents* (Nogent le Rotrou, 1873), pp. i–xiv. See also note 26 below.

[25] Lusignan, 'La transmission parascolaire', pp. 253–60; G. Tessier, 'Le formulaire d'Odart Morchesne', *Mélanges dédiés à la mémoire de Félix Grat* (Paris, 1949), vol. II, pp. 75–102. Before 1515, a guide to the style of the *chancellerie* was published as *La grande stille et prothocolle de la chancellerie de France*, followed in 1527 by *Le guidon des secrétaires*, a formulary for letters close: ibid, p. 102 n. 2.

[26] For manuals and archives, see Boislisle, *Chambre des comptes*, pp. xiv–xv, and P. Contamine, 'La mémoire de l'état: les archives de la chambre des comptes du Roi de France à Paris au XVe siècle', *Media in Francia: Recueil de mélanges offert à K.F. Werner* (Paris, 1989), pp. 85–100, reprinted in P. Contamine, *Des pouvoirs en France 1300–1500* (Paris, 1992), pp. 237–50. Other tools used by officers of the *chambre* included *advaluationes*, containing calendars, comparative tables of currency, extracts from registers of the *chambre* and genealogies of kings of France (Boislisle, *Chambre des comptes*, p. xiv; K. Daly, 'Mixing Business with Leisure: Some French Royal Notaries and Secretaries and their Histories of France, c. 1459–1509', *Power, Culture and Religion in France, c. 1350 – c. 1550*, ed. C.T. Allmand (Woodbridge, 1989), p. 102, note 13). Of those *advaluationes* which I have examined, Paris, BNF MS latin 9848 bears the signatures of, and was presumably owned by, Adam des Champs and Simon Laurens, both clerks in the *chambre*; BNF MS français 4924 was annotated and may well have been owned by Jean Leclerc, also a clerk; and BNF MS latin 6185, a fifteenth-century manuscript, has the coat of arms and signature of Antoine du Boys, son of Jean du Boys (1452–1539), notary and secretary and *maître lai* in the *chambre* in 1496–8. For the du Boys family, see Lapeyre and Scheurer, *Notaires et secrétaires* vol. I, p. 117; vol. II, plate XXXVIII.

today's public perceptions of politicians' private lives; but they should surely be seen in the context of more general attitudes to the connection between political action and morality in the state. Government was a serious and essentially moral business, even if reality failed to live up to the ideal. Christine de Pizan, for example, advised the prince to emulate the Romans, who required petitioners for office to make their requests publicly, on the Field of Mars, but appointed candidates only after their moral conduct had been scrutinized.[27] The *ordonnance* for the reform of justice issued at Montils-lès-Tours in April 1454 warned the *parlement* that failure to administer justice could have grave consequences for the stability of the kingdom.[28] In 1484 the Third Estate reminded the king that he would answer to God for his failure to remedy his people's plight, if he did not relieve them of the burden of wicked officers.[29] Even the ordinance of 1482 in favour of notaries and secretaries in the *chancellerie* repeats earlier requirements that their outward appearance and behaviour should be commensurate with their calling: they were required 'to be dressed respectably according to their estate, not to wear immoral clothing, ... not to play forbidden games, to lead an honest life and not be in dissolute company or scandalous places on pain of severe punishment'.[30] A moral framework for political action is also explicit in Claude de Seyssel's *Monarchie de France*, which, though presented to Francis I in 1515, was the fruit of a political career in royal service stretching back to the reign of Charles VIII.[31]

One favoured method of securing suitable candidates was through election, either through a vote (*voie de scrutin*) or through deliberation and careful choice. Charles V (d. 1380), much admired by Christine de Pizan, who was commissioned to write his biography, had adopted election for certain royal officers (such as the chancellor and officers in the *parlement*).[32] Jean Juvenal des Ursins, as Peter Lewis has noted, follows in the tradition of the Cabochian Ordinance of 1413 in urging the election of as many officers as possible, a principle reiterated in the *Ordonnance* of Montils-lès-Tours in 1454.[33] In 1484, the Third Estate at Tours proposed the election of three worthy

---

[27] *Livre du corps de policie*, pp. xii–xiii, 31, 62–3, 65, 72–4.

[28] *Ordonnances des rois de France de la troisième race* (21 vols, Paris, 1723–1849), vol. XIII, p. 311, clause 118: 'voulans obvier à l'indignation de Dieu et aux grandes esclandres et inconveniens qui pour telle iniquité et pervertissement de justice adviennent souventes-foys ès choses des royaumes et seigneuries'.

[29] *Journal des états généraux*, p. 681. On the pre-eminence of moral concerns, see Krynen, *L'empire du roi*, pp. 144–8, 152–3.

[30] *Ordonnances*, vol. XIII, p. 76.

[31] Claude de Seyssel, *La Monarchie de France*, ed. J. Poujol (Paris, 1961), pp. 11–18, pop popd into English as *The Monarchy of France*, tr. J.H. Hexter and M. Sherman, introd. by D.R. Kelley (New Haven and London, 1981), pp. 3–8, 198.

[32] Christine de Pizan, *Le livre des fais et bonnes meurs du sage roi Charles V* (ed. S. Solente SHF Paris, 1936), 2 vols; F. Autrand, *Charles V* (Paris, 1994), pp. 711–12; eadem, 'Offices et officiers royaux en France sous Charles VI', *Revue historique*, 242 (1969), 313–14.

[33] *Écrits politiques*, vol. I, pp. 542–44. R. Mousnier, *La venalité des offices sous Henri IV et Louis XIII* (Paris, 1971), p. 26 n. 4, suggested that such measures were intended to prevent venality, although he believed that in practice the courts confirmed what the officer's family decided.

candidates for each vacancy, from whom the king should choose the new officer, and that no officer should hold more than a single office. For offices for which election was not required, such as secretary in the royal *chancellerie*, candidates were to prove themselves capable of exercising their functions, or lose them.[34]

The ambition of petitioners was seen as a major impediment to the correct choice of officers. Those who are not 'worthy ... but ambitiously pursue honours, are to be reproved and rejected...', advised Fribois, 'for by labour and not ambition should one increase one's honour'.[35] In the final analysis, the royal will was paramount: having drawn the king's attention to the criteria which he should apply, Fribois concluded: 'However, rational causes may persuade secular princes to dispose of secular offices as they think expedient, according to urgent needs and current circumstances.'[36]

In other cases, there was a lack of consensus as to whether current practice was a vice or a virtue. Was it more advantageous to the *chose publique* for royal officials to be appointed for long periods, or would it encourage complacency and abuses, blurring the fact that the office was the king's to give, and therefore revocable? Or would the instability and disorder consequent on rapid changes of personnel make matters worse? In 1405, Christine de Pizan advocated that offices should not be held permanently, or even for long periods: the Romans changed their officers each year so that they would not be puffed up with pride and evil-doers could be punished. In 1445, Jean Juvenal II was still advising his brother to purge the *chancellerie* of incompetents and the superfluous, with the aim of retaining the best notaries and secretaries, and reducing their number to the statutory fifty-nine.[37]

By 1484, the petition of the Third Estate at Tours alleged that stability in office would be more likely to secure loyal servants for the king, 'pource qu'il n'est riens qui exite ung officier ou serviteur a bien loyaument et diligemment servir, que d'estre asseuré de son estat et de sa vie et loyaument servir son maitre...', not least because otherwise the occupants might be tempted to recoup as much as they could from offices before they lost them.[38] Claude de Seyssel gave a more idealistic gloss to the immovability of officers of justice (particularly the *parlement*) in 1515 by maintaining that 'justice is more authoritative because the officers deputed to administer it are permanent...'. According to Seyssel, judges and officers who knew themselves to be 'irremovable if they do no wrong, acquit themselves in the administration of justice with greater confidence, or if they do not they are inexcusable', although even he had to

---

[34] *Journal des états généraux*, p. 685. Similar demands were voiced in the Cabochian Ordinance: Coville, *L'ordonnance cabochienne*, p. 227.

[35] Fribois, *Abrégé*, f. 70r-v.

[36] 'Toutesvoyes aucunes consideracions raisonnables peuvent mouvoir les princes temporelz a disposer d'aucunes offices seculiers, ainsi qu'il leur semble estre expedient selon les urgentes necessitez et les cas occurrens': ibid. f. 69v.

[37] *Livre du corps de policie*, p. 73; *Écrits politiques*, vol. I, p. 540.

[38] According, however, to Masselin, the clerk of the Estates, an attempt (in the petition of the Third Estate) to include a request for the restoration of Louis XI's officers, dismissed 'sans cause' by his successor, was viewed with great displeasure by the Estates. The response was that the king 'fera a son bon plaisir': *Journal des états généraux*, pp. 683, 706.

admit that the bridle of justice could be bent, both by the king and by corrupt officers.[39]

How secure, then, were officers in the fifteenth century? Once again, theory and practice diverged, and the application of each depended on the type of office in question. In theory an office was the king's, not the holder's. In her study of the *parlement* of Paris, Autrand showed that this principle was asserted in the late fourteenth century by practitioners such as Jean Le Coq (1387–97), but it was also believed that an officer should be maintained in his functions if he had not merited destitution, and that he should not be deprived without due process.[40] Odart Morchesne, author of a formulary dating from about 1427, noted that the clause, *tant qu'il nous plaira*, in letters of appointment (*de don*) demonstrated the king's right to appoint and dismiss, although once again he signalled that 'par ordonnances royaulx nul officier doit estre osté de son office sanz cause et sans estre oy'. However, on the death of the king, offices became technically vacant and holders needed confirmation. Interestingly, Morchesne sidesteps, rather than confronts, the problem of continuity in general by asserting that two specific offices (serjeant-at-arms of the king, and notary) 'sont offices perpetuels de roy en roy, ne les forfait': these offices did not cease on the death of the king.[41]

How did the principle of continuity fare during periods of political crisis, such as the 1417 purge in the *parlement*, the massacres which followed the Anglo–Burgundian entry into Paris in summer 1418, and the division of the royal administration between the Anglo–Burgundian regime in Paris and the administration of the dauphin, later Charles VII, south of the Loire?

If some lost their offices, or, like the notaries and secretaries Jean de Montreuil and the Cols in 1418, even their lives, in these upheavals, others managed to weather the storms. Continuity is clearest in the *parlement* of Paris, where, as Autrand has shown, even in the troubled political period of 1410–30, far more *conseillers* (62 per cent) left the *parlement* because they died through natural causes or took up other offices, than were deprived of office or life (11 per cent). Furthermore, the recovery of Paris by Charles VII in 1436 was marked in general by reconciliation and reintegration of the rival administrations, not by deprivations. Thus Jean Le Bègue (d. 1456/7), *greffier* in the *chambre* retained his office under Charles VI, the Dual Monarchy and Charles VII.[42]

If there seems to be a general consensus that office-holding was becoming more stable in the last years of Charles VII, interpreting the significance of Louis XI's deprivation of some of his father's officers on his accession in 1461 has proved more controversial. Peter Lewis and Philippe Contamine have played down its significance. For example, Contamine demonstrated in 1992

---

[39] 'Encores que (cettui frein) se puisse plier et qu'il y ait imperfection en ladite Justice comme en toutes autres choses humaines...': *Monarchie de France*, p. 118.

[40] Autrand, 'Offices et officiers', pp. 322, 324.

[41] Tessier, 'Le formulaire d'Odart Morchesne', pp. 76, 84–5, 88. See also note 81 below.

[42] F. Autrand, *Naissance d'un grand corps de l'état: les gens du parlement de Paris 1345–1454* (Paris 1981), table 5, and pp. 144–157; for the 'remarkable ... stability in office of civil servants' in the fifteenth century, see Lewis, *Later Medieval France*, pp. 148–9; but cf. G. Tessier and G. Ouy, 'Notaires et secrétaires du roi dans la première moitié du XVe siècle', *Bulletin philologique et historique, 1963* (1966), 863–76, esp. 876, n. 1.

that, among the notaries who had served Charles VII and held their office at Louis XI's accession, 30 were confirmed by the new king. He could only detect ten new appointments and it was not clear that the officers whom they replaced had been deprived of their posts by the king. In the *chambre des comptes*, only one president and five *maîtres* were replaced.[43] On the other hand, Christopher Stocker, and more recently Gareth Prosser, have emphasized the importance and the disruptive effects of the *épuration* of 1461, through which Louis was able to assert the principle that all offices were vacant because of *nouvel advenement*.

In the event, Louis miscalculated and, faced with the War of the Public Weal, had to reinforce his position by a series of gifts and grants.[44] In July 1465, he issued an edict restricting the number of notaries and secretaries and suppressing the offices he had created at his accession 'in ignorance of the foundation and perpetuity' of the college, 'which should not and is not accustomed, by change of lordship, *nouvel advenement* or otherwise, to be increased or diminished, nor the offices of our secretaries said to be vacant or subject to confirmation'. On 21 October 1467, the principle was extended to office-holders generally, because, according to the ordinance, fear of losing their office had cooled their 'zeal and fervour in our service'. Considering 'that in our affairs consists, under our authority, the direction of the acts (*faicts*) by which is policed and maintained the *chose publique* of our kingdom', of which they were the essential ministers, 'like members of a body of which we are the head', the king promised that he would only appoint a new officer if an office was vacated by the death of an incumbent, or by willing resignation. A similar assurance was given to the officers of the *chambre des comptes*.[45]

To judge by these events, Louis XI's attempt to assert his right to take back any royal office had been challenged successfully, and he had conceded the principle that officers could not be removed without good reason and due process. Louis' 'U-turn' was disguised as a return to 'custom' and justified by the special status attributed to officers, because of their good service, and value to the crown. However, his own letters, and the careers of notaries and secretaries under Louis and his successors, reveal cases where kings continued to deprive their officers at will.[46] It seems at least plausible that the so-called *Grande Ordonnance* of 1482, the fullest statement of the privileges of notaries and secretaries,

---

[43] Lewis, *Later Medieval France*, pp. 140–49, 230; P. Contamine, 'Louis XI, la prise au pouvoir, la foire aux places (juillet-septembre 1461)', in his collected essays *Des pouvoirs en France 1300–1500* (Paris, 1992), pp. 131–46, esp. pp. 136–7.

[44] C. Stocker, 'Office and Justice: Louis XI and the Parlement of Paris, 1465–1467', *Medieval Studies*, 37 (1975), 360–86; G. Prosser, 'After the Reduction: Restructuring Norman Political Society and the *Bien Public* 1450–65' (unpublished Ph.D. thesis, University College London, 1996), esp. pp. 191–200. I am grateful to Dr Prosser for allowing me to consult his thesis.

[45] *Ordonnances*, vol. XVI, pp. 335–9; vol. XVII, pp. 25–6; H. Jassemin, *La chambre des comptes de Paris aux xve siècle* (Paris, 1923) pp. 46–9: the assurance made in 1467 renewed a promise to the officers of the *chambre* made in 1407; however, this did not prevent kings from changing the 'ordinary' personnel, while the 'extraordinary' or supernumerary clerks, appointed at the king's pleasure, had even less security.

[46] See, for example, *Lettres de Louis XI*, vol. IX, pp. 230–1, for correspondence concerning Hugues Allegret, whom Louis had replaced as *greffier criminel* in the *parlement* of Paris on 10 Jun 1482.

may have been another opportunity seized, against the background of the king's failing health and a looming minority, to assert the principle that their offices would not be revoked at the king's death. Nevertheless, the aspirations of office-holders to make the stability of their office more permanent had to co-exist with political realities, and it may well be that the threat of insecurity, rather than the onward march of immovability, was more evident to contemporaries than to historians with the benefit of the *longue durée*. In practice, even notaries and secretaries, like officers without the benefit of an *ordonnance* or custom, continued to seek royal confirmation of their offices from the new king, Charles VIII. In spite of the immovability he ascribed to the officers of justice, Seyssel recognized that 'by an unregulated act of will', they could be 'deprived regardless of order'.[47] My own (albeit provisional) conclusion on the events of 1461–65 and the ensuing grants of privileges is that there may have been more at stake for office-holders in the fifteenth century than has sometimes been assumed.

The getting and keeping of the office involved more than the candidate – it was also a family affair, and critics decried the relatives, friends or patrons lurking in the wings. According to Christine de Pizan, officers should be appointed for 'virtue and intelligence'(*sens*); more usually they advanced through the favour or aid of their friends, a practice which she condemns. In similar terms, Jean Juvenal II warned his brother, the chancellor, in 1445 that even in the *parlement* of Paris 'notice is taken of relatives and friends at whose request by devious means' they persuade the king to give them offices there, 'and ... strictly speaking, by doing this [they] are deceiving the king and the public good, a most evil thing to do'. He also advised that officers should have no other office but that which they held of the king.[48]

Yet entry into the royal administration usually required the good offices of a patron, family or *affines*. In fact, Christine had sought patronage for her own son among the royal family, before he eventually entered the *chancellerie*.[49] Half a century later, Fribois seemed to take the operation of favour in the 'market place' for offices for granted: the crucial factor was the suitability of the candidate.[50] For Seyssel, the problem is rather the use of the office. Using it to

---

[47] F. Bluche, *L'anoblissement par charges avant 1789* (Cahiers nobles, XXII, 1962), p. 5, suggested a link between the grant of privileges such as ennoblement through office for secretaries, and political turmoil in 1485. See also Seyssel, *Monarchie de France*, p. 118.

[48] *Écrits politiques*, vol. I, pp. 515–16, 544. Exclusive service of the king by *officiers* in the *parlement* was desired but not enforced in the fifteenth century: however, certain royal offices could not be held simultaneously, appointment to one entailing resignation of the other(s): Autrand, 'Offices et officiers', pp. 295–6.

[49] More obliquely, Noël de Fribois encourages those who have risen from a lower estate not to despise their 'parens et autres amis', but to 'recognize, honour, love, aid and support them in their needs and their affairs', citing the *exemplum* of the conduct of Peter the Lombard towards his mother. Although he does not explicitly address this comment to royal officers, but to 'evesques, arcevesques, prelatz et autres ...', secular and ecclesiastical offices are often coupled elsewhere in the text: Fribois, *Abrégé*, f. 74 v.

[50] Citing a treatise concluding with the quotation from Aquinas, 'quiconques baille a son roy ou prince temporel aucune personne inhabille ou non ydoine ou inutile pour avoir et exercer aucun office, duquel la disposicion et provision appartiengne au prince, est envers luy desloyal', ibid., f. 69r. On the market for offices, see Contamine, 'La foire aux places', pp. 131–46.

enrich, or acquire friends for, the holder, particularly when he is incompetent to exercise his duties, is like 'fire or poison' to the *chose publique*; recourse to an intermediary can also diminish the gratitude – and by implication the loyalty – of the holder to the king.[51]

The relationship between individual, family and office was also problematic. Was office a dignity, like the crown itself, or should it be viewed as maintenance, or as a form of property?[52] Was the inheritance of office regarded in the light of an ecclesiastical benefice, and the promotion of relatives a form of nepotism? In 1406, for example, notaries and secretaries had been forbidden to cede their offices to sons or sons-in-law.[53] On the other hand, the heirs of royal officers might actually be considered the most suitable 'candidates' for office and thus their promotion even regarded as an effective way to secure 'good' servants.[54]

In fact, none of the authors considered here openly cites family links as a positive virtue in providing the king with suitable officers, or draws a direct analogy between the advantages of a hereditary crown and inheritability of royal office. Concerns about nepotism – a vice – may have discouraged them from directly advocating the heritability of office as an advantage for the *chose publique*. Nonetheless, individuals did draw attention to the loyalty displayed by their own families in the crown's service. Thus Jean Juvenal II des Ursins underlines his family's tradition of royal service in *Verba mea auribus* (1452), addressed to Charles VII.[55] In the preamble to the royal ordinance of 1482 (drafted by one of their number), the right of royal notaries and secretaries to pass their office to their heirs, like their other privileges, appears to be a consequence of the good services performed by generations of these royal officers for *la chose publique*.[56] Although hereditary right was not acknowledged in the *chambre des comptes* in the fifteenth century, and in fact contravened the ordinances governing the *chambre*, in practice there are

---

[51] Seyssel, *Monarchie de France*, pp. 151–2.

[52] For the crown as dignity rather than property, see Krynen, *L'empire du roi*, pp. 127–33.

[53] Mousnier, *Venalité*, p. 23, citing O. Morel, *La Grande Chancellerie royale et l'expedition des lettres royaux de l'avènement de Philippe de Valois à la fin du XIVe siècle* (Paris, 1900), p. 72.

[54] For the formation of family groups within the milieu of the *parlement* of Paris by 1454, see Autrand, *Naissance d'un grand corps de l'état*, pp. 266–7. Between 1483 and 1498, two-thirds of the resignations of office in the *parlement* were in favour of relatives and may even have assured the *parlement* of a new officer's competence: F. Autrand in *Histoire de la fonction publique en France: des origines au XV siècle*, ed. M. Pinet (Paris, 1993), p. 405. For examples drawn from the *notaires* and *secrétaires*, see Lapeyre and Scheurer, *Notaires et secrétaires*, vol. I, pp. 67–70, 94–6, 199–203, 249–53; vol. II, plates XXV, XXXI, LXV, LXXVII, for articles about and genealogies for Budé, Chevalier, Le Picart, Petit. Seyssel advocated that the king should advance men of renown, 'preferring them to honorable *charges* and bestowing rewards on them and their children', although it is not clear that he is specifically advocating hereditability of office in this passage: *Monarchie de France*, p. 152.

[55] 'Et si vous avons feu monsr. mon pere et nous ses enffans servis loyalment de nostre povoir...': *Écrits politiques*, vol. II, p. 186.

[56] *Ordonnances*, vol. XIX, p. 63.

examples of offices passing through three, and exceptionally even four, generations of the same family.[57]

The sale of office, however, was seen as a particularly severe barrier to securing the best officers, and concerns about the sale of offices, particularly those
relating to jurisdiction, continued to be expressed in the fifteenth, as they had
in the previous, century. Some offices in the *parlement*, notes Jean Juvenal, are
sold, 'according to some ... which is a damnable thing'.[58] 'If any one is promoted to offices through [venality], virtue and knowledge will be of no account',
the Third Estate at Tours was told, and in their turn reminded the king. Venality
lay at the root of most abuses: more than one office is acquired so that the
holder can take the profit, 'without exercising ... the said offices'; the most
'expert' are not appointed, and those who are, seek to recover the price of the
office through extortion.[59]

Like religious benefices having the cure of souls, offices requiring the exercise
of justice should not be sold (and it should not be forgotten that administering
justice was represented in political thought and literature as a sacred duty of
monarchy, for which the ruler is responsible to God). The exercise of justice,
however, could be defined very broadly to include any office having an element
of jurisdiction, including financial jurisdiction. Thus although the office of
notary and secretary was *impétrable*, and could be obtained on request, through
the grant of royal letters, the clerks or greffiers of the *parlement* formed a special
category through their connection with the supreme court of justice, and in
principle had to be elected.[60]

Fribois singled out venality in his *Abrégé des Chroniques de France*, presented
to Charles VII in 1459, and seemed to extend it beyond offices of justice. He
departs from his usual historical sources (indeed, it is not clear where he found
this information, for which there seems to be no exact historical basis), to attribute to Philip Augustus the prohibition on the sale of judicial office on pain of
fines and loss of office; and alleged that St Louis 'expressly forbade venality or
sale of offices, especially judicial offices', for the 'great and irreparable harm
which could arise from it'.[61] He sees a clear relationship between the appointment of 'suitable' or 'worthy' candidates to office, and the absence of venality.

---

[57] Jassemin, *Chambre des comptes*, pp. 34, 35 n. 1–3, 36.

[58] *Écrits politiques*, vol. I, p. 516.

[59] Discourse of Jean de Rély, canon of Paris, representative of the *prévôté* of Paris, and
elected orator by the Third Estate: *Journal des états généraux*, pp. 209, 685, 687, 695,
718 n. 3.

[60] See for example, Jean Juvenal des Ursins, 'A a a nescio loqui', *Écrits politiques*, vol.
I, p. 513; Seyssel, *Monarchie de France*, p. 150. For general background, see Mousnier,
Venalité, pp. 13–33.

[61] Fribois, *Abrégé*, f. 34r-v: 'Il ordonna que nul ne vendist ne achetast offices mesmement
de justice sur peine de les perdre et d'amende arbitraire et de inhabitilité a jamais point
en avoir ...'. The source is not the Testament of Philip Augustus (1190). The Third
Estate made a similar demand in 1484, that those guilty of venality should lose their
office and the purchase price, and both purchasers and vendors should be 'inhabile a
plus tenir offices royaulx': *Journal des états généraux*, p. 695. According to Fribois,
'Sainct Loys ... avant son partement de l'expedicion d'Auffrique deffendy expresse-
ment venalité ou vendicion d'offices par especial de justice pour les grans maulx et
inconveniens irreparables qui en seulement avenir': Fribois, *Abrégé*, f. 39r. The refer-

His training in canon, as well as civil, law may have alerted him to analogies drawn by canon lawyers between venality and simony. 'Whoever takes a dignity of which he is not worthy commits the crime of forgery (*faulx*); ... those who offer sacks of money ... should not be promoted....'[62] Condemnation of venality was voiced again by Seyssel.[63]

As we have seen, the selling of offices was believed to encourage the most incapable and unworthy candidates. To modern eyes, there might seem to be a narrow distinction between the right accorded to notaries and secretaries to resign their office to a nominee *in favorem*, where it is hardly credible that no money changed hands in the transaction, and the abuse denounced by Fribois. Fribois himself had in fact resigned his wages as notary and secretary in favour of one Jean Thierry in 1444, while retaining the *bourses* (share of the emoluments of the seal).[64] By the second half of the fifteenth century, sale of office (*a proffit*) was tacitly and occasionally openly accepted in the *chambre*.[65] The sale of judicial offices was banned once more by Charles VIII in 1493 and by Louis XII in 1498, the latter acknowledging that the practice had happened in the past, and yet again by the Great Ordinance of Blois (March 1499). In practice, financial needs led to the continuing countenancing of venality; even office-holders in the *parlement* were allowed to resign in return for payment. The distinction between office and property which fifteenth-century writers had striven to maintain became increasingly blurred, as the crown itself became a major beneficiary in the exploitation of royal offices, even if public venality was not formally accepted for another century.[66]

---

ence to Saint Louis might have been a misinterpretation of his reforming ordinance of 1256 as cited by the *Grandes Chroniques*, ed. J. Viard (SHF, Paris, 1932), vol. VII, p. 185: 'Nous establissons que cil qui tendront noz baillies etnoz prevostéz soient si oséz qu'il les vendent ne metent hors de leurs main *sans nostre congié*'. Venality, therefore, is not expressly forbidden, in spite of Fribois' assertion.

[62] Fribois, *Abrégé*, ff. 34r–v, 39r, 69r–70v. For the influence of canon lawyers on attitudes to venality, see C. Lefevre, 'Les juristes au moyen age et la vénalité des charges', *Miscellanea Historica in Honorem Leonis van der Essen* (2 vols, Brussels, 1947) vol. I, pp. 273–85; R. Descimon, 'Les élites du pouvoir et le prince: l'État comme entreprise', *Les élites du pouvoir et la construction de l'État en Europe*, ed. W. Reinhard (Paris, 1996), p. 138.

[63] Seyssel associates venality with 'men not of the legal profession' but 'who have favour at court'; without such intermediaries, the appointee would be obliged only to the king: *Monarchie de France* p. 152; *Monarchy of France*, pp. 91–2.

[64] Paris, BNF MS français. 29310, dossier. 62803, pièce. 6 (pièces originales 2826: Thierry); Lapeyre and Scheurer, *Notaires et secrétaires*, vol. I, p. 131. For later transactions concerning resignations, see C. Stocker, 'Office as Maintenance in Renaissance France', *Canadian Journal of History*, VI (1971), 21–43; and in general, Mousnier, *Venalité*, pp. 22–5, 46–7.

[65] Jassemin, *Chambre des comptes*, pp. 37–9.

[66] R.J. Knecht, *The Rise and Fall of Renaissance France* (London, 1996), pp. 69–70. For a more positive gloss on the development of venality, see C. Stocker, 'Office as Maintenance', passim, and in general, Mousnier, *Venalité*, pp. 7–33. For a longer term perspective, see Descimon, 'Les élites du pouvoir', pp. 149–58, who traces a transformation of what he terms 'customary' into 'legal' venality.

Such differences of opinion, even confusion, surely reflect a gradual evolution of attitudes to royal office and office-holding in the later middle ages comparable to that developing for the crown itself. *Honneur, dignité and office* are often used interchangeably, in the sense of public office itself, or the duties or attributes or status associated with office-holding.[67] In this respect, we might make a fruitful comparison with attitudes to the nature of royal power in the sixteenth century, where apparent contradictions can be seen as part of a debate in progress, rather than static statements of fact.[68] A more systematic study of the vocabulary of offices and office-holding in the Middle Ages than has yet, to my knowledge, been undertaken may illuminate such debates, and the reasons behind them.[69]

Virtue and necessity: the ideal officer

As we have seen, advice literature and political discourse recognized the need for 'worthy', 'expert' officials. Did the fifteenth century witness the development of a genre of advice literature specifically addressed to this group? In general, the answer is negative. Probably the closest approach was *A, a, a, nescio loqui*, Jean Juvenal II's treatise for his brother, Guillaume, the chancellor of France (1445).[70] Jean Juvenal was already experienced in the production of advice literature, and there are interesting parallels between the works he addressed to the king, and the advice he gave Guillaume. Jean Juvenal emphasizes the importance of the office to which Guillaume is called, for 'strictly speaking none should have a chancellor except the king, and the others are only keepers of their lords' seals'.[71] The advice to Guillaume echoes that proffered to the king: he should display moral rectitude, humility, and understanding of his responsibilities as chief counsellor of the king. His duty is clear: 'in all that you do have

---

[67] See for example, Christine de Pizan, where *office* can also have sense of 'task', role, function: so each part of the body politic carries out 'l'office de quoy il doit servir'; also, Fribois, *Abrégé*, where *office, dignité* and *honneur* are not clearly defined and distinguished, but the author is adamant that none should be purchasable (ff. 65r, 68v–69v). Similarly, although judicial office is singled out among royal offices as having peculiar characteristics, the distinction is not made systematically by the authors studied here (see above, pp. 111–12).

[68] See the illuminating comments in Potter, *Emergence of a Nation State*, pp. 36–7, on debates about absolutist or limited monarchy.

[69] I have not been able to consult J.P. Fieschi, 'Les procès d'offices royaux, 1477–93' (unpublished *mémoire de maîtrise*, University of Paris I, 1970), signalled by B. Guenée, 'Les tendances actuelles de l'histoire politique du moyen age français', idem, *Politique et Histoire*, p. 180, n. 1. Dr J. Powis is currently preparing a study entitled *A State of Privilege; Office and Office-Holding in the French Old Regime*. In the meantime, see his penetrating comments in 'Aristocratie et bureaucratie dans la France du XVIᵉ siècle: État, office et patrimoine', *L'État et les aristocraties*, pp. 231–45.

[70] *Écrits politiques*, vol. I, pp. 441–551.

[71] 'Et a proprement parler, nul ne doit avoir chanceiller si non le roy car les aultres ne sont que gardes de seaulx des seigneurs': ibid., pp. 444–5. In 1481, the *parlement* of Paris accused the duke of Bourbon of giving his officers titles, including that of chancellor, which could only be applied to royal officers: Krynen, *L'empire du roi*, p. 407.

regard for the good of [the king] in whose service you are ... sustaining his rights and the *chose publique'*, relieving his subjects from oppression, and thus helping the king to fulfil his coronation oath.[72]

Fifteenth-century kings of France were incited to virtuous acts by the 'mirror' of conduct held up by their ancestors, Clovis, Charlemagne and St Louis. Jean Juvenal also holds up a model for his brother's conduct: their own father, Jean Juvenal I, who had said he would rather beg his bread than remain with the enemy of his lord. Just as Guillaume's office is more exalted than his father's, so he must excel him in virtue.

Interestingly, Jean Juvenal I's career, and his son's attitude to it, is more nuanced and realistic than the images of royal paragons usually held up as models for kings. Sketching a biography of his father, Jean II is uncomfortably aware of the penalties of strict adherence to moral rectitude, when faced with political realities, and his advice to Guillaume is also more practical. Their father would not 'bend his sail to the wind', when confronted with the misgovernment of Charles VI's counsellors. When advised to dissimulate by his friends, he responded that 'he was made that way, and would have to be remade, before he changed'. 'I tell you, ... so that you will take care not ... to resist the will of those at court; ... it is better to be patient and dissimulate and be the cause of less harm', when the consequence otherwise would be 'to lose your estate,' Jean Juvenal advised Guillaume. Even his suggestion that his brother 'look in his [real] mirror' to remind him to hide his choleric nature before council meetings seems to have a practical, rather than a strictly moral, purpose![73]

There is no evidence that Jean Juvenal's text was intended for more general circulation and it survives mainly in later copies.[74] Several notaries and secretaries, however, produced historical works, which could serve as 'a mirror and example' to guide contemporary actions. Like Noël de Fribois, the authors generally addressed their works to the head of the body politic, kings or princes, rather than to their fellow officers, or wrote their historical works as a professional tool, or as a pastime. Some, like Fribois' chronicle, enjoyed a certain vogue within the same milieu, being owned or copied by notaries and secretaries, while Nicole Gilles addressed one 'exhortation' in his *Annalles et Chroniques* (before 1503) to magistrates in the *parlement* of Paris, to uphold the Pragmatic Sanction, and his work may have circulated in that milieu.[75] More powerful royal officers became patrons in their turn, but there is little evidence of a coherent body of advice literature addressed to this group, analogous to 'mirrors for princes'.

Reflected glory: public image and concepts of the chose publique *among royal officers*

The absence of a specific genre of literature addressed to this group might be explained in several ways. Royal officers could have expected to gain general

---

[72] *Écrits politiques*, vol. I, pp. 444, 451, 482.

[73] Ibid., pp. 472, 477, 481–82.

[74] Ibid., p. 437, where the editor identified only one medieval, and nine post-medieval manuscripts.

[75] K. Daly, 'Mixing Business with Leisure', pp. 99–115, esp. p. 114, n. 49.

advice on moral and spiritual conduct from the works which guided any good Christian, and on political conduct from the same texts which could be found in the libraries of kings and noblemen.[76] Professional manuals and the traditions of a particular institution, public expectations of royal officers, and their duties as members of the Christian church provided more specific sources of guidance.[77] On the other hand, it may be that their sense of forming a body within the *chose publique*, and their close association with royalty, encouraged them to look to the same models of conduct as that provided for the king himself.

Royal service was the source of the officers' reflected glory. Those who did not hold exalted office as individuals were associated with the monarchy through public ceremonial. Such opportunities were probably greatest for the *parlement* of Paris, which, as the highest sovereign court, emphasized its association with the king's crucial role as dispenser of justice, even when its own monopoly was mitigated at regional level by the creation of provincial *parlements* during the fifteenth century.[78]

---

[76] There is no systematic study of libraries of royal officers during the fifteenth century. These conclusions are based on the partial studies of groups or individuals: F. Autrand, 'Culture et mentalité. Les librairies des gens du parlement au temps de Charles VI', *Annales ESC* (1973), pp. 1219–44; N. Pons, 'Chancelleries et culture. Les chancelleries parisiennes sous les règnes de Charles VI et Charles VII', *Rapports présentés à la Commission Internationale de Diplomatique, XVIe Congrès International des Sciences Historiques* (Vatican City, 1990), pp. 137–68; P. Hefti, 'La formation d'un humaniste (Clément de Fauquembergue) au début du XVe siècle en France', *Romania*, XCII (1971), 289–325. Nicolas de Baye in 1419 and Jean Budé in the late fifteenth century owned copies of John of Salisbury's *Policraticon* (Paris, BNF MS latin 12966); Budé also owned a manuscript of the *De Regimine Principum* by Giles of Rome (BNF MS latin 6697): see *Journal de Nicolas de Baye*, ed. A. Tuetey, SHF (Paris, 1888), vol. II, p. lxxxii, n. 36; M. C. Garand, 'Les copistes de Jean Budé 1430–1502', *Bulletin de l'Institut de Recherche et d'Histoire des Textes*, 15, 1967–8 (1969), 293–328. For the role of officers of the *chancellerie* as patrons in their own right at a slightly later period, see S. Charton-le Clech, *Chancellerie et culture au XVIe siècle (les notaires et secrétaires du roi de 1515 à 1547)* (Toulouse, 1993).

[77] In 1406 Nicolas de Baye had a picture or board placed in the *grande chambre* of the *parlement* of Paris, with extracts from the writings of prophets and inscriptions taken from philosophers and poets, together with Nicolas's own comments on the duties of magistrates: *Journal de Nicolas de Baye*, vol. II, p. xiv.

[78] A. Viala, *Le parlement de Toulouse et l'administration royale laique 1420–1525 environ* (2 vols, Albi, 1953), vol. I, pp. 409–12, stresses that although ceremonies associated that *parlement* as a body with the crown, particularly on the occasion of royal deaths, the scope and frequency of its ceremonial did not rival that of the *parlement* of Paris. In the *parlement* of Rouen (established in 1499), technically the highest royal court within the province, the magistrates were associated with the king through ceremonies when he made his royal entry into the town, but again, not on the scale of the Paris *parlement*: J. Dewald, *Formation of a Provincial Nobility: Magistrates of the Parlement of Rouen 1499–1610* (Princeton, 1980), pp. 42, 44–5. For the defence by the Paris *parlement* of its special relationship with the crown when faced with the creation of provincial *parlements* in the fifteenth and sixteenth centuries, see B. Guenée, 'Espace et état dans la France du bas moyen âge', *Annales ESC* (1968), 116–25.

By the fifteenth century, however, the notaries and secretaries attempted to forge a comparable identity, through the medium of royal letters and ordinances granting privileges to their confraternity, of which the most highly developed example is that of the *ordonnance* of 1482. After considering 'the great, praiseworthy and commendable services that they have done heretofore, do each day and may do in future for the crown of France, and the necessity of maintaining them for the public good (*pour le bien de la chose publique de nostre royaume*)', Louis XI confirmed the college of notaries and secretaries' existing privileges, and accorded new ones.[79] Louis XI's dismissal of his father's officers on his accession (and the subsequent involvement of the disaffected in the War of the Public Weal) was glossed over with the explanation that the king had not been fully apprised of their privileges.[80] Thus the confraternity of notaries and secretaries is represented in this *ordonnance* as the beneficiary of a long tradition of public service, with a special relationship with the French crown: 'the kings of France have for good and just cause wished to raise the the notaries and secretaries to special privileges, estates, dignities and prerogatives among all their other officers, and above all have retained [them] and all their successors among their household and *familia* and as ordinary, domestic and commensal officers'. The assertion that their office would not be revoked at the death of an individual king associated them with the *office* of kingship, rather than the mortality of the man holding the office.[81]

This association with the crown is displayed in other ways. The births, reigns and deaths of kings in the short chronicles in manuals in the *chambre des comptes* and the *chancellerie* formed the context for the activity of the officers who served there, as well as practical chronological guides to the documents they might be called upon to deal with; the most important events in their professional and family life were also occasionally recorded.[82] The notaries and secretaries who served in the royal *chancellerie* and *chambre des comptes* were particularly prominent in exalting the prerogatives of the crown, not only in the course of their official duties, but through the composition of historical works and of treatises defending royal rights, whether against the Plantagenets (or in

---

[79] *Ordonnances*, vol. XIX, pp. 62-81, esp. pp. 63–4.

[80] For the role of the *parlement*, see C. W. Stocker, 'Office and Justice: Louis XI and the Parlement of Paris (1465–67)', *Medieval Studies*, XXXVII (1975), 360–86.

[81] 'Les roys de France ont a bonne et juste cause voullu eslever en especial privileges, estats, dignités et prerogatives entre tous leurs autres officiers, et par especial ont retenuz lesdits notaires et secretaires et tous leurs successeurs, de leur hostel et famille, et pour les officiers ordinaires, domestiques et commensaulx': *Ordonnances*, vol. XIX, pp. 63–4. In theory, from the fourteenth century, tenure of the chancellor and officers in the *parlement* did not terminate with the death of the king. For changes to the royal funerary ceremony in the fifteenth century, which emphasized the survival of the royal office in spite of the death of individual kings, see R. Giesey, *The Royal Funeral Ceremony in Renaissance France*, Travaux d'Humanisme et Renaissance XXXVIII (Geneva, 1960), pp. 210–14.

[82] Paris, BNF MS latin 9848 (*Advaluatio* of the *chambre des comptes*), ff. 4v–6r, 8r, where Adam des Champs, clerk in the *chambre des comptes* and Simon Laurens, *clerc extraordinaire* (1465–1501), recorded such events, as well as the battle of Agincourt in 1415, and the surrender of Rouen in 1449.

the case of the Dual Monarchy, the Valois), or against the pretensions of those they regarded as fellow subjects, such as the nobility.[83] The association of groups or individuals with the crown was also depicted visually, for example, in the *Retable* of the *parlement* of Paris, in illustrations of Charles VII in the Book of Hours of Etienne Chevalier, or the copy of the French translation of Boccaccio's *De casibus* belonging to Chevalier's son-in-law, Laurent Girard, and perhaps even in the 'two bodies' of Guillaume Juvenal des Ursins, depicted in his manuscript of the *Mer des Histoires*.[84] The ennoblement of individual royal officers through royal service was one of the most striking outcomes of this association, particularly when, in the case of the royal notaries and secretaries, it became open to the whole corps, once they had served for three generations.

Conclusion

For some (particularly themselves), royal officers were faithful servants of the crown, rewarded for their devotion: while for their critics, they were incompetent, rapacious and self-serving! These contrasting images seem appropriate for a group whose functions and social situation were undergoing profound changes during the fifteenth century. If 'by serving the king [royal officials] were serving themselves',[85] it is hardly surprising that the reality should fail to live up to the moral ideal projected for public service. The expectation that royal

[83] For Jean de Montreuil and Alain Chartier, in addition to works cited above, see J. Laidlaw, 'The Arts of Crisis Management: Alain Chartier 1418–1429', *Later Medieval France*, ed. C.T. Allmand (Liverpool University Press, forthcoming). For other officers in the *chancellerie* and *chambre des comptes*, see Daly, 'Mixing Business with Leisure'. For some French apologists on the opposing side, see B. Rowe, 'King Henry VI's Claim to France in Picture and Poem', *The Library*, 4th series, 13 (1932–33), 77–88; A. Bossuat, 'La littérature de propagande au XVe siècle: le mémoire de Jean de Rinel, secrétaire du roi d'Angleterre, contre le duc de Bourgogne (1435)', *Cahiers d'Histoire*, 1 (1956), 131–46.

[84] A. Châtelet, 'Le retable du parlement de Paris', *Art de France*, LV (1964), 60–9; M.G.A. Vale, 'The Livery Colours of Charles VII in Two Works by Fouquet', *Gazette des Beaux-Arts*, LXXIV (1969), 243–48. Cf. in a different context the comments of Rosemary Horrox on a painting of Edward Grimston in the Lancastrian livery collar, and on Reynold Bray's decorative use of symbols of the Beauforts and Tudors whom he had served: 'Service', *Fifteenth-Century Attitudes: Perceptions of Society in Late Medieval England*, ed. R. Horrox (Cambridge, 1994), pp. 61–78, esp. p. 68. On Guillaume Jouvenal des Ursins and the *Mer des Histoires*, BNF français 4195, where he is depicted as chancellor, and as a knight, see P. S. Lewis, 'The Chancellor's Two Bodies: Note on a Miniature in BNF latin 4915', *Journal of the Warburg and Courtauld Institutes*, 55 (1992), 263–5; Lewis is, however, cautious in interpreting this as a conscious representation of the chancellor's dual role as lay official and soldier, as it might be merely 'another example of his family's eccentricities' (265).

[85] P. S. Lewis, *Later Medieval France*, p. 140. The conflict between ideals and reality in attitudes to French royal government and royal officers in France is reminiscent of the 'disparities between theory and practice that fuelled public dissatisfaction with the law' discussed in A. Musson and W.M. Ormrod, *The Evolution of English Justice: Law, Politics and Society in the Fourteenth Century* (Basingstoke, 1999), pp. 161–93, esp. p. 189.

officials should be expert was to some extent justified by gradual, though incomplete, 'professionalization' and specialization within the royal administration. On the other hand, the expectation could not be fully satisfied, given the elasticity of royal office and the multiplicity of purposes which individual royal officers had to fulfil. Royal offices could be sinecures, rewards or even security for loans for those who served the king, or the politically powerful, in other capacities.

It is easy, however, to take too cynical an approach. The political thought and ideas of royal officials as a group have not been studied, but we have some indications of the attitudes of particular individuals or coteries, which show subscription to principles which did not necessarily benefit them, and might menace their political survival. Leaving aside the stories told by Jean Juvenal II about his father, one might cite some of the letters of Jean de Montreuil, who reminded his friend, Gontier Col, in 1400 that those with different gifts might serve the *rei publicae* in different ways according to their talents,[86] and who expressed, in his sixty-third year, gratitude and hope that he would continue to enjoy the bodily strength to serve the king.[87] The irony of his comment, so shortly before his death, was not lost on the annotator of the manuscript of his letters, Jean Le Bègue, who recalled that Montreuil was massacred less than a year after the letter was written. Le Bègue's own annotations reinforce several of the themes mentioned earlier, some shared by Montreuil and Chartier: the corruption of those at court; the need for silence on political events when those in power care neither for faith nor law; the desirability that patrons or advocates should not accept presents.[88]

Perhaps it is appropriate to end with Le Bègue, rather than his better known and more prolix literary colleagues, Montreuil, Chartier and Fribois, who all wrote defending the Valois cause against the English, combining private loyalty and public service in their works. Le Bègue's career spanned the reigns of Charles VI, Henry VI (for he opted to stay in Paris) and Charles VII. In her recent study of the notes he made in his manuscripts, Nicole Pons has traced the impact on Le Bègue of the changes in the *chose publique* which he witnessed in his own lifetime. She suggests that Le Bègue was profoundly affected by contemporary political turmoil, in spite of his own survival, withdrawing from the arena of public affairs, despite his humanist interests, as if disillusioned by political events. For some individuals, at last if not at least, the true route to service of the crown and that of the *chose publique* lay in professional routine and expertise: the exercise of the 'duties' of office, rather than the rewards, as Chartier advised his friend.[89]

---

[86] Jean de Montreuil, *Opera*, ed. E. Ornato (Turin, 1963), vol. I, pp. 207–8, cited in N. Pons, 'Érudition et politique. La personnalité de Jean Le Bègue d'après les notes marginales de ses manuscrits', *Les serviteurs de l'État au Moyen Age. Actes du XXIXᵉ Congrès de la SHMESP (Pau, 1998)* (Paris, 1999), pp. 281–97.

[87] 'Cupientissimus insuper quod possem iure officii rei communi atque regi quantum unquam subservire': Montreuil, *Opera*, p. 334.

[88] Ibid.; Pons, 'La personnalité de Jean Le Bègue', pp. 292–95.

[89] Ibid. pp. 294–95. For Le Bègue's ambitions earlier in life to better himself by marrying the daughter of the chancellor, Pierre Lorfèvre, however, see G. Ouy, 'Le songe et les ambitions d'un jeune humaniste parisien vers 1395', *Miscellanea di studi e ricerche sul Quattrocento Francese*, ed. F. Simone (Turin, 1967), pp. 355–407.

VIII

THE MATERIAL REWARDS OF SERVICE IN LATE MEDIEVAL BRITTANY: DUCAL SERVANTS AND THEIR RESIDENCES

Michael Jones

'KERANIOU, I have seen what you have written to me, and because I also very much want to get the cattle, I am sending Crochen to fetch them because they are such fine animals. Send me by Crochen as much cash as you possibly can so that we can get up to twenty of them, otherwise when you come here from [Callac], you will drink nothing but cider! Crochen will tell you all about the rest of my affairs as usual, so adieu, with best wishes from Branxihen, all yours, J[ean] de Villeblanche.' Thus, on 14 October 1504, Jean, *seigneur* of Plessis Balisson, Châtellier and Plusquellec, writing on friendly, even intimate, terms as the diminutive form of address suggests, to Henri de Kernegues, castellan and receiver of his lordship of Callac (22), in a routine letter of command, similar probably to countless others sent by Villeblanche's *compères* to their own servants in late medieval Brittany.[1] Nevertheless, it is a rare survival of correspondence at this social level – that of the middling nobility or well-off knighthood – in a province not blessed with the great letter collections that have provided so much evidence for recent discussions of service and the relations

---

[1] AD du Finistère, 5 H 449: 'Keraniou, jay veu ce que mavez escrit et comant je aussi envie querir les beuffs je y envoia Crochen pour cest affaire pource que lesdits beuffs soient bien excellans. Envoiez moy par led. Crochen le plus dargent que possible vous sera de faire pour faire venir pres vings ou aultrement quant viendrez de par de sa vous ne boirez que du cidre. Led. Crochen vous dira le par sur an vous recommandant touz mes affaires de par de la touz jours et adieu leur en me recommandant a vous. A Branxian le xiiij^me doctobre [1504]. Le tout vostre, J. de Villeblanche'. The letter is endorsed by Pierre Crochen acknowledging receipt from Henry de Kernegues of five oxen (*boeuffs*) and one cow, worth 43 *livres* on 18 October 1504. Other documents in this small *liasse* include an order from Villeblanche to Kernegues to pay Jean de Ferrières, *maître d'hôtel*, his annual wages of 20 *livres* (29 Sept. 1504), a quittance by Villeblanche to Kernegues for receipt of 50 *livres* (13 Sept. 1504) and a list of expenses Kernegues had incurred since his last account, with details of journeys and other expenses over legal cases. Further accounts for the seigneury of Callac for 1502 and 1506–8, when Kernegues was still the receiver, survive (5 H 438, 439*, 451, 452) as do other particulars for 1503 and 1504–5 (5 H 434 and 450). The departmental locations of places mentioned in this article in Brittany are indicated by the modern administrative code numbers: 22 = Côtes-d'Armor; 29 = Finistère; 35 = Ille-et-Vilaine; 44 = Loire-Atlantique; 56 = Morbihan.

119

of lords and men as fifteenth-century England has done.[2] Indeed, although medieval Breton society was in most respects as hierarchical and conscious of distinctions as elsewhere, I have been struck whilst preparing this paper by a contrast between the haughty tone of many masters and obsequiousness of their servants on this side of the Channel, and a corresponding absence of such attitudes in Brittany, a contrast sharpened not just by a dearth of written evidence but because of genuine differences of behaviour and outlook: that late medieval Brittany was in some respects more egalitarian than late medieval England, though, as we shall see, it was not innocent of fine gradations in social differentiation.[3] Family honour, status, gaining and defending privilege, pique and *amour propre*, play a part in what follows. In particular I will exploit material evidence to show some rewards of service, especially service to the dukes of Brittany, since this compensates in part for the absence of written records. Both in its variety and quality, it raises interesting questions about sources of wealth and its use. Some answers can be advanced, but there is still much to be discovered both with regard to individual families and buildings and about general reactions to visible display of material rewards by the successful.[4]

To put things into perspective, a few facts and figures: late medieval Brittany covered some 35,000 square kilometres, about a tenth of the size of royal France, much the same area as medieval or modern Wales. But it was more densely populated than other Celtic lands, especially around its coastal fringes. In the late fourteenth century it probably contained in excess of a million inhabitants. By 1430 this figure had fallen by some 25 per cent, a decline which continued to the mid-century, after which an uneven but perceptible recovery set in with the population around 1500 once again exceeding a million, perhaps even reaching as many as 1.25 million.[5]

Within this substantial population, and of particular concern in what follows, since one of the most frequent rewards of service was ennoblement, there was already a higher proportion of nobles than found in most other parts of France. Whilst modern estimates, based on extrapolation from the evidence of periodic revision of tax registers during the fifteenth century, commissions for the *réformations des feux*, and from frequent musters (*montres*), of those owing military service, differ from one modern authority to another, there is broad agreement that the total number of Breton noble families in this period certainly exceeded

---

[2] See *Fifteenth-Century Attitudes: Perceptions of Society in Late Medieval England*, ed. R. Horrox (Cambridge, 1994), especially the editor's fine essay, 'Service', pp. 61–78.

[3] J. Gallet, *La seigneurie bretonne (1450–1680). L'exemple du Vannetais* (Paris, 1983), p. 99, illustrates the relatively simple form of the feudal pyramid in Brittany in tabular form.

[4] This paper picks up some themes elaborated at greater length in M. Jones, 'The Late Medieval State and Social Change: a View from the Duchy of Brittany', *L'État ou le Roi. Les fondations de la modernité monarchique en France (XIVe–XVIIe siècles)*, ed. N. Bulst, R. Descimon and A. Guerreau (Paris, 1996), pp. 117–44.

[5] J. Kerhervé, 'Temps des ducs, temps des rois. Manoir et histoire', *Le manoir en Bretagne 1380–1600* (Cahiers de l'inventaire no. 28) (Paris, 1993), p. 34, summarizes population figures; see also J-N. Biraben and A. Blum, 'La population de la Bretagne de 1500 à 1839', *Populations et cultures: études réunies en l'honneur de François Lebrun* (Paris, 1989).

7,000, and by 1500 in all likelihood closely approached 10,000. Michel Nassiet, for example, estimates some 7,940 noble families in 1426 and around 8,800 in the 1480s; an earlier estimate by Pocquet du Haut-Jussé suggested precisely 9,336 at this latter date, while Jean Kerhervé has 'au moment du redressement démographique, 9,000 à 10,000 familles peut-être'. Certainly 3 per cent of the total population enjoyed a measure of noble privilege.[6] Moreover, since there were some 1,300 parishes in the duchy, each parish inevitably contained several families of *noblesse*, newcomers often having to vie with long-established families and jealous commoner neighbours to prove their credentials, especially to claim that freedom from direct taxation conferred by nobility.[7]

In northern Brittany, in particular, it was common for many parishes to have twenty or more such families, and extreme cases are known where ducal commissioners acknowledged more than fifty families claiming nobility in a single parish: for example Plounévez-Lochrist (29) had 54 noble families; Taulé (29), 59; Maroué (22), 57; and Planguenoual (22), 61.[8] Inevitably noble income varied equally disproportionately from those whose annual revenue might be as low as a couple of shillings, to great landholders like the *vicomtes* de Rohan, *comtes* de Léon, or the *comtes* de Laval, *seigneurs* de Vitré, who had hundreds of tenants and rent rolls running to more than 5,000 *livres p.a.*[9] Although the figures must be considered minima, given that they were self-assessed, even if scrutinized by neighbours, at the moment nobles or would-be nobles were summoned to *montres* (when they were supposed to equip themselves with armour and weapons appropriate to their annual income as set out on a scale regulated by ducal *ordonnances* from 1451), it has been calculated that in the Vannetais an average fifteenth-century Breton gentleman probably had an income of around 100 *livres p.a.* (say £20 sterling) or less.[10] Similar figures can be produced for most other parts of the duchy; a recent study has shown that of 260 noble families in Cornouaille, in part of the diocese of Quimper, 75 per cent belonged

---

[6] M. Nassiet, *Noblesse et pauvreté. La petite noblesse en Bretagne XVe–XVIIIe siècle* (Bannalec, 1993), pp. 90–2; B.A. Pocquet du Haut-Jussé, 'De la vassalité à la noblesse', *Bulletin philologique et historique du comité des travaux historiques et scientifiques*, I (1963), 785–800; Kerhervé, 'Temps des ducs', p. 39; cf. the estimate of 3,000 landholders of knightly or gentry rank in England, c. 1300, by C. Given-Wilson, *The English Nobility in the Late Middle Ages* (London, 1986), p. 14.

[7] See Nassiet, *Noblesse*, pp. 85–90, for some problems of determining where the line between commoner and noble status was drawn. He is also usefully publishing a systematic survey of Breton 'feudataires' in 1480: 'Dictionnaire des feudataires des évêchés de Dol et de Saint-Malo en 1480', *Association Bretonne, Bulletin* (1990), 183–203; ibid., (1991), 265–96; ibid., (1993), 221–51; 'Dictionnaire ... Saint-Brieuc en 1480', *Bulletin de la société d'émulation des Côtes-d'Armor* (1996), 7–86; 'Dictionnaire ... Tréguier', ibid. (1998), 3–76.

[8] Kerhervé, 'Temps des ducs', pp. 39–40, and esp. tables in n. 57, pp. 312–3.

[9] Nassiet, *Noblesse*, pp. 46 et seq. for 'la hiérarchie des revenus nobles'. In the diocese of St-Brieuc thirty-nine 'feudataires' claimed that their income from their noble properties was one *livre* or less!

[10] Hervé, vicomte du Halgouët, *Une seigneurie de la sénéchaussée d'Auray. Coëtsal. Le domaine et les seigneurs* (St-Brieuc, 1920); cf. Gallet, *La seigneurie bretonne*, pp. 137–42, where he claims the average income of the 'petite noblesse' was c. 40 *livres*.

Michael Jones

to what has been termed the 'petite aristocratie', with incomes of 40 *livres* to 80 *livres p.a.*, whilst 19 per cent possessed less than 20 *livres p.a.*;[11] in the Vannetais 30 per cent of noble families fell into this latter income group.[12] In north-eastern Brittany in the dioceses of St-Malo, Rennes and Dol, Nassiet found that only 3 per cent of nobles declared incomes of more than 600 *livres*, nearly 17 per cent enjoyed between 100 and 500 *livres p.a.*, but more than 80 per cent of those in the diocese of St-Malo possessed less than 80 *livres p.a.* and that the median average of noble income here was 30 *livres*.[13] Relating this to military obligation and the costs of equipment, he further estimated that 'L'équipement minimal [i.e. for an archer] coûtait donc de l'ordre du triple de la nourriture d'une famille de cinq personnes pendant un an'.[14] These statistics must be kept in mind when considering the scale of rewards enjoyed by those in ducal service.

It is now well-known that the dukes of Brittany in the later Middle Ages created an all but independent state within the kingdom of France; I shall not rehearse all the arguments yet again here.[15] Briefly, from the time of the Breton civil war in the mid-fourteenth century, successive dukes had deliberately and continuously expanded their own household, created major administrative departments, notably a chancery and financial institutions centring on a *chambre des comptes*, overhauled the judicial system, elaborated a hierarchy of courts in eight separate *sénéchaussées* (which led on appeal to the *parlement de Bretagne*), and formed a small standing army, among other practical measures intended to provide them with the means to govern effectively and independently of the crown. With the introduction of regular taxation in the form of hearth taxes, *fouages*, and a raft of indirect levies (*aides, billots, impôts, traites*) on foodstuffs, beverages and other consumable goods, there came regular sessions of the *états* in which issues other than finance could also be discussed by a wide body of the higher clergy and *noblesse*, reinforced by town representatives.[16] Brittany had its own currency and church; its ruler claimed sovereign rights, notably with regard to judgement of *lèse-majesté*; it constituted a separate heraldic march.

At a local level too, urban administration, traditionally supervised closely in Brittany by the duke and his council, also expanded in this period to meet growing demands for action by public authorities on civil and military matters, most notably for physical defence against aggressive neighbours, first the English, especially their garrisons in Normandy and Maine, and latterly the French, while there was the perennial menace of enemies at sea.[17]

---

[11] N. Calvez, 'La noblesse en Basse Cornouaille, XVe–XVIe siècles' (unpublished mémoire de maîtrise, Université de Bretagne occidentale, Brest, 1990).

[12] Gallet, *La seigneurie bretonne*, pp. 137–42.

[13] Nassiet, *Noblesse*, pp. 46–53.

[14] Ibid., p. 51.

[15] See M. Jones, *The Creation of Brittany* (London, 1988); idem, ' "En son habit royal": le duc de Bretagne et son image au XVe siècle', *Représentation, royauté et pouvoir à la fin du moyen âge*, ed. J. Blanchard (Paris, 1995), pp. 253–78.

[16] P.S. Lewis, *Essays in Later Medieval French History* (London, 1985), pp. 127–38, is the best starting point for the Breton estates.

[17] J-P. Leguay, *Un réseau urbain au Moyen Age. Les villes du duché de Bretagne aux XIVe et XVe siècles* (Paris, 1981), pp. 167–90.

In addition, though the subject can again only be mentioned in passing, this pragmatic approach to government was reinforced by an ideological one in which history and myth, together with legal precedent, were used to create concepts of Breton individualism and autonomy. Much of this programme of conscious propaganda was inevitably borrowed from Valois France, though it was given a particular Breton twist: Trojan origins, the use of visual symbols of authority (crowns, royal or imperial robes, coinage, including a gold currency, bearing the *Dei gratia* formula), the panoply of court ceremonial, a chivalric order (the Ermine, founded *c.* 1381), a lively and expanding historiography, written by those close to the ducal family, court or administration in the service of the Breton state, are among its more obvious features. It was aimed at persuading inhabitants of the duchy to think of themselves first and foremost as Bretons and ducal subjects rather than as subjects of the king of France.[18] The strain imposed on their loyalties by dukes who pursued policies at variance with those of the crown is also a theme that has been examined elsewhere;[19] it long suited the Breton *noblesse* to play off Brittany and France, rallying to the duke when it appeared that the crown was about to gain a closer control of the duchy, as happened on at least two occasions in the fourteenth century. Nascent provincial sentiment also helped dukes to stave off similar moves in the fifteenth century until the final Wars of Breton Independence between 1487 and 1491. Then the intervention of all the major western European powers in Breton affairs brought a dawning realization that lasting domestic peace could only be bought by the marriage of Duchess Anne to Charles VIII, paving the way for a closer, permanent union of the duchy and kingdom.

The formation of the late medieval Breton state naturally provided opportunities for the ambitious and able. The expansion of both central government and local administration created offices and other chances for employment and reward which were eagerly seized. The evolution of the *chambre des comptes* provides a clear example of this. A specialized financial system first begins to emerge in the 1260s with local receivers presenting themselves at regular intervals at a limited number of locations before officials delegated by the duke to hear their accounts.[20] If it was the needs of rivals in the Breton succession war that provided an incentive for further development, with more regular attempts at general taxation from the 1340s, the establishment of a proper *chambre des comptes* was one of the first priorities of Duke John IV after his victory at Auray in 1364. It is mentioned for the first time in 1365, the first year in which

---

[18] See Jones, *Creation of Brittany*, pp. 283–307; idem, 'Les signes du pouvoir: l'Ordre de l'Hermine, les devises et les hérauts des ducs de Bretagne au XVe siècle' *MSHAB*, LXVIII (1991), 141–73; idem, ' "En son habit royal" '; J. Kerhervé, 'Entre conscience nationale et identité régionale dans la Bretagne de la fin du moyen âge', *Identité régionale et conscience nationale en France et en Allemagne du Moyen Age à l'époque moderne*, ed. R. Babel and J-M. Moeglin (Beihefte des Francia, Bd. 39, 1997), pp. 219–43.

[19] Jones, *Creation of Brittany*, pp. 329–50; idem, 'Aristocratie, faction et l'état dans la Bretagne du XVe siècle', *L'État et les aristocraties (France, Angleterre, Ecosse), XIIe–XVIIe siècle*, ed. P. Contamine (Paris, 1989), pp. 129–60.

[20] B-A. Pocquet du Haut-Jussé, 'Le plus ancien rôle des comptes du duché, 1262', *MSHAB*, XXVI (1946), 49–68.

it was possible to levy a *fouage* on the whole duchy and to collect customs generally on wine and other merchandise entering or leaving ports.[21] The *chambre* soon had its own seal, and from the 1380s a clerk and a permanent base, the Hôtel de Largoët at Vannes, where it remained until Charles VIII moved it to Nantes. As for its permanent personnel, numbering around ten in 1400, by the reign of Duchess Anne there were twenty officers – two *présidents*, two or three *auditeurs* and the rest clerks or secretaries of accounts – many of whom enjoyed long and successful careers, often accumulating lesser functions which had been created in the *chambre* during the course of the century such as a *procureur*, who protected the duke's interests from the 1440s, an archivist, a paymaster, a *huissier* and two *greffiers*, turning them too into offices, some becoming family preserves. In turn the *chambre* supervised the local receivers of some thirty-five to forty domainial receipts, twenty separate receipts for *fouages* and many other minor receipts and farms created to handle the wide range of direct and indirect fiscality imposed after 1365. Thanks to the herculean labours of Jean Kerhervé, the careers of some 1,500 of these financial officers for the period 1365–1491 have been traced; the vast majority were laymen, a high proportion enjoying noble status, if not from the outset, certainly by the end of their careers.[22] Some, as we shall see, have left tangible evidence of their worldly success, since a career in finance, more so even than the legal profession, was a path to fortune in late medieval Brittany. The same story is repeated in the first half of the sixteenth century as Dominique Le Page's recently published investigation of the careers of a further 400 financial officers makes clear.[23]

The other main central organ of state was the chancery. A permanent writing office had first emerged in Brittany towards the end of the twelfth or beginning of the thirteenth century, but its history before the fourteenth century is sketchy; even the succession of chancellors, for instance, is difficult to establish.[24] In 1305 there were seven resident clerks in the ducal household, providing a growing technical service in preparing and writing documents. A century later their number had doubled, whilst, as in the *chambre des comptes*, careers were increasingly open to married men even if the top jobs of chancellor and vice-chancellor were predominantly held by clerics, with a few notable exceptions, Guillaume Chauvin, chancellor from 1459–81, being the most significant.[25] In 1488 twenty-four named chancery clerks were issued with mourning cloth on the death of

---

[21] J. Kerhervé, *L'État breton au 14e et 15e siècles. Les ducs, l'argent et les hommes* (2 vols Paris, 1987), vol. I, pp. 341–405, is fundamental for the *chambre*; he has recently added a useful documentary appendix: 'La chambre des comptes de Bretagne', *Les chambres des comptes en France aux XIVe et XVe siècles*, ed. P. Contamine and O. Mattéoni (Paris, 1998), pp. 127–79.

[22] Kerhervé, *L'État breton*, and more fully in the unpublished, three-volume, 'Catalogue prosopographique' of his original thesis, 'Finances et gens de finances des ducs de Bretagne, 1365–1491' (Université de Paris I, 1986), of which copies are deposited in all the Breton departmental archives.

[23] D. Le Page, *Finances et politique en Bretagne au début des temps modernes 1491–1547. Étude d'un processus d'intégration au royaume de France* (Paris, 1997).

[24] For the chancery, see Jones, *The Creation of Brittany*, pp. 111–58.

[25] We lack a good study of Chauvin, but see Kerhervé, *L'État breton*, passim, and 'Catalogue', vol. III, pp. 768–73.

Francis II, in addition to the major officers, the chancellor, vice-chancellor and the *maîtres des requêtes*.[26] For a brief period Charles VIII suppressed the Breton chancery and the number of those employed as clerks fell, but Louis XII's reign saw a return to earlier policy. Although the title of chancellor was suppressed in 1514, out of deference to the chancellor of France, other members of the chancery continued to enjoy high social status until changes in the mid-sixteenth century resulted in newly created *présidiaux* taking over its judicial functions, whilst a sovereign *parlement de Bretagne* (erected in 1554) now assumed responsibility for the registration of acts. Like the majority of those serving in the *chambre des comptes* during the transition from ducal to royal rule, few members of the chancery suffered as a result of the change of regime in 1491.[27]

Other sectors of ducal government display similar features to those of the *chambre des comptes* and the chancery. The duke's own household, for example, witnessed a major expansion of its personnel and responsibilities during the course of the century. In 1404, early in the reign of John V (1399–1442), while he was still in the guardianship of Philip the Bold, duke of Burgundy, the latter undertook a thorough overhaul of the ducal *hôtel*.[28] At that point it contained some 160 members; by 1488 it had almost 700 and there were another 120 employed in that of the young princess, Anne.[29] Depending on family circumstances pertaining at any particular point, a number of lesser households buttressed that of the duke, providing additional opportunities for employment that was both lucrative and honourable. Although not as formalized as it was at the Burgundian court, the doubling-up of officers and service by rotation during the course of the year expanded the duke's patronage. Many families of *noblesse* sought places at court, often beginning the process early in life by sending sons to be *enfants de la chambre* or daughters *demoiselles* of the duchess, their welfare, especially their marriages, being a matter of particular ducal concern.[30] It was normal too for the duke's heir and the duchess or dowager-duchesses, of whom

---

[26] *Documents inédits sur le complot breton de M.CCCC.XC.II*, ed. A. de la Borderie (Nantes, 1884), no. XLVII at pp. 85–7; J. Kerhervé, 'Les registres des lettres scellées à la chancellerie de Bretagne sous le règne du duc François II (1452–1488)', *Écrit et pouvoir dans les chancelleries médiévales: espace français, espace anglais* (Textes et études du Moyen Age, Fédération internationale des Instituts d'études médiévales, no. 6, Louvain-la-Neuve, 1997), pp. 153–203, is an important contribution on the chancery's functioning.

[27] See Le Page, *Finances et politique en Bretagne*, esp. pp. 200–49.

[28] Dom H. Morice, *Mémoires pour servir de preuves à l'histoire ecclésiastique et civile de Bretagne* (3 vols, Paris, 1742–6), vol. II, cols 735–40, the original of which is AD Loire-Atlantique, E 5 no. 3.

[29] Kerhervé, *L'État breton*, vol. I, p. 230, after Morice, *Preuves*, vol. III, cols 603–7, and *Documents inédits*, pp. 79–104.

[30] Remarks based on the fragmentary and scattered remnants of the ducal household accounts in AD Loire-Atlantique, B, chambre des comptes, parchemins non classés; AD Ille-et-Vilaine, 1 F 1111–1118; Nantes, Archives municipales, II 120 and 121; and Abbaye St-Guénolé, Landévennec (29), Fonds Lebreton, liasses 4A and 4B.

there were several notably long-lived examples in fifteenth-century Brittany,[31] to have their own *hôtels*, whilst other cadets of the house of Montfort like Richard, *comte* d'Étampes, and Arthur de Richemont, *connétable de France*, younger brothers of John V, sometimes resided at the Breton court with their own body of servants.[32] In a relatively backward economy, the importance of the court and its satellites as consumers of both ordinary and luxury goods needs little emphasis: craftsmen and merchants, especially in the largest towns like Rennes, Nantes and Vannes, were the leading suppliers of their demands, though Parisians and foreigners (notably Italians, Spaniards and Flemings) might also enjoy ducal patronage.[33]

Though Brittany cannot now show the wealth of documentary evidence that is so instructive for Burgundian (or Angevin or even Yorkist) court life in this period, it is clear that it developed equally elaborate rituals and etiquette, with specialized offices dealing with all the multifarious aspects of the duke's private and public life. To take what may appear a relatively minor example, the offices of the *grand veneur* or *maître de fauconnerie* provided substantial financial rewards to their holders, without exception members of the *noblesse*: Mons. Henri le Parisy received 300 *livres p.a.* as the duke's master huntsman in 1434, whilst Jean Dauray drew at least 125 *livres* in 1434–5 as *grant maistre de la fauconnerie*.[34] Fragmentary though surviving household accounts are, they are replete with evidence of ducal generosity to officers from the most senior chamberlains and *maîtres d'hôtel* to lowly clerks and messengers, of gifts over and above their usual wages, either in the form of monetary payments or rewards in kind – a horse, a piece of armour, a robe, an ell of cloth – offered for a particular service.[35] In addition some gift-giving at court was ritualized in the form of New Year's presents (*étrennes*), a practice which seems to reach its apogee in the mid-century, with studied attention to the social status of the recipient and appropriately fine distinctions in quality, workmanship and cost of the gift conferred, though it should also be remembered that reciprocation was expected, thus in part limiting the value of the reward enjoyed by subordinates.[36] Here, perhaps, is more concrete evidence for a deferential society than otherwise found in the written record.

[31] E.g. Isabeau de Stuart (d. 1494), widow of Francis I (d. 1450), and Françoise d'Amboise (d. 1495), widow of Pierre II (d. 1457); Catherine de Luxembourg (d. 1492), third wife of Arthur III (d. 1458); Marguerite, *comtesse* d'Étampes (d. 1465), mother of Francis II, widow of Richard, *comte* d'Étampes (d. 1439), also spent much time at the Breton court.

[32] See Kerhervé, *L'État breton*, vol. I, pp. 226–8.

[33] Well-evidenced in fragmentary accounts among those cited in n. 30 above.

[34] AD Loire-Atlantique, B, parchemins non classés, fragments of the accounts of Auffroy Guinot, *trésorier et receveur-général*, 1433–4. Dauray replaced Alain de Duaut, who was receiving 120 *livres p.a.*, on 24 January 1434; under Francis II, total expenses for these two services cost the duke 4,000–6,000 *livres p.a.*; see Kerhervé, *L'État breton*, vol. I, pp. 257–8.

[35] See n. 30 above.

[36] For ducal *étrennes*, see Morice, *Preuves*, vol. II, cols 1195, 1224, 1260–1, 1395, 1412, 1688, 1724; for more details, see Jones, ' "En son habit royal" ', p. 259 n. 21. For the gift of 'un gros dyamant partie assiz en un annel dor' and 'une chasenette dor' given by Francis, count of Montfort, to his wife on New Year's day 1432, see Landévennec, Fonds Lebreton, liasse 4A no. 54.

As elsewhere before the establishment of standing forces, the ducal household also continued during the century to provide the nucleus of any army the Bretons put into the field. Between the beginning of the reign of Duke Francis II (1458–88) and that of Duchess Anne (1488–1514), in part reflecting growing concern with defence against a powerful neighbour, though also mirroring developments elsewhere, the ducal bodyguard alone grew from fifty-one lances to over 500 men, the captains and lieutenants of whom automatically assumed leading positions in time of war.[37] The marshal and admiral of Brittany were always leading courtiers and members of the ducal council; household messengers were ceaselessly on the road between the duke, his council and captains of castles or those in the field. A *commis* of the treasurer, usually a leading secretary like François Avignon in the middle and later years of Francis II's reign, was attached to the household to make payments directly on the duke's behalf for his 'secret affairs', usually a euphemism for confidential diplomatic missions or for rewarding spies, as the ducal *hôtel* remained the hub of military and diplomatic action.[38]

After 1449 a small professional army, normally consisting in peacetime of 200 lances (600–1,000 men in all) and a respectable artillery corps with more than seventy cannoneers and technical experts, was kept on a permanent footing.[39] In times of crisis like the War of the Public Weal (1465) or the Wars of Independence from 1487, it was able to expand quickly to 600–700 lances, and many of its disciplined and experienced troops provided the officer corps for the amateur forces produced by appeal to those owing traditional feudal service who appeared at the *montres*. It is thus hardly surprising that the ducal household made the heaviest regular demands on his revenues throughout the century, accounting for more than half of expenditure even in a normal year. In this it was no different from the royal household or those of other contemporary French princes.[40] Whilst it is difficult to demonstrate huge individual profits derived from war, it is notable that military service in the ducal *ordonnance* companies appears frequently when discussing possible sources of wealth for the building of many seigneurial residences. Likewise, those who were responsible for administering, paying or disciplining the ducal forces, from the *trésoriers des guerres* and the *prévôt des mareschaux* and their *commis* downwards, were not ill-rewarded for their pains if their homes are taken as evidence.[41]

---

[37] Jones, *The Creation of Brittany*, p. 361.

[38] For Avignon, see Landévennec, Fonds Lebreton, liasse 4A no. 124 and 4B no. 126, and cf. 4A no. 117. A bundle of 85 quittances for payments made chiefly in 1473–4, presented by the executors of Avignon's predecessor, Guillaume Moulnier, when settling his account, survives in AD Loire-Atlantique, B, chambre des comptes, parchemins non classés, rare examples of what must once have been an enormous archive. I am grateful to M. Jean-François Carhaës, *conservateur*, for help in allowing me to see these and other unclassified documents at Nantes.

[39] For the Breton army, see Jones, *The Creation of Brittany*, pp. 351–69.

[40] Kerhervé, *L'État breton*, vol. I, pp. 261–9, 'un gouffre financier'.

[41] For example, the sadly mutilated remains of the once fine *manoir* of La Boullaye en Betton (35) of Olivier Le Baud, *trésorier des guerres*, 1461–78 (Jones, 'Social Change', pl. 7; Kerhervé, *L'État breton*, vol. II, pp. 898–9).

Turning more specifically then to the architectural and archaeological evidence, first a few general remarks to set the context. As the Renaissance châteaux of the Loire valley or the great houses of early Tudor ministers testify, leading servants of early modern states frequently displayed their wealth, dignity and influence in exuberant architectural form.[42] But the habit was already well-established in France by the early fourteenth century at the latest, when the petty Norman gentleman, Enguerran de Marigny, who rose spectacularly to become a leading adviser of Philip IV, only to become a scapegoat under his son, acquired an extensive rural lordship, bought up houses in Paris (with a view to building an impressive *hôtel* conveniently close to the Louvre), and founded a collegiate church at Ecouis (Eure) and numerous other chapels and charitable foundations on his other estates.[43] Successful servants of the Breton state naturally followed suit.

As already indicated, Brittany was a duchy dominated socially as well as numerically by its *noblesse*. To maintain their status, nobles, as Peter Lewis convincingly demonstrated and as Philippe Contamine has recently reminded us, have to live, as far as they are able, nobly, dispendiously and generously.[44] Long before 1400 this meant that nobles in Brittany, as elsewhere, led lives that required appropriate physical locations for the display of their status. For the upper échelons of noble society from at least the eleventh century this usually meant a castle, a fortified residence, a *château-fort* in French, to distinguish it from the later more domesticated Renaissance-style *château*, where defensive attributes were merely symbolic; while for those with more limited means, by the thirteenth century a *maison-forte* might suffice, both often succeeding earlier primitive motte-and-bailey structures on the same site or closely adjacent to it.[45] At the same time, however, considerations of domestic comfort and civil function as much as defensive criteria (or just lack of resources) led many noble families to inhabit simpler, largely undefended dwellings, *manoirs*, the principal purpose of which, besides offering a home to a lord and his family and displaying signs of lordship, was to serve as the centre of an agricultural estate.

Hence, too, their numbers: if there were some forty to fifty *châteaux-forts* in the medieval duchy, it has been calculated that by the fifteenth century there were around 13,000–14,000 *manoirs* (since many families owned more than

---

[42] J. Babelon, *Châteaux de France au siècle de la Renaissance* (Paris, 1989); M. Howard, *The Early Tudor Country House. Architecture and Politics 1490–1550* (London, 1987).

[43] J. Favier, *Un conseiller de Philippe le Bel, Enguerran de Marigny* (Paris, 1963), pp. 33–53.

[44] P.S. Lewis, *Later Medieval France: the Polity* (London, 1968), pp. 187 et seq., P. Contamine, *La noblesse au royaume de France de Philippe le Bel à Louis XII* (Paris, 1997), esp. pp. 38–45.

[45] For the range of noble residences in Brittany, see M. Jones, G. Meirion-Jones, J. Pilcher and F. Guibal, 'The Seigneurial Domestic Buildings of Brittany: a Provisional Assessment', *The Antiquaries Journal*, 69 (1989), 73–110, and G. Meirion-Jones, M. Jones and J.R. Pilcher, 'The Seigneurial Domestic Buildings of Brittany, 1000–1700', *Manorial Domestic Buildings in England and Northern France*, ed. G. Meirion-Jones and M. Jones (Society of Antiquaries of London, Occasional Papers vol. 15, 1993), pp. 158–91.

one).[46] A surprisingly high proportion still survive in some form to the present: the local *savant*, le vicomte Henri Frotier de la Messelière, for example, identified 1,700 manoirs and apparently visited no fewer than 1,300 of them in the *département* of Côtes-du-Nord (now Côtes-d'Armor) alone in the earlier part of last century.[47] Recent, more systematic, surveys of limited areas have confirmed the picture: in ten parishes around Lesneven (29) sixty-eight *manoirs* have been identified,[48] in seven parishes between Aber-Benoît and Aber-Ildut further west in northern Finistère there were no fewer than 112 *manoirs*,[49] and in seventeen modern communes in the cantons of Lézardrieux and Tréguier, representing fourteen medieval parishes, 217 *manoirs* have been identified, forty-nine of which are named in fifteenth-century sources and 134 in the sixteenth (though many certainly had earlier origins), a density of one every ninety-six square hectares.[50] An informative study of the *noblesse* of the southern part of the diocese of Quimper located 282 *manoirs*.[51] Characteristically, many appear in the records for the first time in the period 1364–1420; no fewer than 150 are mentioned in the first surviving *réformation de la noblesse* in 1426–8. Of the sixty-seven which have left identifiable archaeological traces, only one (Kervenéguin en Loctudy, 29) seems to pre-date the civil war which began in 1341. Work done on the project, 'The Seigneurial Domestic Buildings of Brittany, 1000–1700', by a team led by Professor Gwyn Meirion-Jones, of which I have been a part for more than fifteen years, has recently identified a few hitherto unrecognized early *manoirs* with remains from the late twelfth century onwards, but the vast majority of the buildings we have seen date in their current form from the post-civil-war period, above all from the fifteenth century.[52] This was a period in which Brittany witnessed not only a *floraison* of ecclesiastical and military works, but of civil construction (or reconstruction, following damage incurred during the wars of the fourteenth century) on a massive scale.[53]

---

[46] E. Salmon-Legagneur, 'Le manoir breton au XVe siècle: symbole et richesse de la société rurale', *MSHAB*, LXIX (1992), 201–22.

[47] Le vicomte Henri Frotier de la Messelière, 'Les manoirs breton des Côtes-du-Nord', *Mémoires de la société d'émulation des Côtes-du-Nord*, 72 (1940), 247–70; for his papers and sketches, see A. Lejeune, *Répertoire numérique de la sous-série 60 J, Fonds Frotier de la Messelière* (AD Côtes-du-Nord, St-Brieuc, 1989).

[48] T. Cléac'h, 'Les sources de l'histoire des manoirs aux XVe et XVIe siècles. L'exemple du Pays de Lesneven' (unpublished mémoire de maîtrise, Brest, 1991).

[49] M. Créac'h, 'Les manoirs du Léon occidental entre l'Aber-Benoît et l'Aber-Ildut' (unpublished mémoire de maîtrise, Brest, 1991).

[50] P. Pichouron, 'Manoirs et propriétaires au XVe et XVIe siècles dans le Régaire de Tréguier et la seigneurie de Botloy-Lezardre (dans les limites actuelles des cantons de Lézardrieux et Tréguier)' (unpublished mémoire de maîtrise, Brest, 1994).

[51] J-C. Deshayes, 'Les manoirs de la fin de la Guerre de Succession à la fin du XVIe siècle en Cornouaille méridionale' (unpublished mémoire de maîtrise, Brest, 1988), and see also Calvez, 'La noblesse en Basse Cornouaille'.

[52] For example, Le Brégain en La Boussac, 35 (Jones et al., 'Seigneurial Domestic Buildings', 87–8 and below p. 130) and the recently surveyed Fontenay en Chartres (35) and Le Pordor en Avessac (44) are of twelfth- or thirteenth-century origin.

[53] A. Mussat, *Arts et cultures de la Bretagne. Un millénaire* (Paris, 1979), pp. 64 et seq., provides a fine overview; see also his collected papers *Bretagne. Architecture et identités*, ed. Daniel Leloup (Rennes, 1997).

Moreover, although in choosing buildings for particular study, the criteria we have used have principally been architectural or scientific ones – i.e. that there are sufficient material remains for the building to yield significant evidence about its own history as well as for comparative purposes, and, in a more limited number of cases, for dendrochronology to be applied – it has become increasingly clear from archival investigation that many of our *manoirs* were built by those who had served the dukes of Brittany in some capacity or other, confirming a conclusion also reached by other recent commentators.[54]

Among the first in Brittany to adapt to life in a *manoir* were the bishops of the nine Breton sees, many of whom came to own one or more rural residences in the course of the twelfth and thirteenth centuries, the word *manerium* itself first occurring around 1200.[55] But the fashion spread rapidly; other ecclesiastics followed suit as accommodation provided at the priory of Le Brégain (35) shows.[56] Leading nobles, too, began to acquire *manoirs* in addition to their castles, while for the vast body of the plethoric Breton *noblesse* a manor-house became the normal physical expression of their social separation from the rest of the population. For we must remember that most of the latter lived in rural hamlets in single-roomed dwellings shared with their animals, a tradition that lasted in some parts of the province until as late as the 1950s.[57] By comparison, even the simplest medieval *manoir* always displays distinctive features: a common hall (*salle*), an attached chamber (*chambre*) for the lord, usually raised over a cellar (*cave*) or kitchen (*cuisine*), while the greatest late medieval *manoirs* can combine up to four superimposed halls with their corresponding suites of *chambres* and other amenities, an internal chapel, for example, and a wealth of ornamental and decorative features.[58]

---

[54] See Kerhervé, *L'État breton*, vol. II, pp. 892–901; Kerhervé, 'Temps des ducs', pp. 31–3; Pichouron, 'Manoirs et propriétaires', highlights the importance of ducal service in explaining the rise of the Kerleau of Pleubien, Kernec'hriou of Pleudaniel and the Kerousy and Scliczon of Plouguiel in his study of the *régaire* of Tréguier.

[55] For the *palatium* built by Stephen, bishop of Rennes (1169–79), at Rannée (35), see Morice, *Preuves*, vol. I, cols. 672–3, which provides what appears to be the first description of what can be termed a *manoir*: Nos vero ibi palatium lapideum fere centum pedes habens in longitudine, et appendicia et murum in circuitu, propriis sumptibus reedificavimus ... et viridarium quod adjacet palatio proprio sumptu emimus, et in eo plures propriis manibus inseruimus surculos' (Jones et al., 'Seigneurial Domestic Buildings', 109 n. 56). The bishops of Rennes and Nantes usually used three or four *manoirs* at any one time; for that at St-Armel en Bruz (35), see B. Isbled, 'Le manoir de Saint-Armel en Bruz', *MSHAB*, LXVIII (1991), 403–20; M. Décenneux, 'La résidence des évêques de Dol à la fin du moyen-âge', *Annales de la société d'histoire et d'archéologie de l'arrondissement de St-Malo*, année 1977, 232–7.

[56] Jones et al., 'Seigneurial Domestic Buildings', 87–8; Meirion-Jones, Jones and Pilcher, 'Seigneurial Domestic Buildings, 1000–1700', pp. 168–9.

[57] G.I. Meirion-Jones, *The Vernacular Architecture of Brittany* (Edinburgh, 1982).

[58] For what we have termed 'the seigneurial minimum', see Meirion-Jones, Jones and Pilcher, 'Seigneurial Domestic Buildings, 1000–1700', p. 176; for a survey of the main forms, Jones et al., 'Seigneurial Domestic Buildings' esp. 87–98. *Le manoir en Bretagne* provides case studies of some *manoirs* as well as thematic treatment of architectural features and a wealth of illustrative material.

In its fully developed form, the whole ensemble, usually enclosing a courtyard, with or without defensive features such as a fortified gate, walls and a
moat, will include a wide range of agricultural and other buildings – granges,
stables, cart-sheds, sties, an oven, well-head, threshing floor (*aire de battre*) –
usually flanking the main *corps de logis*.[59] It is normally surrounded by gardens,
orchards, meadows and managed woodland (*bois taillis, bois de haute futaye*);
in the Renaissance, *allées d'honneur* and landscaping would confer on seigneurial sites a yet more distinctive appearance. But even in the medieval period, a
dovecot and a mill, with its lake stocked with fish for the seigneurial table, and
a warren are already normally present, and there was some appreciation of
other aesthetic factors. In 1467, for example, the seneschal of Guingamp was
instructed to forbid Jean, *vicomte* de Coëtmen, and his men from chopping
down trees in the wood near Tonquedec 'qui fait a la decoracion et beaute
diceluy [chasteau]'.[60]
To reach finally the nub of this paper, namely the rewards for ducal
servants as revealed in their building activities in the fifteenth century, I
begin with the two seriously excavated Breton seigneurial sites, Lezkelen en
Plabennec (29), and Ste-Geneviève en Inzinzac-Lochrist (56). The first underlines a theme that needs heavy emphasis: that it was often only around 1400
that many Breton motte-and-bailey castles and *maisons-fortes* of earlier times
were finally abandoned for more obviously domestic residences as lords
'descended from the motte'.[61] At Ste-Geneviève there is no trace of a motte,
but there is transition from a previously fortified residence to a largely
undefended *manoir* occuring towards the mid-century; there are also hints of
how ducal service could provide the financial means for a family considering
building (or rebuilding) on a grander scale, since the probable builder of the
new *manoir* was Mons. Henri Le Parisy, whom we have already met as
master of the duke's hunting from 1419–34.[62] The Le Parisy family may be
traced in the Vannetais from at least the late thirteenth century, when Guillaume Le Parisy was farming the ducal mills at Auray. It also provided Jean
Le Parisy, bishop of Vannes from 1312–34, as well as a succession of ducal

---

[59] For a good example, see the particularly full description of Les Fossés en Plélo (22)
given in an inquiry of 1497 (AD Côtes-d'Armor, 32 J). Another is provided by an *aveu*
of 1552 for Le Grand'Cour en Taden (22), ibid., A 71.

[60] AD Loire-Atlantique, B 5, f. 52v.

[61] J. Irien, 'Le site médiéval de Lezkelen en Plabennec: le castel Saint-Ténénan', *Bulletin
de la société archéologique du Finistère*, 99 (1981), 103–19; descriptions of Lezkelen in
1555 and 1601 survive in *aveux* for Coët-Seix-Ploué (AD Loire-Atlantique, B 1721 ff.
41r and 59r); for 'descent from the motte' in Brittany, see Meirion-Jones, Jones and
Pilcher, 'Seigneurial Domestic Buildings, 1000–1700', pp. 164–6.

[62] R. Bertrand, 'La maison-forte de Ste-Geneviève en Inzinzac', *Société d'Archéologie,
Conférences et travaux* (1985–6), pp. 29–42; idem, 'Une fouille en cours: Sainte-Geneviève en Inzinzac-Lochrist', *La maison forte au Moyen Age*, ed. M. Bur (Paris, 1986),
pp. 53–4; idem, 'La vie quotidienne au manoir de Sainte-Geneviève à Inzinzac-Lochrist', *Le manoir en Bretagne*, pp. 212–19.

officers; an earlier Henri Le Parisy, for example, played a prominent role in affairs during Duke John IV's reign.[63]

A clear-cut example of a family that rose swiftly in the world, thanks to employment by the Montfort dukes, is provided by the Carné family, two members of whom laid the foundations of lasting social eminence that even survived the end of the Ancien Régime. The first is Eon de Carné (d. 1462), secretary to John V (1434), *garde des petits coffres* (1433–6, 1447–8), *argentier* (1436–7), *garderobier, trésorier et receveur général des fouages* (1449–51), a post which he held in tandem with that of *trésorier des guerres*, before finishing his career as an *auditeur* in the *chambre des comptes* (1458).[64] Around 1440 he married Jeanne de Trécesson, an heiress whose *château* at Trécesson en Campéneac was rebuilt thanks to Eon's fortunes.[65] The importance of this maternal inheritance in enhancing the family's prestige was recognized by their son, François, who petitioned King Charles VIII in 1494 for permission to assume the name and arms of Trécesson.[66]

Guyon de Carné (d. 1464), Eon's younger brother, succeeded him as *garde des coffres* in 1436 and then linked his fortunes to those of John V's heir by becoming *trésorier* (1439–41) of the future Francis I. As duke, the latter appointed Guyon *trésorier et receveur-général de Bretagne* (1445–6) and a member of his council (1448).[67] As early as 1441 Guyon was in possession of L'Étier en Béganne (56), where armorial bearings on the north *pignon* testify to his building activities.[68] Later L'Étier was briefly held by the most notorious of all those who rose by placing their administrative and financial expertise at the service of the Breton state, Pierre Landais, *trésorier* from 1460–85, who took possession shortly after Guyon's death.[69] However, by 1476, ownership had passed to one of his protégés, Eustache de l'Espinay, member of

---

[63] *Recueil des actes des princes et ducs de Bretagne*, ed. A. de la Borderie (Rennes, 1888), no. clxviii/85 (Guillaume); M. Jones, *Ducal Brittany 1364–1399* (Oxford, 1970), pp. 41 n. 2 (where the older Henri is already the duke's huntsman), 59; *Recueil des actes de Jean IV, duc de Bretagne*, ed. M. Jones (2 vols, Paris, 1980–3), vol. I, no. 321; vol. II, nos. 519n, 599, 737, 820, 1004, 1031, 1171; Kerhervé, *L'État breton*, vol. I, p. 257 (younger Henri).

[64] For Eon's career, see Kerhervé, 'Catalogue', vol. I, pp. 87–8; for the family, see also Gallet, *La seigneurie bretonne*, pp. 135–7, though we must dismiss the idea of an Olivier de Carné as a crusader in 1248.

[65] We lack a good study of this important building; a tradition attributing it to Jean IV de Trécesson, an alleged chamberlain and constable of the duchy *c.* 1370–80, is quite without documentary foundation and conflicts with the architectural evidence.

[66] Morice, *Preuves*, vol. III, cols 755–6.

[67] For Guyon's career, see Kerhervé, 'Catalogue', vol. I, pp. 89–90.

[68] C. Toscer, 'Le château de l'Étier-en-Béganne', *Congrès archéologique de France, 141e session 1983, Morbihan* (Paris, 1986), pp. 54–61, and eadem, 'L'Étier à Béganne: modification de système de circulation', *Le manoir en Bretagne*, pp. 244–9, though the account of the property's descent requires amendment.

[69] AD Loire-Atlantique B 4, f. 84v, and cf. Kerhervé, *L'État breton*, vol. II, pp. 898, 902; Leguay, *Un réseau urbain*, pp. 338–42, also usefully discusses Landais.

Figure 1. The upper hall of L'Étier en Beganne (56): built
by Guyon de Carné (d. 1464), *trésorier et receveur-général
de Bretagne* (1445–6). (Photo Gwyn Meirion-Jones)

another powerful curial family, while Landais' own estate-building activities
were concentrated more exclusively in the Nantais and the Rennais.[70]

Three more *manoirs* owing their current appearance to work undertaken by
servants of John V and Francis I may be briefly mentioned. Perhaps the finest
of all buildings of this kind is Hac au Quiou (22), constructed by Jean Hingant,

[70] Toscer, 'Le château de l'Étier-en-Béganne', p. 54 (l'Espinay); an important councillor
of Francis II (AD Loire-Atlantique, E 131 ff. 61r, 108v, 147r, 164v, 173r, 198r, 217r,
for the period 1460–2), he was in receipt of a pension of 300 *livres* in 1465–6 (Morice,
Preuves, vol. III, col. 145). For Jean de l'Espinay (d. 1524), *trésorier et receveur général
de Bretagne*, 14 April 1489 – December 1491 and April 1498 – 30 July 1524, see

chamberlain and councillor to both dukes. Here a former tower-house, possibly of late thirteenth-century date, has been incorporated into an ambitious rebuilding programme with domestic and display considerations uppermost, though Hingant's fall from grace in 1450 (when he was suspected of complicity in the murder of Gilles de Bretagne) may have caused an interruption in building, since the *manoir* remains unfinished.[71] There is no evidence now for outer defence works (a moat, fortified gate or enclosure) and the *manoir*'s main purpose, apart from its evident quality as accommodation and as a statement of Hingant's arrival among the leaders of Breton society, is as the centre of a flourishing agricultural estate. This he had striven hard to put together in a rational form by purchasing neighbouring land and selling or exchanging outlying properties, a process which (shades of the Fastolf inheritance) led to decades of litigation for his successors.[72]

Less controversially, at Le Plessis Josso en Theix (56), the same process can be seen at work as Guillaume Josso, his brother, Pierre, and the latter's son, Jean, raised a grand manor-house and put together a middling-size estate to go with it. Tradition, dating at least from the eighteenth century, has it that the Jossos owed their fortunes to the marriage of one Sylvestre Josso to Martine de Carné, a match dated variously between 1330 and the early fifteenth century: in 1427 the widow of a Sylvestre Josso certainly held lands at Surzur by right of dower, at which date Mons. Guillaume Josso already held Le Plessis.[73] In the 1430s he became seneschal of Moncontour, a post in which Pierre succeeded him, later becoming *alloué* of Vannes, a leading legal officer for the duke, and he appears in the *parlement* at Vannes in 1451.[74] His income was reckoned at a

---

Kerhervé, 'Catalogue', vol. I, pp. 52–4, and Le Page, *Finances et politique en Bretagne*, pp. 401–5. See Kerhervé, *L'État breton*, vol. II, p. 903, for a map showing the distribution of Landais' properties, including two castellanies, Le Loroux Bottereau (44) and Briord (44), for which he received a licence to crenellate in 1478 (AD Loire-Atlantique, B 9 f. 130v). The early history of this latter estate has to be reconstructed from documents scattered in the AD Loire-Atlantique, B 1853, E 351–354 and 356, while instructive records for its later history also survive in E 733 and 826, including inventories of 1595 and 1657 when Landais' *manoir* still survived, but in the hands of Jean de l'Espinay's descendants. His only building to survive reasonably intact to the present is La Gascherie (La Chapelle-sur-Erdre, 44), possibly built for his daughter and her husband, Arthur Lespervier, *sire* de la Bouvardière, *grand veneur* of Queen Anne, but heavily restored *c.* 1890.

[71] M. Jones, G. Meirion-Jones, J. Pilcher and F. Guibal, 'Un des grands manoirs bretons: le château de Hac au Quiou', *Le Pays de Dinan*, 10 (1990), 171–207, updated in G. Meirion-Jones and M. Jones, 'Hac au Quiou: un des grands manoirs bretons', *MSHAB*, LXXVI (1998), 531–51.

[72] AD Côtes-d'Armor, E 3465 provides the details of the family's dispute with a powerful neighbour, Jean, *vicomte* de Coëtquen, marshal of Brittany.

[73] AD Ille-et-Vilaine, 2 Ec 8 for the family tradition; this *liasse* also includes a register which lists details of marriage contracts from 1422–1650. G. de Carné, 'Le Plessis Josso', *Congrès archéologique de France ... 1983*, pp. 139–42, provides a brief overview; for Sylvestre's widow, see R. de Laigue, *La noblesse bretonne aux XVe et XVIe siècles. Réformation et montres, i, Evêché de Vannes* (2 vols, Rennes, 1902), vol. II, p. 813, and, for Guillaume Josso, p. 815.

[74] *Lettres et mandements de Jean V, duc de Bretagne*, ed. R. Blanchard (5 vols, Nantes, 1889–95), nos 2079, 2177, 2439, 2478; Morice, *Preuves*, vol. II, col. 1565.

Figure 2. Hac au Quiou (22): built in the 1440s by Jean
Hingant, chamberlain and councillor of Dukes John V and
Francis I. (Photo Gwyn Meirion-Jones)

conservative 140 *livres p.a.* in 1464; a will drawn up in 1471 reveals considerable
movable wealth; he had already established a rent of 40 *livres p.a.* to pay for
masses by the Dominicans of Vannes in 1465.[75] Whilst his son, Jean (d. 1527),
does not appear to have held a particular office under the duke, simply serving
in arms when called upon to do so, he further improved family fortunes as an

---

[75] Laigue, *La noblesse breton*, vol. II, p. 832 (income); AD Morbihan, 231 H 4 (will);
  ibid. 49 H 4 (rent). In 1454 a Guillaume Josso rendered an *aveu* to Guyon de Carné,
  sire de l'Étier (Nantes, Archives municipales II, 140).

Figure 3. Le Plessis Josso en Theix (56): the main *corps de logis* built for Pierre Josso, *alloué* of Vannes, *c.* 1450, and late fifteenth-century *enceinte*. (Photo Gwyn Meirion-Jones)

active landlord. Among his acquisitions was half the Étang de Noyalo, which he exploited for milling, as well as for its fishing and wildfowl, including a supply of swans,[76] while among building work he probably undertook was an *enceinte* wall, furnished with gun-loops. In 1553 this briefly kept a posse at bay when the last male member of the line, Guillaume, was besieged at Le Plessis, following an attempt to release his accomplice in several serious crimes, including murder, from the royal prison at Vannes.[77] Leaving aside this colourful history, dendrochronology has furnished firm dates for the Renaissance additions to this house whilst also throwing some light on its mid-fifteenth-century state during the lifetime of Pierre Josso, to whom may be owed the principal *corps de logis*, with its *salle basse* and *salle haute*, originally open to the roof-space before it was ceiled in the mid-sixteenth century.[78]

Le Fretay en Pancé (35) has also yielded some interesting dendrochronological evidence to go with surviving documentation. One of the few Breton licences

---

[76] AD Morbihan, E 1410.

[77] L. Lallement, 'Un événement à Vannes', *Bulletin de la société polymathique du Morbihan, année 1909*, 149–58.

[78] G. Meirion-Jones and M. Jones, 'La résidence seigneuriale en Bretagne: problèmes et progrès récents de la datation dendrochronologique et de son interprétation', *Mondes de l'Ouest et villes du monde. Regards sur les sociétés médiévales. Mélanges en l'honneur d'André Chédeville*, ed. C. Laurent, B. Merdrignac and D. Pichot (Rennes, 1998), pp. 226–8.

to crenellate of which record survives was issued in 1417 to the ducal chamberlain, Pierre de la Marzelière (d. 1462).[79] Member of a family of *ancien noblesse*, who succeeded his father, Guillaume, in 1423, Pierre served successive dukes in many capacities, though usually in military posts. In 1432, for example, he was one of two guardians or governors of the marches towards Anjou, Maine and Normandy; later for services in the reconquest of Normandy he received a pension from Charles VII as well as an increase in the one he had long received from the dukes.[80] Perhaps pressing official duties prevented him from taking advantage of his first licence to crenellate; in any case it was renewed by Francis I in 1442 as his career reached its apogee,[81] and it is to this period that the small, rectangular castle of Le Fretay, with its early artillery embrasures, enclosed within a larger moated *enceinte*, can be dated. Specifically, for an independent lodging range adjacent to the main castle, dendrochronology has conveniently supplied the date 1440–2.[82]

A further licence to crenellate granted in 1453 serves to introduce another work in which military rather than domestic features initially strike any observer. This is the castle of Kerouzéré en Sibiril (29), the fortification of which was justified on the grounds that it would offer protection against English raids, since it lies just a few hundred metres inland from the Breton north coast.[83] As at Le Fretay, it also proved necessary to reissue the licence in 1468, delays in building having apparently ensued because another, more well-established, seigneurial family, the Kermorvans of Coët-Seiz-Ploué (Maillé, 22), had objected to infringement of their rights by the *arriviste* Kerouzérés.[84] In fact, the latter had been rising steadily in the world for almost a hundred years since Jean de Kerouzéré, seneschal of Morlaix in 1385, acquired the *manoir* of Kerouzéré by exchange in 1378.[85]

---

[79] *Lettres de Jean V*, no. 1245^*bis*.

[80] Jones, *The Creation of Brittany*, p. 45, citing *Lettres de Jean V*, no. 1981, and 358n; Morice, *Preuves*, vol. III, cols 1514, 1520–1, 1593–4; C. Roulon, 'Histoire généalogique de la famille de la Marzelière, originaire de Bain-de-Bretagne (Ille-et-Vilaine) d'après les documents retrouvés', *Association Bretonne*, 5e série, 68 (1959), 98–144. *Aveux* presented for Le Fretay from 1393–1603 may be found in AD Loire-Atlantique, B 2148.

[81] *Bulletin de la société archéologique de département d'Ille-et-Vilaine*, IV (1866), 220.

[82] Jones *et al.*, 'Seigneurial Domestic Buildings', 100–1. Seized by the Leaguers in 1592, Le Fretay was partially demolished in 1598 and its state in 1619 is revealed by a detailed description: *Revue historique de l'Ouest, Mémoires*, 8 (1892), 232.

[83] AD Ille-et-Vilaine, 2 Er 269.

[84] AD Loire-Atlantique, B 4 f. 66r and B 6 f. 7v; for more details of the licences, see Jones, *The Creation of Brittany*, p. 53, and, generally, G. Meirion-Jones and M. Jones, 'Trois résidences seigneuriales en haut Léon: Kerouzéré, Maillé et Tronjoly', *Association Bretonne. 123e Congrès à Saint-Pol-de-Léon 1996* (1997), pp. 167–200.

[85] AD Côtes-d'Armor, 89 J 42, contract with Guillaume, *seigneur* de Pencoët and Marguerite Charruel, *dame* de Guerlisquin, 23 August 1378. Among the properties which Kerouzéré acquired on this occasion were those once possessed in Sibiril parish by Hamon de Kerouzéré 'le veill', but their relationship is not stated, nor whether Kerouzéré already held other lands there. What is clear is that he had deliberately seized the chance to hold the *manoir* which bore his own surname, dispensing with lands held in another parish.

Figure 4. Le Granil en Theix (56): the two fifteenth-century ground-floor halls and attached chamber-block of the Le Baron family.
(Photo Gwyn Meirion-Jones)

Here again, as at Hac and Le Plessis Josso, it is possible to trace the stages by which an impressive landed estate was put together piecemeal over several generations. This is most easily illustrated by the fact that around 1400 the family received rents from tenures in the parish of Sibiril covering only 3 hectares, but that by 1461 the figure had reached 38 hectares and, nearly a century later, 266 hectares, while in the same period the lands they farmed out increased from 8 to 427 hectares, to which should be added the home farm, forming by the mid-sixteenth century a domaine of some 640 hectares.[86] Already in 1467 Eon II de Kerouzéré (d. 1476), the probable builder of the castle, declared an income of 500 *livres p.a.*; a document of 1509 confirms this sum and additionally shows income from other estates of a further 500 *livres*.[87] The careers of the medieval holders of this lordship cannot be traced in detail here, but, besides this considerable income derived from their landed estate, it is notable that in

---

[86] H. Lesaulnier, 'La seigneurie de Kerouzéré au bas Moyen Age (1378–1540)' (2 vols, unpublished mémoire de maîtrise, Brest, 1981); Chantal Daniel, *Archives de Kerouzéré et de la sous-série 16 B (jurdiction de Kerouzéré-Trongoff)* (Quimper, 1993) passim.

[87] Rennes, Bibliothèque municipale, MS 499, p. 624 (1467); in 1467 Eon was in receipt of a pension of 300 *livres p.a.* as chamberlain of Francis II (Morice, *Preuves*, vol. II, col. 20), while in 1484–5 Jean III de Kerouzéré had one of 150 *livres* (AD Loire-Atlantique, E 212/17 f. 9v); Lesaulnier, 'La seigneurie de Kerouzéré' vol. I, pp. 136–43 (1509).

Figure 5. Kerouzéré en Sibiril (29): licences to crenellate in 1453 and 1468.
(Photo Gwyn Meirion-Jones)

successive generations they usually held ducal office and were in receipt of many tokens of ducal favour. Specifically, it was particularly the career of Eon I de Kerouzéré, *président du parlement de Bretagne* (1419–33), that really enabled the family to gain the footing that helped it reach the upper ranks of Breton society.[88]

What more modest resources and conventional services might produce by way of domestic building can be exemplified by two more *manoirs* from the Vannetais, Lesnevé en St-Avé (56) and Le Granil en Theix (56), both of which have recently provided good dendrochronological data.[89] Lesnevé belonged to the Benoist family; Jean Benoist was a gentleman of the ducal guard in 1419, while Eon, probably his brother, served in the forces raised to rescue John V from his Penthièvre cousins after they had seized him in 1420. It was Eon who

---

[88] See Kerhervé, 'Catalogue', vol. III, pp. 723–5. It was Eon I who first received permission to hold annual fairs in Sibiril which were a major factor in the family's economic resources (Lesaulnier, 'La seigneurie de Kerouzéré', vol. I, p. 158, and vol. II, pp. 102–5, 110–11, 117, and cf. AD Finistère, 151 J 664 and 665). The underhand means used by Eon I de Kerouzéré to dupe some of his neighbours in building up his estates, is well-revealed in ducal letters of 20 January 1463 obtained by Tanguy de Kermarvan against Eon II de Kerouzéré during the course of a long dispute. These catalogue a sequence of shady legal moves and abuse of power by Eon I as *président de Bretagne* (AD Ille-et-Vilaine, I F 656).

[89] Meirion-Jones and Jones, 'La résidence seigneuriale en Bretagne', pp. 228–33.

held Lesnevé in 1427.[90] There is then a long gap in documents relating to the lordship, but in 1477 another Jean Benoist, a minor at the time of a previous muster in 1464, declared an income of 120 *livres*. In the following forty years, he, too, modestly continued to build up his estates in the customary way.[91] It is probably to his lifetime that the richly ornamented Gothic doorway still surviving in the principal *logis* can be attributed, though it may have been inserted into an older building. More convincingly, beams from a tower block, perhaps intended to provide high-quality accommodation for visitors, since it is located outside the main courtyard, have yielded dates from the mid-fifteenth century, suggesting it may have been built by Guillaume Benoist, who was *sire* de Lesnevé in 1448, or by Jean Benoist, constable of Vannes in 1457.[92]

The owners of Le Granil were marginally richer than the Benoist family: in 1427 *le manoir de Guazeneil* belonged to Jean Le Baron, probably to be identified with Jean Le Baron, *gourme de chambre* of the duke's children in 1421, perhaps son of Raoul Le Baron, *sommelier de chandelerie* in 1404.[93] Once again the records are fragmentary: in 1477 Mons. Alain Le Baron, acting as *tuteur de la dame de Graneil* failed to appear at a muster; in 1471 he had been one of the witnesses to Pierre Josso's will, whilst in 1491 it was with the *sire* de Granil that Pierre's successor reached an accord over the Étang de Noyalo which Le Granil overlooks.[94] The 1477 muster showed that Marguerite Le Baron, *dame* de Granil, had an estimated revenue of 200 *livres*. The same sum was acknowledged in 1481, by when Marguerite, though still in the wardship of Mons. Alain Le Baron, was nevertheless married to Jean de Champballon, one of the fifty men-at-arms of the ducal guard.[95] By 1487 he was captain of the town of Guérande (44) and in 1490 was sent by Duchess Anne on embassy to England; next year his pension was an impressive 400 *livres p.a.*[96] As for the actual *manoir* of Le Granil, two architectural features deserve brief notice: first, a chamber block, with two *chambres*, placed over a semi-sunken *cave*, which has yielded dendrochronological dates which suggest that it was originally erected between 1437 and 1448; second, the unique example of two, late medieval, open ground-floor halls, one of which was ceiled, probably in the seventeenth century.[97] So far it has not been possible to offer a convincing explanation for the occurrence of

---

[90] Morice, *Preuves*, vol. II, cols 1061, 1069; Laigue, *La noblesse bretonne*, vol. II, p. 683.

[91] Laigue, *La noblesse bretonne*, vol. II, pp. 464, 685, 687.

[92] Ibid, vol. II, p. 683 (Guillaume); Morice, *Preuves*, vol. II, p. 1710 (Jean); Meirion-Jones and Jones, 'La résidence seigneuriale en Bretagne', p. 232. An inquiry in 1719 provides a fascinating and very detailed survey of Lesnevé, including the chamber-block (AD Morbihan, B 632, 'Grand et prise de la maison et manoir noble de Lesnevé', 20 ff.).

[93] Laigue, *La noblesse bretonne*, vol. II, p. 824; Morice, *Preuves*, vol. II, cols 738, 1085.

[94] Laigue, *La noblesse bretonne*, vol. II, p. 824, AD Morbihan, 231 H 4 (will); E 1410 (1491).

[95] Laigue, *La noblesse bretonne*, vol. II, pp. 824–5, identifies Marguerite as the daughter of Jean Le Baron and Françoise de Bourne, and wife of Jean de Chamballan/Champballon, *sire* de la Ricardye en Rieux (56) 'de la maison du duc'.

[96] Morice, *Preuves*, vol. III, cols 388, 437, 537, 576, 658–600, 725. After 1491 he remained a member of the queen's bodyguard (ibid., 895; AD Loire-Atlantique, E 214/41 f. 9r).

[97] Meirion-Jones and Jones, 'La résidence seigneuriale en Bretagne', p. 232.

Figure 6. Le Bois Orcant en Noyal-sur-Vilaine: rebuilt for Julien Thierry, *argentier* of Francis II and Duchess Anne, during recent renovation. (Photo Michael Jones)

the two halls, nor to obtain a definite date for the construction of either of them.

One final building may be mentioned to bring us back to the immediate circle of leading servants of Francis II and Duchess Anne in the last days of the independent duchy. Le Bois Orcant en Noyal-sur-Vilaine (35) owes its name to the family of Orcant/Orquant. On the death of Jean Orquant in 1398, his successor presented a description (*minu*) of 'le herbregement et maisons du Boais Orquant ensemble o le herbregement et mesons de la mestairie'. This reveals a typical modest *manoir*, covering a few hectares, and rents worth 47 *livres p.a.*[98]

---

[98] AD Loire-Atlantique, B 2141/1. This sum includes 7 *livres* derived from the customs of Châteaugiron and 11 *livres* owed by the *sire* de Lestou; the demesne at Le Bois Orcant appears to have comprised around 63 *journaux*, approximately 16 hectares, and was worth about 22 *livres p.a.*

When, in 1407, another *aveu* was furnished by Alain du Pé, *sire* de Boisorcant by right of marriage, he acknowledged holding 'le herbergement dou Boais Orquant la ou a present est scisse la meson neuffve', suggesting recent developments, though it is not until 1458 that there is mention of a *salle*, whilst the first definite mention of Bois Orcant as a *manoir* occurs in 1460. Shortly afterwards the Du Pé family, most notable for their military prowess,[99] had released any interest in the property, and, after a period of uncertain ownership, by 1476 it had passed to the celebrated financier, Julien Thierry of Rennes, ducal *argentier* 1477–90.[100] His greatest public service came with a series of impressive loans in the last days of the independent duchy, the military and political débâcle of which he managed to survive with his own fortunes largely intact, as Le Bois Orcant itself now testifies.[101] Its building history is immensely complicated and has not yet been completely elucidated; recently some beams in the *communes*, themselves clearly dated to the sixteenth century, have provided late fourteenth-century dates, perhaps being re-used from the *meson neuffve* mentioned in 1407.[102] Parts of this, or of a successor of which the *salle* of 1458 was an integral feature, are almost certainly incorporated in the present *corps de logis*. Nevertheless, the dates of 1483–1502 and 1489–1508 provided by two beams still *in situ* in the *salle basse*, and by ceiling-beams in the *salle haute* which were cut shortly after 1495, are eloquent evidence for a major refurbishment during Thierry's lifetime, while other dates from different parts of the building, including a series from the rear-kitchens, also reveal rebuilding, perhaps in several stages, in the latter half of the century.[103] Much more should be said about this fine building, especially about developments in the sixteenth and seventeenth centuries, but it can stand as a pre-eminent example of what serious money could

[99] For the Du Pé family of St Jean de Boiseau (44), see le comte de Rosmorduc, *La noblesse de Bretagne devant la Chambre de la Réformation 1668–1671. Arrêts de maintenue de noblesse* (4 vols, St-Brieuc, 1896–1905), vol. II, pp. 455–64. The most prominent member in this period was Jacques Pé, who served with Guillaume de Rosnyvinen in Normandy in the 1450s and then played a prominent role in military affairs under Francis II (see Morice, *Preuves*, vol. III, cols 125, 140, 230, 308, 322; AD Loire-Atlantique E 133/11, E 343). Alain and his successor, Placidas du Pé, *sire* de Boisorcant (d. after 29 Sept. 1460), belonged to a cadet branch.

[100] The first document I have found naming him *sire du Boisorcant* is a purchase of rents on 9 January 1476 (AD Ille-et-Vilaine, 2 El 217).

[101] B.A. Pocquet du Haut-Jussé, 'Les emprunts de la duchesse Anne à Julien Thierry (1488–1491)', *Annales de Bretagne*, LXIX (1962), 269–93; Leguay, *Un réseau urbain*, pp. 338–42, also surveys his career and provides important details from an *aveu* of 1522 on the estate at Le Bois Orcant, by then covering 214 hectares. Appointed *miseur* of Rennes in February 1465 and minter at Nantes at 60 *livres p.a.* on 11 June 1466 (AD Loire-Atlantique B 4 f. 68v), Thierry's career is best documented in Kerhervé, 'Catalogue', vol. I, pp. 104–8.

[102] P. Gandreuil, 'Le Boisorcant à Noyal-sur-Vilaine', *Le manoir en Bretagne*, pp. 258–65, is an inadequate account, both of the descent of the manor and of its architectural history. For a full study, including a resistivity survey, dendrochronology and excavation, see G. Meirion-Jones, M. Jones and R. B. Harris, 'Le Bois Orcan en Noyal-sur-Vilaine: une étude pluridisciplinaire', *Bulletin et mémoires de la société archéologique et historique d'Ille-et-Vilaine*, 103 (2000), 67–123.

[103] Meirion-Jones and Jones, 'La résidence seigneuriale en Bretagne', p. 225.

buy a thrusting *arriviste* like Thierry, incorporating as it did some of the very latest ideas on comfort emanating from the Loire valley, notably in having one of the first upper halls, originally open to the roof, to be ceiled, a fashion that only began to become general in Brittany from around 1500.[104]

To conclude, much of this paper has been impressionistic; it is impossible to estimate with any precision the number of surviving late medieval Breton *manoirs* whose owners served their dukes and what proportion of their investment in building was furnished by wages, pensions, gifts or other resources provided by such employment. It is regrettable that our ignorance is almost complete about total construction costs for any medieval Breton *manoir*: no full accounts survive; contracts, even for limited building work or repairs, are extremely rare; estate or household records provide only a few tantalizing details.[105] Equally, the selection of buildings presented here has inevitably been arbitrary, a small number from a much larger total, one which may itself be unrepresentative, certainly one that cannot be meaningfully treated in a statistical form, though in presenting sites here an effort has been made to span the full range of fieldwork evidence.[106]

The general lineaments of the late medieval Breton state have been well-studied, most magisterially in Jean Kerhervé's *L'État breton*. Thanks in particular to work by Jean Gallet, Michel Nassiet and, again, Jean Kerhervé, the economic fortunes of the Breton *noblesse* at the end of the Middle Ages are now well-understood; some general work has also been undertaken on seigneurial *mentalités* and ideology, though this is an area which deserves more investigation.[107] There is also now a much better appreciation of the general architectural characteristics of the *manoir*.[108] But as the figures quoted for surviving monuments indicate, the task is huge and synthesis difficult.

[104] G. Meirion-Jones, M. Jones and J. Pilcher, 'L'insertion des plafonds dans les salles à charpente apparente en Bretagne: un phénomène des seizième et dix-septième siècles', *Le bois dans l'architecture*, 6èmes Entretiens du Patrimoine. Collection des Actes des Colloques de la Direction du Patrimoine, no. 6. Rouen, les 25 au 27 novembre 1993 (Paris, 1995), pp. 67–80.

[105] At Les Huguetières (44) in 1411, eighty labourers were paid 'a tirer des vieulx murs dudit herbregement pour mettre et emploier la pierre esdits eupvres neufves' (E. Saddier, 'Une seigneurie rurale du pays nantais au XVe siècle: les Huguetières à travers les comptes du receveur', unpublished mémoire de maîtrise, Chambéry, 1975, p. 70), while expenses for repairs at La Chatière en Tremblay (35) in 1452–3 and 1545–5 are found in AD Ille-et-Vilaine, 2 Eg 80. Buris en Chavagne (35) was bought for 911 *livres* in 1510 (AD Ille-et-Vilaine, 2 Eb 11) and Julien Thierry bought Le Plessis Mauhugeon (35) for 1650 *écus* in 1470 and had to sell it for 1200 *écus* in 1471 because of *retrait lignager* (AD Loire-Atlantique, 46 J 4), before successfully acquiring Le Bois Orcant.

[106] Urban property, including some impressive *hôtels*, which many ducal servants possessed, along with their rural *manoirs*, has been ignored here, but see Kerhervé, *L'État breton*, vol. II, pp. 861–82, for a good survey.

[107] See M. Nassiet, 'Signes de parenté, signes de seigneurie: un système idéologique (XVe–XVIe siècle)' *MSHAB*, LXVIII (1991), 175–232, for interesting perspectives.

[108] As a result of work by the *Commission régionale de l'Inventaire Général des Monuments et des Richesses Artistiques de la France* (equivalent to the Royal Commission on the Historical Monuments of England), though cf. Meirion-Jones and Jones, 'Trois résidences seigneuriales' (1997), p. 181, n. 35, for some criticisms of its work; our study of Le Bois Orcant is also eloquent in this regard.

Nevertheless, what I hope this essay demonstrates conclusively is that in a proportion of cases, even if it is an unquantifiable proportion, one of the most important factors in explaining the social circumstances of owners, and how they acquired the means to build their *manoirs*, was ducal service. But there are many others, too, in any rounded view of the place, purpose and function of *manoirs* in a hierarchical society, with its apex in the ducal court: expectations of lordship, displays of authority and wealth, the influence of fashion in determining the style, design and quality of building, not to mention the way in which *manoirs* were lived in and furnished, matters on which interesting Breton evidence can be advanced.[109] Many issues thus happily remain for further investigation both in the archives and in the field.

---

[109] *Le manoir en Bretagne*, passim, provides some valuable evidence, including extracts from various inventories (pp. 33, 220–7, 279, 300–3), although the list could be considerably extended: see M. Jones and G. Meirion-Jones, 'The Breton Gentleman and his Home in the late Middle Ages: Recent Research and Fieldwork', *Traditions and Transformations: Views of the Fifteenth Century*, ed. S.D. Michalove (Stroud, forthcoming); M. Jones, '"Les archives du succès?" Les debuts d'une grande dynastie parlementaire bretonne: les Becdelièvre', *Mélanges Phillipe Contamine*, ed. J. Paviot and J. Verger (Paris, 2000).

IX

SERVICE AND TENURE IN LATE MEDIEVAL SCOTLAND, 1314–1475

Alexander Grant

I

IN late medieval Scotland there would have been numerous forms of service relationships, just as in England or anywhere else in western Europe, and they would have operated in much the same ways as elsewhere. Of these, the most 'different' by comparison with the English equivalents – and therefore the most interesting in the context of the present volume – are probably the ones which are most traditional in historiographical terms, namely the relationships between 'lords' and 'men' within the landowning classes. This paper will therefore look at the Scottish form of what used to be called 'bastard feudalism'. To a readership versed in the voluminous modern studies of late medieval English landed society, the exercise might seem rather old-fashioned, but in Scottish history there is still room for a basic examination of this topic. Much of the best recent work on late medieval Scotland is essentially political,[1] and although this highlights many individual ties between lords and followers, the system, so to speak, lying behind those ties has tended to be taken for granted. There is, indeed, only one thorough account of Scottish 'bastard feudalism', Jenny Wormald's magisterial *Lords and Men in Scotland, 1442–1603*,[2] which deals with bonds of manrent, the rough equivalent to the English indentures of retainer. But most of Dr Wormald's evidence and the bulk of her analysis relate to the sixteenth century; and while she does discuss the later Middle Ages as well, there is, I think, something more to be said about the basis of lord–man relations in that period.

My paper derives from what has become an extremely long-term and much-interrupted research project on the late medieval Scottish higher nobility.[3] It

---

[1] Especially S. Boardman, *The Early Stewart Kings: Robert II and Robert III, 1371–1406* (East Linton, 1996); M. Brown, *James I* (Edinburgh, 1994); C. McGladdery, *James II* (Edinburgh, 1990); N. Macdougall, *James III* (Edinburgh, 1982); N. Macdougall, *James IV* (Edinburgh, 1989). A broader study is M. Brown, *The Black Douglases: War and Lordship in Late Medieval Scotland, 1300–1455* (East Linton, 1998) – ch. 8 is a detailed account of Douglas lordship – but its approach is still essentially political.

[2] J. Wormald, *Lords and Men in Scotland: Bonds of Manrent, 1442–1603* (Edinburgh, 1985). Also, for a fuller version, see her doctoral thesis: J.M. Brown, 'Bonds of Manrent in Scotland before 1603' (unpublished Ph.D. thesis, University of Glasgow, 1974).

[3] It originated with A. Grant, 'The Higher Nobility and their Estates in Scotland, c. 1371–1424' (unpublished D. Phil. thesis, University of Oxford, 1975), but the scope

encompasses the dukes, the earls, the great 'provincial' lords, the lords of parliament (who constituted the lowest rank in the Scottish peerage after that came into existence in the 1440s), and, from the fourteenth and earlier fifteenth centuries, the more important barons (those who seem to have the same kind of position within Scottish landed society as the lords of parliament subsequently had). For convenience, all these 'higher nobles' are referred to here simply as 'lords', following the later Scottish jingle 'lords and lairds', in which the lords are the peers and the lairds are equivalent to the English gentry; there were probably between about forty and sixty of these lords in Scotland at any one time.[4] The period covered by the project runs from 1314 to 1475. It begins with the enactment of the Cambuskenneth parliament of November 1314 (in the aftermath of Bannockburn) that all who were outside Robert I's peace would lose their lands, which brought about a fundamental transformation of the upper levels of landholding society;[5] and it ends with the forfeiture of the earldom of Ross by John MacDonald, Lord of the Isles, in December 1475, the last in a fifty-year sequence of major confiscations that meant that by the later fifteenth century the highest ranks of the nobility had once again been transformed.[6] The intention is to collect and analyse all the documents produced by or for the Scottish lords of that period. So far, from the main sources and repositories, some 2,061 texts have been located and filed;[7] that is by no means an exhaustive total, but it will certainly constitute well over half, and probably the great majority,

---

and time-scale have been greatly extended; much of the post-doctoral research has been carried out in periods of leave generously provided by the University of Lancaster. For a summary of my initial thoughts about my subject, see ch. 5, 'The Nobility', in A. Grant, *Independence and Nationhood: Scotland, 1306–1469* (London, 1984).

[4] The same definition is used as in A. Grant, 'Extinction of Direct Male Lines among Scottish Noble Families in the Fourteenth and Fifteenth Centuries', *Essays on the Nobility of Medieval Scotland*, ed. K.J. Stringer (Edinburgh, 1985), pp. 210–31; the families are listed on pp. 227–31. For the new peerage of the fifteenth century, see A. Grant, 'The Development of the Scottish Peerage', *SHR*, LVII (1978), 1–27. Note that in Scotland 'baron' does not have peerage connotations; it simply meant someone who held an estate 'in free barony', with 'baronial' jurisdiction, including the right to execute thieves. There were always well over 100 barons in late medieval Scotland; only the top twenty or so (roughly, those possessing at least three baronies) have been counted as 'lords'. See Grant, 'Higher Nobility and their Estates', pp. 25–9, 132–48; and *The Court Book of the Barony of Carnwath*, ed. W.C. Dickinson (Scottish History Society, 1937), pp. xiii–xxviii.

[5] *APS*, vol. I, p. 464; *RRS*, vol. V, no. 41; Grant, *Independence and Nationhood*, pp. 26–8, 122–3.

[6] *APS*, vol. II, p. 111; Grant, *Independence and Nationhood*, pp. 123–7, 219–20.

[7] That total does not include notes of transactions for which full or nearly full texts do not survive – of which there are at least half as many again. Among these, a large number come from confirmation charters by the crown or an overlord, where details of the actual transaction are only summarized. Also, the sixteenth-century notes of the early part of the Register of the Great Seal (mostly lost in 1661: see below, p. 147) list hundreds of otherwise unknown transactions, but give no details; see *RMS*, vol. I, App. II.

of the available documentation,[8] at least with respect to full or nearly full texts.

That highlights a major point about the late medieval Scottish lords: how sparsely documented they are. I am sure that the final number of documents relating to them will be no higher than 4,000, and it may well be below 3,000. For the kingdom's greater nobles over a period of 160 years, that is not a very impressive amount of material. Hardly any individual lords are represented by more than about thirty items, while for the two magnates who are by far the best documented, Archibald, 4th earl of Douglas (died 1424), and Sir James Douglas of Dalkeith (died 1420), there are respectively only 111 and 104 full or nearly full texts.[9] One reason for the relative lack of documentation is the disaster of 1661, when the Scottish government records removed to London by Oliver Cromwell were returned in two ships, one of which sank, sending 85 hogsheads of documents to the bottom of the North Sea.[10] Among the major casualties were much of the Register of the Great Seal (which for relative significance could be equated with the English Patent Rolls), most of the sheriffs' accounts, and (probably) almost the entire late medieval records of the royal council and of the Scots parliament in its judicial capacity; although crown records, these would have been full of material relating to Scottish lords. It is also conceivable that magnate records were lost in the wreck, in the form of muniments relating to the earldoms and other great estates which had come into the crown's possession during the fifteenth century.

But that is only part of the explanation. As Bruce Webster has stressed, the relatively un-centralized nature of Scottish government meant that justice and administration were generally carried out locally by the landowners, and records of decisions and actions did not have to be transmitted to the centre.[11] For

---

[8] So far I have searched the following: all the relevant printed sources, as conveniently listed (up to 1960) in *List of Abbreviated Titles of the Printed Sources of Scottish History to 1560*, supplement to *SHR*, XLIV (1963); the MS material collected for the forthcoming and projected *RRS* volumes on 1371–1406, 1406–37, and 1437–60 (my warmest thanks to Dr Athol Murray and Dr Alan Borthwick for help with this); and most of the unprinted material in the National Archives of Scotland (formerly the Scottish Record Office), Edinburgh [NAS], and the National Library of Scotland, Edinburgh [NLS]. I have yet to search collections of unpublished muniments still held privately or locally; but for Scotland those are a much lower proportion than for England, because so many sets of private muniments are in the 'Gifts and Deposits' (GD) section of the NAS. For this paper, documents relating to the church, and letters to and from foreign rulers and lords, have not been counted.

[9] Those figures include a few administrative documents that have not been counted in the overall totals. For the 4th earl of Douglas's documents, see A. Grant, 'Acts of Lordship: The Records of Archibald, Fourth Earl of Douglas', *Freedom and Authority: Scotland c. 1050–c. 1650. Historical and Historiographical Essays presented to Grant G. Simpson*, ed. T. Brotherstone and D. Ditchburn (East Linton, 2000), pp. 235–74; this also notes 23 other 'lost' texts. For James Douglas of Dalkeith's documents, see note 13, below.

[10] D. Stevenson, 'The English and the Public Records of Scotland', *Stair Society Miscellany I* (Stair Society, 1971), pp. 156–70; B. Webster, *Scotland from the Eleventh Century to 1603* (Sources of History, 1975), ch. 5.

[11] Ibid., pp. 149–51.

instance, the central register of 'retours' (equivalent to English inquisitions *post mortem*) survives only from the seventeenth century;[12] if a register was kept before then, it presumably perished in 1661, but it is more likely that the individual retours were simply kept by the landlords concerned, and that once they were obsolete they tended to be cleared out. Out of the countless retours that must once have existed, I have so far noted only 33 for lands held by or from Scottish lords between 1314 and 1475. Other kinds of documents of merely ephemeral significance were probably dealt with in the same way, which would explain why, for instance, next to no financial material has survived for the lords of late medieval Scotland. Even the uniquely businesslike (for late medieval Scotland) Sir James Douglas of Dalkeith had that attitude. Unlike his contemporaries, who usually simply bundled the documents they wanted to keep into 'charter-chests', he had two cartularies drawn up, recording the texts of documents relating to his estates; the first contains 106 items, the second 206, though there is a certain amount of duplication between them. The great majority of these texts no longer exist as originals.[13] In addition, Sir James had his muniments inventoried on four rolls, telling 'where the lord's documents are to be found', and these contain some 433 entries;[14] although a detailed analysis of these rolls has yet to be made, it appears that at least a third of his documents were not included in his cartularies. Not surprisingly, it was mostly items of an ephemeral nature that were omitted, such as preliminaries for conveyances, licences, receipts, and so on, which would have been extremely useful to modern scholars, but in the late Middle Ages were clearly considered dispensable.

The documents that the lords of late medieval Scotland did regard as worth keeping consist chiefly of title-deeds. They are in the form of charters or (less commonly) letters patent, indentures and bonds; and they primarily record the transfer of estates, though some deal with rights and favours, annuities, office-holding and retaining. My files, so far, contain 1,511 of these charters, letters, indentures and bonds: 683 are royal, issued by the crown, and 828 are non-royal, issued either by the lords, or to them by lairds. Eighty per cent of them, that is 1,204 in all (519 royal, 685 non-royal), deal with the transfer of land.[15]

---

[12] Calendared as *Inquisitionum ad Capellam Domini Regis Retornatarum ... Abbreviatio*, ed. T. Thomson (Edinburgh, 1811–16).

[13] The cartularies are bound together as NLS, MS 72, Morton Chartulary. This was printed as vol. II of *Registrum Honoris de Morton*, ed. T. Thomson and others (Bannatyne Club, 1853) [*Morton Reg.*]. Unfortunately, the initial 41 items in the first cartulary (which are mostly very difficult to read, not least because they were badly stained with gall in the nineteenth century) were not included in the printed version. On the other hand, the editors did include various items relating to Sir James and his family which are not actually in the MS cartularies; these came from the Register of the Great Seal and from original documents now in NAS, Morton Papers, GD150. In all, the printed *Morton Reg.*, vol. II, contains 218 items from before Sir James's death in 1420, but I have yet to make a precise correlation of these with the cartulary entries. Most of the 104 texts relating to Sir James himself come from these sources.

[14] NAS, Morton, GD150/77–80 (parts of rolls 150/78 and 150/79 duplicate each other).

[15] Currently, therefore, charters and the like amount to 73 per cent of all the documents in my files (1,511 out of 2,061); those dealing with land transfers make up 58 per cent (1,204 out of 2,061).

Most of those documents (1,117, or 74 per cent) record straightforward conveyances in one form or another, generally in perpetuity, but there are also 37 'wadsets' (mortgages) and leases, and 50 confirmation charters issued by lords have also been included.[16] Of the rest, 103 (7 per cent) are grants of rights, privileges or favours, also usually with respect to land; 74 (5 per cent) grant annuities; 59 (4 per cent) are appointments to office, often in heredity; and 71 (5 per cent) are bonds or indentures in various forms between lords and their men. As for the 550 documents which are not title-deeds in one form or another, 240 of them are items of routine administration which are also almost all connected with land transfers, including 143 'precepts of sasine'[17] and the 33 retours mentioned above; while the remaining 310 cover a very wide range and mixture of topics (among them, marriage agreements and dispute settlements), and can only be categorized as 'miscellaneous'.

The number of documents in my files will, of course, be only a small proportion of those that were actually issued; any detailed local study would quickly demonstrate that many must have been lost. Also, the proportions in the above breakdown are unrepresentative of the documents that would actually have been issued at the time, when routine administrative items would have hugely swamped the charters; but, as has already been said, ephemera were not usually preserved. The result is that research on the late medieval Scottish nobility has to depend heavily on – and be skewed heavily towards – the kind of evidence presented by title-deeds and the like. The situation is much the same as that for historians of twelfth-century England, but without Domesday Book and the Pipe Rolls. Yet what does survive is not absolutely unrepresentative, because it provides an excellent sample of what late medieval Scottish lords would have regarded as their most significant documents; and it also reflects the old-fashioned (in English terms) nature of the landholding system of late medieval Scotland, where charters were at a premium.

II

It is those charters on which the discussion will initially focus: the 1,204 conveyances of land involving late medieval Scottish lords which are noted in my current files. For simplicity, these are all called charters here. Among them, one of the most frequently encountered concepts is that of 'service': the terms occurs, in one context or another, in almost exactly two-thirds of the texts.[18] An example giving a useful starting-point for the discussion is provided by a charter

[16] I.e. charters issued by lords confirming ones issued by their tenants. Here I have only included confirmations which give full or nearly full texts of charters that were issued by lesser landowners and are therefore not already in my files. This is only a very small proportion of surviving confirmations; but in most cases those provide insufficient detail for any analysis.

[17] Precepts of sasine were administrative documents giving instructions for conveyances to be carried out in terms of the relevant charters; in most cases they duplicate existing charters, but far fewer of them have survived.

[18] In 802, which is 66.6 per cent of the 1,204 conveyances.

of 21 June 1433 issued by Sir Robert Erskine of that ilk[19] to Sir William Forbes of Kinnaldy.[20]   Forbes was a fairly important Aberdeenshire laird, and the younger brother of Sir Alexander Forbes of that ilk, who was probably the major figure within the central Aberdeenshire earldom of Mar after the earl himself. As for Erskine, he was a much greater figure, among the top twenty Scottish lords of his generation, and an immediate member of the Scottish peerage when that came into being in the 1440s. Erskine's main estates were in central Scotland, but he also possessed property in Aberdeenshire – and, significantly, he was the senior collateral heir to the earldom of Mar. The earl of Mar was ageing and no longer married; his only child had died in 1430. It is possible, therefore, that Erskine's charter to Forbes was part of a search for supporters in Aberdeenshire and especially in Mar, preparatory to his claiming that earldom on the earl's death.[21] That is a familiar scenario. The kind of transaction, however, will probably not be so familiar to a readership accustomed to tenurial practice in late medieval England. It is a grant, for Forbes's 'faithful service done and to be done' (*pro fideli servicio impenso et impendendo*), of the land of Laskgowan in Erskine's north-Aberdeenshire barony of Kelly, which was to be held in fee and heredity of Erskine and his heirs, by the tenure known as 'blench farm', for an annual payment of 20*s* in lieu of all other demands, and for performing the 'Scottish service' due to the king from a quarter of one davach of land.

Here are references to two different kinds of service. The Erskine–Forbes charter was selected because it refers to Scottish service: since this paper's initial remit is service in late medieval Scotland, that concept needs to be mentioned. 'Scottish service' is one of various phrases used to describe the country's fundamental military obligation, by which every piece of land had to provide a certain number of fighting men.[22] In the late Middle Ages, however, it is an archaic term, occurring in only nine of the lords' charters in my files (of which all but this instance are from the fourteenth century);[23] instead, the general military

---

[19] 'Of that ilk' means 'of the same' – *de eodem* in Latin – and was used when the names of both the family and its main estate were the same: here it means Erskine of Erskine, which was the family's original property in Renfrewshire.

[20] *Collections for a History of the Shires of Aberdeen and Banff*, ed. J. Robertson (Spalding Club, 1843), pp. 392–3.

[21] The earl of Mar died in 1435, and in November 1435 Sir Alexander Forbes agreed to back Erskine's claim: *Abdn.-Banff Ills.*, vol. IV, pp. 188–9 (though he did not keep the agreement: ibid., pp. 189–90). For Erskine's unsuccessful efforts to gain Mar, see McGladdery, *James II*, pp. 19–22, 40–1, 103–4.

[22] A.A.M. Duncan, *Scotland: The Making of the Kingdom* (Edinburgh, 1975), pp. 378–85; G.W.S. Barrow, 'The Army of Alexander III's Scotland', *Scotland in the Reign of Alexander III*, ed. N.H. Reid (Edinburgh, 1990), pp. 132–47; Grant, *Independence and Nationhood*, pp. 154–6; G. Dickinson, 'Some Notes on the Scottish Army in the first half of the Sixteenth Century', *SHR*, XXVIII (1949), 133–45.

[23] Most strikingly, Thomas Randolph held the earldom of Moray for the service of eight knights, plus Scottish service and aid from each davach in Moray, as accustomed: *RMS*, vol. I, App. I, no. 31. See also ibid., vol. I, no. 452; App. I, no. 66; *RRS*, vol. V, no. 294; ibid., vol. VI, no. 202; W. Fraser, *History of the Carnegies, Earls of Southesk* (Edinburgh, 1867), vol. II, no. 60; *Morton Reg.*, vol. II, no. 51; NAS, Miscellaneous Collections, GD1/47/1/75, 'Miscellanea Arblarensie', ff. 31b–32r.

obligation was often referred to as 'forinsec' service (*servitium forinsecum*),[24] or, most commonly, as 'due and accustomed' service (*servitium debitum et consuetum*); in all, such phrases appear in 45 per cent of the charters under discussion here, and it is probably taken for granted in most of the others.[25] What was meant is like the twentieth-century 'national service', which is a reminder that in its basic sense the word 'service', both then and now, has a military meaning – a point that at times has perhaps been overlooked. Be that as it may, 'Scottish', 'forinsec' or 'due and accustomed' service involved an age-old obligation – as the association of Scottish service with the davach, almost certainly originating in a Pictish form of land assessment,[26] demonstrates. It is therefore very like the Anglo-Saxon fyrd, which also, in a way, survived through to late medieval England in the Assize of Arms and the system of recruiting shire levies to the royal armies. But, because of the wars in Scotland and especially in France, English armies were also raised through contracted retinues. That was not done in late medieval Scotland. The contrast is significant in the present context, because in England the practice of raising contract armies played an important part in standardizing and formalizing the way in which lords' ordinary retinues were put together, by means of indentures of retainer and retaining fees.[27] In Scotland, since there were no contract armies, there was no such stimulus towards standardization in lord–man relationships. Instead, as will be seen, lords made a wide variety of arrangements with their followers, just as happened in England before the development of contract armies in the first half of the fourteenth century.

It is the other reference to service, however, that brings us to this paper's chief concern. To repeat, Erskine's grant is stated to have been made in return for the faithful service which Forbes has performed in the past and will perform in the future. Phrases like that, ostensibly setting out the purpose of the grant, were fairly common in late medieval Scotland; they occur in 39 per cent of the 1,204 charters under discussion here, and among the non-royal ones the proportion is just on 50 per cent. These phrases took three basic forms: 'for faithful service done and to be done' (as in the Erskine–Forbes example), in 20 per cent of the non-royal charters; 'for homage and service done and to be done', in 21 per cent of them; and, less commonly, 'for counsel and aid done and to be done (or similar words to that effect), in 9 per cent. In most cases, the phraseology is fairly standard, but sometimes it is amplified and modified; for example, estates were granted 'for his service, counsel and aid most frequently given and to

---

[24] 'Forinsec' derives from the French *forein*, i.e. 'outside or additional to whatever is due to the immediate lord' (Duncan, *Making of the Kingdom*, p. 380); in later medieval Scotland it would always have involved military service to the crown.

[25] That is implied by the fact that royal confirmations of landowners' grants invariably included the phrase '*salvo servitio nostro*', which maintained a general obligation of military service to the crown from all pieces of land. And note that in a subsequent charter conveying Laskgowan, 'Scottish service' was replaced by the commonplace 'service to the lord our king', though the actual obligation would have remained the same: *Abdn.-Banff Ills.*, vol. III, pp. 142–3; and below, p. 179.

[26] G.W.S. Barrow, *The Kingdom of the Scots* (London, 1973), pp. 268–9.

[27] M. Powicke, *Military Obligation in Medieval England* (Oxford, 1962), passim; 'Private Indentures for Life Service in Peace and War 1278–1476', ed. M. Jones and S. Walker, *Camden Miscellany XXXII* (Camden Society, 1994), pp. 12–16.

be given';[28] 'for his diligent labour and gracious service done efficaciously and effectively';[29] 'for his homage and service done and to be done for all the time of his life';[30] 'for his well merited and faithful service done and perpetually to be done';[31] 'for his and his heirs-males' homage, service and special retinue to be done ... in perpetuity';[32] and so on. Whatever the form of words, the basic idea is much the same: that the donor of the land expected service from the recipient – which is, of course, the concept behind what historians used to know as 'feudalism'. While this expectation of service occurs only in about half the conveyances involving late medieval Scottish lords, they would certainly have regarded it as a common concept. But was that merely the result of formulaic verbiage, or did it actually mean something in terms of lord–man relations? That is the main question of this paper.

III

A point to make at the outset is that this question could not be asked at all about late medieval England, because no grants or conveyances like the Erskine–Forbes example were possible there: such a subinfeudation, in fee simple, was prohibited by the statute of *Quia Emptores* of 1290. And although *Quia Emptores* did not prohibit subinfeudation in the case of restricted or conditional grants, that loophole seems not to have been employed by English landowners. Instead, the conveyance of land came to be almost entirely by substitution: the recipient simply replaced the donor, and no tenurial link was established between them. Therefore, while pre-1290 tenurial links could still survive in late medieval England, new subinfeudations did not take place.[33] They could and did take place, however, in late medieval Scotland, where no law equivalent to *Quia Emptores* was ever passed.[34]

---

[28] *... pro suis servicio, consilio et auxilio michi sepius impensis et impendendis*: e.g. John Stewart, Lord Darnley, to his brother, Alexander, 1450: NAS, Great Seal Register, C2/4, no. 23 (incompletely printed in *RMS*, vol. II, no. 350).

[29] *... pro suo diligenti labore et grato servicio nobis efficaciter et effectuose impenso*: e.g. David II to Archibald Douglas, 1369: *RRS*, vol. VI, no. 451.

[30] *... pro homagio et servicio suo nobis impenso et pro toto tempore vite sue impendendo*: e.g., William, earl of Douglas, to John Towers, *c*. 1360: *RRS*, vol. VI, no. 228; or Sir William Crichton of that ilk to Walter Scott, 1437: W. Fraser, *The Scotts of Buccleuch* (Edinburgh, 1878), vol. II, no. 33.

[31] *... pro benemerito et fideli servicio suo nobis impenso et pro suo perpetuo nobis impendendo*: William, earl of Ross, to John Tarrell, *c*. 1364: *RRS*, vol. VI, no. 321.

[32] *... pro ipsius et heredum suorum masculorum homagio servicio et speciali retinencie nobis et heredibus nostris pro perpetuo impendendis*: Sir Duncan Campbell of Lochawe to his second son, Colin: NAS, Register House Transcripts, RH1/2/199.

[33] See, e.g., J.M.W. Bean, *The Decline of English Feudalism* (Manchester, 1968), pp. 79–104; S.F.C. Milsom, *Historical Foundations of the Common Law* (2nd edn, London, 1981), pp. 113–18.

[34] For late medieval Scottish land law, see H.L. MacQueen, *Common Law and Feudal Society in Medieval Scotland* (Edinburgh, 1993); I. Milne, 'Heritable Rights: The Early Feudal Tenures', and H.H. Monteath, 'Heritable Rights: From Early Times to the Twentieth Century', chs 13–14 of *An Introduction to Scottish Legal History*, ed. G.C.H. Paton (Stair Society, 1958); and Grant, 'Higher Nobility and their Estates', pp. 186–211.

The only Scottish check on subinfeudation was a rule that more than half of a fief could not be granted away without the permission of the overlord, who would be either the king or the 'subject-superior' (to use the Scots legal term for a landlord who had vassals holding land of him); if that rule was broken, the overlord could 'recognosce' or confiscate the land into his own possession. This did occasionally happen, but it seems that Scottish conveyances usually had the necessary permission. Sometimes land was granted to be held of the overlord rather than the grantor of the charter, so that the recipient took the place of the grantor in the land-holding chain; but that was fairly unusual, occurring in only 87 (13 per cent) of the non-royal charters that I have noted. With the rest of the non-royal charters, the conveyancing was by subinfeudation – and in over half these cases there was ostensibly an expectation of some form of service in return.

The Scottish conveyancing system, however, was not so simple as that implies, because the grantor of the charter was not necessarily the person making the actual conveyance. Ownership could, in fact, be transferred by surrendering the land in question to the overlord – either the crown or the subject-superior – who would then grant it to the desired recipient. This process is found in twelfth-century England, but it soon ceased.[35] In Scotland, however, it became standard practice, not only for alienating property but also for changing the form of tenure: a landowner could surrender land to his overlord and receive it back under new terms, especially as a 'tailzie' (entail) or jointure.[36] The surrender-and-regrant procedure thus had much the same function as the English use,[37] with the crown or subject-superior having the role of the feoffees-to-use, but legally it was much more stable, because the transactions were ratified by the overlords' charters, which (unlike the use) were recognized by the common law.[38]

When surrender-and-regrant is taken into account, the transactions in the 1,204 royal and non-royal charters being considered here can be analysed as follows. There were 180 outright grants by the crown to lords; the other 1,024 were in effect conveyances among landowners.[39] Of these, 159 (16 per cent)

---

[35] See, e.g. F. Pollock and F.W. Maitland, *The History of English Law before the Time of Edward I* (2nd edn, Cambridge, 1911), vol. I, pp. 329–51, esp. 345; Milsom, *Historical Foundations of Common Law*, pp. 110–12; J. Hudson, *The Formation of the English Common Law* (London, 1996), pp. 100–3, 216–17; and MacQueen, *Common Law in Medieval Scotland*, ch. 1.

[36] Also, the overlord's charter could stipulate that only the formal ownership was conveyed, and that the tenancy of the land (and hence the profits) remained with the original owner for life, in what became known as 'liferent'; that enabled landowners to make what were in effect *post mortem* grants, especially to their children.

[37] See Bean, *Decline of English Feudalism*, ch. 3.

[38] Moreover, the overlords' charters almost invariably contained clauses of warrandice, by which they promised to compensate the recipients of the conveyance if it was successfully challenged – though since any such challenge would be against the overlord's charter and would have to be brought initially in the overlord's court, the likelihood of success would have been slight. For a warrandice case in 1372–3 where the overlord provided compensation, see *Morton Reg.*, vol. II, nos. 130, 136.

[39] Though 339 of these are recorded in charters which were actually issued by the crown.

returned lands to the original owner under new conditions of tenure; and exchanges, wadsets and leases account for another 74 (7 per cent). The remaining 791 were more normal conveyances, transmitting property from one person to another: 385 (38 per cent) of these were substitutions, while 406 (40 per cent) were straightforward subinfeudations. Thus, despite the fact that there was no Scottish equivalent to *Quia Emptores*, transferring land by substitution was in practice almost as common as subinfeudation during the later Middle Ages, so far as transactions involving the lords were concerned.

That conclusion does not apply evenly to the lords' and the lairds' conveyances, however. Where lords were giving land to other lords or to members of their immediate families, substitution was slightly more common: there are 129 instances of it, as opposed to 111 subinfeudations. When they gave land to lairds, on the other hand, it was almost entirely by subinfeudation: there are 246 instances of this, as opposed to only 36 transfers by substitution. But that is completely reversed with respect to conveyances made by lairds to magnates and other lairds: 220 of these were substitutions, only 49 were subinfeudations. Admittedly the charters under consideration here include only a small proportion of the total issued by the lairds of late medieval Scotland. Nevertheless, even with that caveat, the pattern seems clear: the lords employed both kinds of conveyance when transferring land to their equals, but generally subinfeudated when granting land to lairds; while the lairds, in contrast, tended not to do that, for most of their conveyances were outright alienations. The likely explanation of this pattern is that although the lords themselves maintained the practice of subinfeudation, they usually prohibited their tenants from doing so, and insisted, instead, on land transfers at that social level being made by substitution. The late medieval Scottish conveyancing system appears therefore to have been controlled by the lords in order to maintain their tenurial lordship.

The fundamental question still remains, however: did that tenurial lordship have any real importance in terms of lord–man relations, or was it merely a technicality? The history of landownership in thirteenth-century England, before 1290 and *Quia Emptores*, suggests a negative answer.[40] What operated there seems to have been a conveyancing system pure and simple, without any lord–man significance. The words *quia emptores* – 'because purchasers' – bring that out clearly: subinfeudation was prohibited partly because it had become a purely commercial practice, in which, when lands were sold, vendors maintained their superiority not out of any sense of viable lordship but because they hoped for future profit from the 'feudal incidents' of wardship, marriage and relief after the purchasers died; and partly because if used shrewdly it enabled them to avoid the obligations of service and incidents which they owed to their own overlords.

Furthermore, according to A.A.M. Duncan's important discussion of 'Fief and Service' in twelfth- and thirteenth-century Scotland,[41] the situation was the same north of the Border. Although during the twelfth century Scottish subinfeudation was usually for 'feudal' knight or sergeanty service (which must, of course, be distinguished from the 'forinsec' service owed generally to the

---

[40] See, e.g., Bean, *Decline of English Feudalism*, ch. 1.
[41] Duncan, *Making of the Kingdom*, ch. 15.

crown),[42] Professor Duncan believes that its significance soon rested solely in the incidents. This is supported by the fact that in Scotland traditional 'feudal' land tenure came to be known as tenure 'by ward and relief', or simply as 'ward-holding'. Moreover, the obligation of service and incidents was often commuted for an annual cash payment (plus double on inheritance), which emphasizes the commercial side of Scottish landownership. Such fiscal tenure was called 'feu farm', denoting both the yearly payment ('farm') and the fact that the land was not leased but was held in fee, heredity and perpetuity (i.e. in 'feu'). It became increasingly common, so much so that eventually, in the eighteenth century, feu farm became the only way of owning land in Scotland. That remained the case until 1974; and indeed much Scottish landowning (of houses and gardens as well as estates) is still technically 'in feu', that is by a form of 'feudal' tenure, nowadays. But if such 'feudal' tenure is essentially a lawyers' fiction at the beginning of the twenty-first century, that, claims Duncan, was already the case during the thirteenth:

This tired structure [the thirteenth-century conveyancing system] was scarcely more significant of social relationships than the ruinous feudal pile which conceals lucrative legal incompetence today. It existed as a form to enable two basic kinds of transaction to take place: sale of land outright, and irredeemable loan of land at a fixed rate of interest, the feu duty.[43]

In this view, the most important aspect of the charter granting land was the warrandice or guarantee that would be promised by the grantor. Also,

the conveyance was completed by the giving of homage and sasine [equivalent to English *seisin*] and was renewed in each generation by the same ceremonies. Even better if it were renewed each year by a symbolic transaction, the handing over of gloves or spurs, to remind the parties and outsiders that a title and guarantee of title still existed. Hence, even with outright sales, there was point in preserving an empty or *blanche* feudal render.[44]

From that '*blanche* feudal render' there evolved tenure in 'blench farm' (as in the Erskine–Forbes charter of 1433). It is a version of feu-farm tenure in which the payment was symbolic – a penny (most commonly), a pair of spurs, a rose, a glove, a hawk, a pound of pepper, and so on – and had only to be rendered if specifically requested.[45]

For Duncan, therefore, the pattern of lordship revealed by the Scottish medieval charters has little or no significance for lord–man relations. He argues that while the followings of thirteenth-century lords included many men who held land of those lords, that was simply accidental: the fact that they were tenants of the lords simply brought them into the latter's spheres of influence, as a result of which they entered the lords' service. In other words, the actual tenancies

---

[42] Barrow, *Kingdom of the Scots*, ch. 10, 'The Beginnings of Military Feudalism'.

[43] Duncan, *Making of the Kingdom*, p. 408.

[44] Ibid.

[45] Spelled out, e.g., by Thomas, earl of Mar, in 1358 × 9, when he gave John Forbes land to be held 'for faithful service . . . without homage or ward [and] relief or suit-of-court . . . rendering annually one penny sterling . . . if it is claimed, in name of blench farm, standing for all kinds of other services, customs, aids, exactions or demands which could be demanded . . . from the said land': *RRS*, vol. VI, no. 323.

did not by themselves create lord–man relationships; these were the product of geographical proximities, not specific tenurial links. It is a powerful argument which has been highly influential, especially among Scottish medievalists who believe that in the past excessive emphasis has been placed on strictly 'feudal' aspects of the twelfth and thirteenth centuries.[46] And it has been followed for the later medieval and early modern periods by Wormald in *Lords and Men*. She too sees the tenurial ties as largely meaningless, and believes that lord–man relations had to be constructed on the basis of much more personal connections.[47] Therefore she provides a chapter on 'The Rise of the Personal Bond' – which, when fully risen, is represented by the 800 or so bonds of manrent and maintenance from the period 1442–1603 that she has identified and analysed in depth.

At first sight, the evidence of the late medieval lords' charters backs up the Duncan–Wormald line of argument. The conveyances by substitution, where lands were alienated completely (as in the England of *Quia Emptores*) could be regarded as sales, and the phrases about homage and service and faithful service could be ignored. And, therefore, when the same phrases appear in charters recording subinfeudations, they could be disregarded there as well – so that those conveyances, too, could be sales. Also, with the non-royal charters, it could be that the crucial aspect was the warrandice clause, which is included in virtually every one (royal charters did not include warrandice, but the great seal probably gave sufficient guarantee). As for the obligations imposed upon the recipients, while 'forinsec' military service to the crown was frequently stipulated and generally implied, military service to a lord was stipulated only once, in *c.* 1325.[48] Otherwise, the traditional 'feudal' obligation was simply indicated by the catch-all phrase 'due and accustomed service', a version of which occurs in 362 (35 per cent) of the 1,024 conveyances between landowners;[49] presumably it was not significant enough to spell out precisely. In 29 charters, however, the obligation is said to be 'wardship, marriage and relief' or 'ward and relief': that shows that when aspects of traditional 'feudal' tenure *were* specified, they were usually the incidents.[50] But it was more common for both the 'feudal' service and the incidents to be cancelled; that happened 461 times, in 45 per cent of the conveyances.[51] Sometimes – though in only 34 cases – the replacement tenure

---

[46] See, e.g., R.D. Oram, 'Gold into Lead? The State of Early Medieval Scottish History', *Freedom and Authority*, ed. Brotherstone and Ditchburn, pp. 32–43. But for a challenge to Duncan's views, see K.J. Stringer, *Earl David of Huntingdon, 1152–1219* (Edinburgh, 1985), pp. 89–90.

[47] Wormald, *Lords and Men*, pp. 11–13, 46–51.

[48] *Morton Reg.*, vol. II, no. 50: Duncan, earl of Fife, to Sir William Douglas of Lothian; for the service of half a knight. Knight-service to the *crown* is, however, specified in eight charters, all from before 1375.

[49] I include a few cases where land was to be held for the equally catch-all phrase 'homage, service, ward and relief' – which is given as a synonym for 'due and accustomed service' in a charter of 1432: NAS, Lindsay, GD203/2/6.

[50] E.g., *RRS*, vol. VI, nos. 216, 217, 231; *RMS*, vol. II, nos. 228, 370, 1428, 2034. The phrase generally occurs together with the requirement of suit-of-court; probably the 'feudal' military service part of the obligation was being cancelled.

[51] That leaves 172 conveyances (17 per cent of the 1,024 total) where no specific reference was made to tenure: these include the wadsets and leases, and charters stating that the lands were to be held in the same way as before the conveyance.

was feu farm. Blench farm, however, was the norm: there are 342 instances of it, of which 264 are in the non-royal charters. The remaining 85 record conveyances in which all that was required was suit to the overlord's court; as with blench farm, other obligations were apparently waived. More often than not, therefore, lands were conveyed with merely a token recognition of superior lordship – as was spelled out by Thomas Stewart, earl of Angus, in 1360, who said that a blench farm of spurs was 'in name of recognition of this our grant', or by George Dunbar, earl of March, in 1396, who said that his requirement of three suits-of-court was 'in name of cognition of our lordship and as a sign of the subjection of [the recipient and his heirs]'.[52] The conclusion, therefore, could easily be that the late medieval lords' charters have little or nothing to do with lord–man relations.

However, there is another way of thinking about these charters. Twenty-eight of them (3 per cent) state explicitly that land was being bought or sold, often including forms of the clause 'know that we have sold ... in our great and urgent necessity'.[53] In 16 cases, lords sold land – most spectacularly in 1372, when Thomas Fleming, earl of Wigtown, sold his earldom (modern Wigtownshire) to Sir Archibald Douglas for £500![54] Two other significant sales, for £200 and 200 merks respectively, were by Sir Thomas Erskine of that ilk in 1385, and by Alexander Leslie, earl of Ross, in 1401, in both cases to raise money towards the reliefs they owed the crown.[55] Andrew, Lord Gray, had to sell land three times, in 1461, 1462 and 1472;[56] William, 8th earl of Douglas, had to do so twice, in 1451 and 1452;[57] and eight other lords had to make single sales.[58]

---

[52] W. Fraser, *Memorials of the Montgomeries Earls of Eglinton* (Edinburgh, 1859), vol. II, no. 5; W. Fraser, *Memorials of the Family of Wemyss of Wemyss* (Edinburgh, 1888), vol. II, no. 25.

[53] *... noveritis nos ... vendisse ... in magna et urgente necessitate nostra ...*

[54] W. Fraser, *The Douglas Book* (Edinburgh, 1885), vol. III, no. 327; also *RMS*, vol. I, no. 507.

[55] NAS, Rothes, GD204/701, summarized in HMC, *4th Report*, p. 494, no. 13; Fraser, *Carnegies of Southesk*, vol. II, no. 44. 'Merk' is the Scots form of mark, and, strictly speaking, should not be used before *c.*1390, when Scottish currency ceased to be known as sterling; but for clarity it has been applied generally in this paper. Note that, conversely, I have used the simple £ symbol to represent the £ Scots after *c.*1390 as well as the £ sterling before then.

[56] W. Fraser, *The Melvilles Earls of Melville and the Leslies Earls of Leven* (Edinburgh, 1890), vol. III, no. 45; *RMS*, vol. II, no. 895; NAS, Rollo, GD56/10.

[57] NAS, Great Seal Reg., C2/4, no. 150 (summarized, *RMS*, vol. II, no. 502); Fraser, *Douglas Book*, vol. III, no. 422 (the latter transaction took place just a month before James II killed him).

[58] Sir Walter Oliphant (1375); Patrick Graham, earl of Strathearn (1406); Sir James Dunbar of Frendraught (1424); Robert, Lord Erskine (1441); Sir Alexander Ogilvy of Auchterhouse (1454); George, Lord Haliburton (1471); George Leslie, earl of Rothes (1472); and Archibald, earl of Angus (1475): *RMS*, vol. II, nos. 279, 1222; *Abdn.-Banff Ills.*, vol. III, 135–6; ibid., vol. IV, pp. 322–3; HMC, *4th Report*, p. 496, no. 34; NAS, A.P. Melville WS, GD1/349/2; NAS, Montrose, GD220/1/A/1/6/8; and transcript in collection for *RRS, 1371–1406*, dated 22.2.1424, from MSS Viscount Arbuthnott, bdle 2, no. 18.

Conversely, there are 14 instances of purchase, by 11 separate lords.[59] The transactions conform well enough to the Duncan model; when lords purchased land
it was alienated outright to them, and when they sold, it was generally by subinfeudation and mostly in blench farm. But surely the main point about these
conveyances is that they were described as sales. That demonstrates that the
landowners of late medieval Scotland did not necessarily avoid stating in their
charters that land was being sold – and hence that conveyances about which this
is *not* stated should not automatically be regarded as sales. That, of course,
applies to the vast majority of the charters under consideration here.

Admittedly the point could be taken too far. There are cases where contracts
exist to prove that what look like straightforward grants of land were really sales.[60]
Also, among the charters of Archibald, 4th earl of Douglas, there are four that
apparently record ordinary grants of land but were probably issued as securities
for debts incurred as a result of his captivity in England in 1402–8.[61] Thus
hidden commercial transactions cannot be ruled out. But if, for instance, most
of my total of 246 straightforward subinfeudations made by lords to lairds in
this period were actually sales,[62] then that would imply a significant economic
imbalance between the greater and the lesser landowners, which is surely
implausible. Moreover, if sales of land really were so common as Duncan
claims, then it is extremely surprising that many more of them have not come
to light – especially for the mid-to-late fifteenth century, when the wording of
the charters seems to be more explicit.

Such considerations make the case against taking the charters at face value less
compelling. There are signs, indeed, that care was taken over the phraseology
describing the grants. 'Service' and 'homage' phrases are never included in charters where the transactions were described as sales; they are rarely found when
lairds granted land to lords;[63] and they are invariably omitted when, as was quite
common, land was granted by a kinsman or a husband 'in free marriage' (in which

---

[59] Twice from other lords – making 28 cases of buying or selling in all. The 14 purchases
were by: Sir Colin Campbell (1361, twice); Sir Duncan Wallace (*c.* 1368); Sir Simon
Preston (1370); Adam Forrester (1376, 1385); Sir John Lyon (*c.* 1377; twice); Sir William Graham (1406); Sir Patrick Ogilvy of Auchterhouse (*c.* 1421); Sir William Hay of
Erroll (1413); Sir George Crichton of Cairns (*c.* 1430); James, Lord Hamilton (*c.* 1462);
and Laurence, Lord Oliphant (1468): *RMS*, vol. II, no. 965; *RRS*, vol. VI, no. 391;
Abdn.-Banff Ills., vol. III, 364–5; Fraser, *Douglas Book*, vol. III, no. 389; Fraser, *Carnegies of Southesk*, vol. II, no. 44; HMC, *Hamilton Report*, no. 20; NAS, Abercrombie
of Forglen, GD185/6/6/2, s.d. 4.1.1422; NAS, Montrose, GD220/1/A/1/6/8; NAS,
Whitehills, GD143/1/2; NAS, Reg. House Trans., RH1/2/87, s.d. 16.8.1361 and
11.11.1361; ibid., RH1/2/139; and transcripts in collection for *RRS, 1371–1406*, from
earl of Strathmore's muniments at Glamis Castle, Box 3, nos. 60, 62.

[60] E.g. *Morton Reg.*, vol. II, nos. 143, 202, 207.

[61] Grant, 'Records of Fourth Earl of Douglas', p. 240.

[62] For these, see above, p. 154.

[63] That is the norm, though there are a few exceptions from the period before the 1440s,
when there was no formal distinction between the men I describe as lords and the
more important lairds (i.e. those who, like the lords, possessed baronies and so were
barons). References to 'counsel and aid', or the like, do however occur quite often in
laird–lord charters; but that was a different concept.

no obligation of any kind, not even blench farm, was ever imposed). Furthermore, grants 'in free marriage' were not commercial, at least not in the way that sales of land were; their purpose was to endow the husband and wife, often in jointure. Similarly, when lords granted land to their sons, one intention may have been to avoid inheritance dues – though in such cases the overlords may have charged compensatory amounts for permission – but the main purpose must have been simply the endowment of their immediate kindred. But it should follow that, if grants to wives and sons are not to be regarded as sales, that could also be said about grants made to the known followers or retainers of a lord.

Some charters, indeed, can hardly be anything else than grants of land in reward of service. In 1409, for example, the 4th earl of Douglas gave an estate in Stirlingshire to a prominent member of his affinity, Sir William Crawford, because Crawford had acted as deputy-warden of Edinburgh Castle for the earl during his captivity in England.[64] More strikingly, in 1369 William, earl of Ross, granted a davach of land in Ross to Hugh Munro of Foulis, head of one of the earldom's leading families, 'for his faithful service done and to be done during his time, and also for the laudable service done to us by his father, lately killed in our defence';[65] the land was to be held 'as freely as any land in Scotland is granted by any earl or baron for good deeds'. Or, thirdly, consider the fascinating charter from David Lindsay, earl of Crawford, to Herbert Johnstone in 1464, giving him property in Dumfriesshire to be held 'for his faithful service to us at the time when we were held captive by James, late [9th] earl of Douglas ... and especially for freeing and abducting our person from captivity at the hands of the said James'.[66] These transactions were not sales of land; the introductory passages must surely be taken at face value. Conversely, an explanatory phrase was pointedly left out of the charter of 1365 by which Robert Stewart, earl of Strathearn, gave Foulis in Strathearn to David II's stepson, John Logie, whom it is safe to say he hated; this grant, which can hardly have been a sale, was probably forced on Stewart by David II.[67]

---

[64] NAS, Reg. Ho. Chrs., RH6/225; summarized in Fraser, *Douglas Book*, vol. III, no. 356.

[65] ... *pro fideli servicio suo nobis impensis et pro suo tempore nobis impendendis et eciam pro laudabili servicio patris sui nuper pro nostra defensione interfecti nobis impensis*: NAS, Munro of Foulis, GD93/6; cf. *Calendar of Writs of Munro of Foulis*, ed. C.T. McInnes (Scottish Record Society, 1940), no. 6. Here and hereafter, quotations from manuscript sources are given in the original Latin as well as in English translation.

[66] ... *pro sui fideli servitio nobis tempore quo tenebamini captivus per Jacobum quondam comitem de Douglas ... et precipue pro liberatione et abductione persone nostre de captivitate et manibus dicti Jacobi*: NAS, Great Seal Reg., C2/6, no. 87; summarized in *RMS*, vol. II, no. 786.

[67] W. Fraser, *The Red Book of Grandtully* (Edinburgh, 1868), vol. I, no. 72*. It was probably an element in the amends that Stewart had to make for leading a rebellion in 1363, partly out of hostility towards David II's marriage to Margaret Logie (née Drummond). Stewart did call Logie his 'dearest kinsman', but that must have been through gritted teeth. Also, in 1366, he agreed to detach the lands of Logie from the earldom altogether; again that was no doubt on David II's insistence: *RRS*, vol. VI, no. 353. For Stewart and Logie in general, see Boardman, *Early Stewart Kings*, pp. 15–22. Once Queen Margaret and John Logie fell out of David II's favour in 1369, Foulis was probably taken back by Stewart; when he himself was king (Robert II), Foulis was in the hands of the next earl of Strathearn, his son David: *Exch. Rolls*, vol. III, pp. 34–5.

Now, one significant aspect of the charters by the earls of Ross, Crawford and Strathearn is that Munro, Johnstone and Logie were to hold their lands in blench farm. This demonstrates that blench-farm tenure does not have to indicate that land was being sold and only a token superiority retained. Instead, it could have reflected the financial significance of the 'feudal' incidents in a different way: cancelling them by means of blench farm would have been a valuable form of patronage from the lord (albeit enforced patronage in the Stewart–Logie grant). This was spelled out in 1402 by the 4th earl of Douglas, who declared that although William Sinclair used to hold Carfrae in Lauderdale from the earl for homage and service, suit-of-court, ward, relief and marriage, now, 'on account of the tenderness which we have for the said William, and not without cause, we ... grant Carfrae ... in blench farm ... for a pair of spurs ... if requested'.[68] Douglas, however, would not have meant Sinclair to stop serving him; thus when the earl was on parole from his English captivity, Sinclair was one of his hostages.[69] Therefore, the service that was waived in the conversion to blench farm can only have been a specified 'feudal' obligation from the land, not the more general service that any lord would expect from his men. This is also demonstrated by a charter of 1448 from Sir Laurence Abernethy granting land in Banffshire to John Auchinhove, for homage and service, ward and relief, suit-of-court and a pound of pepper a year if demanded; here, the pepper can only have been in lieu of the formal 'feudal' service,[70] while general service was presumably still required. It seems safe to conclude, therefore, that in the frequent cases where grants in blench farm were said to be for 'faithful service', 'homage and service' and the like, there was not necessarily any contradiction between the concepts.

Occasionally, however, grants in blench farm or its equivalent were made which cancelled the incidents but nonetheless required specific military service. In 1346, for instance, King David II gave the barony of Alloa in Clackmannanshire to his 'ally' (*confederatus*), Sir Robert Erskine,[71] 'for performing half the service of one knight and three suits-of-court a year ... for all other service ... and demands'; David 'expressly conceded' for Erskine's heirs that the land would be 'free and quit of ward, relief and marriage ... for ever'.[72] Among the non-royal charters, in 1360 William, earl of Sutherland, granted land in the earldom to his brother, Nicholas, 'for his faithful homage and service ... rendering the service of one knight per year for all service, exactions or demands whatsoever'.[73] In 1426, William Douglas, earl of Angus, gave part of Kirriemuir

---

[68] HMC, *Milne-Home Report*, no. 591; and cf. no. 590.

[69] Grant, 'Records of Fourth Earl of Douglas', pp. 246, 250.

[70] *Abdn.-Banff Ills.*, vol. II, p. 228; blench farm is not actually mentioned in this charter, presumably because the obligations were much more than 'blench'.

[71] Grandfather of the lord of the 1433 charter with which this discussion began.

[72] *RRS*, vol. VI, no. 327. 'Half a knight's service' presumably equated to the service of a man-at-arms. 'Ally' probably had retaining connotations (Wormald, *Lords and Men*, p. 90); earlier, in 1360, Erskine was called David II's 'dear bachelor': *RRS*, vol. VI, no. 233.

[73] Ibid., vol. VI, no. 307. The term 'blench farm' is not mentioned, but this is obviously the same form of tenure, except that the knight's service takes the place of the token render.

barony, in Angus, to William Giffard, 'for rendering therefrom annually ...
homage for the said lands and the service of one *armiger* [man-at-arms or
esquire] in both peacetime and war, and one suit-of-court three times a year ...
and one silver penny ... in name of blench farm'.[74] And, most strikingly, there
is a grant from 1384×8 by James, 2nd earl of Douglas, to his bastard son,
William (ancestor of the dukes of Buccleuch), giving him the barony of Drum-
lanrig in Dumfriesshire, for performing 'the service of one knight in our army,
in name of blench farm only, for all other secular services, exactions or
demands'.[75] These three territories were presumably to be held for the service
of a knight or *armiger* on a flexible basis (which would obviously have suited
the earls) and without any of the other obligations and incidents normally
associated with traditional military tenure. It is difficult to say whether or not
that can be described as a form of 'feudal' tenure, and it probably does not
matter; the significant point is that these charters show that land certainly could
be held in fourteenth- and fifteenth-century Scotland for a purely physical obligation and nothing else. They may be exceptional documents, but they demonstrate that at least some of the late medieval Scottish lords believed in a direct
relationship between land tenure and military service.

IV

Another way to approach the fundamental problem addressed in this paper is
to ask the following: if land grants by lords to lairds did not have any significance for lord–man relations in late medieval Scotland, then on what institutional basis were lords' retinues recruited and kept together? That immediately
brings us to Wormald's analysis of bonds of manrent in her *Lords and Men*. As
she explains, in the term 'manrent', *-rent* is a form of the northern English
suffix *-raed*, meaning '-ness',[76] so manrent simply means 'man-ness'. One of its
early senses takes that particularly literally, as sexual intercourse; but by the
late Middle Ages in Scotland it had come specifically to denote the relationship
between a man and his lord. From the mid-fifteenth century onwards, that was
formally created by presenting the lord with a sealed written promise to be his
man: in other words, by giving him a bond of 'man-ness' or manrent. In return,
the lord would promise to maintain the man, or give him 'maintenance' – which
in Scotland did not have the same connotation of lawlessness as it acquired in
England, but was simply a neutral term for standard 'good lordship'. Again,

---

[74] *Reddendo inde annuatim nobis et heredibus nostris ... homagium pro predictis terris et servicium unius armigeri tam temporis pacis quam guerre et una secta ter in anno ... et unum denarium argenti ... in nomine albe firme*: NAS, Great Seal Reg., C2/2, no. 112; summarized in *RMS*, vol. II, no. 111. The land had been resigned by Giffard, and was regranted with a tailzie in favour of the rising lord, Sir Patrick Ogilvy of Auchterhouse. Thus Giffard was probably giving or selling Ogilvy the reversion of the land, and it is quite likely that the earl was really aiming the special form of tenure at Ogilvy.

[75] HMC, *15th Report*, App. VIII, p. 8, no. 2.

[76] Hence 'liferent' = 'life-ness': the possession of land for life. The most common modern usage of the suffix *-raed* is in 'hatred', which in fifteenth- and sixteenth-century Scots was *hatrent*.

from the mid-fifteenth century, that was commonly put in writing, as a 'bond of maintenance'. Thus, together, a bond of manrent and a bond of maintenance correspond to the two halves of the English indenture of retainer; the technical difference is that in Scotland the two documents do not have identical wording, since the bond of manrent represents only the man's undertaking, and the bond of maintenance the lord's.[77]

Wormald found that the earliest document giving a promise of manrent like that was issued, in the vernacular, by Thomas Fraser of Lovat (near Inverness) to Alexander MacDonald, earl of Ross and Lord of the Isles, on 18 January 1442. Fraser states that he has

becummyn and becummys lele man ande trew to ... my lorde Sir Alexander of Ila erle of Ross ande lorde of the Ilis ... ande ... sal mak to my saide lord lele and trew service at all my gudely powar ... Ande giff [if] it happin me ... to brek my manrent and obelysing made to my forsaide lorde the erle I obeliss me ... to pay to my saide lord ... fyftene hundir markis of gude and usuale monay of the kinrike of Scotlande.[78]

The weight of that penalty clause raises a question about what had been going on between Fraser and Earl Alexander; but whatever the circumstances, it is the first recorded usage of 'manrent' in this sense, and hence the first of the known bonds of manrent. Thereafter, they were increasingly common for more than a century and a half, until the early 1600s (long after indentures of retainer ceased in England). For most of those one-and-a-half centuries, the issue of bonds of manrent and, reciprocally, maintenance, was the standard way of creating and consolidating lord–man relationships – beyond those of agnatic blood kinship – in Scotland.

From about 1442, therefore, it would appear that bonds of manrent and maintenance represent the main cement in Scottish lord–man relationships. But what of the previous period? Between 1314 and the date of the first known bond of manrent – which is almost as long a time as that in which the bonds of manrent flourished – what held such relationships together? For the present, the answer implied in the previous section, that they may have been cemented through grants of land in return for service, will be set on one side. Instead, what Wormald has called 'the rise of the personal bond'[79] must be discussed. The practice of making written promises of service did not spring up *ab initio* in about 1442, but already existed in the later fourteenth and earlier fifteenth centuries, when men undertook to give *retinencia*, or retinue-service,[80] to their lords, generally in documents known as 'letters of retinue'.

So far, my files contain 19 examples of, or references to, promises of retinue-service made before the date of the earliest known bond of manrent in 1442.[81]

---

[77] Wormald, *Lords and Men*, pp. 1–3, 14–24, 47–51, 60, 102–3, etc.

[78] Ibid., p. 17; printed in *Acts of the Lords of the Isles, 1336–1493*, ed. J. and R.W. Munro (Scottish History Society, 1986), no. 37.

[79] Wormald, *Lords and Men*, ch. 3.

[80] In Scotland, *retinencia* (like manrent) was what a man gave a lord; 'his *retinencia*' was the man's state of being retained. Hence it seems wrong to pop pop it as '*retinue*', because the words 'his retinue' would normally mean the lord's following.

[81] Also see Wormald, *Lords and Men*, pp. 35–9, for examples of other, less specific, bonds.

Nine are from the later fourteenth century. The first is an obligation by John Kennedy of Dunure in *c.* 1366, to be '*de retinencia*' to Queen Margaret Logie and her son John Logie for life, and to warn them of all plots against them, especially in Annandale.[82] Six others concern Sir James Douglas of Dalkeith and his immediate family. In 1372, Sir James made an indenture, in French, with William, 1st earl of Douglas, by which he promised 'his dwelling[83] and *retinance* for all the time of his life' to the earl, 'with eight men-at-arms and sixteen archers, as well in war and peace against all living except the king'.[84] Then, in *c.* 1391, Sir James's illegitimate son, James Douglas of Aberdour, gave his father a letter of retinue which runs, in so far as it can be read:[85]

Be it known to all men through these present letters that I James Douglas of Aberdour and Bucht am obliged and oblige myself [. . .] these my letters that from this day forth [. . .] for all the term of my life I shall be and become to my reverend lord and father Sir James of Douglas lord of Dalkeith of dwelling, that is to say [. . .] or of retinue, at the will of my forenamed lord with all my [. . .] in all times as well of war as of peace against all living men [. . . allegiance?] outtaken [to?] the king, for [. . .] reward made to me through the fornamed my lord [. . .] of the which the whole [. . .].

Two other letters of retinue were also given to Sir James, by Richard Brown and John Stewart of Craigie, but these texts are lost.[86] Also, in 1386, Sir James's brother, Henry Douglas of Lochleven, promised John Stewart, earl of Carrick (eldest son of Robert II), that he would give 'his *retinencia* and faithful service' to Carrick's son, David, the future duke of Rothesay; and sometime between 1398 and 1402, Rothesay himself had a similar promise from James Douglas junior of Dalkeith (Sir James's heir).[87] And there are two more fourteenth-century instances of retaining agreements, showing 'service and *retinencia*' being

---

[82] J. Riddell, *Inquiry into the Law and Practice in Scottish Peerages before and after the Union* (Edinburgh, 1842), vol. II, p. 982 (cf. *RRS*, vol. VI, no. 354 for the date). Riddell gave the Erroll charter-chest as his source, but the document has not been found.

[83] Printed as 'dem*a*eie' and (later in the text) as 'deuio²', which I read as *demurere* (or *demeurre*) and *demour*, like the forms of *demore* which are common in contemporary French-language indentures from England (e.g. 'Private Indentures', ed. Jones and Walker, nos. 47, 48, 50, 51, etc.), and corresponding to the term 'dwelling' which is common in vernacular Scottish bonds.

[84] *Morton Reg.*, vol. II, no. 129; the format is unusual for Scotland, and resembles an English indenture of retainer. See 'Private Indentures', ed. Jones and Walker, pp. 11–12; Wormald, *Lords and Men*, p. 43; and Brown, *Black Douglases*, p. 144.

[85] NLS, MS 72, f. 117v. Unfortunately the text, in the Morton cartulary, is badly damaged. It is in fourteenth-century Scots, but I do not trust my palaeography enough to be sure of the precise versions of some of the semi-legible words used here; therefore, since their gist is clear enough, I have modernized the wording.

[86] Brown's letter is listed in one of the inventory rolls of Sir James's muniments: NAS, Morton, GD150/78, m.1, 13th item. Stewart's letter is noted in the table of contents of the Morton cartulary, immediately before the letter from James Douglas of Aberdour (NLS, MS 72, ff. 45r and 133v, item 204); but the folio on which it was written has been cut out of the cartulary, probably in the fifteenth century (ibid., between ff. 117 and 118).

[87] No contracts survive, but the obligations of *retinencia* are recorded in *Morton Reg.*, vol. II, nos. 179, 214.

given to Sir Andrew Leslie of that ilk by his cousin and namesake in 1390,[88] and 'special *retinencia*' being owed to Sir William Lindsay of Byres by William Elphinstone in 1397.[89]

Next, there are significant references to retinue-service in two important political indentures from the early fifteenth century. First, when Robert Stewart, duke of Albany, the governor (i.e. regent) of Scotland, imposed his authority on Sir Gilbert Kennedy of Dunure in 1408, part of the settlement was that Sir Gilbert 'haf made his dwelling and speciale retenew with our said lorde ye gouvernor'.[90] Secondly, in 1420, Duke Murdoch (Robert's son and successor as duke of Albany and governor) made an indenture with Alexander Stewart, earl of Mar, concerning the latter's responsibilities in northern Scotland, in which it was stated that Mar 'is becum man of speciale feale and retenue' to Duke Murdoch, and 'salle giffe his letter therupon till [to] our forsaid Lord the Governour in deu forme under his seille'; while Mar's son, Thomas, was also to become the duke's man, and similarly give 'his letters of retenewe in due forme'.[91]

The other eight instances of retaining contracts from the earlier fifteenth century are more prosaic. In 1406, Duncan, earl of Lennox, was given a letter of retinue by Arthur of Ardencaple.[92] In 1408, Alexander Cumming promised to be 'lele man and trew for al the days of his live' to Thomas Dunbar, earl of Moray, though he was not to enter Moray's service until the expiry of his current contract with the earl of Mar in five years' time.[93] In 1413, Sir Patrick Gray gave a letter of retinue to Alexander Lindsay, earl of Crawford, becoming the earl's 'man of special retinue' for life.[94] In 1414 and 1432, Sir Duncan Campbell apparently had promises of 'special *retinencia*' from Ranald of Craignish and from Colin Campbell, his second son, respectively.[95] In 1428, Thomas Kirkpatrick gave a letter of retinue to the 5th earl of Douglas;[96] and in 1430, Alexander Ogston did likewise to Sir Alexander Forbes of that ilk.[97] And finally, in

---

[88] NAS, Rothes, GD204/718.

[89] W. Fraser, *The Elphinstone Family Book* (Edinburgh, 1897), vol. II, no. 10. The date is from an accompanying precept of sasine (ibid., no. 9); but the charter's witness list includes the duke of Albany and the earl of Crawford, titles which did not exist until 1398. Since the charter is only known from a crown inspection of 1424, later clerical error is probably to blame.

[90] *Facsimiles of the National Manuscripts of Scotland* (London, 1867–71), vol. II, no. LXI.

[91] *Abdn.-Banff Ills.*, vol. IV, pp. 181–2. The indenture was renewing an agreement made between Mar and Duke Robert of Albany. It also refers to Duke Murdoch's 'lettres baunde and seill ... of mantinance helpe and suppleie in deu forme and in effect as quhilum [= late] our Lord the Governor hes fader did', which seems to indicate the existence of 'bonds of maintenance in due form' in the years before 1420.

[92] W. Fraser, *The Lennox* (Edinburgh, 1874), vol. II, no. 43.

[93] *Abdn.-Banff Ills.*, vol. IV, pp. 175–6.

[94] *The Scots Peerage*, ed. J.B. Paul (Edinburgh, 1904–14), vol. IV, p. 271, quoting from the MS Draft Inventory of Gray Writs in the Lord Lyon's Office, Edinburgh, no. 9. The original may be among the Gray muniments at Darnaway Castle, but it has not been located.

[95] NAS, Reg. Ho. Trans., RH1/2/87, s.d. 4.6.1414; ibid., 1/2/199.

[96] NAS, Crown Office Writs, AD1/41.

[97] NAS, Forbes, GD52/1077.

1432, Forbes himself made an indenture with Alexander Lindsay, earl of Crawford, which referred among other things to 'his retinue' to the earl.[98]

Chronologically, the next known Scottish retaining document is that of January 1442, between Alexander MacDonald, earl of Ross, and Hugh Fraser of Lovat – the earliest bond of manrent. As might be expected, however, the terminological change from letters of retinue to bonds of manrent was not immediate. In March 1442, two months after the MacDonald–Fraser bond, Walter Ogilvy agreed to become 'speciale man of retenew' to Sir George Leslie of Rothes, and to give him a letter of retinue.[99] And in 1444, John Kennedy of Blaucharn and his son contracted to become the men of Sir Gilbert Kennedy of Dunure (grandson of the Gilbert mentioned above) for the following ten years.[100] Neither of those documents mentions manrent, but, otherwise, it is hard to see any difference in the lord–man relationships that were being established: Fraser, Ogilvy and Kennedy of Blaucharn were all becoming the men of their lords. Moreover, it should be stressed that the use of the term 'manrent' is not necessarily taken as a *sine qua non* for the bonds of manrent listed by Wormald. It is not found in the bond given in 1444 by James Forbes to Alexander Seton, Lord Gordon, which simply states that Forbes 'becummys mane' to 'my redoubtit lord' Gordon;[101] or in the indenture of 1452 by which Archibald Douglas of Cavers and his son 'ar becummyn men, and, be thir lettres, becummys men of speciale retenew' to George Douglas, earl of Angus (who had appointed them keepers of Hermitage Castle);[102] or in the 1457 'bande of retenew' of James, Lord Hamilton, to the earl of Angus, by which he became the earl's 'man of speciale seruice and retenew'.[103] These examples indicate that there can have been no significant difference between the early bonds of manrent and the previous letters of retinue;[104] the terminology may have been changing, but only slowly.

That said, the 19 instances of promises of *retinencia* found before 1442 do not amount to an impressive total. Originally, however, there were probably many more. But, as was stressed at the beginning of this paper, Scottish landowners tended to keep their title-deeds but to be less worried about other records; hence letters of retinue and the like may well have been cleared out or lost once they were no longer relevant.[105] That is borne out by the example of late medieval England, from where, apart from the Gaunt and Hastings material, only 156 indentures of retainer survive:[106] a huge number of English retaining agreements must have been lost, and much the same no doubt happened in

---

[98] *Abdn.-Banff Ills.*, vol. IV, p. 393, note; from NAS, Forbes, GD52/1044.

[99] This is from an extremely complex indenture, summarized below, p. 172.

[100] NAS, Ailsa, GD25/1/34; mentioned by Wormald, *Lords and Men*, pp. 50–1, but not included in her list of bonds of manrent.

[101] *Abdn.-Banff Ills.*, vol. IV, p. 395; Wormald, *Lords and Men*, p. 278.

[102] Fraser, *Douglas Book*, vol. III, no. 82; Wormald, *Lords and Men*, p. 173.

[103] HMC, *Hamilton Report*, no. 59; Wormald, *Lords and Men*, p. 174.

[104] Cf. Wormald, *Lords and Men*, p. 46: 'Early Stewart "retinue" was indeed the forerunner of manrent'.

[105] In practice they would only have lasted, at most, for the lifetimes of the parties involved; each generation would have had to create its own relationships.

[106] 'Private Indentures', ed. Jones and Walker, pp. 35–179.

Scotland.[107] The point can be illustrated from the Douglas of Dalkeith material, where six of the nine fourteenth-century retaining agreements were found. Only that between the earl of Carrick and Douglas of Lochleven is an original document;[108] the one between the duke of Rothesay and the younger Douglas of Dalkeith is known from a later royal charter, and the sources for the other four are Sir James's cartulary and inventory rolls. Thus five out of six of the originals have been lost. Also, the text of John Stewart of Craigie's letter of retinue has disappeared from the cartulary, and Richard Brown's letter was never copied into it, being simply noted in the inventory rolls.[109] Since Sir James Douglas of Dalkeith left the best preserved collection of lay muniments in late medieval Scotland, it is reasonable to conclude that similar losses of original documents relating to retinue-service would have happened among the muniments of other lords, who, so far as we know, did not keep cartularies or inventory rolls. Thus it is quite likely that the issue of letters of retinue was common practice – as is indicated by the two references in the indenture between Murdoch, duke of Albany, and the earl of Mar to letters of retinue 'in due form'; by an ordinance of council-general of January 1399 that everyone had to assist and obey the king's lieutenant (the duke of Rothesay) 'nocht agaynstandande any condiciounis of retenewis'; and by James I's requirement in 1435 that everyone at parliament had to give their 'letters of *retinencia* and fealty [*fidelitas*]' to his queen.[110] And, if it was common for men to give letters of retinue to their lords in the later fourteenth and earlier fifteenth centuries, then it would appear, obviously, that such letters played a major part in cementing Scottish lord–man relationships during the period before 1442, just as bonds of manrent seem to have done thereafter.

V

There is, however, one significant difference (terminology apart) between the letters of retinue and the bonds of manrent. Whereas, as Wormald has shown, with almost 90 per cent of the bonds of manrent and maintenance there was no tangible reward from the lord whatsoever, merely intangible 'good lordship',[111] about half the pre-1442 letters of retinue noted above involved financial rewards, mostly as annual fees.[112] Although the figures involved are low (9 out of 19), the difference may be significant. By the Douglas of Dalkeith–earl of

---

[107] See ibid., p. 10, and also Wormald, *Lords and Men*, pp. 2–3, 73, for the clearing out of obsolete bonds of manrent.

[108] NAS, Morton, GD150/50.

[109] See above, note 86. The inventory rolls also include references to a 'letter of David Lang about his service to the lord [of Dalkeith]', an 'obligation of John Clerk ... about his service to the lord', an indenture with Richard Brown, and four other indentures which could have had to do with retaining: NAS, Morton, GD150/77, m.3; GD150/78, m.1.

[110] *Abdn.-Banff Ills.*, vol. IV, pp. 181–2; *APS*, vol. I, p. 573; vol. II, p. 23. A council-general had almost the same status as a parliament.

[111] Wormald, *Lords and Men*, pp. 23–4, 66, 103.

[112] Above, pp. 163–5. References for the nine transactions listed in the rest of this paragraph are given in notes 84–5, 87–8, 92–3, and 97–8.

Douglas indenture of 1372, for instance, Earl William was to give Sir James 600 merks sterling at the rate of 200 merks a year; that was, in effect, a substantial lump sum. Henry Douglas's contract with Carrick, and James Douglas's with Rothesay, brought them 50-merk and £40 annuities respectively. James Douglas of Aberdour apparently received a 20-merk annuity from his father for retinue service;[113] and that is what Sir Andrew Leslie gave his cousin, too. In the fifteenth century, the earl of Lennox promised Arthur Ardencaple a 3- or 4-merk annual fee;[114] the earl of Moray promised Alexander Cumming 'resonable reward efter his seruice as his consale ordanys'; Sir Alexander Forbes gave Alexander Ogston 'a certane soume off mony'; and the earl of Crawford in effect gave Forbes a £20 retaining fee.[115]

Furthermore, among the pre-1442 royal charters there are texts of 13 grants of annuities in return for 'service and *retinencia*' or the like. The earliest is £20 a year from David II to Sir William Ramsay in 1362, 'for so long as he is in our retinue'.[116] Next, Robert II (1371–90) gave Sir James Douglas of Liddesdale (later 2nd earl of Douglas) and Sir Thomas Erskine annuities for 'special *retinencia*' of 200 merks and 50 merks respectively in 1380, and one of 40 merks to Sir Patrick Gray in 1381.[117] Then, under Robert III (1390–1406), there were the following grants for 'special *retinencia*': 40 merks to Sir David Lindsay (later 1st earl of Crawford) and to Sir John Montgomery in 1391; 40 merks to Sir William Stewart of Jedworth in 1392; 200 merks to the king's brother, Robert Stewart, earl of Fife, 100 merks to Fife's son, Murdoch Stewart, and £20 to Thomas Dunbar, earl of Moray, in 1393; 50 merks to another royal brother, Walter Stewart (later earl of Atholl), in 1397; £40 to Sir James Douglas junior of Dalkeith in 1402 (continuing the grant by the late duke of Rothesay mentioned above); and £20 to Sir Alexander Ogilvy of Auchterhouse in 1404.[118] In addition, the royal charters and the exchequer records from the reigns of Robert II and III provide evidence of about seventy other annuities (though not all were paid to lords).[119] While these are not stated to have been for retinue service, in most cases they went to men who probably belonged to the royal household or affinity; so they can surely be regarded as royal retaining fees, too. Indeed, since all but one of the 'special *retinencia*' annuities was for service

[113] In the younger James's letter of retinue (above, p. 163), the final point about his reward implies he had been given a lump sum, but the previous (even more illegible) item in the cartulary is a grant to him from his father, dated 1391, of a 20-merk annuity: NLS, MS 72, f. 117r. The letter of retinue was very probably a quid pro quo (and the annuity gives a likely date).

[114] Initially 4 merks, but it was to go down to 3 after his father died, presumably because Arthur would inherit land.

[115] Forbes was to rent land from Crawford for £81 a year, of which £20 was to be kept back 'for his fee and his retinue' to the earl; that was the equivalent of a £20 retaining fee.

[116] *RMS*, vol. I, no. 109.

[117] Ibid., vol. I, nos. 640, 646; *Exch. Rolls*, vol. III, p. 49.

[118] *RMS*, vol. I, nos. 812, 842, 868, 869; *Exch. Rolls*, vol. III, pp. 280–1, 340–1, 437, 597; *Morton Reg.*, vol. II, no. 214.

[119] And a number of others can be traced back to the reigns of David II and Robert I.

to the heir to the throne,[120] that might be the only thing that was 'special' about them.

Can something similar be said about other annuities issued by the lords? There is, unfortunately, less evidence about these; I have, so far, found only 27 annuities granted by lords (apart from the eight already mentioned)[121] in the entire period between 1314 and the date of the first known bond of manrent in 1442,[122] and over half seem not to involve lord–man relations. Yet some, at least, probably did have such a function: most obviously, the 40-merk annuity promised by the 4th earl of Douglas to Sir Herbert Maxwell in 1407, along with an obligation 'to supowelle and defende ... Syr Harbarte in all his ryghtwys cause, als we awe to do to our man and our kosyn'.[123] And, however the other annuities are interpreted, one point is clear: the concept of consolidating retaining relationships through money payments, mostly in the form of annuities, would certainly have been well known in late fourteenth- and early fifteenth-century Scotland.

That changed dramatically, however: following Robert III's death in 1406, the practice of granting annuities appears to have died out almost completely. Under the Albany governorships (1406–24), existing hereditary annuities ceased to be paid when their recipients died; and when James I returned from his English captivity in 1424 he cancelled all that were left.[124] No new crown annuity was granted until April 1452, when James II gave 100 merks a year to George Douglas, earl of Angus – presumably as part of the urgent search for support after the killing of the 8th earl of Douglas less than two months earlier.[125] After

---

[120] The exception is the earl of Atholl's annuity after 1397 (*Exch. Rolls*, vol. III, p. 437); and it is not impossible that here a reference to service to the king's son was accidentally omitted from the exchequer's version of the grant.

[121] I.e. those where annuities or fees were paid, but excluding the two lump sums.

[122] It might have been different had any of the lords' financial records survived; after all, a high proportion of the crown annuities are found in the exchequer records, not in the charters.

[123] W. Fraser, *The Book of Carlaverock* (Edinburgh, 1873), vol. II, pp. 417–18. The 4th earl's other annuity, £40 to Alexander Stewart, earl of Mar, 'for his service and benefit (*beneficio*)', may not have involved the same kind of lordship, but there was no doubt a patronage element: NAS, Mar and Kellie, GD124/1/423. Nine other possibly significant annuities are: earl of Strathearn to John Murray, 10 merks for counsel and labour, *c.* 1329 (NAS, Abercairny, GD24/5/1, no. 5); Sir Michael Wemyss to David Wemyss, 6 merks, *c.* 1332 (Fraser, *Family of Wemyss*, vol. II, no. 8); earl of Wigtown to William Boyd, 12 merks for life service, 1371 (*RMS*, vol. I, no. 492); earl of Strathearn to Henry Douglas, 1377 (NAS, Morton, GD150/34d); Sir Thomas Erskine to William Erskine, £20 for faithful service, 1384 (NAS, Mar and Kellie, GD124/7/2); Sir David Lindsay to William Ogilvy, £20 for homage and service, 1390 (*RMS*, vol. I, no. 819); countess of Angus to Patrick Lindsay, £5 for good will and deeds, 1389 × 97 (ibid., vol. II, no. 195); Walter Ogilvy to Patrick Ogilvy, 10 merks for counsel and aid, 1421 (ibid., vol. II, no. 113); and David Hay of Yester to his brother, Edward, 12 merks, for faithful service, 1437 (ibid., vol. II, no. 210).

[124] This is clear from *Exch. Rolls*, vol. IV, passim.

[125] *RMS*, vol. II, no. 540; the money was from the Haddington customs, and Angus was also given all the customs of North Berwick. For the political situation in 1452, see McGladdery, *James II*, ch. 4–5; Brown, *Black Douglases*, ch. 13; and Grant, *Independence and Nationhood*, pp. 192–5.

that, the only other crown annuity I have noted was a grant of 400 merks a year by James III to William Sinclair, earl of Caithness, in 1470.[126] As for the lords, their annuity grants did not cease quite so sharply, but I have found only seven between 1400 and 1442,[127] and only three thereafter: the 20-merk annuity from Sir Gilbert Kennedy of Dunure to John Kennedy of Blaucharn in 1444 that has been mentioned already, and ones of £10 and 20 merks from Laurence, Lord Oliphant, to, respectively, Silvester Rattray in 1469 and Humphrey Murray in 1471.[128]

The reason was probably economic change. During the later fourteenth century, booming wool exports had pushed the crown's customs revenue, and hence its overall income, to what for Scotland were unprecedented levels. As a result, Robert II was able to afford over £2,000 on annuities – far more than his predecessors – and Robert III spent almost as much. But by 1400 the economic climate had deteriorated seriously: during the fifteenth century wool exports fell to less than a third of what they had been, and the customs plummeted – just as happened in England, but earlier.[129] Thus it is not surprising that existing crown annuities were cancelled and new ones were not granted. The lords were hit by the economic changes, too. In the post-Black Death era, their rents had fallen, but until about 1400 there was some compensation for that in the income they would have had from selling wool produced on their estates, while many benefited from the crown annuities.[130] Thus they probably had some money to spare, and in a period of falling rents, fixed annuities may have been more attractive to recipients than grants of land. Conversely, after the economy contracted in the early fifteenth century, they would have been much less able to afford annuities; and since the value of the Scottish currency was falling (by about 80 per cent from 1375 to 1475), fixed annuities would not have been so worth having.

At first sight, therefore, the trend appears to fit in neatly with Wormald's finding that in the case of nearly 90 per cent of the bonds of manrent and

---

[126] Initially for 50 merks, but soon increased to 400 (*RMS*, vol. II, no. 998; *APS*, vol. II, p. 101). This was connected with Sinclair's resignation of his earldom of Orkney (held of Norway before 1469) to the Scottish crown: see R. Nicholson, *Scotland: The Later Middle Ages* (Edinburgh, 1974), p. 417. I have yet to search the post-1424 *Exch. Rolls* thoroughly; these may contain evidence of other crown annuities.

[127] I.e. the four fifteenth-century ones listed in note 123, and three others (*RMS*, vol. I, no. 936; vol. II, nos. 65, 195).

[128] NAS, Ailsa, GD25/1/34 (Sir Gilbert was also to pay 10 merks a year to Blaucharn's son and heir, and Bishop James Kennedy of St Andrews, Gilbert's brother, was to add another 2 merks); J. Anderson, *The Oliphants in Scotland* (Edinburgh, 1879), no. 25 (this was just for three years; if Lord Oliphant's mother died in the mean time, the fee was to go up to £20); ibid., no. 30. There are also two references to unspecified amounts of money being paid as (presumably annual) fees: ibid., no. 22 (1468); and W. Fraser, *Memoirs of the Maxwells of Pollok* (Edinburgh, 1863), vol. I, no. 50. All of these were in bonds of manrent or maintenance.

[129] See E. Gemmill and N. Mayhew, *Changing Values in Medieval Scotland* (Cambridge, 1995), esp. pp. 19–24, 371–81; also Grant, *Independence and Nationhood*, pp. 77–87, 236–40. Totals for royal annuities have been calculated from *Exch. Rolls*, vols. II–III, passim.

[130] Grant, 'Higher Nobility and their Estates', pp. 261–3, 267–70.

maintenance there was no concrete *quid pro quo* from lord to man. It could be argued that, in the later fourteenth and earlier fifteenth centuries, there was a tendency for lord–man relationships to be consolidated not only through letters of retinue but also though the payment of annuities; but that by the 1440s (or slightly earlier) annuities were no longer being paid. Instead, what men now wanted and received from their lords was much vaguer, if more important: the general support, favour and maintenance that can be summed up by the phrase 'good lordship'.[131] This might tally, too, with what was going on in England. Whereas in the fourteenth and early fifteenth centuries English lords generally gave their men retaining fees or annuities, in the late fifteenth century rewards could be less tangible; the Hastings retainers, for example, were not paid annuities but were simply promised 'good lordship'.[132]

VI

The above arguments should not, however, be regarded as conclusive, for a very different scenario can be suggested. To begin with, consider the royal charters. Although during the first half of the fifteenth century all kinds of grants by the Scots crown to its lords seem to have ceased – the rule against alienating crown property during royal minorities was followed in 1406–24 and 1437–49, while in 1424–37 the notoriously ungenerous James I gave no significant patronage[133] – in the second half of the century the situation changed, especially after James II's conflict with the earls of Douglas. Between 1450 and 1475, 32 grants of crown lands to various lords have been noted (and, as the Register of the Great Seal shows, many more went to lairds). Admittedly, that was not on the same scale as in the earlier fourteenth century, when the Bruce kings granted out vast amounts of territory to their followers during and after the Wars of Independence;[134] nevertheless it shows that, so far as the kings' rewards to their supporters are concerned, the long-term trend of the hundred years between 1375 and 1475 was not simply away from annuities, but actually back towards the granting of land.

Can that also be said about the Scottish lords? It is now time to consider the idea – set on one side at the beginning of section IV – that land grants could, after all, have been a significant way of cementing lord–man relations in late medieval Scotland. A start may be made with the Sir James Douglas of Dalkeith material. As has already been seen, the letter of retinue which he received from

[131] Wormald, *Lords and Men*, pp. 23–4 (though that phrase was rare in Scotland).

[132] W.H. Dunham, *Lord Hastings' Indentured Retainers, 1461–1483* (Connecticut Academy of Arts and Sciences, 1955), pp. 47–66; but the Hastings indentures may have been exceptional: 'Private Indentures', ed. Jones and Walker, pp. 24–6.

[133] What are technically five crown grants of land can be found in 1424–37, but in each case the underlying circumstances mean that none of them really counts: *RMS*, vol. II, nos. 44, 47, 76, 93; W. Fraser, *The Red Book of Menteith* (Edinburgh, 1880), vol. II, pp. 293–5.

[134] For the fourteenth century, my files contain 67 outright crown grants of land from the years 1314–50 (though note Duncan's caveat, in *RRS*, vol. V, p. 3); 54 from 1351–75; 18 from 1376–1400; and only 3 (all before 1406) from 1401–25.

his illegitimate son, James of Aberdour, was almost certainly reciprocated by the grant of a 20-merk annuity in 1391.[135] But in 1411, this annuity appears to have been exchanged for a grant of land, which is stated to be for the younger James's 'homage, service and special *retinencia*'.[136] Clearly, therefore, Sir James made no distinction between using an annuity and using land to back up a retaining tie. And while that is the only one of his land grants to mention retaining specifically, two others are worth comment. In 1377 he procured the resignation of land in his barony of Kilbucho, Peeblesshire, and gave it, for 'homage and bodily (*corporaliter*) service', to Andrew, son of John, who may have been a minor retainer.[137] At about the same time, he granted £10 worth of land in East Lothian to Andrew Ormiston for life; unfortunately, full details of this charter do not survive, but since Ormiston witnessed several of his charters and almost certainly belonged to his affinity, the life grant perhaps represents a retaining fee.[138]

Grants by other lords provide fuller and clearer examples of this. The most striking is that from Sir William Lindsay of Byres to William Elphinstone in 1397. It was cited above as an instance of a promise of special *retinencia*; but the full details are that Elphinstone, like Douglas of Aberdour, was given an estate in Stirlingshire in return for homage, service and special *retinencia*: here is another retaining fee in the form of land, albeit partly deferred because Lindsay kept the tenancy of it for his own lifetime![139] Likewise, when Sir Patrick Gray of Broxmouth became the 2nd earl of Crawford's 'man of special retinue' in 1413, he was granted 'as his fee of the said earl the toun of Alyth' (near Perth).[140] The undertakings of 'special *retinencia*' to Sir Duncan Campbell by Ranald of Craignish in 1414 and by his son Colin Campbell in 1432 were in return for Sir Duncan's grants of part of Lochawe and all of Glenorchy respectively; both grants were for 'homage, service and special *retinencia*'.[141] And further north on the west coast, in 1415, Donald MacDonald, Lord of the Isles, issued a charter of land in Caithness and Sutherland to Angus Mackay of Strathnaver, for his 'homage, *familiaritatem*,[142] and service against all men [with no exception of allegiance to the crown!] ... as Angus has stated in his letters patent'[143] – which must in effect have been a letter of retinue. Similarly, in 1427 Donald's successor, Alexander, Lord of the Isles, gave a charter of Barra and part of Uist in the Hebrides to Gilleonan MacNeill, 'for homage and faithful

---

[135] Above, note 113.

[136] *RMS*, vol. I, no. 932 (James Douglas of Aberdour and of Roberton are the same person).

[137] *Morton Reg.*, vol. II, nos. 146, 150. Sir James paid Alice Threepland £5 for the resignation, but she was to enjoy the proceeds of the land for the rest of her life, so Andrew was in effect being given the reversion.

[138] *RMS*, vol. I, no. 657; this charter survives only in an abbreviated crown confirmation. For Ormiston as witness, see Grant, 'Higher Nobility and their Estates', p. 333.

[139] Fraser, *Elphinstone Book*, vol. II, no. 10; above, note 89.

[140] *Scots Peerage*, vol. IV, p. 271.

[141] NAS, Reg. Ho. Trans., RH1/2/87, s.d. 4.6.1414; ibid., 1/2/199. Colin Campbell also had to provide ships for his father's service.

[142] Which I take to be membership of and service in the Lord of the Isles's *familia*.

[143] *Acts of the Lords of the Isles*, no. 19.

service ... against all men and women of whatever status or condition they shall be, both in war and in peace, going both by land and by sea'[144] – a requirement of active service that must surely be taken seriously! Those last two charters are hardly 'normal' in fifteenth-century Scotland, but while the Lords of the Isles may be regarded as exceptional,[145] it should be remembered that fifteen years later it was Alexander, by then earl of Ross, who received the first known bond of manrent. Finally, back in Lowland Scotland, in the indenture of March 1442 between Sir George Leslie of Rothes and Walter Ogilvy, Ogilvy became Leslie's 'speciale man of retenew' for life, and promised to be with Leslie in peace and war whenever required, to provide a letter of retinue, and to side with Leslie against the lord of Gordon; in return, Leslie granted Ogilvy land in Fife, to be held until equivalent land was granted in Kincardineshire – with the proviso that, when Leslie managed to make the earl of Crawford give Ogilvy a certain other estate, then the land granted by Leslie would be surrendered, while Leslie would cancel the retinue-service and return the letter of retinue.[146] Here land and retaining seem inextricably interlinked – just as, in less complicated ways, they are interlinked in the other documents cited here. Although these are only a tiny proportion of the lords' charters from this period, what they show is that, as late as the mid-fifteenth century, letters of retinue or promises of *retinencia* were just as likely to have been given in return for grants of land as for annuities or cash.

Since, however, the Leslie–Ogilvy indenture was made after January 1442, it ought to be counted as a bond of manrent. The equation of letters or bonds of retinue with bonds of manrent has already been discussed, but another instance of that should be mentioned here: the bond issued by Gilbert Kennedy of Ardstinchar to Sir Gilbert Kennedy of Dunure in 1447, stating that he became man to his beloved master, Sir Gilbert, 'in manred and seruis of retinue', and that if his heirs would not give their letters of retinue in the same form, then the land which Ardstinchar had received for his manrent had to be surrendered.[147] This not only illustrates the retinence–manrent equivalence, but also provides a particularly striking example of land being granted in return for *retinencia* – or manrent.

Now, as has been stressed already, out of the *corpus* of known bonds of manrent, almost 90 per cent did not involve any concrete *quid pro quo* in either money or land.[148] But the great majority of these bonds date from the sixteenth century, and, in the light of the 1442 Leslie–Ogilvy and 1447 Kennedy–Kennedy

---

[144] Ibid., no. 21.

[145] See ibid., nos. 61 (1456) and 96 (1469), for two other charters with similarly ferocious service clauses; and in general A. Grant, 'Scotland's "Celtic fringe" in the Late Middle Ages: I, The MacDonald Lords of the Isles and the Kingdom of Scotland', *The British Isles 1100–1500: Comparisons, Contrasts and Connections*, ed. R.R. Davies (Edinburgh 1988), pp. 130–4.

[146] NAS, Rothes, GD204/657; badly summarized in HMC, *4th Report*, p. 495, no. 20. The background to this exceedingly complex indenture is probably the Crawford–Ogilvy–Gordon rivalry that affected eastern Scotland in the 1440s and 1450s: see, e.g., McGladdery, *James II*, pp. 34–7, 61–4, 76–8.

[147] NAS, Ailsa, GD25/1/35; Wormald, *Lords and Men*, p. 170.

[148] Ibid., p. 23: 'One-tenth were given for land, and a mere handful for money ...'

transactions, it should be asked how far that applies to the earliest ones, which for the purpose of this paper will be taken to be those dating from before the end of 1475. From that period I have counted 47 bonds of manrent (or retinue) and maintenance involving lords.[149] In two cases, lords gave what could be called semi-tangible returns for the bond: one was a bailieship, the other a grant of fishing rights.[150] Three were in return for annuities, and a fourth refers to a fee.[151] With no fewer than 14, however, there is a connection with land: in 10 instances the bond is said to have been made in return for a land grant of some sort,[152] and in the other four that is implied.[153]

Furthermore, although on 30 September 1444 James Forbes, heir to Sir Alexander Forbes of that ilk, gave what looks like a standard bond without any tangible *quid pro quo* to Alexander Seton of Gordon, on exactly the same day the lord of Gordon granted Forbes lands in his Aberdeenshire barony of Cluny.[154]

---

[149] Thirty-eight are listed in Wormald, *Lords and Men* (pp. 170, 173–4, 176, 267, 275, 277–80, 298, 328, 346, 350–2, 355, 359, 375, 402–3; that includes 'lost bonds' where sufficient details are recorded). I would add the following (the lord's name is given first): George Leslie and Walter Ogilvy, 23.3.1442 (NAS, Rothes, GD204/657); Gilbert Kennedy and John Kennedy, 2.7.1444 (NAS, Ailsa, GD25/1/34; in Wormald, *Lords and Men*, pp. 50–1, but not as a bond of manrent); earl of Crawford and William Boner, 3.5.1446 (NAS, Fotheringham of Powrie, GD121/2/3/3, s.d.); earl of Crawford and David Fotheringham, 2.1.1450 (ibid., 121/2/3/4, s.d.); Lord Maxwell and John Maxwell of Pollok, 6.2.1453 (Fraser, *Maxwells of Pollok*, vol. I, no. 41); earl of Angus and Andrew Ker, 7.12.1457 (Fraser, *Douglas Book*, vol. III, no. 437); Lord Graham and John Ogilvy, 10.7.1462 (NAS, Montrose, GD220/1/A/1/10/4; bond of fealty); earl of Crawford and John Auchinleck, 16.3.1467 (*RMS*, vol. II, no. 1038); Lord Darnley and John Maxwell of Pollok, 20.11.1471 (Fraser, *Maxwells of Pollok*, vol. I, no. 50).

[150] Earl of Angus and Andrew Ker, 7.12.1457 (Fraser, *Douglas Book*, vol. III, no. 437); Lord Graham and John Ogilvy, 10.7.1462 (NAS, Montrose, GD220/1/A/1/10/4).

[151] Sir Gilbert Kennedy and John Kennedy of Blaucharn, 2.7.1444 (NAS, Ailsa, GD25/1/34); Lord Oliphant and Silvester Rattray, 18.6.1469 (Wormald, *Lords and Men*, p. 351); Lord Oliphant and Humphrey Murray, 5.9.1471 (ibid., p. 352); Lord Oliphant and Robert Mercer, 6.8.1468 (ibid., pp. 350–1).

[152] George Leslie and Walter Ogilvy, 23.3.1442 (NAS, Rothes, GD204/657); Gilbert Kennedy and Gilbert Kennedy of Ardstinchar, 23.4.1447 (Wormald, *Lords and Men*, p. 170); earl of Crawford and David Fotheringham, 2.1.1450 (NAS, Fotheringham of Powrie, GD121/2/3/4, s.d.); King James II and 9th earl of Douglas, 16.1.1453 (Wormald, *Lords and Men*, p. 359); Lord Maxwell and John Maxwell of Pollok, 6.2.1453 (Fraser, *Maxwells of Pollok*, vol. I, no. 41); earl of Erroll and Alexander Hay, 3.12.1458 (Wormald, *Lords and Men*, p. 275); earl of Crawford and John Auchinleck, 16.3.1467 (*RMS*, vol. II, no. 1038); earl of Morton and Hugh Douglas, 15.5.1468 (NAS, Morton, GD150/142; cf. Wormald, *Lords and Men*, p. 346); earl of Huntly and Lord Forbes, 8.7.1468 (*Abdn.-Banff Ills.*, vol. IV, 405–6; cf. Wormald, *Lords and Men*, p. 279); earl of Angus and George Hume, 27.11.1470 (ibid., p. 176).

[153] Earl of Crawford and William Boner, 3.5.1446 (NAS, Fotheringham of Powrie, GD121/2/3/3, s.d.); earl of Angus and Archibald Douglas, 24.5.1452 (Fraser, *Douglas Book*, vol. III, no. 82; cf. Wormald, *Lords and Men*, p. 173); Lord Gordon and Alexander Seton, 10.4.1470 (Wormald, *Lords and Men*, p. 298); Lord Darnley and John Maxwell of Pollok, 20.11.1471 (Fraser, *Maxwells of Pollok*, vol. I, no. 50).

[154] Wormald, *Lords and Men*, p. 278; *Abdn.-Banff Ills.*, vol. IV, pp. 395–6.

Similarly, when William, Lord Forbes, made four bonds with the 1st earl of Huntly (as Alexander Seton had become) on 8 July 1468, one was said to be in return for land in the barony of Aboyne,[155] while the rest made no mention of land; but on the same day, Huntly granted Lord Forbes three different territories in Cluny and Midmar baronies, which can surely be linked with the other three bonds.[156] Lastly, on 29 June 1472 Alexander Dunbar gave his manrent to the 2nd earl of Huntly, while on 16 July in the same year Huntly gave Dunbar a charter of lands in Cluny; although in this case the documents were not issued simultaneously, and the lands had to be resigned by previous owners, nonetheless the transaction probably reflects Huntly's maintenance of Dunbar.[157]

In all, therefore, some kind of *quid pro quo* was either certainly or probably involved in 25 (53 per cent) of the 47 early bonds of manrent, and in 19 cases (40 per cent) it had to do with the possession of land. The pattern shown by these early bonds, therefore, is very different from that produced by the great bulk of them after 1475. It is a pattern that corresponds well, however, with the evidence from the royal grants. Just as land was being used again for crown patronage after 1450, so too, the early bonds of manrent reveal, it was being used in the lords' patronage of their men. As a consequence, it is impossible to argue that, down to 1475, men were generally content with simply receiving 'good lordship' from their lords. Instead, it appears that there was at least as strong a demand for more tangible rewards, sometimes in cash but more commonly in the form of real estate.

VII

The implications of that are far-reaching indeed. In the case of the Gordon–Forbes bonds, we know about the connection with land grants only because both charters and bonds issued on the same day have survived. What if that had not happened? If the charters had been lost, we would be unaware that lands had been granted in return for the bonds, which would have been a pity, but not necessarily serious; on the other hand, if the *bonds* had been lost, then there would be nothing to show that the charters had any lord–man significance – which is a most important point. In themselves, the grants that Alexander Seton, earl of Huntly, made to the Forbeses are very like the great majority of late medieval Scottish lords' charters. The tenure of the estate granted in 1444 was by suit-of-court with ward and relief, and the tenure of those granted in 1468 was by suit-of-court alone; in both cases the conveyances were said to have been made for 'homage and service done and to be done' by the respective Forbeses. There is nothing to make those conveyances appear

---

[155] This one is therefore included among those listed in note 153.

[156] Wormald, *Lords and Men*, p. 279 (Gordon, nos. 4, 5, 7); *Abdn.-Banff Ills.*, vol. IV, pp. 404–5. Between these sets of grants, Huntly also granted other lands in Cluny barony to James, Lord Forbes (as the 1444 recipient had become): ibid., vol. IV, pp. 400–1. No bond is recorded, but the grant is said to have been because Forbes received the order of knighthood at Huntly's hands – which indicates another kind of lord–man tie.

[157] Wormald, *Lords and Men*, p. 280 (Gordon, no. 8); *RMS*, vol. II, no. 1065.

significant. In fact, the standard forms conceal transactions which had a genuine lord–man significance – but of how many other conveyances might that be said? Since, as was pointed out at the beginning of this paper, title-deeds tended to be preserved much better than were ephemeral documents including bonds, the answer might well be, a very considerable number.

Another set of documents illustrates this even more clearly. It starts with a bond of 2 January 1450 by which David Fotheringham of Powrie bound his son and heir, Thomas, to be the 'man of special retinue' to the nine-year-old son and heir of Alexander Lindsay, earl of Crawford, in return for the lands of West Broughty near Dundee.[158] Here, the bond refers to the grant of land, whereas the actual grant of the land of West Broughty, on 15 January 1450, does not mention the bond, and at first sight looks like yet another straightforward subinfeudation: it is for homage and service, and requires due and accustomed service.[159] Then, thirty-one years later, in 1481, Earl Alexander's son, David, now 5th earl of Crawford, issued a charter to his 'kinsman and familiar esquire', Thomas Fotheringham, granting him the lands of West Broughty following Thomas's own resignation, plus other land in Inverarity barony (Angus), all to be held directly of the crown instead of Crawford. At first sight that looks like an outright alienation, presumably a sale, and it is not obvious that we should give credence to the clause explaining why the charter was granted: 'for his faithful service, and gracious and continuous labours done by him to us from our youth, and graciously over a long space of time'.[160] Yet that must be accurate – which makes the alienation renouncing Crawford's right of lordship into a piece of lord–man patronage. Without their fathers' bond, that would never have been recognized.

The point may be developed further. It means, surely, that when lords' charters state that land was granted for service, there is a distinct possibility that such statements ought to be believed – or, at least, that generally we do *not* know that we should *not* believe them. Furthermore, it raises significant questions about the concept of homage. The standard view is that this was a 'tired' and essentially meaningless concept not to be taken seriously.[161] Yet homage, or Latin *homagium*, comes from the French *homme*, meaning man. Therefore, literally, homage means 'man-ness' – in which case, is it any different from manrent? For the sixteenth century, the answer would certainly be yes; by then, homage was obsolete, relating to the technicalities of land tenure, while manrent was about vital lord–man relations.[162] But, earlier, the distinction may not have been quite so clear. One of the conclusions of the previous section was that, during the mid-fifteenth century, there was no significant difference between the older concept of the letter of retinue and the newer one of the bond of manrent; the one simply evolved slowly into the other. Can much the same be suggested about the terms 'homage' and 'manrent'?

[158] NAS, Fotheringham of Powrie, GD121/2/3/4, s.d. 2.1.1450.
[159] NAS, Great Seal Reg., C2/4, no. 70; cf. *RMS*, vol. II, no. 393.
[160] NAS, Great Seal Reg., C2/10, no. 15; cf. *RMS*, vol. II, no. 1497. Thomas Fotheringham was a frequent witness to the earl's charters: e.g., ibid., vol. II, nos. 776, 1078, 1169, 1448, 1522.
[161] See above, pp. 154–5.
[162] Wormald, *Lords and Men*, pp. 24–5.

Wormald argues powerfully against that. Despite the etymological similarity, she cogently claims that the two concepts were entirely separate: that homage was an act (one *did* homage to one's lord), whereas manrent was a situation (one is *in* the state of being the lord's man).[163] But it will probably be necessary to agree to differ over this point. I am not entirely sure that I have grasped the subtleties in the linguistic usages, and am not convinced that all the lords of mid-fifteenth-century Scotland would have done so. Instead, it may be proposed that, during the era when the vernacular was replacing Latin as a vehicle for all but the most formal documents, there was too much laxity of language for precise distinctions to be made; after all, late medieval Scottish charters, in either language, exhibit such fluidity and inconsistency in so many other aspects that it seems inadvisable to expect absolute precision over this point. And if, by the mid-fifteenth century, Latin had become simply a technical language so far as the secular law of real property was concerned, then what did contemporary lords and lairds think that *homagium* meant when they put it into Scots – if not 'manrent'?

The equation of the two is indicated, it may be suggested, by the 5th earl of Douglas's charter to Thomas Kirkpatrick in 1428, which stated that Kirkpatrick had given him not simply a letter of retinue, but *litteras homagii et retinencie*.[164] Would the translation of that into fifteenth-century Scots have produced a version of 'letters of homage and retinue', or 'letters of manrent and retinue' – and is there really a significant difference between those two phrases? Similarly, consider two charters issued by William Hay of Erroll (after 1452 1st earl of Erroll). In 1432 he granted land in Fife to his kinsman, Nicholas Hay, to be held *in wardam, relevium, humagium* [sic] *et servicium*, which, translated literally, is 'in ward, relief, homage and service'. Then, in 1456, he confirmed his original grant for Nicholas's son, Gilbert; but now the charter was in Scots, and states that the tenure is by 'service of ward and relief mantrent [sic] and service'.[165] *Wardam* is 'ward', *relevium* is 'relief', *servicium* is 'service' – but *humagium* has become 'mantrent'. Is that last translation meant to convey a significant difference?[166] It seems much more likely that the two terms are being equated, implying that *homagium* and manrent meant much the same thing to contemporaries.

Be that as it may (and the linguistic niceties of mid-fifteenth-century Scots, not to mention the extent to which secular landowners understood them, are extremely difficult to grapple with), if the term manrent had not been used in that 1456 confirmation, the obligation of homage and service in William Hay's charter of 1432 would normally be considered routine verbiage. Or, to put it another way, did the fact that in 1456 the land was said to be held for manrent, whereas in 1431 it was said to have been held for *homagium*, mean that there

---

[163] Ibid., pp. 15–27.
[164] NAS, Crown Office Writs, AD1/41; but cf. Wormald, *Lords and Men*, pp. 50–1. Whether this was a single document, or more than one, is unclear; *litteras* could have either meaning.
[165] NAS, Lindsay, GD203/2/6, and GD203/8; partly printed in HMC, 5th Report, pp. 624–5.
[166] See Wormald, *Lords and Men*, p. 19.

was a significant difference in the ways by which Nicholas and Gilbert Hay held it, and in their relationships with their overlord, the earl of Erroll? That appears to me to be extremely doubtful. Yet, if *homagium* and manrent are seen to have much the same meaning in late medieval Scotland, then the phrase 'for homage and service . . .' in a grant of land has to be regarded as a potentially meaningful concept.

VIII

That brings us back, finally, to the fundamental question posed in this paper: did tenurial lordship have any significance in terms of lord–man relations, or was it merely a technicality? My answer now has to be that in some cases it certainly did have a real importance, and that in many others that possibility must be entertained seriously. As has just been suggested, this could even apply generally to grants by subinfeudation said to have been made in return for homage and service. And in that case, the same would have to be said about similar grants made 'for faithful service done and to be done', and the like. Taken to an extreme, that could apply to well over half the charters in my files. That is, of course, excessive: it would be unrealistic to claim that every phrase about homage and service, faithful service, and so on, invariably indicated a meaningful lord–man tie (though at times that seems to be taken for granted by those historians who currently write so illuminatingly on late medieval Scotland's political history). On the other hand, what I would suggest is that at least a reasonable proportion of the land grants from lords to men in late medieval Scotland may well have had such a significance.

Having arrived at that answer, I must emphasize that there is no intention to portray late medieval Scotland as an example of what used to be thought of as traditional 'feudal' society. The fact that a man held land of a lord does not mean that he necessarily belonged to the latter's retinue or affinity; in that respect, I am happy to agree with Duncan's analysis.[167] But a *new* grant of land by a lord is a different matter. When – as no doubt happened afresh in each generation – late medieval Scottish lords set about recruiting and constructing their affinities, then the absence of a Scottish equivalent to the statute of *Quia Emptores* meant that they were not prohibited by law from making subinfeudations of land in return for or as rewards of service from the members of those affinities, if they chose to do so – and I suggest that many of them often did so choose.

Such subinfeudations may, from the mid-fourteenth century until the later fifteenth, have been accompanied by the issue of letters of retinue or bonds of manrent by the recipients; many of those letters and early bonds are linked with grants of land, though the sparsity of the actual examples, and the likelihood that countless letters of retinue have been lost, mean that certainty is impossible on this point. Alternatively, it may be that many promises of retinue-service to a lord by his men were made orally, in some kind of ceremony[168] – though how would that have differed from an act of homage or an act of fealty? Perhaps

---

[167] Duncan, *Making of the Kingdom*, p. 408; see above, p. 155.

[168] As implied by Wormald, *Lords and Men*, pp. 47–8.

the frequent use of the word 'special' in connection with *retinencia* was intended to indicate a closer or stronger tie than what was normally implied in the wording of the charters – though again, the evidence is inconclusive, because late medieval Scottish lords were not at all consistent in their use of the terminology. But whatever the case, attention should be drawn here to the observation by Michael Jones and Simon Walker on English indentures of retainer, that they 'were the most formal and explicit, but by no means the most common, of these bonds of service . . . nor were they always a necessary adjunct to the exercise of lordship'. In other words, lord–man ties did not have to be based on formal indentures or contracts in late medieval England; Professor Jones and Dr Walker point as well to tenurial relationships (which had a 'residual influence'), annuities, grants of livery and appointments to offices as means of rewarding good service.[169] The same is surely true of late medieval Scotland – with the difference that north of the Border there was far less cash available for rewarding service, and no legal restriction on using land instead.

The use of land grants as reward for service is particularly evident in the documents of arguably the greatest (certainly the best-known) of all Scotland's late medieval magnates, Archibald, 4th earl of Douglas (1400–24).[170] They demonstrate that Douglas seems not to have bothered with letters of retinue, or even with 'special *retinencia*' phrases; yet there is no doubt that he had one of the largest and most powerful affinities ever seen in Scotland. Many of its members were long-term Douglas tenants, which no doubt brought them into his sphere of influence and hence into his service; that is in line with Duncan's argument. But what is most significant is that many of the retinue, and almost all its leading figures – not to mention his mistress[171] – received new grants of land from the earl. With respect to the 4th earl of Douglas, therefore, it is clear that that was one of the main methods of distributing patronage within the affinity. And there is no reason to believe that the earl was unique in using land-grants in this way.

Earl Archibald's grants of land did not, however, create absolutely permanent ties between the families making up his affinity and subsequent earls of Douglas. After his death at Verneuil in 1424, it is clear that his son and successor, the 5th earl of Douglas, had to reconstruct a new affinity for himself, and that many of the sons of the 4th earl's erstwhile followers took service elsewhere, especially with the king.[172] Similarly, in north-east Scotland, despite both the Gordon–Forbes grants and the Forbes–Gordon bonds, during the sixteenth century relations between the two houses were distinctly tense, and at times dissolved into open feud.[173] And if Sir Robert Erskine of that ilk had hoped to

---

[169] 'Private Indentures', ed. Jones and Walker, pp. 12–13.
[170] The exigencies of space and time have precluded a detailed examination of the documents of Earl Archibald, such as was sketched in the final part of my original conference paper. A full-length version of this has, however, now been published elsewhere, and interested readers are referred to that (Grant, 'Records of Fourth Earl of Douglas'; see above, note 9); the points made here derive from it.
[171] Fraser, *Douglas Book*, vol. III, no. 60.
[172] That is beyond the scope of my essay on the 4th earl, but it is discussed well in Brown, *Black Douglases*, ch. 11.
[173] K.M. Brown, *Bloodfeud in Scotland, 1573–1625* (Edinburgh, 1986), pp. 110–12; Wormald, *Lords and Men*, pp. 23, 73, 77, 117–18.

bind William Forbes of Kinnaldy to him by the gift of Laskgowan in 1433 with which this paper started, then he was mistaken, for in 1435, only two years later, William alienated the land to Gilbert Menzies, burgess of Aberdeen, in return for the sum of £68.[174] As those examples show, grants of land would not have been any more successful than other methods of consolidating lord–man ties; individual factors no doubt always determined the success or failure of the relationships. That, of course, is why the traditional, idealistic and unrealistic concept of 'feudal' ties has no relevance for late medieval Scottish history.

So long as that caveat is borne in mind, however, it is possible to conclude that in late medieval Scotland the concepts of service and land tenure probably did commonly go hand-in-hand, as least on a short-term or lifetime basis; and that the form of the service would usually have been general and unspecific rather than strictly regulated. That is likely to have been the case, in particular, with respect to many of the 246 straightforward subinfeudations that I have found made by lords to lairds between 1314 and 1475, and, also, to many of the 111 subinfeudations made to family members or to other lords. It is impossible, however, to be sure about the precise extent of the practice. All that can be said is that *some* land grants were definitely employed, in various ways, to cement *some* individual lord–man relationships in late medieval Scotland – and that many other land grants would very probably have been used for the same purpose. Such a conclusion would, no doubt, apply both to the period discussed in this paper and to the preceeding twelfth and thirteenth centuries as well.[175] But whether, in that case, late medieval Scottish landowning society should be regarded as 'feudal', as 'bastard feudal', or as something else is a question which I, for one, would prefer to leave unanswered.[176]

[174] *Collections for ... the Shires of Aberdeen and Banff*, p. 393; *Abdn.-Banff Ills.*, vol. III, p. 143. Forbes's conveyance of Laskgowan was by substitution, which Sir Robert Erskine ratified in 1437, not by a straightforward confirmation, but by his own charter granting Laskgowan to Menzies following Forbes's resignation: ibid., vol. III, pp. 142–3. This presumably gave Menzies a stronger title, and also perhaps made a clearer statement of Erskine's lordship. It also stated that the grant to Menzies was 'for faithful service done' to Erskine, which may simply have been token phraseology.

[175] Cf. D. Crouch, 'From Stenton to McFarlane: Models of Societies of the Twelfth and Thirteenth Centuries', *TRHS*, 6th ser., V (1995), 179–200, esp. 194–8.

[176] I am most grateful to Dr K.J. Stringer for his kindness in reading and commenting on various drafts of this paper, and indeed for all his advice on this subject over the years; and my thanks go also to the editors of this volume, for their patience and encouragement in so many ways.

INDEX

ERRATA

Due to an error while processing computer files to printed plates the following text needs to be corrected:

p.15, n.57 the last sentence should read:
Nevertheless she remained in their service for a whole year from her contract date: Borthwick IHR, CP.E.89, translated in *Women in England*, pp. 73, 78.

p.19, n.75 should read:
University of Leeds, Brotherton Library, Ripon Chapter Act Book 432.1, translated in *Probate Inventories of the York Diocese 1350-1500*, ed. P.M. Stell L. Hampson (York, n.d.), pp. 294-6.

p.75, line 19 should read:
discussion had reached the necessary Act of Resumption. Its preamble sets

p.162, n.80 should read:
In Scotland, *retinencia* (like manrent) was what a man gave a lord; 'his *retinencia*' was the man's state of being retained. Hence it seems wrong to translate it as *'retinue'*, because the words 'his retinue' would normally mean the lord's following.

Lightning Source UK Ltd.
Milton Keynes UK
UKHW021807110722
405703UK00003B/369

9 780851 158143